REGIONS APART

For our students

REGIONS APART
The Four Societies of Canada and the United States

Edward Grabb AND James Curtis

OXFORD
UNIVERSITY PRESS

1904 ❧ 2004

100 YEARS OF
CANADIAN PUBLISHING

OXFORD

UNIVERSITY PRESS

70 Wynford Drive, Don Mills, Ontario M3C 1J9
www.oup.com/ca

Oxford University Press is a department of the University of Oxford.
It furthers the University's objective of excellence in research, scholarship,
and education by publishing worldwide in

Oxford New York
Auckland Bangkok Buenos Aires Cape Town Chennai
Dar es Salaam Delhi Hong Kong Istanbul Karachi Kolkata
Kuala Lumpur Madrid Melbourne Mexico City Mumbai Nairobi
São Paulo Shanghai Taipei Tokyo Toronto

Oxford is a trade mark of Oxford University Press
in the UK and in certain other countries

Published in Canada
by Oxford University Press

Library and Archives Canada Cataloguing in Publication

Grabb, Edward G.

Regions apart : the four societies of Canada and the United
States / Edward Grabb and James Curtis

Includes bibliographical references and index.
ISBN 0-19-541691-0

1. Canada—Social conditions.   2. United States—Social conditions.   3. Canada—Civilization.
4. United States—Civilization.   5. Social values—Cross-cultural studies.   6. Canada—History—Errors,
inventions, etc.   7. United States—History—Errors, inventions, etc.   8. Regionalism—Canada.
9. Regionalism—United States.   10. National characteristics, Canadian.
11. National characteristics—American.   I. Curtis, James F., 1943–   II. Title

HN50.G72 2004   971   C2004-903610-6

Cover Design: Brett J. Miller
Cover Images: Comstock/Getty Images (flags) and
Digital Vision © 2003 (satellite image of North America)

1 2 3 4 - 08 07 06 05

This book is printed on permanent (acid-free) paper ∞.

Printed in Canada

TABLE OF CONTENTS

PREFACE xi

1 **Introduction** **1**
   Plan of the Book 5

PART I **CANADA AND THE UNITED STATES:**
        THEORETICAL PERSPECTIVES **9**
        Introduction 9

2 **Previous Perspectives: Founding Fragments and**
   Revolutionary Origins **11**
   Hartz's Theory of European Founding Fragments 11
   Lipset's Origins Thesis: The Defining Moment of the
      American Revolution 20
   Summary 25

3 **An Alternative Perspective: Deep Structures and the**
   Four Sub-societies of Canada and the United States **26**
   The Concept of Deep Structures 27
   Deep Structures and the English Heritage 31
   Identifying the Deep Structures of the English Societies 46
   Canada and the United States as Four Sub-societies 53
   Summary and Conclusion to Part I 57

PART II **HISTORICAL MYTHS AND HISTORICAL EVIDENCE** **59**
         Introduction 59

4 **Liberty, Liberalism, and the Myth of**
   American Individualism **61**
   The Concept of Liberty in Pre-revolutionary America 61
   The Myth of American Individualism 65
   Summary 73

5   **English Canada and the Loyalist Myth**   74
    The Loyalist Migration and Canadian Toryism   74
    Counting the Loyalists   76
    How Loyal Were the Loyalists?   77
    Were the English-Canadian Colonists 'Americans'?   81
    Tory Values: Comparing the Elite and the Larger Population   83
    Summary   86

6   **Canadians and Americans: Historical Comparisons**   87
    Class Structure and Economic Background   88
    Ethnic Composition and Sources of Immigration   89
    Religion in Canada and the United States   111
    Patterns of Urbanization   116
    Political Culture and Organization   118
    Summary   127
    Conclusion to Part II   129

PART III ENDURING MYTHS AND CONTEMPORARY REALITIES   135
    Introduction   135
    Samples and Data Sources   136
    Research Questions   138

7   **Moral Issues: Religion, Family Values, and Crime**   140
    Religion and Religiosity   140
    Family and Sexual Values   147
    Crime and the Law   153
    Summary   165

8   **Individualism, Collectivism, and the State**   166
    Collectivism and the Role of the State   168
    Attitudes about Individualism, Statism, and Collectivism   180
    Summary   192

9   **Social Inclusion and Tolerance toward Minorities**   193
    Mosaic and Melting Pot   195
    Patterns of Immigration and Racial Composition   197
    Socioeconomic Attainments of Immigrants
       and Ethnic Minorities   200
    Comparative Research on Attitudes toward Minorities   205
    Summary   214

10   **Political Attitudes and Political Action   216**
      Political Interest and Political Behaviour   219
      Political Trust and Confidence in Government   228
      Feelings of Interpersonal Trust and National Pride   230
      Summary   232

11   **Voluntary-Association Involvement and Activity   234**
      Previous Research   234
      Results from the World Values Surveys   238
      Summary   241
      Conclusion to Part III   242

12   **Conclusion   247**
      Deep Structures Revisited   248
      How Many 'Nations' Are There?   255
      Elites and Masses   259
      National Differences: Comparing the Extremes   262
      Past, Present, and Future: Convergence,
          Divergence, or Both?   266

      APPENDIX I   275

      APPENDIX II   281

      APPENDIX III   284

      REFERENCES   287

      INDEX   315

PREFACE

This book, in a sense, has been a long time in the making. As Canadian social scientists, we have devoted most of our efforts over the last three decades or more to trying to understand the workings of our own society. In the process of doing so, however, we have also found ourselves being regularly drawn to the pursuit of other research, to studies that directly compare Canada with its southern neighbour. The same impetus has been common among other Canadian academics, of course, beginning with the now-classic works of such noted figures as S.D. Clark (1948, 1968) and Gerald Craig (1968). It is also evident in the writings of many later scholars. These include J.L. Granatstein and Norman Hillmer (1991; Granatstein 1996), Jeffrey Reitz and Raymond Breton (1994; Reitz 1998), John Herd Thompson and Stephen Randall (1994), Wallace Clement and John Myles (1994), Neil Nevitte (1996), Keith Banting and colleagues (1997), and others. Especially in recent times, Canadian journalists and social commentators have shown a similar fascination with comparing Canada and the United States, as is evident in interesting and thought-provoking books by Richard Gwyn (1985, 1995), Will Ferguson (1997), Jeffrey Simpson (2000), Michael Adams (1997, 2003), and James Laxer (2003).

This wealth of research and commentary may be the clearest indication of just how important the Canadian–American connection is, certainly for those of us living north of the border. Indeed, for Canadians, the comparison of the two nations is almost inescapable, given the great influence that the United States has had on our society during much of our shared history, not to mention the predominant role that the United States now plays in the world as a whole. However, as we shall attempt to show in this volume, a close comparison of the two countries is extremely enlightening, and probably essential, if we are to establish a deeper and fuller understanding of both Canada and the United States, and of their respective locations in the larger spectrum of nations.

Hence, individually, together, and in collaboration with other colleagues, we have been engaged since the 1970s in a series of analyses that compare Canadians and Americans, and at times other populations, on a range of sociological and historical questions. In part, the present volume represents the culmination of this long-term project. Even so, while the current study revisits some of the themes and questions that we have considered in the past, its main goal is to build from this previous work and to weave it into an overarching and more comprehensive analysis, involving new conceptual insights and a much wider range of historical and recent evidence.

As we outline further in Chapter 1, our analysis is organized around a set of three interrelated problems, which are examined in three parts that form the core of the book. First, in Part I, we reconsider existing theoretical perspectives, and also offer an alternative approach for thinking about and understanding how Canada and the United States emerged and developed. Then, in Part II, we provide a detailed analysis of historical evidence, particularly on the question of whether the two societies arose from distinct or similar historical origins. Our third concern, as presented in Part III, is to conduct a multifaceted comparison of contemporary research on Canada and the United States. In this section of the book, we review and assess the results of many previous studies. We also consider extensive findings and information obtainable from government agencies, opinion poll organizations, and other publicly accessible sources. In addition, we conduct our own analyses of representative sample survey data collected in the two nations. This rich array of attitudinal measures, behavioural evidence, and social-structural indicators, which covers a period of more than three decades dating from the 1970s and in some cases earlier, allows us to provide what we hope is one of the most thorough and wide-ranging contemporary comparisons of the two societies that has been attempted in recent years. Finally, we conclude the book with a reiteration of the main findings, an overall assessment of what the evidence really tells us about Canada and the United States, and suggestions for the direction that further research should take as we look toward the future of both nations.

We wish to express our gratitude for the contributions that a number of people have made in the preparation of this volume. First, we reserve a special thanks for our long-time co-author and colleague, Doug Baer. Because of other commitments, Doug was unable to participate in the writing of this book. However, his work on the sample survey data used in Part III, particularly on the data from the World Values Surveys, was most valuable to us and is much appreciated. Doug also conducted multivariate analyses of these data. Although we do not present the multivariate results here, Doug's work was helpful for confirming that the bivariate findings reported in Part III are largely unaltered by controls for the effects of other variables. The reader will see, as well, that many of our collaborative pieces with Doug are well represented in the literature reviews and discussions found throughout the book.

Several of our other colleagues, at the University of Western Ontario, the University of Waterloo, and elsewhere, have been exceptionally generous in devoting their talents and time to reading and commenting on the manuscript. First among these is Kevin McQuillan. Kevin's thoughtful assessments of all the early drafts, his extensive knowledge of both historical materials and contemporary sources, and his unflagging encouragement of the project have been instrumental in keeping us on track since the book's inception. The same vote of thanks goes to Jeff Reitz, whose thoroughness and attention to detail in the reading and evaluation of the manuscript have been remarkable. Jeff helped us in avoiding several errors or omissions, and offered suggestions that significantly strengthened parts of both the analysis and the conclusions. We owe a similar debt to Sam Clark. Sam provided us with many useful sources, particularly for the theoretical and historical sections of the volume. He also raised some thought-provoking questions, posed constructive and incisive criticisms, and read the various chapters with a care that is the mark of a true colleague. We also thank our four anonymous reviewers for their suggestions, which led us to make some notable improvements in the final version of the manuscript. Others who graciously took the time from their busy schedules to read parts of the book, to offer helpful suggestions, or to provide additional references and recommendations include Mike Carroll, Ron Gillis, Peter Neary, Anton Allahar, Michael Gardiner, John Myles, Bill Avison, Rod Beaujot, Jerry White, Paul Whitehead, Julie McMullin, Paul Maxim, Cecil Van Bolhuis, Kym Hunt, Shannon Thomson, Daryl Boshart, Kathleen Hunter, Lorne Dawson, and Leah Ross.

Our work has also been greatly facilitated by the people at Oxford University Press Canada, particularly Lisa Meschino, David Stover, Phyllis Wilson, and Rachael Cayley. We are gratified by their faith in the project and thankful for their consistent support in bringing it to fruition. We also thank Megan Mueller who, before going on to other pursuits, originally signed us to write the book and offered helpful comments and encouragement in the initial phases of the process.

It is important, as well, that we mention four special individuals, for their outstanding research assistance. First, we thank Julie Dembski, for her able and unerring secretarial work. Second, we appreciate the assistance of Catherine Corrigall-Brown, who conducted a number of bibliographic searches for us, especially in the early stages of the project. Third, we are grateful to Tom Perks, for his diligent library work and his skill in constructing the tables presented in Part III. Finally, we thank Monica Hwang, whose exceptional industry, perseverance, intelligence, and ingenuity were invaluable for enabling us to work with what we believe are among the best and most up-to-date references, statistical information, and data sources that are currently available on the subject of Canada and the United States. To the extent that our analysis is a comprehensive one, a great deal of the credit goes to Monica.

In closing, if we may, we would like to send our best wishes to the folks at Quehl's Restaurant in Tavistock, Ontario, which is half-way between our home bases in London and Waterloo. Thanks, especially, to Kim Ziegler and Sue Festoso, for your warmth and hospitality, and for putting up with us all these many years.

E.G.G. and J.E.C.

CHAPTER 1

✍

INTRODUCTION

This is a book about myths. One of its main goals is to consider some of the central elements in the national mythologies of Canada and the United States—the enduring images, impressions, and symbols that, according to many observers, provide the most compelling representations of the two countries and their national characters. But this book is also about realities. Indeed, its principal purpose is to go beyond a recounting of these prevailing myths, and to assess their accuracy or applicability, using a wide range of both historical and contemporary evidence.

In the chapters that follow, we shall concern ourselves with some important features of the social structures of both nations, including their political and legal systems, economic organization, demographic composition, and so forth. At the same time, though, our primary focus in much of the analysis will be on the Canadian and American cultures, especially as reflected in the values, beliefs, and behaviours of the two populations. For most social scientists, of course, the social structures and culture of a nation are thought to be closely intertwined. This basic perspective goes back at least as far as the classic works of Karl Marx and Max Weber, both of whom, in different ways, sought to understand the often complex and reciprocal causal connections that can arise between the economic, political, religious, and other social structures of different societies, on the one hand, and the ideologies or belief systems that prevail in those societies, on the other hand (see, e.g., Grabb 2002: Chapters 2 and 3). In the present analysis, we take the same general theoretical approach, for we also see cultural and social-structural realities as inextricably linked, and we argue that the core values and beliefs that operate within a society are both conditioned by and reflected in the workings of its major social structures.

One of the main contentions in this book is that, while the myths that have arisen about Canada and the United States have some basis in reality, all too often what has been thought to be true about the countries and their peoples does not stand up to careful investigation. In other words, although there is an element of truth in some of the images and beliefs that people hold about Canadians and Americans, we shall find that a surprisingly large number of the most influential depictions that have emerged over the years prove, on closer inspection, to be exaggerations or distortions. In numerous cases, in fact, they are simply wrong. Still, as misleading as many of the myths have been, they also provide a very useful set of benchmarks for the analysis that follows. These lingering ideas have guided and informed so much of the existing research and commentary about Canada and the United States that they serve as essential starting points from which to move toward a more accurate and more thorough understanding of what truly constitutes these two societies and their cultures (see, e.g., Curtis and Tepperman 1990).

An obvious thing about myths is that they are usually quite familiar and well known. Moreover, at least in the Canadian case, many of them appear to be accepted as correct by a considerable portion of the nation's population. Leading Canadian intellectuals have played a significant role in promoting this acceptance. However, some of the most commonly held views and beliefs that Canadians have about themselves actually stem from the ideas of noted scholars and observers from other countries, especially those writing in the United States. In fact, as we shall see, most of the best-known images of Canada have developed as counterpoints to several time-honoured myths about the United States, especially those surrounding the American Revolution. Almost from the beginning of the two societies, it seems, Canadians have largely been defined in comparison with, and often in contrast to, their neighbours to the south. As a result, many of the existing studies of Canada's history and culture, either explicitly or implicitly, have entailed hypothesizing about and testing for similarities and differences between Canadians and Americans.

The present volume proceeds from and builds upon this same research tradition. The comparative approach, of course, has long been embraced as a method of analysis in the social sciences, not only in studies of Canada and the United States, but also in more general analyses. These include the writings of such renowned scholars as Tocqueville, Weber, Marx, and others (see, e.g., Hartz 1955: 4, 25; Lipset 1990: xiii; Bendix 1960: 463, xxiii). The essence of this tradition has been succinctly captured by Edgar T. Thompson, whose early studies of the American South consistently held to the view that 'a society, any society, is best understood in the perspective of other societies and their histories' (Thompson 1975: xiii). In voicing this belief, Thompson aptly alludes to the famous rhetorical question of Rudyard Kipling: 'And what should they know of England who only England know?' (See Bartlett 1968: 874.) In our analysis, we take much the same position. It is not possible to know Canada well without also knowing a good deal about other countries, particularly the

United States. To achieve a full understanding of our own society requires that we have a clear sense of the American nation, with which we have been closely tied and perpetually compared from our earliest days.

Before continuing, we should first comment on some of our geographic terminology, which, judging by the comments of certain reviewers of this book, could weigh on the minds of some readers. The first issue concerns the use of the words 'Canada' and 'Canadian'. Strictly speaking, Canada was the name given by the British to the old province of Quebec. In 1791, Canada was divided into Lower and Upper Canada, which later became Canada East and Canada West, and finally Quebec and Ontario. Quebec and Ontario, of course, are now two of the ten provinces that form the modern country of Canada. For clarity and simplicity throughout our analysis, 'Canada' refers to the entire national territory north of the border with the United States, and 'Canadian' denotes any member of the population living in this territory. A second concern involves the words 'America' and 'American'. In its original and fullest meaning, 'America' refers to all of the lands in the Western hemisphere, not just the United States, and 'American' is a term denoting a person who inhabits any one of these lands. However, while we are well aware of the original meanings of these words, and discuss them ourselves in Chapter 2 and elsewhere, for ease of description and to vary the phrasing in the text, we also, in later chapters, employ the two terms in what have become their commonly accepted usages today, i.e., to refer to the United States and to any of that nation's inhabitants. A third issue concerns the term 'North America'. Here, too, we are aware that, by most geographic definitions, the continent of North America includes not only the United States and Canada, but also Mexico and, in some formulations, Greenland and the Central American countries. Let us simply make it clear that, while we have scrupulously endeavoured not to imply that Canada and the United States constitute the entire continent of North America, we are solely concerned in the present analysis with a comparison of Canada and the United States, and use 'North America' primarily to refer to the regions of the continent that form these two countries.

If we review the prevailing images that have been used to characterize Canadian society over the years, it soon becomes apparent that many of these images are quite complimentary to both Canada and its citizens. At the same time, though, many of these same views also seem to have a double edge. Thus, for instance, while it is widely believed that Canadians are a polite and respectful people, it is often argued that these alleged qualities may also make Canadians too passive and too ready to let their governments take care of them. A related perception is that Canadians are peace-loving and law-abiding, but that they, in turn, may be too willing to believe and to obey whatever their leaders tell them. In a similar fashion, it is often contended that Canada is a caring nation, in which the government provides extensive assistance to help disadvantaged groups, including the poor, the elderly, and the infirm, but that this may occur in a way that at times discourages such liberal-democratic values as individual initiative, self-reliance, and personal responsibility. Yet another pervasive belief is that Canada is unusually tolerant of and receptive to human diversity, especially ethnic, linguistic, regional, and cultural distinctiveness, but that, partly as a result of these virtues, Canadian society is also highly fragmented, and lacks any strong sense of national unity, identity, or vision. In such illustrations, it is evident, as well, that there is an implicit, if not explicit, comparison of Canada and the United States, with Americans typically being thought to be the opposite of Canadians in all of these areas. These are just some of the most familiar perceptions and assumptions that have become part of the folklore in our two countries. In subsequent chapters, we will reconsider these and other well-known images, and will conduct analyses that bear on each of them.

Most of the views and opinions about Canadians and Americans that we address in this analysis involve characterizations that apply to today or to the recent past. However, as is typical of myths, virtually all of these ideas can ultimately be traced to events and occurrences from much earlier times. Several noted writers have pointed to the late eighteenth and early nineteenth centuries, especially the period during and immediately after the American Revolution, as a pivotal time in the development of the societies that would eventually become Canada and the United States. While we concur with much of this literature, we also argue, in contradistinction to some prominent researchers and commentators, that there are equally significant defining moments and historical events that came well before the era of the Revolution. We suggest that, in important respects, certain occurrences and circumstances that predated the American War of Independence served as common roots in the establishment and subsequent development of both societies. Here we refer to the periods of European, especially British, colonization and related influences going back at least as far as the late seventeenth and early eighteenth centuries. Furthermore, we contend that there were significant historical events that took place, not just before the Revolutionary period but afterward, as well. The American Civil War is one of the prime examples of important later events that were crucial for shaping both societies. This topic and others are discussed in depth as part of our general review of historical arguments and evidence. In this introductory chapter, however, we draw the reader's initial attention to these central points, because they serve as recurring themes in much of our theoretical and historical analysis, and also provide insights into the patterns of findings in the research on contemporary comparisons of Canada and the United States.

PLAN OF THE BOOK

The main body of this volume comprises three interconnected parts, although each of these segments could be viewed as a 'booklet' on its own. The first of these deals with theoretical issues, the second focuses on historical research, and the third concentrates on contemporary evidence and recent interpretations. Thus, Part I begins with a detailed review and assessment of the two major competing theses about the beginnings of the two countries. As outlined in Chapter 2, the first of these approaches is the European 'founding fragment' perspective, which is represented in the work of Hartz (1955, 1964) and in the broadly similar arguments of McRae (1964) and Horowitz (1966). In somewhat different ways, each of these writers suggests that Canada and the United States began as generally kindred societies, except for a 'touch of Toryism' that permeated the northern nation. The second leading perspective that is discussed in Chapter 2 is Lipset's quite different 'origins' or 'revolution-counterrevolution' interpretation, which contends that fundamental and enduring differences between the two societies developed specifically out of the American Revolution (see, e.g., Lipset 1963a, 1963b, 1964, 1968, 1979, 1985, 1986, 1989, 1990, 1996).

Building from this review of existing approaches, we then offer an alternative theoretical interpretation, as outlined in Chapter 3. Our interpretation partly complements but also goes beyond each of the earlier perspectives. As is discussed in detail later, we suggest that, for some time prior to the Revolutionary era itself, the English-speaking colonies in Canada and the American North or Northeast were influenced by a set of common 'deep structures', along with related values, institutions, and forms of social organization, that were fundamental to the early development of both societies and that have had a lasting influence in these regions, right up to the modern era. A central hypothesis is that the two sets of British colonies that would ultimately become present-day Canada and the United States were marked in indelible and still influential ways by their shared connections with England. This early English or British influence is evident not only in the cultures and value systems of the two societies, but also in many of the social-structural characteristics that have come to define each nation. We argue further that, in other regions, especially French Canada and the American South, many of these common influences were largely negated by, or overlaid with, other quite different social, economic, and political forces. Such forces took these two regions in directions that diverged from English Canada and the northern United States, and influenced their populations in ways that distinguished them rather clearly from the peoples inhabiting the rest of North America. The ultimate result of this process was the creation of four relatively separate regional entities or 'sub-societies' within the territories that would eventually become Canada and the United States.

Part II of the book, which includes Chapters 4, 5, and 6, is an extensive presentation and assessment of historical research bearing on the theoretical perspectives discussed in Part I. Of special concern throughout these chapters is the period of history running from the latter part of the eighteenth century to the middle of the nineteenth century. Various writers suggest that this span of about 100 years was the formative era for both Canada and the United States, and perhaps is the most crucial period to study if we are to comprehend the underlying nature of the two countries, both historically and in the modern age. As we shall discuss, it was during this time that several pivotal events took place. These include, in particular, the English defeat of the French in Canada, the American Revolution, the American Civil War, and the arrival of millions of immigrants on the North American continent. These critical occurrences shaped the nature of the two societies in fundamental ways, and had implications for both nations that are, in some respects, still apparent today.

Part III of the analysis focuses on Canada and the United States in the contemporary period. Here we present evidence dealing with a series of issues that have emerged from the more recent literature on the two societies, with our findings presented in five distinct but interrelated chapters. Our main purpose is to assemble and test a series of hypotheses about Canadian and American differences that have arisen from this literature. In addition, however, as suggested above, we go beyond most of the research in this area by theorizing about and assessing the existence of key regional distinctions within the two societies, specifically between Quebec and the rest of Canada and between the American South and the rest of the United States.

We test the applicability of this four-regions model, along with the more conventional two-nations comparison, using numerous sources of data and statistical information. These sources include representative sample surveys that were administered in the two countries, especially the Canadian and American waves of the World Values Surveys (WVS) from the early 1990s (see Inglehart 1997). For some of our comparisons, we also use supplementary data from other sample surveys that were taken both before and after the WVS. In addition, we conduct extensive reviews of past and recent literature comparing the two societies on a broad set of issues. A large portion of our analysis deals with what are generally thought to be cultural differences between the nations. These differences are judged primarily by comparing the attitudes, beliefs, and behaviours exhibited by the two peoples. However, as noted previously, such cultural indicators are typically assumed to have significant and reciprocal causal connections with the political, economic, and other social-structural characteristics of the two countries. We share this view. For this reason, we compare the two societies and the four regions, not only from the point of view of attitudes and behaviours, but also with respect to such social-structural variables as size of government and government-spending, levels of economic inequality, patterns of immigration and ethnic composition, and so on. Many of these elements of our analysis draw on a large and diverse array of statistical evidence that is available from government research bureaus and other agencies in both nations.

The main themes to be considered in Part III are as follows. In Chapter 7, we begin by looking at a set of related topics dealing with the general question of morality or moral conservatism. Here we compare the two nations and the four sub-societies on such issues as religious involvement and religiosity, family values and sexual morality, and problems of crime and the law. A principal issue to be explored is the claim by some observers that present-day Americans, especially those living in the US South, have a more conservative and restrictive view of these concerns, while Canadians, particularly Quebecers, are more liberal, egalitarian, or permissive on such questions. Chapter 8 is devoted to the study of individualist versus collectivist values, including the extent to which the two populations and the four sub-groups vary in their views on individual self-reliance, personal self-confidence, and the role of government. This part of the analysis will allow us to assess the widely accepted argument that Americans have a deep commitment to personal independence, as well as a strong dislike for government authority, whereas Canadians favour less individual freedom and a more prominent government presence in their lives. In Chapter 9 we assess a third category of issues, which fall under the broad title of social inclusion and tolerance. Our central goal here is to present evidence about the rights and opportunities that are afforded to ethnic and other minorities in both countries. In this section of the analysis, we test the perception that Canadians are more accepting of minority rights and ethnic pluralism than are Americans. We also look at the question of whether there are important regional differences on these issues within the two societies. Our research in Chapter 10 concentrates on the extent to which the national populations vary with respect to their approaches to politics and political behaviour. The analysis in this chapter focuses particularly on the allegation that Canadians are much more passive, submissive, and trusting toward their government leaders and political structure than are Americans. In Chapter 11, we look closely at the question of social involvement and voluntary action in each nation. Of special interest in this final section of Part III is the long-standing assumption that Americans are significantly more engaged with and involved in the voluntary sector than are their Canadian counterparts.

The concluding chapter of the book, Chapter 12, offers an overview of the important national and regional differences and similarities that we have identified in the analysis. In addition, we address several continuing debates about the nature of Canada and the United States and the links between these debates and the myths, both past and present, that have shaped our understanding of the two nations. We also discuss how our own findings bear on these debates and consider the implications of our research for future analyses of the Canadian–American reality in the twenty-first century.

PART I

_⁓_

CANADA AND THE UNITED STATES

THEORETICAL PERSPECTIVES

INTRODUCTION

At least from the time of Tocqueville (1835, 1840), observers and researchers from various fields have sought to understand and explain the historical beginnings and underpinnings of North America's societies. Although much of the early literature concentrated exclusively on the United States, some of these accounts also provided comparative assessments of the relationship between the United States and Canada (e.g., Tocqueville 1835: 362, 445, 448; see also Bryce 1887, 1889, 1921a, 1921b; Hanna 1902). More recently, a considerable amount of historical work has been generated that directly compares the two nations (e.g., Bell 1992; Bell and Tepperman 1979; Craig 1968; Errington 1994; Granatstein and Hillmer 1991; Horowitz 1966; Lower 1946; Thompson and Randall 1994; Smith 1994; Stuart 1988; Underhill 1960). This research has made significant contributions to the documentation, description, and interpretation of the notable events in the shared past of Canada and the United States.

While a variety of important insights and conclusions can be gleaned from this body of research and commentary, there are two prominent theoretical perspectives that have generally been the most influential interpretations of how and why Canada and the United States developed as they did in both the early and the later stages of their histories. The first of these perspectives actually has at least three variants: the original formulation of Louis Hartz (Hartz 1955, Hartz et al. 1964) in the historical literature, and the broadly similar interpretations developed by Kenneth McRae (1964) and Gad Horowitz (1966) in political science. These three approaches overlap and complement each other in several ways, and so are sometimes referred to in combination (see, e.g., Forbes 1987: 287; Brym 1989: 58). The other leading account, and the major rival to the first set of perspectives, is one that has emerged from the sociological literature, in the work of Seymour Martin Lipset (1963a, 1963b, 1964, 1968, 1979, 1985, 1986, 1989, 1990, 1996).

In Part I of this volume, our purpose is to outline, assess, and build from these prominent theoretical approaches. Chapter 2 begins with Hartz's original work, which focuses on the founding influences of European colonization in North America, and the 'fragment' nations that allegedly arose out of these influences, as the main factors in the evolution of Canada and the United States into distinct societies. As part of this analysis, we also consider the revisions and supplements to Hartz's perspective that have been provided by both McRae and Horowitz. We then review Lipset's 'origins' interpretation, which points to the crucial importance of the American Revolution as the central event, or defining moment, underlying the formation of both Canada and the United States. Following this overview of previous theories, we proceed in Chapter 3 to suggest an alternative perspective. This chapter begins by extracting what we believe are the most useful contributions, both from the two leading theoretical interpretations discussed in Chapter 2 and from a number of other sources. We then redirect these ideas toward a different, though partly complementary, interpretation. This interpretation argues for the enduring influence of what might be called the common 'deep structures' that both societies carried within them prior to their disconnection from one another around the time of the American Revolution. We also consider important events that occurred subsequent to the revolutionary period, and discuss how these later events may have had an equally significant impact in shaping the two nations.

CHAPTER 2

꿇

PREVIOUS PERSPECTIVES

FOUNDING FRAGMENTS AND REVOLUTIONARY ORIGINS

HARTZ'S THEORY OF EUROPEAN FOUNDING FRAGMENTS

A half-century ago, Louis Hartz embarked upon a set of influential historical analyses that sought to explain the founding of so-called 'new societies'. Hartz was especially concerned with those societies that came into existence during the era of European exploration and colonization after the mid-1500s. His principal examples in this ground-breaking work included the United States, English and French Canada, Australia, Dutch South Africa, and the nations of Latin America (Hartz 1955; Hartz et al. 1964).

According to Hartz, all such New World societies are 'fragments' of their European parent nations, pieces that, after being broken off from their Old World progenitors, then developed separately from them. His main thesis is that, although all of the fragment societies changed over time and moved beyond the circumstances of their original founding, they did so largely 'without inhibition' from their forebears, untouched in important ways by the political events and social upheavals taking place in Europe in later years (Hartz et al. 1964: 9). In Hartz's view, each fragment was planted on 'new soil' and was 'detached' from the key forces shaping its Old World parent; as a result, each one evinced a considerable amount of cultural 'immobility', conserving and reinforcing the original core values and institutions that characterized its beginnings (Hartz et al. 1964: 3). As Horowitz puts it, Hartz's thesis is one in which 'the ideology of the founders is thus frozen, congealed at the point of origin' (Horowitz 1966: 145).

Liberalism in North America

Probably the best-known and most influential illustration of Hartz's general theory of European fragments is his analysis of the rise of 'liberalism' in North America. We should begin by noting that liberalism is a word which has been used in different and even contradictory ways by various writers over the years.

Throughout the latter half of the twentieth century, as Hartz himself suggests, the idea of liberalism has become linked with 'all sorts of social reform connotations' (Hartz 1955: 4). These connotations have meant that liberalism in the present day is normally associated with what might more appropriately be termed 'left-liberalism', i.e., a system of thought that favours significant government involvement in and control over the lives of individual citizens in society, especially through an often extensive array of state-directed and publicly funded social-welfare programs.

In the context of Hartz's work, however, the concept of liberalism has quite another meaning, one which is almost the opposite of this more recent usage, and which today is more apt to be referred to as 'conservatism' (e.g., Pocklington 1985: 63–4; Gwyn 1985: 162; for some discussion, see Grabb, Baer, and Curtis 1999; Lipset 1996: 35–9). That is, instead of signifying a system in which all people are greatly influenced and constrained by government and other outside authorities, Hartz's liberalism, on the contrary, refers to individual freedom from undue external constraints. Here Hartz is explicitly influenced by the idea of 'liberty', as defined by the seventeenth-century English political philosopher, John Locke (Hartz 1955: 4, 59–60; also Forbes 1987: 290).

Locke believed that, in an imagined or hypothetical 'state of nature', all people ideally should enjoy 'natural liberty', including the right to think, speak, and act freely, without being subject to the will or power of other individuals or groups (Locke 1690: 301). At the same time, however, Locke agreed that the 'perfect freedom' implied by this hypothetical state of nature is not feasible in reality, because if all individuals are allowed to act completely as they wish, without regard for the wishes of others, clashes among people must inevitably occur and these clashes will nullify the very liberty that all of us desire (1690: 287). Thus, for Locke, the 'state of liberty . . . is not a state of licence', in which each person is free 'to do as he lists, to live as he pleases, and not to be tied by any laws' (Locke 1690: 288, 302). On the contrary, liberty in a society or community requires some system of government, i.e., a formal political and legislative structure that has the legal capacity to 'restrain the partiality and violence of men' and thus to safeguard universal freedom (1690: 294). Such 'freedom of men under government' should also be 'by consent' of the governed, with 'a standing rule to live by, common to everyone of that society and made by the legislative power erected in it' (Locke 1690: 301–2). Locke's only real worry about the role of government was that it too should be regulated, with a 'limited power' that protects the people's natural rights from possible abuses by government leaders themselves (Locke 1690: 302, 371–2; for some discussion, see McClelland 1996: 234–9).

These questions concerning the priority that should be granted to individual rights relative to government authority, and to personal freedom relative to the collective good, are central issues to be addressed in subsequent sections of this volume. For now, however, we can note that Hartz's idea of the liberal society is one marked by liberty or liberalism 'in the classic Lockian sense' (Hartz 1955: 4). In such a society, as long as citizens have a regard for the natural rights of each other, with some limited but effective government power to help ensure that these rights are protected, each person can have the opportunity to achieve what might be called 'life, liberty, and the pursuit of happiness'.

The latter phrase is a familiar one, of course. It comes from the Declaration of Independence, the now-famous document drafted by the revolutionary leaders of the thirteen American colonies, which in 1776 rebelled against British rule and ultimately constituted the original United States of America. It may come as no surprise, then, that the United States, especially in its founding years, has often been viewed as the quintessential example of what Locke meant by a liberal society, a nation of free individuals living in a virtual state of nature. Locke himself appears to suggest as much when he says that, 'in the beginning all the world was America' (Locke 1690: 319; see Hartz 1955: 61). However, it is important to note that 'America' here is a reference to the colonial regions of the Americas in general, especially North America. This comment is not about the United States of America, which did not exist as a nation until almost a century after Locke wrote these words.

In any event, Hartz largely agrees with those who see the United States as a prime illustration of a liberal society. From Hartz's perspective, the new nation that arose in the thirteen American colonies did so in a kind of 'time capsule', or perhaps more precisely a 'time and space capsule', largely unaffected by important events unfolding in Europe and elsewhere. Hartz argues that 'America represents the liberal mechanism of Europe [more specifically, England] functioning without the European social antagonisms' (Hartz 1955: 16; see also Hartz et al. 1964: 33). These antagonisms include, first of all, the clash between aristocratic and 'bourgeois' factions, such as those that occurred in the late feudal or early modern era; a key example here is the English Civil War involving the forces of King Charles I and Oliver Cromwell in the mid-1600s (see Hartz 1955: 23, 35, 38, 43). In addition, Hartz's interpretation is that, because of the absence of this first kind of class conflict, American liberalism never acquired any real exposure to a second key form of class antagonism—between the bourgeois and proletarian classes of capitalist society. As a result, Hartz suggests, Marxist-inspired socialist movements never gained much support in the United States, in both the early and the later stages of America's development (see, e.g., Hartz 1955: 6, 9, 35, 50–2, 76; Hartz et al. 1964: 7, 39). Hartz's view is that the avoidance or repudiation of such conflicts in colonial America was possible precisely because America represented a new and geographically detached fragment, a place 'where land was abundant and the voyage to the New World [was] itself a claim to independence' (Hartz 1955: 18, 64–6). Thus, such a place and time provided ideal circumstances and conditions for liberalism to grow.

Nevertheless, while Hartz sees the thirteen American colonies as a near-perfect setting for the rise of liberalism, he also notes that this is clearly not the only liberal fragment in the Americas, or the only new society where liberal values and institutions would take root and flourish. He argues that 'for all of the magical chemistry of American liberal society, we are dealing with social materials common to the Western world' more generally (1955: 17). In particular, he points to English Canada as the other major example in North America of an essentially liberal society (Hartz et al. 1964: 3, 7, 9, 16n.).

Hartz sees a common lineage of liberalism in the United States and English Canada and traces it directly to their development as colonies of England from the early 1600s onward. For Hartz, both English Canadians and Americans were among the first people to implement core liberal ideas that originated, at least in prototypical form, in England itself. Some of these ideas include: a belief in the virtues of independent, and typically small-scale or middle-class, 'bourgeois' capitalism; a 'discovery of the "self"', or the individual person, as a real and distinct entity existing apart from the community; and a related preference for individual 'self-help', as opposed to an emphasis on collective rights and responsibilities, especially in economic matters (see, e.g., Hartz et al. 1964: 9, 12, 35). Hartz goes on to suggest, as well, that English Canadians were like Americans in being 'inveterate individualists', who were imbued with much the same 'egalitarian feeling' and 'democratic spirit' (Hartz et al. 1964: 35, 91, 34).

In Hartz's estimation, any differences between American and English-Canadian liberalism are really a matter of degree. That is, while both societies espoused similarly liberal outlooks and tendencies, in the United States these sentiments allegedly were more 'intense', whereas in English Canada (and in another liberal fragment, Dutch South Africa) they were somewhat more 'restrained' (Hartz et al. 1964: 71, 91). For Hartz, the more moderate liberalism of English Canadians is mainly attributable to their not joining in the rebellion against Britain, and so not experiencing an outright separation, or 'sharp break', from their Old World influences (Hartz et al. 1964: 81). In particular, the continued ties to their European parent meant that the people of English Canada faced prolonged exposure to such 'Tory' beliefs as the legitimacy of monarchical or aristocratic pre-eminence in various aspects of life, a belief that was central to Britain's long-established class distinctions, social hierarchies, and imperial political arrangements (see, e.g., Hartz et al. 1964: 40, 91–2).

Hartz posits that this so-called 'Tory streak' or 'Tory touch' in English Canada is also partly due to the 'loyalism' shown by a number of American colonists at the time of the Revolution (Hartz et al. 1964: 34, 91). Hartz's reference to loyalism here concerns one of the more significant repercussions of the American War of Independence: the migration of thousands of residents out of the thirteen American colonies during and after the war, and the settlement of many of these refugees in parts of what would later become the Canadian Maritimes, Ontario, and Quebec. This group of migrants would come to be known as the loyalists, with some of their number eventually being granted official status as 'United Empire Loyalists' (Upton 1971: 52–3). Like other writers we shall consider, Hartz seems to assume here that the very fact of their exodus from the thirteen colonies, along with their failure to show active support for the rebellion, is sufficient grounds for concluding, not only that these refugees from the Revolution were loyal to Britain, but also that their loyalism was proof that they had a greater commitment to Tory values and institutions than did those Americans who chose to remain in the thirteen colonies (Hartz et al. 1964: 40, 91).

Other Societies in North America

Within the larger North American context, there are two other elements that Hartz's analysis seeks to incorporate. The first of these is French Canada, and the second is the southern United States.

French Canada

Hartz contends that French-Canadian society was a complete and self-contained fragment of the Old World, but one which was essentially quite different from those that formed the United States and English Canada. Rather than being a liberal fragment, French Canada (along with various new societies that arose in Latin America) originated as a 'feudal' fragment, or what John Commons called 'a bit of medieval France, picked out and preserved for the curious student of social evolution' (Commons 1907: 97; see Hartz et al.1964: 27).[1]

The social structure of 'New France', as it was called then, was dominated by both a strong Roman Catholic clergy and a privileged class of landholders, or 'seigneurs', whose property rights, while not identical to those of aristocrats living in France itself, were sufficiently similar that the society resembled its European feudal parent in many respects (see, e.g., McRae 1964: 223–5). According to Hartz, French Canada grew from the seeds of this enduring feudal

---

1.   Here and elsewhere, the terms 'feudal' and 'feudalism' are used in the relatively broad sense employed by writers like Marx and Weber, to refer to any form of economic system in which a ruling aristocratic class relies on a commoner class of serfs as a source of labour. This usage departs from the more precise definitions employed by some historians specializing in this area of study (see, e.g., Clark 1995: Chapter 8; Comninel 2000: 9–15).

past, maintaining much the same culture and traditions and remaining largely isolated from the new ideas and momentous events that would reshape France and other parts of Europe after the 1600s (Hartz et al. 1964: 3–4). Of particular importance in this era were the liberal, anti-monarchical, and democratic ideas that became increasingly powerful during the eighteenth-century period known as the Enlightenment, and that were central to the eventual overthrow of France's king, Louis XVI, and his aristocratic consorts during the French Revolution of 1789 (see, e.g., Hartz et al. 1964: 13, 16n., 21).

Hartz notes that subsequent influences did play a part in changing the French-Canadian feudal fragment, including its eventual exposure to Enlightenment thought, but he contends that, by that time, the 'underlying tide of traditionalism' had been so well-entrenched in French Canada that such ideas did not 'cut deep' (Hartz et al. 1964: 17n.). As a result, then, French Canada evolved as a society quite unlike those emerging in the English-speaking societies of North America, with a structural, cultural, and institutional bedrock that lacked the strong motive force of liberalism found elsewhere.

The American South

This brings us to the fourth and final element in Hartz's delineation of the founding components of what are now Canada and the United States. This element is the American South. However, unlike the other three societies discussed to this point, Hartz does not conceive of the southern United States as a full-fledged fragment in its own right. Instead, he sees it as a segment within the larger liberal fragment that comprises the United States as a whole. Hartz does agree with those who say that the South, because of its plantation economy, the institution of slavery, and the extraordinary gap between the 'slaves at the bottom and a set of genteel planters' at the top, is the one part of early America that comes closest to the feudalism of 'Old World Europe' (Hartz 1955: 52, 8). At the same time, however, he contends that 'it has never really been Europe'; instead, it is 'an alien child in a liberal family', 'tortured and confused' because it is headed by a 'frustrated aristocracy' confronted with the contradictions between its slave-based economy and way of life, on the one hand, and its essential American commitment to the Lockian ideas of liberty and individual freedom, on the other hand (Hartz 1955: 8). Thus, while Hartz agrees that 'there may be an "aristocratic" touch to the American South' because of 'the elitism of racial biases' that developed there, he maintains that this region of the United States was still a liberal society, like the rest of the nation, with a common revolutionary past and a shared bourgeois or capitalist ethic that put it 'a long step away from the old English feudal order' (Hartz et al. 1964: 34, 59, 100).

Variations on Hartz's Thesis: The Work of McRae and Horowitz

Building from Hartz's original founding-fragment thesis, a number of other writers have sought to understand and explain the founding of new societies using a generally similar approach. There are two principal examples of this research that focus primarily on the historical beginnings of Canada and its relationship with the United States. These examples are to be found in the works of two Canadian scholars, Kenneth McRae (1964) and Gad Horowitz (1966).

McRae on the Structure of Canadian History

McRae's assessment of the structure of Canadian history parallels Hartz's view in several ways, although there is at least one important difference that should be noted. McRae and Hartz are in agreement, first of all, with regard to the French-Canadian fragment. Both writers see New France as a vestige of European feudalism in most important respects, 'a closely controlled projection' of the 'highly centralized' monarchical regime that was ruling France during the time that the colony became established (McRae 1964: 221). Also, following Hartz, McRae believes that English Canadians and Americans were quite similar during their early histories. In particular, McRae concurs with Hartz when he asserts that, like their counterparts in the thirteen colonies, the pre-revolutionary English population to the north, most of whom lived in Atlantic Canada at the time, were 'fundamentally American in outlook' (McRae 1964: 234). However, in the same passage, McRae also notes that, in his view, the refugees from the Revolution—the so-called loyalists who left America for the Atlantic region, Ontario, and Quebec after the outbreak of war—likewise carried with them 'much of the original liberal heritage of the American colonies' (McRae 1964: 234). To McRae, then, the English-Canadian population, not only the small number who inhabited the Canadian regions before the Revolution but also those who came later from the thirteen colonies themselves, adhered to a similar form of Lockian liberalism in their religious, economic, and political lives. They were 'by the very circumstances of their foundation born free . . . with a prevailing ethos of religious dissent, individual freedom, and limited government' (McRae 1964: 222).

It is on this latter point that we find the main difference between Hartz and McRae. Specifically, McRae takes issue with, or at least seeks to soften, Hartz's 'Tory touch' hypothesis regarding the impact of the loyalist migration to Canada at the time of the Revolution. Although he is not entirely explicit on the point, Hartz's thesis implies that the émigrés included 'servile monarchists', who held strongly Tory or anti-liberal beliefs and who were sufficiently numerous and influential that the loyalists, as a group, were serious 'enemies of the notion of liberty' (McRae 1964: 235). In contrast, McRae's reading of the historical evidence is that the migrants were decidedly liberal in outlook, much like the Americans who stayed behind in the thirteen colonies themselves (McRae 1964: 235–6).

McRae's analysis maintains that whatever differences can be discerned between the Americans and English Canadians in this regard are quite minor. For example, McRae contends that the loyalists and other members of the English-Canadian population generally agreed with the American opposition to many of the policies imposed by the British imperial authorities during this period; however, the English-Canadian opposition to British rule was marked by more 'moderation' and 'compromise' than was shown by the revolutionaries (McRae 1964: 239). Thus, while McRae agrees that the loyalist refugees and other English inhabitants of Canada were not exactly like their American cousins, he is convinced that they were far more similar than different. Moreover, while McRae notes that the two populations obviously differed from each other on the issue of whether or not to revolt against Britain, he also indicates that for him, and in contrast to Hartz's apparent inference, being loyal to Britain and being committed to Tory or anti-liberal values are not the same thing (see McRae 1964: 238–40). This is a point to which we shall return in subsequent sections of the analysis.

Horowitz's Analysis of Liberalism, Toryism, and Socialism

Writing shortly after both Hartz and McRae, Horowitz picks up the main threads of the founding-fragment thesis and seeks to modify and extend the argument. Not surprisingly, there are numerous parallels and areas of congruence between Horowitz's approach and those of the other two writers. For example, like the other two perspectives, Horowitz's analysis proceeds from the premise that the pre-revolutionary American colonies, as well as the early United States in the period after the Revolution, represented an almost pure Lockian liberal fragment, with little or no feudal or Tory presence in the population (Horowitz 1966: 151, 155). In addition, although his commentary on French Canada is brief, Horowitz seems to agree with Hartz and McRae that French-Canadian society is best understood as a distinctively feudal fragment, with 'pre-Enlightenment Catholic' values and outlooks (Horowitz 1966: 155, 145).

However, there are some significant disagreements between Horowitz and the other two writers, especially McRae, when comparisons are made of English Canada and the United States. In general, Horowitz's rendering of the Hartzian argument places greater emphasis on the same differences between English Canada and the United States that McRae's analysis seeks to downplay (Horowitz 1966: 151–2). Thus, while Horowitz agrees that, from the perspective of a comparison of societies throughout the world, the differences between

English Canada and the United States are 'minor' or 'subtle', he also believes that, from a narrower perspective focusing on the two societies alone, they are 'of absolutely crucial importance' (Horowitz 1966: 148–9).

Horowitz's main concern in taking this alternative stance is to argue against the view of both Hartz and McRae that, because both English Canada and the United States began as liberal fragments, neither nation developed a strong socialist political movement in later years (Horowitz 1966: 148–9). In contrast to this argument, Horowitz contends that English Canada has, indeed, experienced a viable socialist movement, and has done so despite its founding liberal ideology and other similarities to the United States. Horowitz suggests that Canada's socialist movement is most clearly represented in the rise of the Co-operative Commonwealth Federation (CCF), which later evolved into the New Democratic Party, a socialist political party that has no parallel in the United States (Horowitz 1966: 149–50).

As part of his critique of McRae's approach, Horowitz argues that one of the main reasons why socialism has found some success in English Canada is because of the very same Tory touch that McRae tends to discount, but that Hartz believed was a distinguishing feature of English Canada's historical origins (Horowitz 1966: 150–1). Horowitz argues that this Tory streak has had a 'continuing influence on English-Canadian political culture' and has helped to differentiate it from American political culture in a number of ways (Horowitz 1966: 150–1). In particular, according to Horowitz, the allegedly greater Canadian acceptance of conservative or Tory-style collectivism, whereby individual rights are often subordinated to group or community needs, is a key reason why, as Hartz's thesis implies, left-wing or socialist collectivism (e.g., the rise of the welfare state) has also been generally more palatable to Canadians than to Americans (Horowitz 1966: 154). In a similar way, Horowitz believes that this connection between Toryism and socialism is also behind the peculiarly English-Canadian phenomenon known as the 'red Tory'. This term refers to those individuals who, despite being members or leaders of pro-capitalist political parties, such as the old Progressive Conservative Party or the new Conservative Party of Canada, for example, are often, at the same time, supporters of government-funded and quasi-socialist programs to assist the poor and other disadvantaged groups (see Horowitz 1966: 157–9).

Overall, then, Horowitz's approach can be distinguished from the other two perspectives primarily because it puts greater stress than either Hartz or McRae on the importance of the so-called Tory streak for establishing and maintaining significant differences between English Canada and the United States, both past and present. For Horowitz, 'the foundations of English Canada are American liberal' but 'the superstructure is British', with 'non-liberal British elements [that] have entered into English-Canadian society together with

American liberal elements at the foundations [emphasis in the original]'
(Horowitz 1966: 156).

LIPSET'S ORIGINS THESIS: THE DEFINING
MOMENT OF THE AMERICAN REVOLUTION

The leading alternative to the various founding-fragment interpretations of the
historical relationship between Canada and the United States is the 'origins'
thesis offered by the noted American sociologist, Seymour Martin Lipset.
Beginning some four decades ago, Lipset has written extensively on Canadian
and American society, and is widely viewed as the major contributor to the
study of this topic in the sociological literature (Lipset 1963a, 1963b, 1964,
1968, 1979, 1985, 1986, 1989, 1990, 1996).

We shall find that there are some areas of overlap between Lipset's historical interpretation and those posed by Hartz, McRae, and Horowitz. In addition, however, there are several crucial differences, especially with respect to
the implications of certain historical events for understanding and characterizing the development of Canada and the United States into two separate societies. In this section, we begin with a presentation of Lipset's general thesis,
with a special focus on what he believes are the main differences in the core
values of Canadians and Americans. In the process of explicating Lipset's interpretation, we also make specific comparisons between his approach and those
offered by the founding-fragment theorists, in an attempt to demonstrate their
major areas of similarity and disagreement. This comparative assessment will
serve as the prelude to Chapter 3, in which we outline an alternative perspective for understanding the historical relationship between Canada and the
United States and the significance of this relationship for shaping the two societies, both past and present.

National Beginnings: Revolution and Counter-revolution

Perhaps the most obvious similarity between Lipset's thesis and the analyses
of Hartz, McRae, and Horowitz is that Lipset also sees the American Revolution as a major factor in the original formation of the United States and Canada.
Lipset's approach differs, however, in that he clearly believes the American
War of Independence was an even more crucial occurrence than do the other
writers. Lipset contends, in fact, that the single event of the American Revolution was unique in human history. He argues that, 'in starting from a revolutionary event' and in being 'the first major colony successfully to revolt
against colonial rule', the United States was an exceptional and unprecedented
creation, 'qualitatively different from all other countries' (Lipset 1996: 18,
77–8; 1963a: 2). Indeed, because of the Revolution, the United States would

be the 'first new nation' of the modern world, 'the most "modern" and purely bourgeois culture', and also 'the most democratic country' (Lipset 1963b; 1996: 79; for some debate and discussion, see Horowitz 1973; Wood 1992; Koschmann 1997; Nelles 1997; Nolan 1997).

And what of the American Revolution's effects on Canada? For Lipset, again, the supposed impact on Canadian society is much more telling and far-reaching than has generally been suggested by the founding-fragment theorists. It will be recalled that Hartz, McRae, and, to a lesser extent, Horowitz all conclude that, compared with the United States, Canadian society did not differ or change radically in the wake of the Revolution. Instead, Canada continued to be similar to American society, in that it was essentially liberal, or else liberal with a Tory touch. Lipset, on the other hand, contends that, as a result of the Revolution, Canada became a 'counter-revolutionary' bastion of non-liberal Tory values and institutions, and henceforward remained distinct from the United States in a number of fundamental ways (see Lipset 1990: Chapter 1; also Lipset 1968).

There is no question, of course, that the period of the American Revolution saw some momentous changes in the political and social structures of the societies developing in the eastern portion of North America. First of all, the United States arose as an independent nation in the late 1700s, after a prolonged military conflict in which many of the inhabitants of the thirteen colonies south of the St Lawrence River combined to overthrow British rule in that region. Second, most of the population to the north, both English- and French-speaking, did not join in or actively support this conflict and continued to live, instead, as subjects of the British Crown. Third, both during and after the Revolution, a number of the southern colonists emigrated to the north, settled in areas of what are now the Canadian Maritimes, Ontario, and Quebec, and came to be called the loyalists. Lipset's analysis touches on other aspects of the two nations' pasts, including the opening of the western frontiers in both countries in the 1800s (Lipset 1963a: 521; 1964: 183). However, it is these founding events that provide the core of his argument for how and why the United States and Canada evolved into distinct societies.

Before continuing, we might raise the question: how can the American Revolution be seen as the historical beginning or defining moment for both countries? Canada, after all, was not constituted as a nation until more than 90 years after the American Declaration of Independence and more than 80 years after the Revolutionary War itself. To Lipset, however, 'the institutional characters' of the two societies, if not their actual nationhood, were defined or 'set' during the Revolution (Lipset 1968: 51). From this perspective, the United States was founded on and still embraces its revolutionary values and ideals, while Canada has always been a society shaped by its initial counter-revolutionary rejection of these same values and ideals. While at times acknowledging that there are now many similarities between the two nations and their populations, Lipset has maintained that even today Canada and the United States continue to be significantly different societies and cultures, and that their differences stem largely from the 'indelible marks' left by the Revolution and the two peoples' divergent responses to this event (Lipset 1990: 1; 1996: 18).

We can see, then, that Lipset's primary concern in his analysis of the Revolutionary era is to determine what this formative period tells us about the guiding principles and fundamental beliefs of the two societies. Central to his thesis is the claim that, especially for the loyalist émigrés and the English-speaking settlers already living in Canada, the choice not to support the War of Independence from England was an explicit indication that the Canadian people at the time had disavowed the values of the Revolution and were strongly committed to a distinct set of Tory ideas and beliefs instilled in them by their European parent. The central questions to address now are: what precisely were the core values of early American society, in Lipset's estimation, and how were these values different from their Canadian counterparts?

A Conflict of Values: American Liberalism and Canadian Toryism

Lipset often uses the term 'Americanism', or the 'American Creed', to denote the set of founding or defining values of the United States (see, e.g., Lipset 1963b: 178; 1979: 25; see also Myrdal 1944). In his first theoretical work on this issue, Lipset argues that the ideas of 'equality' and 'achievement', which are taken from Parsons' set of 'pattern variables', essentially characterize the American value system (Lipset 1963a, 1963b, 1964; see Parsons 1951). These two values are core elements of the American Creed, and can be contrasted with the ideas of 'elitism' and 'ascription', which he sees as the main guiding principles of early Canadian society. In using these ideas, Lipset is basically arguing that, by the time of the Revolution, Americans in general had a strong desire both for equal political rights as free citizens in a representative democracy, and for equal opportunity to achieve success and prosperity as self-reliant individuals in a relatively open economy. By comparison, he suggests that most Canadians were content with an elitist system in which they were obedient subjects of a monarchical government, and in which economic success was based on a structure of ascribed or inherited privilege (see, e.g., Lipset 1968: 37–42, 44–50, 60; 1990: 13–18, 20–2; 1996: 31).

Since his initial characterization of the American Creed and its Canadian Tory counterpart, Lipset has altered and expanded his list of dominant values on at least two occasions (Lipset 1990, 1996). His most recent version identifies five key values that constitute the American Creed. These five values are:

'liberty', 'egalitarianism', 'individualism', 'populism', and 'laissez-faire' (Lipset 1996: 19–23, 31; for an alternative version, see Lipset 1990: 26–34).

Unfortunately, Lipset does not provide complete definitions for these concepts, an omission that makes the theoretical contribution of his work at times inconsistent or ambiguous. Nevertheless, based on his inclusion of such ideas as populism and laissez-faire in the set of dominant values, it seems clear that Lipset believes most Americans place a high value on personal freedom from external constraints in their political and economic lives, especially those imposed by big government. The remaining three concepts on his list—liberty, egalitarianism, and individualism—appear, as well, to underscore his view that Americans cherish individual autonomy and independence in general, and not just in the economic and political spheres of existence (see also Lipset 1968: 57–8). For example, according to Lipset, one other key area of life where freedom and autonomy are especially cherished by Americans is religion (Lipset 1996: 19–20, 93; also Lipset 1968: 52–3, 248–51).

Lipset's underlying intention in delineating the five core components of the American Creed becomes more comprehensible if we note that he sees a common conceptual thread running though all of them. That common thread is the idea of 'liberalism' (Lipset 1996: 31). Lipset further clarifies his view by adding that he is referring to liberalism in the 'eighteenth- and nineteenth-century meanings' of the term. Thus, Lipset definitely does not believe that the American Creed is equivalent to liberalism in the modern sense. As was discussed earlier in this chapter, modern liberalism denotes a preference for a strong government presence in people's everyday lives, an idea that is probably more appropriately referred to as 'left-liberalism' and that is almost the reverse of what Lipset means here.

It is notable that Lipset uses the idea of liberalism as the centrepiece in his delineation of the dominant values of American society. At first glance, this may appear to be quite consistent with Hartz's founding-fragment thesis, which, as we have seen, also treats liberalism as the core idea or guiding principle of American society. However, it is important to be aware of one major difference between Lipset's and Hartz's approaches in this regard. We should recall that Hartz uses liberalism 'in the classic Lockian sense' (Hartz 1955: 4), which means that, for him, liberalism is not synonymous with 'licence', or any situation in which individuals are at liberty to do whatever they wish. On the contrary, the Lockian view is that unrestrained individual freedom ultimately undermines the liberty of others, and is therefore the mortal enemy of true liberalism.

Although Lipset occasionally alludes to Locke in his discussions (see, e.g., Lipset 1990: 8), his analysis generally does not address the issue of whether some form of external control or regulation is necessary for ensuring genuine liberalism in society. In those few instances where he does address this question, Lipset seems to take the opposite view to that of Locke and Hartz. For example, Lipset contends that it is basic to the American liberal tradition to show 'disdain' for state authority, even to the point of criminal disobedience of the law (Lipset 1996: 21, 26, 46). The one real restraint that Lipset's version of American liberalism emphasizes is the application of 'moral individualism'. Moral individualism appears to stem from people knowing their moral responsibilities to others, in part as a result of their religious affiliations and voluntary interactions, from which they develop a sense of how to regulate their own behaviour (Lipset 1996: 275–7). In general, though, Lipset portrays American liberalism as a value system that allows individuals to do largely as they wish, with relatively little regard for the role of legitimate, especially state, authority in protecting the rights of others. This version of what constitutes American liberalism is different from that suggested by Locke, Hartz, and the other theorists that we have discussed to this stage. We shall consider the larger significance of this issue later in this volume.

We now have a sense of Lipset's portrayal of the American Creed, and have noted his belief that the driving force behind this dominant American value system is a certain brand of liberalism. So far, however, we have not paid much attention to outlining Lipset's assessment of the dominant values that have shaped Canadian society historically, other than noting that his early writings depict Canada as a Tory land of elitism and ascription. At different points in his research, Lipset has provided additional and somewhat varied lists of terms to describe Canada's basic values or organizing principles (see, e.g., Lipset 1963b: 249; 1968: 32; 1990: 8). Probably the best way to understand his latest views on Canadian values is to take the five elements from his most recent version of the American Creed and to think of the Canadian 'creed' as comprising their opposites.

If we were to compare Canadians and Americans in this way, we would find the following kinds of contrasts. Lipset would say, first of all, that while Americans have long favoured populism, a form of government based on mass popular involvement and a distrust of centralized state power, Canadians have favoured an elite-controlled system of government and have tended both to trust and to respect their political leaders. Second, where Americans have generally promoted a laissez-faire or free-market approach to business activity, Canadians have accepted and even encouraged what he calls 'statism', a system that entails more government regulation of business and more extensive state involvement in economic and social life. Third, while Americans have always embraced egalitarianism, in the specific sense of ensuring equality of opportunity for all citizens (but not an enforced equality of result or condition for everyone), Canadians have acceded to a more corporatist, often government-directed, 'noblesse oblige' approach, in which the gap between the rich and the poor is eased by elite action, especially the use of state-funded welfare programs. Fourth, where Americans have cherished unbridled liberty for everyone to do more or less as they wish, even if this means negative consequences for other people, Canadians have generally preferred to live within well-defined legal and moral constraints, so as to protect the community from the wilful, self-interested, or criminal behaviour of some citizens. Finally, where Americans have been deeply committed to individualism, Canadians have been more supportive of collectivism, with a stronger sense that individuals are part of, and have obligations to, the larger collectivities or communities to which they belong (see Lipset 1990: 8–9, 13–16; 1996: 19–23).

SUMMARY

We have reviewed the two major theoretical approaches in the literature that have sought to account for the historical emergence and subsequent development of Canada and the United States as separate societies. As we have seen, there are some basic similarities, but also some significant differences, between the founding-fragment interpretations of Hartz, McRae, and Horowitz, on the one hand, and Lipset's origins thesis, on the other hand. Among the key differences is that, compared with the other writers, Lipset attaches far greater salience to the impact of the American Revolution on both societies, and also sees certain historical events, especially the loyalist migration, as proof of a much more fundamental and radical split between a strongly liberal United States and a decidedly Tory or anti-liberal Canada. One other important contrast we have discussed concerns Lipset's conception of American liberalism, which we have seen is quite distinct from the Lockian concept used in the analyses of Hartz and the other founding-fragment theorists. In the next chapter, we consider how elements from these previous perspectives can be used as the basis for developing a different approach to understanding the historical development of Canada and the United States.

꩜

CHAPTER 3

AN ALTERNATIVE PERSPECTIVE

DEEP STRUCTURES AND THE FOUR SUB-SOCIETIES OF CANADA AND THE UNITED STATES

The main purpose of this chapter is to present an alternative to the founding-fragment and origins perspectives. Our approach builds upon certain aspects of these prominent theories, but also draws on and extends several useful arguments offered by other theorists and observers working in the same general area of study. Some of the ideas provided by these additional sources help us both to supplement and to go beyond existing theories in a number of important respects. We shall apply the general concept of 'deep structures' as a means for characterizing and illuminating what we believe are the major social-structural and cultural forces that lie at the roots of Canada and the United States. From our perspective, many of these forces are in fact of Old World origin, and their effects are largely traceable to a time long before the American Revolution. Along with taking a closer look at these early influences from the Old World, we also add to and extend the contributions of the established perspectives by considering the impact of important events that came to pass after the Revolutionary War itself.

We begin with a discussion of the theoretical origins and basic meaning of the concept of deep structures. Once we have established a working understanding of what this concept signifies for the purposes of the present analysis, we then focus our attention on the specific question of the deep-structural forces operating in the English-speaking societies. Here we engage in a detailed review of the observations provided by a range of noted classical and more recent thinkers concerning the English heritage in both Europe and North America. The principal aim of this review is to uncover the numerous instances in which well-known observers over the years have argued for the existence of core ideas, principles, practices, and forms of social organization that are shared by Canada and the United States, and by the established English-speaking democracies in general. As part of this review, other issues are considered, especially the important sources of divergence within the two nations in regard to these central ideas and patterns of social organization and social structure. The most crucial differences concern the distinctive position of French Canada and the significant division between the northern and southern United States. We then highlight four major deep-structural principles, or deep structures, that we believe have been common to the English-speaking nations, and indicate how these principles may be used as part of an alternative perspective for understanding the historical development of Canada and the United States. Based on these considerations, we conclude Chapter 3 by outlining how these factors have contributed to the development of four distinct sub-societies within the Canadian and American nations.

THE CONCEPT OF DEEP STRUCTURES

The term 'structure' or 'social structure' is one of the most widely used and familiar ideas in the social sciences. For most social theorists, including Marx, Weber, and other major figures in the field, this concept is generally used to denote the relatively enduring and recurring patterns of relationship or interaction that arise among sets of social actors. Over the years, theorists and researchers have found that this conception of social structure has been quite useful for studying a wide range of topics, including everything from small-scale social organizations, like the nuclear family, to large-scale social entities, such as entire economies or political systems (for some discussion, see Grabb 2002: 96–100).

Nevertheless, in spite of its prevalence and apparent utility, this view of social structure has been subject to question by some social theorists. A number of critics, including the set of writers that are typically referred to as structuralists (e.g., Lévi-Strauss 1968, 1969; Chomsky 1965, 1973; Althusser 1972, 1974; Bhaskar 1978, 1979), have advocated the need to go beyond, or at least beneath, the more obvious and superficial representations of social life that are captured in the conventional idea of social structure. These critical assessments are not in total agreement on a number of issues. However, one point on which virtually all of them seem to concur is the importance of getting at the 'deep structures' that, in their view, both underlie and give rise to the apparent or 'surface' social structures that people observe around them (for some discussion, see Scott 1995; Collins 1988; Kurzwell 1980).

There is certainly a good case to be made for searching out and unveiling the social realities that operate below the immediately visible evidence of human interaction. Some would argue, in fact, that the main strength and purpose of sociological analysis in general should be to penetrate the superficial observation of everyday life and to find the more fundamental processes and influences that may be hidden beneath (e.g., Collins 1992; see also Dahrendorf 1997: 21). Still, questions arise as to what aspects of this underlying reality we should concentrate on in such investigations, and how far below the surface we should delve to find them. Such questions demonstrate that the exact meaning of deep structures, not to mention their precise social location, has been a matter of some debate. While it is not our goal to attempt a complete resolution of this debate, we suggest that, across the various discussions in this area, there is sufficient common ground on which to arrive at a conception of deep structures that is understandable, and that is also practicable for the purposes of the present analysis.

Perhaps the main point of agreement among those who focus on deep structures is their shared interest in studying the fundamental signs, codes, guides, or symbols that people use to give meaning to their social interactions. At their most basic level, these signs, codes, guides, or symbols amount to language itself—the very words we utter, the rules of grammar and syntax we employ, and the patterns and styles of speech we adopt in our communication with others.

Given the central role of language in most discussions of deep structures, it is perhaps not surprising that one of the pioneers in this area was a linguist: the French structuralist, Ferdinand de Saussure. Saussure was among the first to argue that language is more than just a 'name-giving system' of words, but instead exists as an underlying structure, a 'system of signs that express ideas', which are conveyed using more or less shared 'laws', 'habits', or guides for communication among social actors (Saussure 1915a: 16, 72, 77–8, 127). By applying such guides, and by using more or less the same set of signs, people are able to engage in meaningful interaction with each other. Moreover, Saussure contends that the interactive process by which language structures develop makes it clear that language is an inherently collective phenomenon, not an individual creation (1915a: 19). At times he seems almost to equate language with a 'collective consciousness' (conscience collective, in French) (Saussure 1915b: 98; 1915c: 140) or what in some translations of his work is called 'the collective mind of the community of speakers' (Saussure 1915a: 96, 19; see also Collins 1988: 304). The point Saussure apparently wants to convey here is that the language that people speak in society is, in a sense, the symbolic embodiment of what the general population of that society thinks, feels, and believes.

It should be remarked, as well, that although people normally employ the components of language in a conscious and purposeful way, at times individuals are not fully aware of the operation of these components, even though individuals use them on a regular basis (Saussure 1915a: 72). For example, children, as well as many adults, are often able to engage in and understand communications that are based on formally correct grammar and sentence construction, even if they have received little or no training in the basic rules and rudiments of their language (see also Johnson 1960: 85). This is but one illustration of the ways in which language structures can exist and operate beneath the surface of everyday reality and human consciousness.

We can see in Saussure's analysis the direct influence of his famous contemporary and countryman, Emile Durkheim (see Collins 1988: 302–4; Kurzwell 1980: 171). Durkheim, of course, is one of the major figures in classical sociology. He also speaks of the existence of a 'collective consciousness' or a 'common consciousness' in human societies (Durkheim 1893: 39). Especially in early times, but to some extent in the modern age, as well, this consciousness binds society's members together and provides each person with a sense of shared identity and purpose. Clearly, Durkheim's concept of the collective consciousness closely resembles Saussure's depiction of language as the collective mind or consciousness of a community of speakers. The major difference is that Durkheim locates the collective consciousness, not so much in the signs and guides of a shared language, but in an embedded system of shared values, 'the totality of beliefs and sentiments common to average members of a society' (Durkheim 1893: 38–9).

Despite this difference, however, the parallels between Saussure and Durkheim here are both obvious and noteworthy. Each theorist is pointing to an important source of shared identity and social cohesion that arises from a set of commonly held ideational influences. Each writer argues, moreover, that this set of ideational influences is a collective, not an individual, creation that, in a way, exists apart from any one person's mind or consciousness (Saussure 1915a: 14; Durkheim 1895: 3). Such influences are prime examples of what both Durkheim and Saussure call a 'social fact', a compelling social force that is not tied to the life of any individual but that effectively has 'a life of its own' (Durkheim 1895: 3; 1893: 39; Saussure 1915b: 77). In a sense, as well, both writers are pointing to factors that may be more cultural than they are structural, having to do with the shared symbols of language and values that have long been thought by social scientists to epitomize what is meant by the concept of culture (see Tylor 1871: 1; Williams 1960: 22; Johnson 1960: 10, 85; Carroll 2001: 41–2). For this reason, although we follow established practice by continuing to use the term 'deep structures' to denote these bases for shared identity, we should note that they might as easily be referred to as 'deep cultural structures' (see Dahrendorf 1997: 48).

Finding these similar themes and conceptions in the classical linguistics of Saussure and the classical sociology of Durkheim has some important implications for developing a working understanding of deep structures. Such overlaps might be viewed by some writers as proof that language structures exist at an even deeper level than social structures and are actually the basis for their creation (see, e.g., Chomsky 1965, 1973; Giddens 1976; Habermas 1984; see also Collins 1988: 314–15). From this perspective, the set of shared values in a society may exist as a 'social fact', but in the end is mainly just a by-product of language. However, it is also possible to reverse this argument. In other words, because language is an inherently collective or social creation, its essential elements—its laws, signs, habits, codes, and so on—are themselves social products that are generated and shaped by people interacting with each other according to relatively similar values and orientations to the social world. According to this alternative argument, then, cross-national differences in important aspects of language—in the cadence, speed, and amplitude of typical speech patterns, for example, or in the vocabularies, idioms, and metaphors used by most speakers—are largely outcomes, rather than causes, of variations in the deep-seated values or world views of the different societies and their peoples.

In the present analysis, we take the position that both of these approaches provide parallel and valuable insights into what is truly captured by the idea of deep structures. In particular, each perspective makes the crucial point that, in order to comprehend social structures and social processes, we must look for and attend to those underlying influences that are often so pervasive in our existence, and so much a part of our everyday lives, that they can escape our immediate consciousness or awareness. We suggest that the deep-structural forces operating in any specific society will normally involve both the fundamental markers and meanings provided by a common language and the underlying guides and credos found in long-standing systems of values and beliefs. In turn, these core values will have an important role in both shaping and being shaped by the political, economic, and other social structures, or forms of social organization, that constitute the society in question.

In our view, the patterns of development of the nations that began as former English colonies provide some of the best evidence to support this argument. Indeed, one of our principal contentions throughout this volume is that the English-speaking democracies have emerged as similar societies, and that this has occurred, in part, because of the comparable deep-structural influences that they experienced from being steeped in the same language, and also because of the deeply ingrained values and institutions that they have shared as a result of their more or less common English or British heritage. While these two types of ideational influence are not identical, each is in many ways constitutive of the other. Furthermore, in combination, both kinds of factors have had enduring and recurring impacts. As a result, although there is no question that the English societies of the New World have evolved into independent nations, and can be distinguished from their European parent and from one another in some notable ways, we argue that these differences at the 'surface' have not negated a number of deep-seated structural and cultural commonalities. On the contrary, we suggest that some of the effects of their shared English origins have been quite resilient through extended periods of history and survive in certain pivotal features of their present-day cultures, social structures, and national characters.

DEEP STRUCTURES AND THE ENGLISH HERITAGE

Over the years, various writers have considered how the common heritage of the English-speaking nations may have played an important role in defining the character or ethos of these societies. We have already seen one such analysis in Hartz's thesis of founding fragments. However, some observers contend that the underlying connections between England and her New World offspring may run even deeper than this thesis implies, and stem from events and developments that took place centuries before the period of history that Hartz's perspective has emphasized. Three early illustrations of this way of thinking can be found in the writings of Churchill, Tocqueville, and Montesquieu.

Churchill's Historical Perspective

Sir Winston Churchill is best known to us as a statesman, an orator, and arguably the most important historical figure of the twentieth century. Although Churchill was not a trained academic, he was a Nobel Prize winning author, with a lifelong interest in understanding the linkages between England and its former colonies, especially the United States. This interest may be partially attributed to his family lineage, for his mother was American and two of his great-grandfathers fought in the American Revolution, on the American side (see Churchill 1999: ix–xi).

Churchill was fond of emphasizing, in both his speeches and his numerous scholarly writings, the many 'ties of blood and history' binding the English nations to one another (Churchill 1998: 816; see also 1947, 1956a, 1956b, 1957, 1958). He believed that the main sources of this 'English-speaking unity' were what others would call deep-structural factors, having to do with the sustained 'ties of intellect and spirit' coming from the common 'law, language, [and] literature' that the English societies have long shared (Churchill 1998: 973, 816).

The bonds of language and literature, of course, have facilitated the continuous interchange of ideas among the countries, with the result that their political, economic, religious, and other institutions have often been guided and influenced by similar ideas and orientations. With respect to their shared views about law, Churchill is one of many writers to perceive in the newer English societies the legacy of ancient legal principles (e.g., Montesquieu 1748: 571–2, 608; Tocqueville 1835: 46–7, 286–7; Bryce 1921b, II: 5; Schlesinger 1964: 158; Pocklington 1994: 111; Bailyn 1992: 30–1; Shain 1994: 112, 321; Dyck 2002: 344). The exact origins of these principles are diverse and, in some instances, rather obscure. Many appear to date back to the ninth century and beyond, at a time when Britain was populated by a range of distinct and frequently warring peoples, including Saxons, Danes, Angles, Jutes, Celts, and others. In the late 800s, the Saxon king, Alfred the Great, established a Book of Laws, or 'Dooms', that sought to combine customary laws and codes from these numerous and disparate sources (Churchill 1956a: 111, 120). However, it was not until the twelfth century, during the reign of King Henry II, that a system of laws common to all of Britain began to take hold. Somewhat like Alfred before him, Henry drew upon early Anglo-Saxon and Danish-Scandinavian legal traditions to establish what would come to be known as the English Common Law. This set of laws and regulations was also influenced by ideas that are traceable to Frankish and Norman legal customs found in parts of what is now modern-day France (Churchill 1956a: 217). The result was a set of practices and procedures that are today virtually universal across the English-speaking nations, but that in many cases are still not found in the legal systems of other societies, including some democracies. Among the principles adopted from the Common Law are the use of trial by jury, the appointment or election of independent judges, the reliance on legal precedents when passing judgments, the right of accused individuals to face their accusers, the requirement that all testimony be given in a public forum, the establishment of rules concerning the admissibility of evidence, and so on (Churchill 1956a: 215–25). Churchill asserts that this system 'was all transported . . . to the New World', by pioneers who 'took it with them when they crossed the Atlantic'; moreover, despite some modifications over time, this was essentially the same system of law that had 'governed the lives and fortunes of twelfth-century Englishmen' (Churchill 1956a: 223; 1998: 973).

Churchill contends that the legal systems of the English societies are guided by a similar regard for the general principle of 'equity', as epitomized by the right of all citizens to enjoy legal equality or equal justice under the same laws (Churchill 1998: 973, 879). He believes that some historical evidence of this shared principle can be found by comparing two famous documents: the American Constitution of 1789 and England's Magna Carta, or 'Great Charter', of 1215. At first, this comparison might seem peculiar, since the American Constitution was mainly the creation of common people seeking to establish their basic rights under a new democracy, whereas the Magna Carta was largely an invention of English nobles trying to protect their rights from the abuses of their feudal monarch, King John. However, as Churchill notes, there is little question that parts of the American Constitution 'are an echo of the Magna Carta'. For example, the 5th and 14th Amendments to the Constitution assert 'that no person shall . . . be deprived of life, liberty, or property without due process of law', that no state shall deprive any person of these same rights, and that no state shall 'deny any person within its jurisdiction equal protection of the laws' (Churchill 1998: 973, 879; see also Churchill 1947: 78; 1956a: 242–57; 1999: 417). Much the same principle of equal justice is represented in article 39 of the Magna Carta, which states that 'no free man shall be seized or imprisoned, or stripped of his rights or possessions, or outlawed or exiled, or deprived of his standing in any other way . . . except by the lawful judgments of his equals, or by the law of the land' (Wood 1999: 251).

What may be most striking about the similarities in these two documents is their demonstration that, almost 600 years before the American Revolution, English people had already sought and gained some recognition that every 'free man' should have the same access to such basic rights as representation and equal protection under the law (see also Churchill 1956a: 254–7; Wood 1999: 254–7). As various writers have noted, including the classical philosopher David Hume, the Magna Carta did not signal the start of a smooth and easy transition to the creation of an official English bill of rights or constitution (Hume 1754; see also McClelland 1996: 409; Shain 1994: 162; Churchill 1956a: xvi–xix; Schama 2000: 161–2; Breay 2002; Pocock 1987). It would take many years, marred by wars and civil strife, before England would establish a formal document outlining the legal and political freedoms of its people. Even so, the passages from the Magna Carta noted above imply that Britain was probably ahead of most other societies of that time in seeking to achieve this goal (see Wood 1999: 257; Churchill 1956a: 256; Schama 2000: 162). Eventually, the emphasis on legal equality or equal justice embodied in these words would ultimately find its way into the constitutions of every other English democracy of the modern era.

In his discussions of the English heritage, Churchill also contends that, apart from the idea of equity under the law, there are many basic political rights and freedoms that have also formed part of the 'joint inheritance of the English-speaking world', and that are still unknown in many other countries today (Churchill 1998: 879). These include the right to free elections, the use of secret ballots, the opportunity to choose among multiple political parties, the establishment of courts of justice that are formally independent from outside political influence, the protection of free political debate and dissent, the provision for checks and balances in the powers of different branches of government, and others (Churchill 1998: 879–80, 691–2; 1999: 423). All of these rights and freedoms underscore, in one way or another, what for Churchill is the most important inheritance characterizing the 'common conceptions among the English-speaking peoples'; that legacy is 'the love of personal freedom' and 'individual liberty' (Churchill 1998: 816; 1999: 423).

In suggesting that personal freedom or individual liberty lies at the core of what defines the character of the English societies, Churchill was aware that he was expanding on a theme that has been the subject of other writers for several centuries. Some of this work was touched on earlier in this chapter, in our brief review of John Locke's conception of liberty. As we noted then, Locke believed that people in their natural state should enjoy the liberty to think, speak, and act freely, with the understanding that these freedoms also depend on everyone being subject to commonly agreed-upon laws enforced by a limited but effective government authority. Until now we have discussed Locke's ideas about liberty mainly in connection with their relevance to the American colonies. However, it should be noted that at times he also speaks specifically of the 'people of England' themselves, and their 'love of their just and natural rights' (Locke 1690: 155). In general, then, Locke's views on liberty are quite consistent with those of Churchill. Both men see true liberty as deriving from mutually accepted legal and political rights and freedoms, and both suggest that this idea has a long tradition in the English-speaking world.

Montesquieu and English Liberty

Another classical observer who has provided a similar perspective on the importance of liberty in the English context is the French philosopher, Montesquieu. Montesquieu's definition of liberty is very close to that of Locke and Churchill. Liberty is 'the right to do everything the laws permit'; this idea, however, should never be confused with 'doing what one wants' regardless of the society's laws or the rights of others (Montesquieu 1748: 155). For Montesquieu, as for Locke and Churchill, the liberty of the individual depends on a recognition of the rights and freedoms of all people (see also Montesquieu 1748: 242, 325).

Montesquieu lived and wrote during a crucial era in European, especially English, history, in a time roughly equidistant between the English Civil War of the middle 1600s and the American and French Revolutions of the late 1700s. He was actually a committed monarchist himself, and opposed Oliver Cromwell's short-lived establishment of Parliament as 'the supreme power' in England, following the overthrow of King Charles I in 1648 (Montesquieu 1748: 22n.; see Churchill 1956b: 285–6; Schama 2001: Chapter 3). Nevertheless, Montesquieu recognized in the England of his day the beginnings of a special, indeed an unprecedented, form of society, based on the core democratic value of political liberty. He notes, in particular, that England in that period was the 'one nation in the world whose constitution has political liberty for its direct purpose' (Montesquieu 1748: 156). As a result, England was also 'the freest country there is in the world' and English subjects were among 'the freest people that have ever lived on earth' (Montesquieu, cited in Althusser 1972: 105n.; Montesquieu 1748: 204).

An obvious question to ask is: what led England to occupy this special place among the world's nations? For Montesquieu, part of the answer to this question lies in factors that we have discussed earlier. Most notable here is the long-standing English experience with popular representation and involvement in law and governance, dating back to the Common Law and the Magna Carta. These deep-rooted influences led to an English constitution that he saw as unique, because it established a government in which the monarch, nobles, and commoners exercised separate and therefore countervailing powers, and because it also provided for a judicial system of courts and judges that could operate largely independently of government control (Montesquieu 1748: 156–7). Montesquieu's views on this question are somewhat similar to those of Locke, who also suggested that the separation or balance of powers was important for ensuring political liberty (Locke 1690: 344–5, 356–7).

It turns out that the various branches of the English government in Montesquieu's time were probably more interconnected and interdependent than he believed, so that the concept of a complete separation of powers may be something of a 'myth' (see, e.g., Althusser 1972: Chapter 5). Still, it does appear that English politics exhibited more pluralism or balance in its power structure than other nations in this period (see McClelland 1996: 332–5). In addition to this relatively pluralist political system, Montesquieu also observed that English customs and institutions had long fostered or tolerated what has been called 'the spirit of turbulence in the common people', or the willingness of the mass of the population to engage in unruly and even riotous actions when their governments were thought to be unjust or tyrannical (McClelland 1996: 334; see also Wood 1992: 12–15; Macfarlane 1978: 168–73). These considerations lend credence to Montesquieu's argument that, during his time, the English were unique among the peoples of the world in treating liberty, at least in some elementary form, as a guiding principle for deciding how society should be structured.

Another part of Montesquieu's explanation for the distinctive quality of English liberty concerns the rather mundane, though undeniably fundamental, factors of climate and geography. First of all, he argues that, as a northern people, the English faced the exigencies of a difficult and hardy existence. These hardships spurred them to be more vigorous, adventurous, and self-reliant than many of their European rivals, and, in turn, caused them to be less tolerant of control by arbitrary authority, either from within or from outside their borders (Montesquieu 1748: 231, 242). Furthermore, given England's situation as a large island country, the population of necessity had to rely on control of the seas to survive and to prosper. Thus, the English turned their adventurous and self-reliant spirits toward the use of sea-power, which was their prime means for establishing themselves as a dominant nation, both politically, militarily, and economically (Montesquieu 1748: 328).

Montesquieu's argument for the role of climate and geography may seem suspect, since we can easily identify many other northern nations, and yet Montesquieu does not believe that any of them developed the same commitment to liberty that he saw among the English. Nevertheless, some elements of this thesis should not be rejected out of hand. It has been suggested, for example, that one reason why early England's comparatively free political and legal institutions were able to develop was because they did so 'largely without outside interference' or 'the threat of constant upheaval' stemming from fears of war and invasion (Wood 1999: 268). Max Weber has similarly argued that England's 'insular position' meant that the nation had less of a need to maintain 'a great national army' (Weber 1927: 164; see also Sayer 1992: 1391; Stanbridge 1997: 30–1). Weber's analysis suggests, as well, that inhabiting an island may have played a role in making it possible, or necessary, for the English to venture into a free-enterprise capitalist economy sooner and more fully than other European nations (Weber 1927: 98–9, 156–7; 1947: 277–8). Research by Hopcroft tends to support this argument (Hopcroft 1999: 87–9; see also Macfarlane 1978: 46–9, 195–6, 201–2).

Overall, then, it is an interesting speculation that the position of England as a somewhat remote and northern island nation, which was both dependent on and highly proficient at the exercise of sea-power for its existence, could have played a role in enabling the English principles of liberty to take root and evolve with time. Being relatively insulated and protected in these ways, especially from the more authoritarian tendencies of its neighbour countries, English society may have been in a position to develop the deep structures of liberty and freedom that Montesquieu and others have attributed to it.

It is noteworthy, as well, that Montesquieu sees England's seafaring activities as pivotal in spreading the English way of life to other parts of the globe, especially the English-speaking societies of the New World. Paralleling Churchill to some extent, Montesquieu argues that England gave 'the form of its own government to the people of its colonies' (Montesquieu 1748: 329). In addition, he mentions how the English preference for freedom of commerce and its consequent economic prosperity were exported elsewhere, and he also hints at the spread of England's religious traditions, including its allegedly greater tolerance for religious diversity and dissent compared with other countries. To Montesquieu, the English are unique here, as well, for they are 'the people in the world who have best known how to take advantage of each of these three great things at the same time: religion, commerce, and liberty' (Montesquieu 1748: 343).

Tocqueville's Views on America and Canada

To this stage in our analysis of the deep-structural features of the English heritage, we have considered arguments suggesting that England was, by many centuries, the first nation to pay heed to and at least partially develop certain basic principles of individual liberty and legal equality. These ideas are now fundamental watchwords of all the English-speaking democracies. We have also seen that, during the period from the late 1600s to the middle 1700s, some prominent thinkers and observers, including Montesquieu and to some extent Locke, wrote about the unique emphasis on the values of liberty and freedom to be found in both England and its New World colonies. Montesquieu's analysis, in particular, suggests that these core values had the opportunity to take root in the English-controlled areas of North America for many decades prior to the American Revolution.

Almost a century after Montesquieu, another famous French writer and intellectual, Alexis de Tocqueville, provided his own special insights into the nature and significance of the English heritage, especially in North America. Tocqueville's analyses have come to be widely cited and revered, especially by the many American social scientists who have sought to fathom the founding principles of the United States. Tocqueville is also one of the only classical writers to discuss the development of the southern United States as a distinct society within the larger American nation. What is not often recognized, however, is that Tocqueville's work does not deal solely with the United States, but also makes some incisive observations concerning the societies that emerged in both English Canada and French Canada.

Tocqueville's major work on the subject is Democracy in America, which was published in two volumes, the first in 1835 and the second in 1840. His analysis was based on his travels, both in the United States and in parts of what are now Ontario and Quebec, during the early 1830s. Thus, Tocqueville's writings offer us a first-hand account and assessment of how the new American nation, as well as the British-controlled areas to the north, evolved during the 50-year period following the American Revolution. An important aspect of Tocqueville's analysis is that, like the other commentators we have discussed, he sees the English heritage as playing a fundamental role in defining the core elements of what he often refers to as 'Anglo-American' society (Tocqueville 1835: Chapter 2). Furthermore, in his view, these influences are apparent, not only in the colonial period prior to the formation of the United States as an independent country, but also for many years afterward.

The English Influence: Language, Law, Politics, and Religion
One of the first factors Tocqueville emphasizes in his assessment of the colonists who settled America in the 1600s is that, with few exceptions, they all 'spoke the same language' (Tocqueville 1835: 29). As we have found with other analysts, then, Tocqueville expressly recognizes the important deep-structural impact of language in promoting the common heritage of the English-speaking societies. This 'tie of language' in his view 'is, perhaps, the strongest and most durable that can unite mankind' (Tocqueville 1835: 29, 176, 333).

Tocqueville goes on to argue that the English colonists also shared a common bond in the legal and political traditions that they brought with them from the parent country. Thus, as with some of the other writers we have already discussed, Tocqueville speaks of the English belief, harkening back to the Magna Carta and the Common Law, that everyone should be placed 'under the protection of the laws' (Tocqueville 1835: 29, 41). He also comments, like Montesquieu, on the history of popular upheaval in England, which provided the English people with a 'political education', teaching them to be 'more conversant with the notions of right and principles of true freedom than the greater part of their European contemporaries' (Tocqueville 1835: 29).

Tocqueville perceives an especially important Old World English influence in the 'doctrine of the sovereignty of the people'; this idea, which was 'deeply rooted in the habits of the English' of Europe, stressed the right of local communities, shires, or townships to have autonomous powers from those of the central national government (Tocqueville 1835: 29, 42, 58; see also Churchill 1956b: 285; Wood 1999: 267–8). Thus, the principle of 'municipal liberty', as he sometimes calls it, was yet another idea that was adopted from Britain and that then 'penetrated into the laws and customs of the English' of North America (Tocqueville 1835: 435). This precept, which holds that authority in a community or a society must ultimately lie, not with any king or ruler, but with the people, soon became prevalent in America. According to Tocqueville, it may be the single most important Anglo-American principle, for it 'is always to be found, more or less, at the bottom of almost all institutions', even though it 'generally remains there concealed from view' and 'is obeyed without being recognized' (Tocqueville 1835: 57). In such passages, we can see quite clearly the deep-structural imagery that Tocqueville employs when characterizing the founding principles of the early United States, and when underscoring their origins in the English heritage.

Tocqueville makes a related argument regarding another key feature of the Anglo-American perspective on liberty. He connects the idea of municipal liberty with the belief that all people should have the right to associate freely in voluntary groups and organizations. Some of these are official organizations or 'permanent associations', such as the councils that administer the laws of the 'townships, cities, and counties'; in addition, however, 'a vast number of others are formed and maintained by the agency of private individuals' to deal with all manner of concerns about such issues as 'public safety, commerce, industry, morality, and religion' (Tocqueville 1835: 198–9). Tocqueville remarks that no other country in the world has been as successful in implementing this principle of free association as has the United States (Tocqueville 1835: 198). In subsequent chapters, we will look further at the question of voluntary association involvement, and consider evidence on the extent to which the contemporary United States differs from other societies in this respect. In the present context, however, it is important to note Tocqueville's belief that 'the right of association was imported from England', and so is yet another American principle that grew from old English roots (Tocqueville 1835: 201).

Tocqueville indicates one other factor that is particularly important to consider when seeking to understand both the American conception of liberty and the fundamental American character. That factor concerns religion and the principle of religious freedom. He suggests that religion and liberty were intertwined in America from the beginning of colonization, in large part because of the many Puritans and other Protestant 'dissenters' among the early English settlers. These were people who, when faced with religious persecution in Europe, went to the New World so that they could 'live according to their own opinions and worship God in freedom' (Tocqueville 1835: 33, 45). Tocqueville argues that the religious teachings of these groups were important, not only for establishing religious freedom in Anglo-America, but also for promoting a general love of liberty in other areas of life. Thus, he says that religion is 'the first of their political institutions', because it is so intimately connected with American views about political liberty (Tocqueville 1835: 316–18). He expresses similar ideas about the close relationship between religion and law in America. For example, although the early system of laws was at times incomplete in defining citizens' rights and responsibilities, so much so that 'the law permits the Americans to do what they please', the moral restraints of religion were sufficiently strong and pervasive that they helped to temper the 'imperfections of human nature' (Tocqueville 1835: 314, 377). According to Tocqueville, the influence of religion, when combined with the unusually strong Anglo-American fear of disapproval by others in the community, meant that the population at that time tended not to commit 'rash or unjust' actions that would threaten the liberty of others (Tocqueville 1835: 314; 1840: 275).

Tocqueville also believed that these constraining influences of religion and public opinion operated in concert with a widespread American belief in 'self-interest rightly understood'. This idea denotes a form of enlightened self-interest, in which people pursue their own goals and desires while at the same time paying heed to the general welfare or the public good (Tocqueville 1840: 129–31; see Diggins 1984: 242–4). The mixture of people's adherence to religious teachings, their desire for community approval, and their enlightened pursuit of individual interests produced a society that, in Tocqueville's opinion, was generally marked by a high degree of both personal freedom and public 'virtue' (see Tocqueville 1840: Chapters 8 and 9).

In making these observations, Tocqueville is taking a position that seems largely consistent with those of Locke, Montesquieu, and other writers that we have discussed. He is suggesting that genuine liberty does not take root and develop in societies where people do whatever they desire, but rather in those settings where liberty is exercised with due regard for the rights and aspirations of other citizens (see also Tocqueville 1835: 44–5). If there is a difference between Tocqueville and other writers on this issue, it may be in his apparent view that the Americans of his time relied more than other peoples on the moral authority of religion and the community, and less on the law or government power, for regulating and guiding their behaviour.

In a variety of ways, then, Tocqueville is convinced that religion has had a profound significance for the American people that is not evident in other societies. As we shall discuss in later chapters, various writers have taken these observations by Tocqueville as proof that the United States is unusual or even unique in this way. For now, though, we should note Tocqueville's assessment that the special importance attached to religion in American life also finds its roots in the old English heritage of Puritanism and Protestant dissent (Tocqueville 1835: 33). Even Tocqueville's argument that Americans were unusual in being able to combine the 'spirit of religion' with 'the spirit of liberty' (Tocqueville 1835: 45) closely resembles an earlier assessment that Montesquieu once made about their English ancestors. As we noted previously in this chapter, Montesquieu believed that the English were the one people in the world who were most adept at uniting religious matters with the idea of liberty, and also with commercial or business interests (recall Montesquieu 1748: 343).

In spite of the many linkages that can be drawn between the thirteen American colonies and their English past, some analysts might expect that most or all of these commonalities would have dissipated with the revolutionary break from Britain. However, Tocqueville's travels in North America generally led him to draw the opposite conclusion. More than a half-century after the American Declaration of Independence, Tocqueville still perceived that the 'point of departure' for the United States, the factor that most clearly separated the American nation from other countries, was the good fortune of its people in having English 'ancestors' and 'forefathers', who 'gave them the love of equality and freedom' (Tocqueville 1835: 300–1).

For Tocqueville, what eventually would make the United States somewhat different from England over time were not its core principles, which he saw as largely identical to their English counterparts. Instead, Tocqueville suggested that the English ideals of liberty, equal justice under the law, and popular sovereignty, when combined with the natural advantages of America's New World setting, would be the main basis for any subsequent divergence between the United States and its European progenitor. In particular, because the American populace inhabited a 'boundless continent', with vast amounts of both space and resources, they were able to enjoy a level of material prosperity that was unknown to the ordinary people of England or Europe in general (Tocqueville 1835: 301).

It is interesting that, in another of his famous works, The Old Regime and the Revolution, Tocqueville makes a similar observation to explain why the English themselves had been able to surpass the rest of Europe. He attributes England's greater success historically to its relatively free legal and political institutions, which emphasized 'political liberty' and 'equality before the law', and to its much higher level of economic freedom and 'material prosperity' compared with all the other Old World nations (Tocqueville 1856a: 94, 105, 300–2; 1856b: 282–4, 364–5; see also Macfarlane 1978: 166–7). The only real point of departure between England and the United States in this respect was that the amount of material well-being and the potential for economic growth were even greater in America than they had been in the English parent nation.

The prosperity of the United States, in which 'Nature herself favors the cause of the people', in turn helped to weaken any popular discontent or unrest that might pose a significant internal threat to the stability of the new republic (Tocqueville 1835: 301, 302). In addition, if we set aside the relatively brief conflict with Britain during the War of 1812, the United States also faced virtually no external threats from hostile neighbours during the period of history that Tocqueville considered (Tocqueville 1835: 299, 301). These happy circumstances allowed the American people a freedom of action that was not possible in the Old World societies.

In time, then, these differences would mean some disparity in the paths of development of the United States and its English parent. Even so, Tocqueville emphasizes that this does not diminish the deep-structural imprints of the English heritage on the American nation. Regardless of their differences in natural advantages and material resources, both societies embraced similar 'habits of the heart', which have found their way into the 'laws and customs of the Anglo-Americans' (Tocqueville 1835: 310, 332). To

Tocqueville, these factors are far more important for understanding the character of the United States than is the physical geography or resources of the country (Tocqueville 1835: 333–5).

Slavery and the American South
In his outline of the principles that define the character of the United States, it is clear that Tocqueville's analysis really identifies two different Americas. While he speaks of the Anglo-Americans in general as a people who are imbued with the long-standing English emphasis on liberty, legal equality, and popular sovereignty, he also notes very early in his assessment that another America exists within this larger whole. Consequently, he says that there are two distinct 'branches' of Anglo-America growing in quite divergent directions, 'the one in the South, the other in the North' (Tocqueville 1835: 30–1).

Tocqueville believed that the main reasons for this divergence derived from the institution of slavery, and its far greater prevalence in the southern than in the northern United States. He contends that 'almost all the differences which may be noticed between the characters of the Americans in the Southern and in the Northern states have originated in slavery' (Tocqueville 1835: 379). From the earliest colonial times, agriculture in the North typically had been based on smaller-scale farms, run by mainly self-sufficient families, most of whom owned no slaves and, apart from using some hired labourers, did all the work themselves (Tocqueville 1835: 375). In contrast, agricultural operations in the South tended toward much bigger landed estates, or plantations, that relied heavily on slave labour to harvest the large crops of cotton, fruit, sugar cane, and tobacco that were the staples of the economy in that region (Tocqueville 1835: 385–6).

Tocqueville suggests that the pattern of large landholding in the South was a consequence of southerners maintaining a closer and more prolonged adherence to laws of inheritance borrowed from the Old World English aristocracy. Of particular importance in this case was the law of 'primogeniture', which required that all lands were to be inherited by the eldest son in each family, and which meant that big tracts of land were not divided into smaller holdings and distributed among multiple heirs (Tocqueville 1835: 49–51, 380). Whatever the reason for the large estates, however, slavery was deemed to be acceptable by those who established the plantation system, presumably because slave labour was both cheap and plentiful.

Tocqueville argues that the combination of large estates and slave ownership led to the establishment of a quasi-feudal society in the American South, headed by a class of landowners very much like the Old World nobility. He posits that the wealthy families of the South eventually came to resemble 'the noble families of some countries in Europe', forming 'an aristocratic body' and an 'American nobility' unto themselves (Tocqueville 1835: 380–1). It is also notable that, even though primogeniture was abolished in the United States after the American Revolution, the culture and institutions of plantation life were sufficiently well entrenched that the social and economic structures of the southern states continued to be quite distinct from those in the northern regions. In addition, while the shipment of new slaves to America was officially stopped in 1807, the number of slaves already living in the country by that time was large enough to ensure that the plantation economy in the South could sustain itself through natural increase among the slave population (see Steckel 2000: 434–6). Thus, in spite of the common 'English character' and 'English foundation' of the peoples that inhabited the northern and the southern regions of the American Union, there nonetheless emerged two distinct societies with 'very different characteristics' (Tocqueville 1835: 32).

Here Tocqueville is suggesting that, in the process of accepting and institutionalizing their slave-based plantation society, the people of the American South were adding some distinct deep-structural elements to their otherwise English core principles. In particular, although southerners prized their English-inspired sense of liberty and independence as much as any other American citizens, theirs would become a self-destructive and 'idle independence', born of an increasing reliance on others to do their work for them (Tocqueville 1835: 379). Tocqueville contends that, while slavery obviously 'degrades' and 'dishonors' the labour of those who are enslaved, it also promotes a way of life that has equally damaging effects on the slave masters, breeding in them 'idleness, ignorance, and pride' and benumbing their 'powers of the mind' (Tocqueville 1835: 31, 211). Tocqueville believed that the paucity of major manufacturing industries, railroads, canals, and shipping operations in the South was partly due to the relative lack of energy, talent, and industriousness displayed by the economic and political leaders in that region (Tocqueville 1835: 379, 407). He asserts that the circumstances of the American South implanted the same weaknesses in the personality and character of whites in general, not just the slave holders, because all white southerners at the time were reared in a society that, on a daily basis, taught them that hard labour was beneath them, and that they were immutably superior to those who happened to have black skin (see Tocqueville 1835: 381, 386). To Tocqueville, as well, the fact that virtually all American slaves were black made for a 'calamity' that was even worse than the slavery of ancient Greece or Rome, for example, because in the American setting slavery was tied specifically to the 'prejudice of race, and the prejudice of color' (Tocqueville 1835: 371–2). Consequently, over time the belief in the supremacy of one race over another became deeply ingrained and reinforced in the habits and culture of the American South, producing a society that, in important ways, was fundamentally distinct from the rest of the United States. Therefore, although Tocqueville's analysis bears some similarities with the Hartzian idea that the American South was a liberal 'fragment' with aristocratic or feudal influences, it appears that Tocqueville saw more than just a 'touch' of feudalism in this part of the United States, and a much clearer gap between the two Americas that the institution of slavery helped to produce.

English Canada and French Canada

We have reviewed Tocqueville's main arguments concerning the influence of the core English principles of liberty and freedom on the development of the American character. We have also seen how, in his view, these same principles were to have quite different meanings and consequences in the American South, especially because of the corrupting effects of slavery and racism in that part of the United States. Before concluding our assessment of Tocqueville's work, however, we should also discuss some important observations that he has to offer about two other societies that had been well established in North America by the time of his analysis. These are English Canada and French Canada.

First, based on his first-hand observations of the English Canadians and their American neighbours, Tocqueville states unequivocally that these two Anglo-American populations shared a great deal in common. To begin with, even though English Canada's climate and geography are less hospitable than many parts of the United States, especially the American South, English Canadians nevertheless were surrounded by most of the same natural advantages as were the Americans. They too occupied a land with a wealth of untapped resources and almost unlimited room for population growth and economic development. In addition, except for some concerns about possible American inroads into their territory, the people of English Canada were similarly insulated from serious threats by hostile neighbours. However, for Tocqueville, the most important parallels between the English Canadians and the Americans stem from their common English heritage, especially their core principles and general life orientations. Dating from the era in which both societies were still English possessions, they shared, along with 'all the British colonies', many 'striking similarities'; these included much higher levels of 'internal freedom' and 'political independence' than were granted in the colonies of other nations, and a sense of liberty that pervaded even 'the middle and lower orders' of the class structure (Tocqueville 1835: 29–30, 37, 41, 48, 57–8). These common English influences meant that, despite their more prolonged history as colonial subjects, the English Canadians harboured much the same beliefs in basic democratic ideas as did the Americans. Tocqueville also comments on the similarly strong commitment to free enterprise and the superior commercial success of the English peoples, in both Canada, the United States, and England itself (Tocqueville 1835: 362n., 439, 445). The latter linkage is just one of the many 'moral and intellectual causes' that he suggests as the reasons why these societies are similar to each other, and different from the other countries of the world (Tocqueville 1835: 439). Such common bonds ultimately led Tocqueville to the conclusion that the English-speaking population of Canada residing north of the new American nation 'is identical with that of the United States' (Tocqueville 1835: 448).

As for his views on French Canada, Tocqueville's commentary is brief but again unambiguous. He clearly believed that the French of North America constituted a distinct people, with a heritage and world view that were markedly different from those of the English. His remarks on this question seem especially noteworthy, given his own French heritage. Somewhat like Montesquieu before him, Tocqueville offers the candid opinion that the French, along with the other European peoples, have been surpassed by the 'British race', which is 'very superior to them in civilization, industry, and power' (Tocqueville 1835: 449, 331). He says that 'there was a time when we [the French] also might have created a great French nation in the American wilds, to counterbalance the influence of the English on the destinies of the New World' (Tocqueville 1835: 447). Instead, however, the Old World French system of governance, which was transported to New France, failed to give each person 'the habit of thinking and governing for oneself' (Tocqueville 1835: 448n.). He also argues that 'the government never adopted the great principles which can render a colony populous and prosperous' (Tocqueville 1856a: 281). As a result, the French were relatively less able or less willing than the English, both in Canada and in the United States, to be 'masters of commerce and manufacture' and so were less successful in their economic activities and business ventures (Tocqueville 1835: 448n., 362n.).

Thus, Tocqueville concluded that 'the 400,000 French inhabitants of Lower Canada' (i.e., Quebec) were very different from the English Canadians or the Americans of his time, and constituted 'the remnants of an old nation lost in the middle of a new people' (Tocqueville 1835: 448). This image of French Canada as a remnant of an old nation is quite close to that posed by Hartz and McRae who, as was discussed earlier, see French Canada as a feudal fragment imported from old France. Tocqueville was convinced that, in contrast to the French Canadians, the 'new people' that surrounded them, i.e., the Anglo-Americans of Canada and the United States, were destined to be a major force for social change, helping to promote the English way of life, not only in North America but throughout most regions of the globe (Tocqueville 1835: 449–50, 445).

IDENTIFYING THE DEEP STRUCTURES OF THE ENGLISH SOCIETIES

We have now considered a series of historical analyses that, although they differ on certain specific issues, all make parallel arguments concerning the links between the English-speaking nations of the New World and their European forebears. Each of these assessments supports the view that, from the earliest stages of their histories, the New World English societies, especially in North America, have been marked or influenced by core principles, along with related forms of social organization and social practice, that originated with their Old World English past. It should be remarked, however, that none of the classical and other scholars that we have discussed to this point uses the exact term 'deep structures' when discussing these central ideas or guiding precepts of the English societies. On the other hand, the numerous references made by Tocqueville, Churchill, and others to 'deeply rooted' habits or customs, and to enduring 'ties of intellect and spirit', come very close to evoking the same imagery.

Some more recent historians have also hinted at the concept of deep structures, or similar influences, in their analyses of England specifically. For example, Pocock has suggested that, at least since the Middle Ages, English society was shaped by an 'ideology' involving 'the common-law mind', which was 'rooted in habits of mind' and 'bred by education and practice' among certain segments of the population (Pocock 1987: 279). Likewise, Macfarlane has expressed his agreement with Tocqueville, Montesquieu, and others that England was, from very early times, quite different from the other European nations, and that these differences 'lay deep in the structures of [the] country' (Macfarlane 1978: 181, 165–9). Macfarlane maintains that England's distinctiveness 'was not merely a matter of geography and language, but was rooted deep in its laws, customs, and kinship systems' going back to medieval times (Macfarlane 1978: 175). His research leads him to conclude that England was unique historically, both because of the long-standing influences of the Common Law, and because the English people for many centuries had generally experienced greater economic independence and material well-being than other Europeans (Macfarlane 1978: Chapter 7). Macfarlane argues that, in combination, these factors fostered individualistic patterns of thought and practice among the English population, especially in economic matters. Hopcroft's (1994, 1999) extensive analyses of agrarian change in medieval Europe lead to a similar conclusion. She finds, in particular, that English peasant farmers were more likely than those in other parts of Europe to have the legal right to 'freehold'—to possess and work their own lands, separately from the manorial estates of the aristocracy. She notes, as well, that this form of economic organization dates back to the twelfth century, when 'freeholders were granted substantial legal rights under English common law'; as Hopcroft's research reveals, these developments meant that, with the exception of the Netherlands, England was 'unique in the feudal world' (Hopcroft 1999: 84–5; see also Macfarlane 1978: 171; Comninel 2000: 4–5, 23–4; Kerridge 1969; Hyams 1980).

While these analyses, in varying ways, underscore the distinctive and deep-seated features of the English cultural heritage and patterns of social organization, to our knowledge, there is only one analyst who has explicitly employed the term, deep structures, when discussing the character of all the English nations. That writer is the noted contemporary sociologist, Ralf Dahrendorf. In a collection of essays (Dahrendorf 1997), Dahrendorf mentions the idea of deep structures on a number of occasions. Although his references to this idea are brief, his conception is clearly consistent with that suggested in the overall discussion to this point. Dahrendorf sees deep structures, or what he sometimes calls 'ligatures', as the connecting social and cultural links that lend common meanings to people's lives (Dahrendorf 1997: 21, 30–2). These links help to bind together the members of a single nation, and also provide connections among those nations having the same key characteristics in common.

Dahrendorf concurs with the classical and other writers we have considered in arguing that the English societies share a distinctive set of deep-structural influences, especially with regard to basic principles and forms of democracy. Drawing on an argument originally made by the American diplomat, Jeane Kirkpatrick, Dahrendorf asserts that 'democracy . . . far from being a universal trend or even need, was really a form of social and political organization peculiar to the Anglo-Saxon world: to Britain, the United States, and the temperate Commonwealth countries' of Canada, Australia, and so on (Dahrendorf 1997: 31). He then asks the question: 'what are the deep structures' that have made it possible for 'democracy', which he also calls the 'the open society' and 'the society of citizens', to thrive in these nations?

Although Dahrendorf does not offer a systematic answer to this question, his commentaries point to a number of ideas that resonate with those that we have found in the works of the classical writers. Of particular note in Dahrendorf's assessment are the long-standing commitments in the English democracies to: liberty under the rule of law; equal legal and political rights of citizenship; free forms of debate and association, which allow for civil dissent and constructive social conflict; and the acceptance of religious differences and other social or cultural diversity (Dahrendorf 1997: 16, 20–4, 26–33, 39–42, 55–9; see also Dahrendorf 1979, 1988). These ideas are quite similar, in fact, to four main themes that recur throughout most of the classical writings and more recent analyses that we have considered in this chapter. On this basis, we suggest at least four closely related principles that appear to have left deep imprints on the both the cultures and the social structures of the English societies. These are liberty, legal equality, popular sovereignty, and pluralism.

First, let us consider the concept of liberty. Virtually all of the writers that we have considered have argued that liberty, or the general right of individuals to exercise personal freedom in their daily lives, is a guiding principle of the English societies. In their discussions of the English conception of liberty, most of these researchers and commentators place special emphasis on two types of liberty. One of these is political liberty, including the right of the people to some form of representation, autonomy, and influence with respect to their government. The other is economic liberty, especially the right to own property and to have some degree of economic independence.

Among all the approaches that we have reviewed, the only perspective that does not treat liberty as a core English principle is Lipset's origins thesis. Although his analysis is ambiguous in places, Lipset includes liberty, or liberalism, as an integral component of the American Creed, but he apparently does not see this idea as a central precept of the English nations in general. We have also found that, again except for Lipset, each writer believes that liberty in the English tradition is subject to important conditions or restrictions. In other words, the English version of liberty does not mean the absolute freedom or licence for people to do whatever they wish. On the contrary, true liberty requires the recognition that everyone should have the opportunity to enjoy basically the same freedoms. Because of this stipulation, liberty must therefore be tempered by various constraints, especially those that come from generally agreed-upon rules, regulations, practices, and customs. While many or most of these restrictions are found in formal laws that are created and enforced by government, some derive from and are fostered by other less official but often equally binding influences. As Tocqueville suggests, for example, these other constraints may include the moral suasion of religious teachings, the need or desire to conform to community standards of behaviour, and perhaps also the recognition by most people of the mutual advantages of enlightened self-interest.

The second key principle that emerges from the analyses that we have reviewed is legal equality, or equal justice. This idea, which in some form dates back at least to the time of the Common Law and so may have the deepest roots of all, emphasizes that every person should be afforded the same treatment, the same restrictions, and the same protection under the law. A related aspect of the principle of legal equality, as suggested in the Magna Carta and elsewhere, is that legal statutes are ultimately the 'law of the land', or the nation as a whole, and are not to serve the special interests of particular ruling groups or individuals. This conception of the law operates in coordination with the English idea of liberty, for, as we have already noted, laws are among the major means for guarding against the possibility that liberty will degenerate into licence, or the unregulated freedom for people to do whatever they want.

The third major principle that is consistently mentioned in discussions of the English heritage is the belief in popular sovereignty. This concept has a long pedigree, having been a subject of discussion and debate since the time of Plato (see, e.g., McClelland 1996: 292). However, in the context of the English-speaking democracies, this idea has a particular meaning or connotation. The English view of popular sovereignty suggests that, in the same way that English law is said to come from the nation, or society in general, so too does government power stem, in the last analysis, from the people as a whole, and not from a ruling elite or political leader. Churchill is among those who have argued that this principle, which maintains 'that the people should rule', is another feature of 'the ancient wisdom' that other nations have adopted from the English (Churchill 1947: 78). As we have discussed, the concept of the sovereignty of the people was also believed by Tocqueville to be perhaps the single most important legacy that the Anglo-Americans inherited from their English ancestors. It is interesting that, some 25 years after Tocqueville made his observations about the sovereignty of the people in the early United States, American President Abraham Lincoln offered what may be the best definition of this central idea. In his famous speech in 1863, to commemorate the battle of Gettysburg during the American Civil War, Lincoln spoke of his fervent hope that his own nation would continue to defend 'government of the people, by the people, and for the people'. This phrase captures the essence of what is meant by the concept of popular sovereignty (see Rodgers 1987: 91–2).

The fourth and final core English principle that we wish to emphasize is pluralism. Although this concept is not used explicitly by the writers that we have considered in this chapter, we believe that the term, pluralism, serves as a useful rubric for subsuming a broad set of ideals or values that previous analysts have attributed to the English societies. We also suggest that pluralism is an idea to which the English-speaking societies have consciously and increasingly aspired, as these nations have moved into the modern age.

Essentially, the ideals that we associate with pluralism in this context all emphasize the basic principle that, in a free society, people should have the right to be different, and that, as a consequence, everyone should both expect and accept that there will be some degree of social diversity in the general population. Pluralism, in this sense, is a natural extension or culmination of the other three core principles that we have identified, especially the concept of liberty. As suggested earlier, the English version of liberty is always subject to certain constraints imposed by law, government, custom, and so on. Nevertheless, even with such constraints, liberty in the English sense is meant to denote a range of freedoms. In other words, as long as individuals generally recognize both the rule of law and the rights of others, people should then be at liberty to act and to associate relatively freely, across various spheres of social life. This means, for example, that people should have reasonable latitude to think or to do as they like when it comes to politics, business, religion, and so on. A logical consequence of this arrangement, however, is that individuals must also be prepared to accommodate themselves to those who have different political, economic, and religious orientations. Ultimately, then, a free society necessarily entails some degree of pluralism in this general sense.

In a variety of ways, such noted observers as Montesquieu, Tocqueville, and Churchill have all commented on this aspect of the English cultural and social-structural legacy. According to these writers, the deep-seated and relatively broad acceptance of both liberty and pluralism, albeit in limited and often imperfect forms, has meant that, compared with other nations, the English societies historically were able to progress further and to be more successful in a range of endeavours, including the development of democratic political institutions, the promotion of economic growth and free enterprise, and the acceptance of both religious diversity and freedom of religious thought.

Some Qualifications

In general, then, we will proceed from the view that liberty, legal equality, popular sovereignty, and pluralism constitute the major deep-structural commonalities to be found in the English-speaking societies. In posing this argument, however, we should emphasize a number of qualifications or clarifications.

First, some comments are required about whether the core principles under discussion here are more accurately described as 'British', rather than 'English'. In other words, is it the case that these ideas were born from the experiences and heritages of all Britons, including the Scots, the Irish, and the Welsh, and not the English alone? On this question, some writers have contended, for example, that the central precepts of the American Revolution were at least as Scottish, or 'Scotch-Irish', as they were English (Hanna 1902, I: 90–104; see also Jackson 1993: 119–27, 131–4). To clarify our own position on this issue, the application of the 'English' label in the present analysis is meant, for the most part, to be inclusive of these other British groups, and is not intended to suggest that only those from England itself were the sources or the harbingers of these ideas.

Second, our reference to these four principles as English deep structures does not mean that generally similar values and ideals have never been established as important precepts in other nations. Although it is not a specific goal of our analysis to pursue this topic, there is little question that all or most democratic societies now subscribe, in some measure, to similar ideas. France is probably the most obvious example of a non-British nation that historically attempted to entrench many of the same precepts in its political, social, and economic institutions. This is evident, for instance, in the principles of 'liberté, égalité, and fraternité', which formed the rallying cry of the French Revolution of 1789. At the same time, however, our position is that, compared with other countries, the English societies probably benefited from an historical 'head start' in recognizing such key ideas, in entrenching them in formal constitutions, and in making them integral features of the lives of their citizens. With respect to the principle of popular sovereignty, for example, there is considerable evidence that, under 'the British form of participatory governance', English parliamentary assemblies were able to constrain the powers of their monarchs far more effectively, and at a much earlier stage of history, than were their French counterparts (Stanbridge 1997: 50, 29–35; see also Brewer 1989; Briggs 1977; Corrigan and Sayer 1985; Sayer 1992; Wolfe 1972).

Third, we do not contend that the four deep-structural principles outlined here are timeless or immutable, that their exact meaning and significance in the English democracies have not evolved or adapted with changing circumstances. In Chapter 2, for example, we noted how the English conceptions of liberty and liberalism have varied across different times and historical contexts, a point that we consider at greater length in Part II of this book. Partly because of the ways in which their orientations to the four core principles have developed, we also suggest that the basic character of the English democracies has been rather different from that of other democracies. This assertion does not mean that we accept the view of some commentators that the English enjoy an inherent 'superiority' relative to other peoples (for some discussion, see Clark 1995: 18–21). However, we do contend that both England and the English-speaking societies have generally been distinct from other countries in a number of important ways. In particular, it is clear that the English nations of today are much closer to a liberal-democratic political, economic, and social system than to the more left-leaning or social-democratic model that prevails in such societies as the Scandinavian countries of northern Europe. This is one of the distinctive features of the English societies that will be considered in subsequent sections of this volume.

As a final point of clarification, our identification of the four deep-structural influences with the English heritage does not imply that these ideas have all been put into practice in the English societies in some complete or perfect sense. The concept of pluralism is probably the most problematic in this regard, because it is the one core principle among the four that the English countries have been least successful and most belated in establishing as a reality for their peoples. There are obvious instances in the histories of the English nations of religious, racial, and other forms of intolerance and factional strife, some of which we discuss in Parts II and III. These include, for example, the problem of slavery, especially in the United States, and the treatment of the aboriginal populations in virtually all of the former English colonies. In the history of Britain itself, there have also been significant instances of religious intolerance and ethnic hostility affecting Irish Catholics, the Scottish Highland population, the Jewish minority, the Welsh, and other groups (see, e.g., Kearney 1989: 128, 152, 174). These events serve to refute any claims that the English countries have always embraced or consistently achieved what we refer to here as pluralism.

However, notwithstanding such clear exceptions, we suggest that pluralism and the other three deep-structural principles have generally had a more sustained role in shaping or conditioning the development of the English societies than has occurred in most other countries. Turning the causal sequence around, we also argue that, in a reciprocal way, the political, economic, legal, and other social structures within the English nations have been more effective than those in most other societies in promoting and realizing such values as pluralism and individual liberty. Historical research by a number of writers supports this basic argument. Goldstone, in particular, has concluded that, in the late 1600s, England began to lead the way in the development of both constitutional democracy and industrial capitalism. This occurred because of a combination of factors, including some that were fortuitous and even accidental. Nevertheless, among the main reasons suggested by this body of research was England's somewhat greater and earlier acceptance of religious tolerance, political pluralism, economic liberalism, and scientific innovation compared with other nations (Goldstone 2000: 175, 180, 183–7; see also Goldstone 1987, 1991; Kishlansky 1996; Jacob 1988; Sayer 1992). Given these considerations, it is our view that, especially in their more recent histories, the English-speaking nations have probably been more successful than most other countries of the world in both supporting and attaining individual freedom, the rule of law, popular sovereignty, and such pluralist ideals as tolerance and universal rights of citizenship.

There is additional evidence supporting the thesis that there is something distinctive, perhaps even unique, about the English nations, including their forms of social organization and their guiding principles. For example, in his historical survey of world 'peasant societies', Daniel Thorner concludes that the only areas of the world that never had peasantries, but instead began as societies of independent settler immigrants, were those colonized by England, in other words, Australia, New Zealand, English Canada, and the United States

(Thorner 1968: 504; see Macfarlane 1978: 202–3). Other research has determined that it was 'predominantly the British white settler societies of the United States and Canada (and Australia and New Zealand)' that were most successful in establishing independent democracies, because of their early and sustained experience with self-government when they were English colonies (Lipset et al. 1993: 168; Ibbitson 2004). Evidence from more recent times reveals the same pattern. Weiner, for example, found that, since the end of the Second World War, every one of the world's nations (with a population of at least one million) that had succeeded in becoming an independent democracy was 'a former British colony' (Weiner 1987: 20, 31; see also Lipset 1994: 5).

Of course, just how successful and how committed the English societies have been in implementing each of the four deep-structural principles should be seen an empirical question, as should the issue of whether these nations differ from each other, or from other countries, in these respects. In subsequent chapters, we consider historical and contemporary evidence that will help us to judge whether the people in two of the English-speaking societies, Canada and the United States, have different orientations toward these core ideas. It should be acknowledged that all of the democracies, English or otherwise, have had difficulties at times in establishing the principles of liberty, legal equality, popular sovereignty, and pluralism as pervasive realities in the social structures of their societies. The historical record of every democracy reveals instances in which some groups and individuals have not been granted the freedoms, tolerance, and basic human rights that are implied by these core principles. And, even now, some groups continue to experience discrimination or disadvantage within democratic societies. In spite of such problems, though, we maintain that, compared with any other system that humankind has yet devised, some form of democracy clearly comes closest to these elusive goals. In other words, we agree with Churchill's famous observation that 'democracy is the worst form of Government except all those other forms that have been tried from time to time' (Churchill 1947: 78).

CANADA AND THE UNITED STATES AS FOUR SUB-SOCIETIES

Now that we have highlighted the four underlying principles that are the focus of our analysis, the final concern in the rest of this chapter is to offer, in brief outline, an alternative perspective on the early development of Canada and the United States. The major themes that inform this perspective follow directly from our foregoing review and analysis of the work that has been done on this question by leading classical and contemporary writers.

To begin with, our general argument is that Canada and the United States, despite their eventual emergence as independent nation-states in the modern era, have always been kindred societies, because of shared deep structures stemming from their common English origins and heritage. It is also our view, however, that the underlying historical similarities between the two countries were from the earliest times overlaid with and complicated by two important factors, both of which we have touched on in previous sections of Part I. First, there is the enduring reality of French Canada as a distinct society within the larger Canadian nation. Second, there is the evident division that has existed between the southern and the northern United States. From our perspective, these internal distinctions have meant that the two countries developed historically as a configuration of four interrelated but separate 'sub-societies', which include English Canada, French Canada, the American North, and the American South.

One issue we might comment on before proceeding further is that, although we have delineated four major sub-societies within the two nations, we also contend that two of these elements, namely English Canada and the northern United States, were quite similar historically. In fact, based on a range of historical material that we consider in Part II of this volume, we believe it is probable that, in their early stages of development, these two societies were largely indistinguishable from each other in many important respects.

Pre-revolutionary Influences on Canada and the United States

The prime conclusion that we have drawn from our review of classical commentators and other noted observers is that there is a common old English heritage linking the Canadian and American nations. Thus, it should be clear that, in our estimation, many of the factors that have shaped the two countries go back to a time long before the era of the American Revolution. We certainly agree with those analysts who have said that the American Revolution was a significant factor in the creation of the two countries. However, we do not see this particular event as the most important occurrence for defining either nation. This assertion seems to us to be demonstrably true for Canada, and arguably true for the United States, as well. Our position is that the American Revolution was significant for Canadian society, but was really just one element in the intricate mix of historical and social influences that, over the longer term, have determined Canada's pattern of development. For the United States, of course, it seems undeniable that the Revolution was one of the most crucial moments in its history. Even in the American case, however, as we shall discuss, a strong claim can be made that other events have been at least as significant, if not more so.

One of our main contentions is that the populations of English Canada and America were generally similar from the beginning of permanent English colonization of the New World. This argument differs substantially from

Lipset's origins thesis, which implies that the two peoples were quite distinct, even during the period prior to the Revolutionary War. On this issue, our views are closer to the founding-fragment perspectives of Hartz and McRae who, as we have seen, argue that English liberalism had a similar impact on all the English colonies of North America. However, our analysis differs from the founding-fragment approaches in some other respects. For example, we have sought to build from and go beyond the founding-fragment arguments, by tracing some aspects of the English influence to even earlier events in the distant past, and by specifying more explicitly the main ideas and principles that we see as integral to the old English heritage.

The Distinctiveness of French Canada

Although our analysis devotes considerable attention to understanding the English influence in the New World societies, it is also important to recognize another key factor that has helped to define the North American experience. That factor, as alluded to previously, is France's significant role in the development of French Canada, dating back as far as the late sixteenth and early seventeenth centuries. This topic receives almost no attention in Lipset's origins thesis, but is discussed by some of the founding-fragment theorists, most notably McRae and Hartz. On this issue, our perspective generally parallels the founding-fragment approaches. We argue that the deep-structural forces operating in French Canada historically were fundamentally different from those that affected the development of English Canada and the United States. French Canada's early social structures were guided by quasi-feudal influences that originated in Old World France, and that involved ideas and values that were generally at variance with the principles of liberty, legal equality, popular sovereignty, and pluralism that eventually showed their effects within the English sub-societies.

Here it is helpful to recall that, although Tocqueville's discussion of this issue is relatively brief, he makes much the same observation. According to Tocqueville, French Canada by the middle 1800s was still an old society, one that lacked the emphasis on political liberty, business entrepreneurship, religious diversity, and so on that was emerging in both the United States and English Canada. We would add that, even after Quebec's inclusion as one of the founding provinces of Canadian Confederation in 1867, French Canada continued to display a character that made it distinct from the other sub-societies that were developing around it. As is discussed in Parts II and III of our analysis, much of the French distinctiveness is tied to French Canada's deep-structural divergences from the rest of North America, including its different language, its different religious tradition, and its different world view compared with the English populations. While the magnitude of these differences has undoubtedly reduced substantially in modern times, certain residual effects seem to be evident still. For example, as we note in subsequent chapters, one likely remnant from the past may be the relatively greater French-Canadian emphasis on the principle of collective as opposed to individual rights, especially as embodied in recent Quebec government policies to promote Quebecois nationalism and the pre-eminence of the French language in that province. We also discuss how French Canada's history and heritage have helped to promote a form of society that, in the contemporary period, is more social democratic and less liberal democratic than the other three regions of North America.

Post-revolutionary Influences and the American South

We have already indicated that our historical approach to the study of Canada and the United States differs from others in that we emphasize a number of significant influences that predate the American Revolution, in some cases by several centuries. The second major difference between our perspective and other approaches is that we also place considerable emphasis on events that took place after the American War of Independence. In this respect, we differ markedly from Lipset, whose origins thesis focuses almost entirely on the Revolution and devotes very little attention to later events or issues. As will be apparent from our previous discussion, some of the founding-fragment theorists do consider the period after the Revolution, and briefly comment on subsequent events, such as the American Civil War. In general, however, these analysts, especially Hartz and Horowitz, are similar to Lipset in concentrating mainly on the American Revolution and its immediate aftermath. Both Hartz and Horowitz place particular emphasis on the loyalist migration to Canada during and after the Revolution, and on the so-called Tory touch or streak that this occurrence allegedly introduced into the Canadian population.

Our perspective also considers the significance of the loyalist migration, although our conclusions do not conform with those of several prominent theorists, especially Lipset, but to some extent Hartz and Horowitz, as well. To anticipate some of the historical research and analysis presented in Part II, we contend that any claim that there was a pronounced Tory streak among the loyalist émigrés is simply not borne out by the evidence. In addition, though, our perspective looks well beyond the implications of the loyalist exodus, and considers historical events and episodes that occurred later, and that were almost certainly more important for shaping both nations. Clearly, there have been many pivotal factors in the post-revolutionary period that have jointly affected both the United States and Canada, a number of which we discuss in Part II. However, if we confine our attention to the crucial formative period of about 100 years following the American Revolution, then the single event that was probably the most important for the later development of the United States, and in some ways Canada as well, was the American Civil War in the 1860s.

Especially given the lasting consequences and repercussions of this conflict for the American population, it is surprising that, apart from some discussion of its implications by Hartz, the Civil War receives virtually no attention from the most prominent theorists who have written on the origins of Canada and the United States. This omission is understandable in the case of McRae and Horowitz, whose main concern is with the Canadian historical experience. However, it is difficult to account for this oversight in Lipset's research, except to say that it again may reflect his singular interest in and focus on the Revolution as the only formative event of real consequence for defining the United States. The other writer of note on this question, of course, is Tocqueville. We have found that, prior to the Civil War, Tocqueville placed considerable weight on the implications of slavery for the development of the United States, especially the American South. It is also noteworthy that, even though he completed his analysis of democracy in America many years before the outbreak of the Civil War, Tocqueville was prescient in anticipating that such a conflict might well be fought in the United States over the existence of slavery (Tocqueville 1840: 270).

From our perspective, then, the Civil War is crucial because it represents the culmination of the divergent evolution of two quite distinct sub-societies growing within the bosom of the early United States, one slave-based, quasi-feudal, and southern, the other more essentially Anglo-American, small-scale capitalist, and northern. In our view, this conflict, along with the social conditions and ideological differences associated with it, contributed to deep-seated and enduring differences which, although they have certainly reduced with the passage of time, still reveal vestiges of themselves today. This is another key issue that we shall reconsider later in this analysis.

SUMMARY AND CONCLUSION TO PART I

In this chapter, we have reviewed and assessed the works of a number of classical writers, as well as several more recent commentators and researchers. Based on this analysis, we have argued that it is possible to identify at least four deep-structural influences, or core principles, that were crucial to the social-structural and cultural development of Canada and the United States. These four principles are liberty, legal equality, popular sovereignty, and pluralism. We have also argued that, while Canada and the United States have generally come to share these same values and ideas, the two countries have also been marked historically by significant internal divisions, which have given rise to four comparatively distinct components or sub-societies. These regional elements, which include English Canada, French Canada, the American North, and the American South, have tended to vary in their level of commitment to or experience with English core principles or deep structures. We suggest that, historically, English Canada and the American North were the most similar among the four sub-societies, and, until recently, have also come closest to realizing the ideals of liberty, legal equality, popular sovereignty, and pluralism. The American South, especially because of the distinctive social and economic conditions associated with slavery in that region, as well as the longer-term consequences of this distinctiveness in the wake of the Civil War, was for some time far less likely than either English Canada or the American North to accept or promote most of these same ideals. As for French Canada, because of its quite divergent deep-structural influences stemming from its different language, religious legacy, and quasi-feudal heritage, this sub-society also showed a weaker commitment to these core English principles, at least during its early history.

Having addressed these theoretical issues, we are now in a position to conduct an empirical analysis of the similarities and differences across the Canadian and American nations and the four internal regional sub-societies that we have identified. In Part II of this volume, we move to a detailed assessment of the historical evidence bearing on our perspective, and on the approaches posed by Lipset and the founding-fragment theorists.

PART II

∾

HISTORICAL MYTHS AND HISTORICAL EVIDENCE

INTRODUCTION

In Part I, we outlined and assessed the leading theoretical perspectives on the historical development of Canada and the United States. We concentrated, in particular, on the founding-fragment approaches of Hartz, McRae, and Horowitz, and on Lipset's historical origins thesis. Based on our analysis of these interpretations, as well as an extended review of prominent classical and recent writings that have addressed similar issues, we then posed an alternative 'deep structures' perspective for understanding how and why Canada and the United States emerged as they did, beginning with the early colonial era.

In Part II, our central goal is to offer a detailed presentation and analysis of historical evidence pertaining to these different perspectives. We shall discuss a number of significant episodes and developments that can be identified in the common past of Canada and the United States. Because no part of this common past has attracted more interest from social researchers than has the era of the American Revolution, considerable attention is devoted to this key period. We then look at other crucial occurrences, with a focus on major events during the nineteenth century that helped to shape the two nations. We also comment briefly on more recent times, including several developments that influenced both countries in the latter part of the twentieth century.

We begin in Chapter 4 by reviewing the research of various historians and other social scientists who have sought to characterize the population of the thirteen American colonies in the period up to the Revolution. Of special interest is the evidence provided concerning the level of commitment in the American populace to the core principles of liberty, legal equality, popular sovereignty, and pluralism. Among the key issues we address is the question of whether some of the claims about the early colonists in North America have been based on certain inaccuracies or misunderstandings regarding the meaning of concepts like liberty and liberalism. Here we also discuss related research on what has been called the 'myth of American individualism' (Shain 1994).

In Chapter 5 we turn to another crucial historical question. Here we consider the significance of the loyalists, the group of people who migrated out of the thirteen colonies in the period during and after the War of Independence. As discussed in Part I, most of the major theorists have emphasized that these refugees from the American Revolution had a significant influence in defining both the character of the two societies and the subsequent relationship between the Canadian and American peoples. This emphasis is especially pronounced in Lipset's analysis, which, as we have noted, portrays the events of the Revolution, and especially the loyalist exodus, as the single most important factor in establishing a fundamental and permanent split between a revolutionary American nation and a counter-revolutionary Canada. We have seen that writers such as Hartz and Horowitz have also stressed the loyalist migration as a crucial development, because, in their view, this event brought a Tory touch or streak to the northern British colonies that has always made English Canada somewhat different from the United States. In this part of the discussion, we consider an array of evidence and analysis that will help us to adjudicate the overall accuracy of these arguments. We also assess the extent to which such claims form part of what has sometimes been referred to as 'the loyalist myth' (Bell and Tepperman 1979; see also Knowles 1997).

The final element of our historical analysis, as outlined in Chapter 6, is a detailed depiction of the social backgrounds and composition of the Canadian and American populations for the period of time between the American Revolution and the latter half of the nineteenth century. In addition to comparing Canada and the United States in general, we also look at internal differences among the four components or 'sub-societies' that are integral to the formation of the two nations. We review evidence dealing with a variety of socio-demographic and institutional factors, in an attempt to determine just how similar or how different the two societies and their peoples were in this important period. The main bases for our comparison include class and economic structure, ethnic composition and sources of immigration, religious influences, urbanization patterns, and political organization and political culture. This comparison will provide a means for assessing the extent to which the populations of the two societies, as well as the four sub-societies internal to them, differed from each other in their commitments to or experience with English core precepts, ideas, and social institutions.[1]

---

1.   Part II includes some revised excerpts from articles previously published in the Canadian *Journal of Sociology* (Grabb, Baer, and Curtis 1999) and the *Canadian Review of Sociology and Anthropology* (Grabb, Curtis, and Baer 2000). We are grateful to both journals for granting their permission to use these excerpts.

❧

LIBERTY, LIBERALISM, AND THE MYTH OF AMERICAN INDIVIDUALISM

In previous chapters, we determined that, according to a broad spectrum of prominent writers and commentators, the concept of liberty has long occupied a central place among the key principles of the English societies. The one major dissenting voice in this group of analysts has come from Lipset, whose delineation of the American Creed suggests that both liberty and the related idea of liberalism were essentially unique to the United States, and not fundamental to the national characters of either England or English Canada.

The research presented in Chapter 4 is an attempt to reconcile these discrepant views on the significance of the concept of liberty in the English nations. We look at evidence and analysis provided by a number of historical researchers who have addressed this question. The initial focus is on those studies that have considered what the colonial inhabitants of pre-revolutionary America actually understood or meant by the idea of liberty. It is argued that much of the apparent disagreement between Lipset's viewpoint and the other perspectives is due to some basic misunderstandings about the definition of liberty, and to the changing meanings and connotations that have been attached to this term in different historical periods. In addition to looking at the concept of liberty, we also consider research that has been done on the related idea of individualism. Here we suggest, once again, that certain misconceptions, combined with some misreading of the historical record, have contributed to most of the confusion and disagreement about the salience of this idea in the early development of English North America.

THE CONCEPT OF LIBERTY IN PRE-REVOLUTIONARY AMERICA

In our analysis to this point, we have discussed liberty primarily 'in the Lockian sense', i.e., to indicate the general right of people to exercise personal freedom, subject to the rule of law. However, evidence from a number of sources suggests that this definition was not the only or even the most common meaning that the Anglo-Americans had attached to the concept of liberty by the time of the Revolution.

Research by several historians indicates that the inhabitants of English North America tended to use the word, liberty, to designate a quite restricted and specific set of rights or practices, rather than to describe the more generalized conception of personal freedom suggested in Locke's writings. For example, Appleby has found that liberty was used by the early Americans to refer to the simple economic right to own private property or personal possessions, and also to the basic right of local communities to have some degree of political autonomy (Appleby 1984: 16–20; see also Appleby 1992: 124–5; White 1978: 20–9, 221–54; Diggins 1984: 60–1; Fischer: 783–8, 897–8). The latter meaning roughly parallels Tocqueville's notion of 'municipal liberty' or local popular sovereignty, which was discussed in the previous chapter. Appleby notes, as well, that the related idea of 'liberalism' was not used by or known to most Americans during the late 1700s, although it apparently was familiar to many Europeans by that time (Appleby 1992: 10). This finding suggests that the concept of liberalism, especially the version that is typically attributed to Locke, was not a prevalent idea among the Anglo-American population in the period of the Revolution.

Probably the most comprehensive study that has yet been conducted on the meaning of liberty in colonial America arrives at essentially the same conclusions as those of Appleby (Shain 1994). This research is based on an extensive analysis of printed materials that have survived from that era, including newspaper editorials, political pamphlets, religious sermons, so-called 'political' sermons, personal diaries, and various public documents. Only a relatively small proportion of the populace could read and write at that time, so that such records may not precisely represent the thoughts and outlooks of the people as a whole. Nevertheless, since these documents were produced by individuals who were outside the elite, and closer in status to the mass of the population, their 'lived testimonies' probably provide a more reliable and accurate reflection of the commonly held values and beliefs of the period than do any other sources (see Shain 1994: xvi, 6–8).

Like Appleby, Shain finds that Locke's idea of liberty, in the sense of general individual freedom, was definitely not the most widely recognized meaning of the term in English North America during the late 1700s. In addition, Shain shows that at least seven other usages for liberty were evident in the popular discourse of the time. Two of these usages parallel those noted by Appleby, having to do with economic liberty, especially the property rights of independent families, and with political liberty, in the sense of local community self-government or popular sovereignty. Among the other types of liberty that

Shain delineates, perhaps the most notable is 'spiritual liberty'. This term might seem to imply a general right of religious freedom or religious tolerance, but in fact denotes a more limited idea, in which religious people (specifically Christians) are free to live a righteous existence according to the dictates of their faith (Shain 1994: 168–9, 179–80; see also Bryce 1921b, I: 56; Fischer 1989: 9–11, 199–205, 783–8, 897–8).

Based on his analysis of all the various types of liberty, Shain's overall conclusion is that liberty was certainly a cherished principle among the Anglo-Americans of the late eighteenth century, but was also an idea that, in its numerous meanings, consistently involved significant restrictions on personal freedom (Shain 1994: 162–3). Some of these strictures were imposed by government, especially at the local level, and so are similar to those that Locke himself believed were necessary to prevent liberty from turning into 'licence'. Nevertheless, over and above such legal constraints, Shain finds a more pervasive and all-encompassing set of restrictions in pre-revolutionary America, deriving from community-imposed religious and moral standards of what was considered proper or orderly conduct (see Shain 1994: Chapters 5, 6, and 7). We have already seen that Tocqueville found somewhat similar pressures for community approval operating in the post-revolutionary United States (recall Tocqueville 1840: 275). However, the limitations on individual liberty that Shain points to in the period prior to the Revolution appear to be more stringent and more binding than those that Tocqueville observed in later years. During this earlier era, then, it seems certain that individual liberty or personal freedom was not the overriding concern or primary guiding principle of most Anglo-Americans.

This is not to say that the Lockian idea of individual liberty enjoyed no currency in the period leading up to the War of Independence. For some people, including several founding figures of the Revolution, Locke's ideas were significant. Thomas Jefferson, for example, who drafted much of the Declaration of Independence and who later served as the third President of the United States, held views about liberty that were clearly influenced by Locke's conception, and by the broadly similar ideas of Montesquieu (McClelland 1996: 336, 355–8; Schlesinger 1964: 158; Shain 1994: 186, 248; D'Souza 2000: 179–81; Wood 2002: 59). Even the famous phrase that Jefferson included at the beginning of the Declaration of Independence, concerning life, liberty, and 'the pursuit of happiness', was originally coined by Locke (Bryson 1994: 42). Such influences are evident in the ideas of another early President, John Adams, as well as other prominent leaders of the early American nation (McCullough 2001: 121, 245; Diggins 1984: 32–4; Bailyn 1992: 27–8). Research also suggests that, after the revolutionary period, Locke's 'liberal premises' were more widely known and embraced by an increasing proportion of educated people in the larger population (Wood 1992: 236, 239; 2002: 59, 102–3; see also Shain 1994: 192; McClelland 1996: 356).

Nevertheless, the historical evidence generally indicates that, although liberty was a salient principle in colonial America, for most people the term stood for a different set of ideas from those that it came to signify in later decades. It would be well into the nineteenth century before liberty would refer to the general sense of personal freedom that we typically associate with Locke's conception. Thus, when Locke penned his views on liberty in the late 1600s and early 1700s, he was, in a very real sense, 'ahead of his time', at least as far as most English North Americans were concerned.

The findings we have reviewed raise significant questions about some of the major theoretical perspectives that were discussed in Chapter 2. In the case of Hartz's founding-fragment thesis, the evidence goes against his claim that the English colonies of the New World constituted a liberal fragment in the Lockian sense, although it does appear that the Anglo-Americans of this period were indeed imbued with liberal ideas of the more modest and limited type indicated by Shain and others (see Shain 1994: 10–12, 21; Appleby 1992: 125, 327).

The historical evidence poses far more serious difficulties for Lipset's thesis, however. First, we should recall that the concept of liberalism in Lipset's version of the American Creed, which he calls 'the revolutionary ideology' of the United States, does not emphasize the limited legal or governmental constraint on individual behaviour that Locke saw as essential for true liberty. Thus, in showing that liberty in the thirteen colonies was a significantly more restricted idea than Locke envisioned, the research of Shain and others indicates that Lipset's views about core American values at the time of the Revolution are less accurate than those suggested in Hartz's account.

The second difficulty in Lipset's analysis is his argument that the founding American Creed amounts to 'liberalism in its eighteenth- and nineteenth-century meanings' (recall Lipset 1996: 31). The problem with this assertion is its implication that the meaning of liberalism was invariant across these two centuries of history. The research that we have reviewed indicates that, on the contrary, the predominant meanings and connotations of both liberty and liberalism differed considerably in the eighteenth century from those that prevailed in the nineteenth century. Specifically, although Locke's ideas about liberty and liberalism probably became more central to the dominant American value system as the country progressed through the decades of the 1800s, the type of liberty that most Americans fought for in the Revolution of the late 1700s was almost certainly a different idea. In fact, it is quite possible that the majority of the Americans who rebelled against England were really seeking the same basic rights and the same limited forms of liberty that had previously been given to the English in Europe.

The latter argument has been made by several historians and commentators over the years. McClelland speaks of the numerous writers who have concluded that the Revolution was fought mainly over 'the rights of Englishmen which the Americans thought were being denied to them', and over the simple desire of 'Englishmen living abroad . . . to be treated exactly as Englishmen at home' (McClelland 1996: 355, 422; see also Schlesinger 1964: 158; McPherson 1991: 46–7; Schama 2001: 473, 2002: 46; Harrison and Friesen 2004: 86). This view is consistent with Churchill's assertion that the American Declaration of Independence 'was in the main a restatement of the principles' that the English people themselves had fought for in the late 1600s (Churchill 1957: 189). Similar observations were made by prominent Americans of the time. For example, Shain has noted Thomas Jefferson's assertion that, in seeking to protect their rights to popular sovereignty, political representation, and legal equality, the American revolutionaries were not establishing 'new principles, or new arguments', but were largely restating the existing rights of English subjects (Jefferson, cited in Shain 1994: 247). Likewise, McCullough has commented on John Adams's belief 'that American freedoms were not ideals still to be obtained, but rights long and firmly established by British law' (McCullough 2001: 59). Similarly, Langguth (1988: 68–9) has noted that another famous patriot, Patrick Henry, expressed the firm view that the colonists had brought to America 'all the liberties of the people of Great Britain', with 'the same privileges as if they had been born in England and still lived there'.

There is one historian who has taken a somewhat different stance. He maintains that, although the American colonists and their leaders believed that 'they were simply protecting what Englishmen had valued from the beginning of their history', the revolutionaries were in fact bringing to fruition ideas that would go beyond old English principles (Wood 2002: 58; see also Bryson 1994: 31). Nevertheless, the fact that so many American colonial leaders held to this view raises the intriguing prospect that the Revolution might never have occurred if King George III had given the same rights and protections to the Anglo-Americans as those that were enjoyed by his subjects at home.

THE MYTH OF AMERICAN INDIVIDUALISM

We can see, then, that there is a considerable body of historical research and analysis suggesting that the guiding principles of the people living in the thirteen colonies at the time of the American Revolution were very similar to those found in England itself. Central to these principles was a limited form of liberty, which was constrained by a strong awareness of community standards of thought and behaviour, coupled with a belief in popular sovereignty, self-government, and local autonomy. Overall, this research paints a picture of pre-revolutionary America that is rather different from those provided by either Hartz or Lipset.

One question to ask at this point is: why have the leading perspectives of Hartz and especially Lipset apparently missed the mark in their portrayals of the Anglo-American character in this period of history? As we have seen, much of the answer to this question may be traceable to some misunderstandings about the meaning of key ideas like liberty and liberalism, which more recent studies and more comprehensive historical research have brought to light. A related factor to consider concerns the 'myth-making' that sometimes occurs in historical analysis.

Shain's (1994) research on the revolutionary era appears to have identified just such a myth. He concludes that much of the writing about the early United States, especially with respect to the Revolution, has encouraged what he calls 'the myth of American individualism'. The concept of individualism in this context is a natural extension of, and in many ways is synonymous with, the nineteenth-century version of liberalism suggested in Lipset's analysis. Indeed, it has been argued that, in order to distinguish this conception of individualism from other meanings and usages, it may be preferable to combine the terms 'liberalism' and 'individualism' and to use 'liberal individualism' as a label for this particular idea (Shain 1994: xiv, 324–5; for some discussion, see also Grabb, Baer, and Curtis 1999; Grabb, Curtis, and Baer 2000).[1]

Individualism in this sense amounts to a general belief in the 'freedom to do what one wishes' (Shain 1994: xiv) or, as another author has phrased it, 'the freedom to do anything you damn well please' (Ferguson 1997: 100). In essence, such a principle maintains that all people should largely be free to live and to act as they see fit, without extensive collective or community restrictions on their personal behaviour. Shain contends that this is actually quite a modern idea, and was not a prevalent sentiment in revolutionary America. However, he suggests that, over the years, more recent commentators have often come to accept the erroneous view that the American population of that time was both liberal and individualistic in the modern sense. This myth has arisen primarily because some prominent academics and popular observers have engaged in an 'anachronistic' interpretation of the historical record (see Shain 1994: 117), in which past references or allusions to liberty, liberalism, and similar terms have been read with 'modern eyes', leading to the belief that such words stood for the same principles then as they do today.

---

1.   Other types, some of which are similar to the idea of liberal individualism described here, include 'utilitarian', 'rugged', 'modern', and even 'narcissistic' individualism (see, e.g., Bellah et al. 1985; Christian and Campbell 1983; Lukes 1973; Shain 1994; Triandis et al. 1990; Williams 1960).

In fact, there is compelling evidence that the modern idea of liberal individualism was rarely known in the English North America of the late 1700s and early 1800s. We turn now to a review of this evidence. First, we look briefly at the research that has been done on the central values of the revolutionary leaders and other members of the American elite. We then consider studies that have concentrated on the ideas and perceptions of the general population. Finally, we conclude our analysis of American individualism by examining the views of some prominent outside observers of the United States during the period after the Revolution.

Elite Values: Republicanism and the Public Good

Our analysis to this point has generally proceeded from the view that one of the best ways to judge the core principles of a society is to understand the values and outlooks that predominate in the overall population. However, some would claim that, in order to identify the central precepts of a nation, it is preferable to examine the ideas and world views that prevail among the country's elite leadership. Such an assertion is similar to the 'dominant ideology' thesis found in early Marxism (see Marx and Engels 1846: 59; Gramsci 1928; for some discussion, see Abercrombie, Hill, and Turner 1980; Wright, Levine, and Sober 1992). This perspective suggests that, because the elite or dominant group has the most power to shape a nation's key social institutions and long-term priorities, the ideas of the dominant group also provide the best gauge of that society's core values and guiding principles.

There are plausible arguments on both sides of this debate. Hence, it is advisable to look at both the mass of the population and the elite when assessing the core ideas and values of the early United States. In gauging the elite viewpoint, it is interesting to note, first of all, that many of America's revolutionary leaders themselves believed that their conceptions of the country's central principles should hold sway. Thomas Jefferson, for example, once stated that the ideas of ordinary Americans 'must never be considered when we calculate the national character' (see Wood 1992: 28; also Shenkman 1988: 32–3). John Adams, Alexander Hamilton, and George Washington are some of the other famous people who offered similarly elitist opinions about the ideas of the American people, at times describing them as 'the common herd', 'the unthinking populace', or 'the grazing multitude' (Wood 1992: 28; see also Bryson 1994: 54–9).

In any event, those researchers who have studied the written records left by the leaders of the early United States have found that these prominent figures generally did not place a high value on liberal individualism. On the contrary, most evidence indicates that the national elite favoured a far more group-oriented and socially responsible set of principles and values. As we have already discussed, some degree of Lockian individual liberty was both accepted and encouraged by several of the Revolution's leaders, including Jefferson, Adams, and others. For the most part, however, the national leaders apparently felt strongly that, both for themselves and for the American people in general, it was important to restrain individual desires and interests, and to place primary emphasis on civic responsibility, service to the community, and the general well-being of the people (Bellah et al. 1985: vii–viii, 143; Shain 1994: 157; Williams 1960: 451–2; Wood 1992: 104; Langguth 1988: 438).

These same sorts of priorities are reflected in the idea of 'republicanism', which is one of the central principles that were embraced by many members of the national elite. Republicanism is a concept that, like several others we have discussed, has had multiple meanings at times (see Wood 1992: 95–6; Appleby 1992: 320–4; Rodgers 1992). In this case, however, the word is used in the classical Greco-Roman sense, or in the Renaissance meaning associated with Rousseau, and refers to the belief that free individuals have a responsibility to participate in serving the public good, so as to promote a better society (Bellah et al. 1985: 252–4, 335; Shain 1994: 272–3; Wood 1992: 104; Appleby 1992: 21–3, 290–1). Here, as well, we find that the guiding principles of revolutionary America, at least as they were reflected in the views of the elite leadership, apparently placed the highest value, not on people's freedom to do as they wish, but on subordinating individualistic desires and self-interested motives to the interests of public service and the collective good of society in general.

'Local Communalism' and the American People

If we turn our attention to the American people as a whole, we find evidence that a somewhat different set of principles and practices tended to predominate within the general population. Research suggests, first of all, that the republicanism favoured by many key members of the national elite was not highly valued by the average American in this period (Wood 1992: 189, 216, 222; also Shain 1994: xvi, 137). In fact, in later years, virtually all of the noted founders of the United States, as well as many religious leaders, expressed disappointment that the republican sense of public service had apparently not taken a sustained hold on the American citizenry (Wood 1992: 333–5, 365–7; Bellah et al. 1985: 252–6).

Instead, there is relatively strong and consistent evidence that the prevalent belief system in the general public at that time was a form of what Shain has called 'local communalism' (Shain 1994: xviii, 37–8, 48–9). In other words, American society in the revolutionary period was steeped in a set of values that placed primary emphasis on an adherence to the standards of small-town community life, or 'collectivism within a smaller group' (Pekelis 1950:

67). In this setting, neither unconstrained individual liberty, nor a strong republican commitment to serving the nation as a whole, was greatly encouraged or widely evident (Wood 1992: 20).

This characterization of the Anglo-American population is broadly similar to Tocqueville's assessment. However, the forces of community conformity that Shain and others have identified in the late 1700s were probably stronger than those that Tocqueville found in his travels through America in the 1830s. It appears that most people paid even closer heed and allegiance to their local governments than to their national leaders in the revolutionary period, and harboured 'a marked distrust of elites' situated outside their own communities (Shain 1994: 55). This pattern of 'intense localism' seems to have continued for many years beyond the Revolution (see, e.g., Clark 1968: 209–10). Not until the American Civil War and the disputes over state autonomy, or 'states' rights', is there evidence that local communalism began to be replaced by a moderate individualism and a more republican-inspired national vision. In fact, many analysts have argued that, even into the twentieth century, most Americans continued to be primarily oriented to local community life (see, e.g., Shain 1994: 55, 64–5, 115, 243; Leuchtenberg 1958; Appleby 1974: 337–8, 415–16; Wood 1992: 120; Bellah et al. 1985: 42; Foote 1989; Reed 1982, 1983; Gibbins 1982: 12–13; McPherson 1991: viii, 7–8).

Shain's depiction of the early United States as a highly localized society is quite plausible when we consider the composition of the American nation during this era. The vast majority of the populace were rural settlers, dependent on a predominantly agricultural economy for survival and living in scattered and relatively isolated communities. Estimates suggest that only five per cent of the population lived in towns and villages of more than 2,500 people (see, e.g., Chandler 1977: 17; Stuart 1988: 46, 55; Wood 1992: 58, 131, 312). Even as late as 1870, less than 25 per cent of Americans resided in centres of this size (Bender 1978: 12). These figures indicate that, for decades after the Revolution, only a small proportion of citizens lived in the kinds of settings where they would be likely to have the same experiences and develop the same outlooks as their more informed, cosmopolitan, and urbane national leaders (e.g., Wood 1992: 189, 229).

Crucial to the small settlements that characterized virtually all of the United States during the revolutionary period were the community churches. Most churches and religious organizations fostered reformed-Protestant or other Protestant-sectarian beliefs, which played a major role in shaping the world views of the local populations. It is true, as Lipset and others have noted, that there was a wide and diverse range of sects from which American colonists were free to choose their preferred denomination (Lipset 1996: 19–20; Wood 1992: 1, 112, 332–3; Appleby 1974: 312). However, it also appears that, within each of these denominations, the religious teachings themselves were 'morally demanding' and 'restrictive', and did not place a high value on individual freedom and self-expression; on the contrary, most of these churches regarded the 'autonomous self' as 'at the core of human sinfulness' (Shain 1994: xvi, 3, 37–8, 86). In addition, even though some religious sects, most notably the Quakers (Fischer 1989: 429–34, 595–600; Shain 1994: 71–3), clearly advocated the tolerance of different faiths, there were many groups, including the New England Puritans, the Virginia Anglicans, and others, who seem to have been quite intolerant of those that differed from themselves (see, e.g., Bryce 1889, II: 555; Hanna 1902, II: 1–2, 17–19; Wood 1992: 17, 20; Appleby 1974: 312; Fischer 1989: 232–5, 333, 430, 821; D'Souza 2000: 181–3).

At this stage in the analysis, it is instructive to ask what this evidence tells us about the impact of the four deep-structural English influences on the population of the early United States. That is, to what extent were the principles of popular sovereignty, liberty, legal equality, and pluralism operative among the Anglo-Americans of this era? First, the findings of Shain and others certainly support the conclusion that local popular sovereignty and municipal autonomy had become pervasive social realities by this time. The evidence is also consistent with the view that, during the first few decades of the American republic, the average citizen experienced both legal equality and liberty, at least in the limited forms that we have discussed in this chapter. Nevertheless, the research we have reviewed suggests that the power of the local community, especially in the spheres of politics and religion, typically placed significant restrictions on personal rights and freedoms. These communal influences probably had the most negative consequences with respect to the core principle of pluralism, or what we have previously referred to as the basic right to be different. Given the research noted above, which indicates that some forms of religious intolerance and other kinds of communal restrictiveness were evident at this time, it seems certain that, in many parts of the new United States, there was still a clear discrepancy between the core principle that individuals should have the right to be different from each other and the actual practice of intolerance towards people of diverse religious and other backgrounds.

One factor that may have helped to counterbalance both the pressures for communal conformity and the problems of intolerance was the opportunity for resettlement provided by the openness of the country at the time (see, e.g., Wood 1992: 311). This allowed for what has been called 'the simple expedient of physical separation' (Fischer 1989: 822). In other words, those persons who sought freedom from a particular community's restrictions on, or rejection of, their beliefs and behaviours could often relocate to other communities, or even establish a completely new settlement of their own. Under these circumstances, different groups presumably would have been able to pursue what might be called a 'separate but equal' approach with respect to each other's ethnic and religious diversity, with people being relatively free to follow their own way of life while also allowing others to do the same, albeit in separate communities.

The capacity for people to change locations was probably especially important for giving individuals the chance to achieve economic liberty or self-reliance, because it often meant that they could own their own land. Throughout the revolutionary period and beyond, most Americans existed in similar economic circumstances, making their living in agriculturally based hamlets, or in free-standing farmers' homesteads of one or a few families. In turn, it seems plausible that being economically self-reliant or independent in these settings would also generate an increasingly strong belief in the virtues of economic individualism.

Still, it does not follow that the growing commitment to economic individualism would automatically lead to an equally individualistic or open outlook regarding other spheres of life, including religion or moral values. Here we should note Tocqueville's comments on the 'general equality of condition among the people' of early America, which he saw as one of the major consequences of the economic freedoms and the bountiful resources that the nation provided for its citizens (Tocqueville 1835: 3, 30–1). At the same time, however, Tocqueville believed that these material equalities or economic uniformities in the new American nation were also conducive to uniformities in the 'opinions' and 'habits' of the populace (see Tocqueville 1840: 272–5). Thus, Tocqueville expressed serious concerns that minority ideas or dissenting beliefs were being stifled by the 'tyranny of the majority' in the early United States, so much so that he knew of 'no country in which there is so little independence of mind and real freedom of discussion as in America' (Tocqueville 1835: 273).

Given these considerations, it seems unlikely that the economic independence enjoyed by the American people in that period was in itself sufficient to overcome local-communalist restrictions on individualism. Even the relative ease of mobility and freedom to relocate at that time may not have helped in this regard. In fact, one possible consequence of the opportunity to move elsewhere was to promote the spread of local communalism more widely, creating a myriad of diverse settlements, each with its own distinct set of particularistic ideas and intolerant outlooks (Shain 1994: 95; see also Bender 1978: 69; Appleby 1974: 312; Fischer 1989: 821–3; Blessing 1999: 455–6). Thus, one historian has noted that, for some decades after the Revolution, even along the expanding American frontier, most communities, especially religious ones, 'took a downright dim view of individualism' and discouraged 'individuals who wished to be different' (Shenkman 1988: 117–18).

The Views of Outside Observers: Tocqueville and Chevalier

One final means for judging whether or not individualism was an influential idea in the early United States is to consider the first-hand observations of outside visitors. Two commentaries that are especially helpful and pertinent are those of Tocqueville and his countryman, Michel Chevalier. These two writers, in fact, were the first ever to use the word 'individualism' to describe the value system of the American population (Shain 1994: 84, 91–2). Indeed, the word, individualism, did not even appear in the English language until their works were translated from the original French (Chevalier 1839; Tocqueville 1840).

The timing of these translations in itself raises serious doubts about how influential the idea of individualism could have been in the thinking of the American people during the Revolution, given that these works did not appear in English until some 50 years after the War of Independence. Moreover, it is probable that, even in these instances, the use of the term 'individualism' was an unintended misrepresentation by the two foreign commentators. As Europeans who had never experienced the small-town community orientation of revolutionary America in their own country, both Chevalier and Tocqueville chose the French word, 'individualisme', in an attempt to label what was essentially local communalism. The French word easily, if mistakenly, became 'individualism' in English translation. However, the present-day sense of this idea was not the meaning that these writers wished to convey in their original descriptions of the prevailing American ethos during the period after the Revolution (Shain 1994: 84–5, 90–3, 117; see also Diggins 1984: 239, 242–3).[2]

This point seems especially clear in Chevalier's analysis, which stresses the 'spirit of locality' as the utmost concern among Americans in that era, and which contrasts this orientation with the more centralized and national conception of democracy found in France at the time (Chevalier 1839: 116; see Shain 1994: 93–4). Tocqueville defines the 'individualism' of Americans in similar terms, as the tendency of 'each member of the community to sever himself from the mass of his fellows', 'to draw apart with his family and friends', forming 'a little circle of his own' and leaving 'society at large to itself' (Tocqueville 1840: 104; see Bellah et al. 1985: 37). Observations by other European writers, including the Swiss-German churchman, Phillip Schaff,

---

2. An examination of dictionary sources seems to confirm Shain's conclusions about the origins of the term 'individualism'. For example, The Oxford Universal Dictionary on Historical Principles (London: Oxford University Press, 1955: 993) indicates that the word first appeared in its French form, 'individualisme', around 1835, which is in the same period that Chevalier's and Tocqueville's observations on the United States were written in French and then translated into English.

provide a similar image of a highly localized and communal American society (Schaff 1855: 60, 214; see Shain 1994: xvii, 120–1). Several decades after these commentaries, Lord Bryce, the noted English historian and observer of the United States, continued to remark on the issue, again emphasizing the 'purely local' nature of America in that period of history (Bryce 1887: 24 ; see also Errington 1994: 15; Stuart 1988: 29; Wood 1992: 229). All of these observations by early historians and visitors parallel the other evidence that we have reviewed in this section of our analysis. Thus, we have a clear sense that the Anglo-American populace, during the revolutionary era and beyond, was more strongly committed to localized, small-town collectivist values than to liberal individualist beliefs.

SUMMARY

In this chapter, we have been primarily concerned with assessing the extent to which certain forms of liberty and individualism were important guiding principles in the American population around the time of the Revolution. We have found that most of the evidence, especially the more recent research of a number of prominent historians, indicates that neither individual liberty nor the modern conception of liberal individualism were widely held ideas or values in this period of American history.

Instead, it appears, first, that the elite leaders of the United States adhered to a more limited and socially responsible conception of liberty, which was closely tied to the 'republican' belief in serving the public good and the nation as a whole. Second, in the larger population, the research indicates that people generally espoused a quite restricted idea of liberty, and were mainly committed to a system of local community values, with a strong emphasis on conformity to collectively sanctioned, rather than individually determined, standards of thought and behaviour. There is reason to believe that, as the new nation developed, more of the American populace did acquire a greater desire for personal liberty or individualism, especially in the economic sphere, along with a less localized and more national sense of identity and allegiance. These changes, however, evidently did not take place until well into the 1800s and beyond. In fact, it appears that the focus on local community concerns, along with the commitment to the values of small-town America, has lingered to some degree right into the modern era.

❧

ENGLISH CANADA AND THE LOYALIST MYTH

We should now have a clearer understanding of the core ideas and guiding principles that influenced the development of the United States during the late 1700s and early 1800s. Our next task is to consider what was happening in the English-Canadian colonies at about this same time. It is evident from previous sections of our analysis that, according to most of the prominent theorists who have studied this question, the single most important development that affected the Canadian colonies in this period was the loyalist migration.

In Chapter 5, we are mainly concerned with determining who the loyalists really were, and how their core ideas and beliefs compared with those of their counterparts in the thirteen American colonies. Our review of the available evidence and commentary that deal with these questions will allow us to weigh the relative merits of the different views on the loyalists that are provided in the founding-fragment perspectives and in Lipset's origins thesis. Of special interest are the competing claims concerning the following issues: whether the loyalists had a strong commitment to 'Tory' ideas and principles; whether they instead were essentially liberal but with a Tory touch; or whether they were actually guided by a set of values that were basically the same as those of the American colonists, involving a mix of local-communalist ideas and some limited forms of liberty, legal equality, popular sovereignty, and pluralism. The evidence we consider will also help to address the question of just how loyal the loyalists were to the English monarchy and way of life. Central to this part of the analysis is the attempt to demonstrate that much of what has been said and written about the loyalists by various writers has contributed to another recurring and largely misleading myth, this time about the fundamental nature of early Canadian society and its historical relationship with the United States.

THE LOYALIST MIGRATION AND CANADIAN TORYISM

The loyalist migration out of the American colonies, both during and after the Revolution, is the major factor in Lipset's historical explanation of Canadian–

American differences. It is also a key issue for most of the founding-fragment theorists, especially Hartz and Horowitz. Lipset's argument, as we have noted previously, is that virtually all of those who left the thirteen American colonies for Canada not only were loyal to Britain but also adhered strongly to a belief in Toryism or Tory values. Here Toryism refers primarily to a set of principles emphasizing collectivism, elitism, ascription, and deference to hierarchical authority (see, e.g., Christian and Campbell 1983: 8, 24–6, 30–1; Lipset 1990: 212). As we discussed in Chapter 2, such ideas are close to being the antithesis of Lipset's version of the American Creed (Lipset 1996: 31–2, 91–3). Thus, Lipset's contention is that the refugees from the Revolution who flowed into Canada, being thoroughly versed in traditional anti-liberal and anti-individualist beliefs, were quite unlike the inhabitants of the newly formed United States.

Based on the research reviewed in Chapter 4, some significant doubts must be raised about Lipset's general argument. That is, given the research of Shain, Appleby, and others, it seems certain that, apart perhaps from their economic outlook, the American people themselves were not particularly liberal or individualist, at least in the sense that Lipset uses these terms. Nevertheless, if Lipset is correct in his contention that the loyalist émigrés were even less liberal and more Tory than those who remained in the new American nation, then the migration of the loyalists into the northern colonies of British North America may well have been important for establishing a major social and cultural division between the English Canadian and American peoples at that time. If the founding-fragment interpretations, especially those of Hartz and Horowitz, are correct, then the loyalist refugees should have instilled a notable but more minor Tory influence in Canada. Finally, if the deep-structures interpretation we have outlined is closer to the mark, then the loyalist migration should have had little impact in reshaping or distinguishing the value systems of the two societies, since all of the English-speaking colonists, whether loyalist, American, or otherwise, would have held to much the same set of core English principles and beliefs.

In order to evaluate these arguments, it is necessary to address a series of questions about the loyalists. We first consider estimates on how many loyalists there were, because the size of this group is one important gauge of how influential their migration may have been, both for the Canadian colonies they moved to and for the American states they left behind. We then address the question of how loyal to Britain the loyalists actually were, and also consider the related issue of whether loyalism should reasonably be viewed as synonymous with a commitment to Tory values. Next, we examine the possibility that both the loyalists and the English-speaking inhabitants who were living in Canada prior to the loyalist arrival were in most respects really 'Americans'.

Finally, we conclude our analysis of the loyalists by considering whether the whole question of Toryism and loyalism should take into account the distinction between the elite leadership and the general population of the English-Canadian colonies during the revolutionary era and afterward.

COUNTING THE LOYALISTS

Our initial task is to estimate the number of Americans who moved into the Canadian colonies during and after the War of Independence. Although some writers disagree about the exact size of the loyalist contingent, there is little doubt, first of all, that the migrants represented just a small fraction of the Americans who had serious misgivings about the Revolution. The revolutionary leader and future American president, John Adams, estimated that only about a third of the population truly supported the break with Britain, with another third largely indifferent and the remaining third opposed (Shenkman 1988: 84; Hanna 1902, I: 84). Analyses by historians suggest that the anti-revolutionary proportion was somewhat smaller, comprising between 20 and 30 per cent of the populace, or about 500,000 people (e.g., Condon 1984: ix, 20; see also McRae 1964: 237; Moore 1994: 27, 244). In either instance, it is clear that the vast majority of those who opposed the war with Britain appear to have done so passively or tacitly, since most estimates indicate that no more than 100,000 American residents moved elsewhere during this time (Smith 1968; Wood 1992: 176; Thompson and Randall 1994: 15; Osborne and Swainson 1988: 25).

As to why most anti-revolutionaries chose to stay in the thirteen colonies, the reasons are undoubtedly varied and complex. Many were reluctant to leave long-established homes, kinship or friendship ties, and economic interests. Although they risked possible confiscation of their lands and other serious forms of persecution, many who stayed on could avoid or minimize such penalties by keeping their dissenting views to themselves. Others could find protection through their wealth or social networks. In the latter regard, research suggests that the American colonists who opposed the Revolution did come disproportionately from the more well-to-do and influential strata (Wood 1992: 176–7). In the minds of many of these people, it presumably made sense to hang on, in the hope that the rebellion might fail, or at least be resolved in such a way that they could eventually revert to their previous way of life. Whatever the explanations, relatively few of the Revolution's detractors appear to have 'voted with their feet' by departing from the United States. This point is important to bear in mind, because it belies the assumption that the goers and the stayers in the thirteen colonies can be easily divided into revolutionaries and loyalists, or into liberals and Tories.

It is also significant that, of the roughly 100,000 Americans who did leave during the revolutionary era, more than half, or perhaps 60,000, abandoned North America altogether, many of them returning to Britain and others moving to Bermuda, the West Indies, and elsewhere (Condon 1984: 1; Stuart 1988: 23; Noel 1990: 9; Thompson and Randall 1994: 15; Bell and Tepperman 1979: 45; Senior and Brown 1987; Upton 1971: 43; McRae 1964: 237). This contingent may have included the most steadfastly loyal British subjects of all the émigrés. Although speculative, this hypothesis seems plausible if we consider that the loyalist elite leaders and top bureaucratic officials, most of whom would have been fervent proponents of British ideas and interests, were heavily represented among those who chose not to go to Canada (Bell and Tepperman 1979: 53; Craig 1968: 93; Upton 1971: 44).

Although estimates vary, these considerations lead to the conclusion that about 40,000 refugees came to Canada from the United States in the revolutionary era. This group greatly outnumbered the approximately 15,000 English-speaking people already living in the Canadian settlements at the time (Bell and Tepperman 1979: 45; Wynn 1987: 221; Errington 1994: 158; Thompson and Randall 1994: 17; Simpson 2000: 2; Moore 1994: 157). It is also notable, however, that the original loyalists were themselves quickly outnumbered, both by the arrival of the so-called 'late' loyalists in the period up to about 1815, and especially by the increasing influx of immigrants who came directly from Scotland, Ireland, England, and elsewhere throughout the first half of the 1800s. As a result, the loyalists formed only a small proportion of the more than 300,000 people living in English Canada by 1815, and an even smaller percentage of the more than 600,000 who were there by 1835 (McRae 1964: 245; Gwyn 1985: 25; Craig 1963: 47, 124, 228; Talman 1946: lxii).

HOW LOYAL WERE THE LOYALISTS?

The next issue to address is whether and to what extent the refugees from the American colonies were truly loyal British subjects. First, as suggested previously, there is some basis for concluding that this group of émigrés, those who stayed in North America but moved to Canada, may have had a weaker sense of loyalty to Britain than the 60,000 Americans who moved elsewhere in the British Empire. It is quite possible, as well, that those who came to Canada were no more loyal to Britain than many of the anti-revolutionaries who stayed on in the thirteen colonies. In relative terms, then, it is paradoxical that those who migrated to Canada are normally labelled 'the loyalists' by most writers.

Of course, there is little doubt that many of the 40,000 who came north did identify strongly with their British heritage. Especially among the early waves of refugees, there were a large number of genuine loyalists (Errington

1994: 4–5, 8; McRae 1964: 239). Included here were at least some of those who had been powerful economic and political figures in the thirteen colonies and who, as noted earlier, probably felt the closest ties to Britain (see, e.g., Bell and Tepperman 1979: 53; Condon 1984: ix–x; Upton 1969). In addition, an estimated 8,000 former Americans fought in the British army during the War of Independence and, with the possible exception of conscripts, most of these individuals presumably embraced the loyalist label (Shenkman 1988: 84; Stuart 1988: 10; Moore 1994: 118–19; see also Talman 1946).

Apart from these instances, however, it is far less clear whether loyalty to Britain was uppermost in the minds of the refugees who came to Canada. For example, thousands were members of different native tribes, especially Mohawks and Six Nations Iroquois, many of whom left New York and other neighbouring states for parts of what is now southern and eastern Ontario. Although these tribes were military allies of the British, they clearly saw themselves as independent nations, and chose sides in the Revolution only after weighing their own strategic options and interests. Craig (1963: 5) is one of the many historians who have noted that the native tribes generally 'regarded themselves as the allies, not the subjects, of the British king' (see also Knowles 1997: 15; Moore 1994: 175–7; Bell 1992: 40–3; Craig 1968: 99; Wynn 1987: 220; Frideres 1988: 61–5; Upton 1971: 52). In addition, the migrants included many who belonged to various ethnic and religious minorities, among them Quakers and Mennonites, whose main purpose was to escape persecution and intolerance of their beliefs in the United States (Craig 1963: 44–7; Gwyn 1985: 19; Shain 1994: 112–13; Thompson and Randall 1994: 15–16; Nelson 1961: 88–91; Stuart 1988: 7; Wise 1971: 66; Christiano 2000: 77–83). Much the same can be said for the 3,000 or more African-American freedmen and runaway slaves numbered among the refugees (Wynn 1987: 220; Thompson and Randall 1994: 14–15; also Stuart 1988: 168–9; Bell and Tepperman 1979: 67; Condon 1984: 190–3; Moore 1994: 151–2, 207–8). Thus, while bonds of fealty to Britain may have motivated some of these people, it is likely that other concerns, including the simple need or opportunity to find a more hospitable place to live, explain why many members of these groups moved to Canada.

Given that ethnic and religious minorities accounted for a significant part of the loyalist migration, it might appear that, in a relative sense at least, the Canadian colonies at that time were a setting in which the values of tolerance and pluralism were more widely held than in the United States. However, there is evidence that, in general, the loyalists probably carried with them many of the same local-communalist tendencies that Shain found in the American population during this period. For example, Knowles's research shows that the loyalist contingent who settled the St Lawrence River region of Ontario in the 1780s 'were divided, at their own request, according to ethnicity and religion', with different areas allotted to Catholic Highlanders, Scottish Presbyterians, German Calvinists, German Lutherans, and Anglicans (Knowles 1997: 18; see also Adamson 1994: 432). Such arrangements suggest that, like their counterparts in the United States, the loyalists and the other English colonists may have accepted the rights of distinct groups to co-exist, but not the principle that these different groups should automatically be expected and encouraged to intermingle or integrate with each other (see also Moore 1994: 235–6; Christiano 2000: 77–83).

Another important point to consider when discussing the loyalists is that a significant proportion of those who fled the thirteen colonies stayed only temporarily in the British-held territories in any case. Some went back to their original homes after the Revolution, while others, especially in later years, used Canada as a transit point on the way west to the opening American frontier (see, e.g., Harris and Warkentin 1974: 111, 188; Thompson and Randall 1994: 16; Stuart 1988: 33–4; Condon 1984: 20; McRae 1964: 237; Knowles 1997: 17–18). Often faced with poverty and segregation even in their new Canadian homes, a number of the African Americans eventually returned to Africa (Wynn 1987: 220; Cross 1971: 156; Condon 1984: 192; Moore 1994: 209, 214, 219–220). This evidence raises further doubts about how important allegiance to Britain was for many of the people who came to be known as the loyalists.

Economic necessity and issues of class provide yet another explanation for much of the American exodus into Canada during the revolutionary era. We have already noted that a significant number of the more powerful and wealthy refugees from the thirteen colonies either returned to Britain or went elsewhere in the British Empire. By comparison, the evidence indicates that those who chose Canada as their new home were more broadly based, and represented a cross-section of American colonial society at the time. Most came from rural backgrounds and worked as small farmers, artisans, or labourers. For example, a report written in 1786 for the Loyalist Claims Commission described the refugees as people who, while they were typically 'farmers' and 'landholders', were generally not 'persons of great property or consequence' (see Knowles 1997: 15, 17; McRae 1964: 236). In addition, almost all were illiterate, with only a few having more than a rudimentary education. In other words, most were ordinary people of modest means (Bell and Tepperman 1979: 47–9, 52–3; Wynn 1987: 220, 229; Skelton 1965; Stewart 1990; Thompson and Randall 1994: 15; MacKinnon 1986: 57–65; Noel 1990: 9; Errington 1994: 5, 14; Upton 1971: 50–51; Talman 1946: xxiii–xxvi).

If anything, Canada's loyalists, on average, may have been somewhat poorer than other North American colonials, since their property and possessions in many cases were either taken from them or had to be left behind (see

MacKinnon 1986: 67–9; Condon 1984: 2–3; Moore 1994: 110–16). Another point of note is that, unlike the loyalist gentry, these individuals often could not afford the cost of passage back to Britain, even if they wanted to return, and very few had economic prospects in the Old World in any event (Upton 1971: 46). In comparative terms, most of the refugees who moved to Canada could hope for better opportunities by staying in the colonies, where they had a chance to own their own land. These observations suggest that the motivations for this group to come to Canada probably stemmed as much from economic incentives as from a feeling of loyalty to Britain. Thus, for example, Craig (1968: 104) has pointed to 'land hunger' as a key reason for coming to Canada, especially among the later loyalists who arrived after the end of the Revolutionary War (see also Stuart 1988: 24, 33; Errington 1994: 5, 15; Akenson 1984: 52; Knowles 1997: 20–1).

Such considerations put into perspective another issue, which concerns the oath of loyalty to Britain taken by those people who were new arrivals to Canada during the revolutionary era. The swearing of this oath has at least two possible interpretations. In some instances, such as those involving former soldiers who fought for the English, it is plausible to view the oath as a genuine expression of loyalty to the mother nation. The consequent granting of parcels of land to such veterans can also be seen as an appropriate reward for their allegiance and service. In other cases, however, the causal sequence probably operated in reverse. In other words, because a formal statement of loyalty to the British Crown was a prerequisite at the time for obtaining legal entitlement to land in Canada, some who took the oath almost certainly did so as an expedient means for acquiring property (see Wise 1971: 65–6; Noel 1990: 10–15; MacKinnon 1986: 118; Stanley 1976: 145–8; Upton 1971: 51; Moore 1994: 245–6). Once again, the latter pattern may have been particularly common among the later groups of refugees who flowed into Canada after the Revolution, people who were 'far more attracted by cheap land than by loyalty to Britain' (Harris and Warkentin 1974: 116; see also Clark 1959: 231; Bell and Tepperman 1979: 80–1; Craig 1968: 104; Wynn 1987: 221; Noel 1990: 5; Stuart 1988: 33; Talman 1946: xxviii–xxx).

Thus, while it is incorrect to question the loyalty of all of Canada's loyalists, it also seems clear that their commitment to Britain was neither total nor uniform across all of their number. As some have suggested, the reasons for their exodus from the United States were as varied as the people themselves. For many, the move to Canada really meant that they feared the excesses and uncertainties of the new American republic more than the prospect of continued British governance, and not that they were especially faithful English subjects (Wynn 1987: 220–1; Thompson and Randall 1994: 15; Nelson 1961: 88–91; Craig 1968: 92–3).

WERE THE ENGLISH-CANADIAN COLONISTS 'AMERICANS'?

These observations lead to another central reason for concluding that the refugees who left the United States for Canada had mixed allegiances to Britain. Research indicates that, apart from the economic motivations we have already discussed, a large number of those who chose Canada as their new home, rather than England or elsewhere, did so because they had acquired a deep attachment to an 'American' way of life. Here, of course, the word, American, is used in its broader original sense, and not in its narrow present-day meaning, as a label for citizens of the United States. The latter usage, though now predominant, can be misleading, and has made it easier for some analysts to overlook the basically American experience of most of the inhabitants of the Americas, including Canada's loyalists (see Bryson 1994: 60). On this point, it is helpful to recall that the majority of those who fled the thirteen colonies for Canada, not to mention those who already occupied the northern settlements, had been born in the New World themselves. For example, McRae (1964: 235–6) estimates that 90 per cent of those who fled to the Maritimes were American-born, as were about half of those who moved to Ontario (see also Smith 1994: 34–6, 42; Knowles 1997: 17; Adamson 1994: 432). Indeed, a large proportion came from families who had lived in North America for several generations (see, e.g., Bell and Tepperman 1979: 81; Clark 1968: 64–5; Errington 1994: 6, 37). It would be surprising if the identities and perspectives of this group had not shifted away from England and toward a more North American emphasis with the passage of time.

These considerations clarify why so many researchers have concluded, in contrast to Lipset's account, that the loyalists and other Canadian settlers of that period were, first and foremost, not Britons but Americans. Many historians agree that the English-speaking colonists in Canada were 'not in any real sense British' but were imbued with a fundamental 'Americanness' (Errington 1994: 5–7, 21, 136). It has similarly been remarked that their 'immediate experience' was American and that they had a 'basically optimistic colonial-American view' (Noel 1990: 31). It has even been argued that their American identity was 'their single most important characteristic' (Gwyn 1985: 17; see also Akenson 1984: 114; Wynn 1987: 214, 259; Clark 1968: 226; MacKinnon 1986: 67, 135; McRae 1964: 234–5; Morton 1961: 102; Thompson and Randall 1994: 16; Shenkman 1988: 84; Smith 1994: 43; Harrison and Friesen 2004: 90).

In the revolutionary period and afterward, foreign visitors to Canada frequently made similar observations about the Canadian colonials. For many of these observers, the typical English Canadian was really a 'Yankee', just one that happened not to support the war with Britain (Bell and Tepperman 1979:

76, 82; also Bradley 1968: 168; Smith 1994: 34–5; Morton 1963: 194–5; Craig 1968: 105). Comments by some travellers from the United States suggest that Americans usually did see themselves as quite distinct from (and at times superior to) French Canadians. When discussing the English-speaking population, however, American travellers often stated that the Canadians were much like themselves, with a similar spirit of 'independence' and even 'insubordination' (Stuart 1988: 124, 141, 159; Clark 1959: 227; Errington 1994: 47; Knowles 1997: 18; Ajzenstat 2003: 6).

These opinions offered by outside observers are clearly at odds with Lipset's portrayal of the English-Canadian colonists, which depicts them as a people with a profound respect for established authority. To some extent, these impressions from first-hand witnesses also fail to support the arguments posed by Hartz and Horowitz, who suggest that the English-Canadian population was touched by a Tory belief in deference to elite leaders. However, the accounts provided by foreign visitors are quite consistent with the deep-structures argument, and also with McRae's version of the founding-fragment perspective, in suggesting that the English Canadians and the Americans were very similar to one other, especially in their independent outlook and insubordinate attitudes toward the British authorities.

The findings provided by some eminent historians lead to the same conclusion. Wood, for example, has asserted that all Englishmen in the eighteenth century, including those living in England itself, 'were known throughout the Western world for their insubordination, their insolence, their stubborn unwillingness to be governed'. He adds that 'any reputation the North American colonists had for their unruliness and contempt for authority came principally from their Englishness' (Wood 1992: 12–13; see also Christian and Campbell 1983: 40–3; Craig 1963: 47–8; Condon 1984: ix–x, 38). In his research on the Ontario loyalists, Knowles finds the same air of disobedience, even among some of the loyalist military regiments (Knowles 1997: 18; see also Harrison and Friesen 2004: 28).

Observers who have noted the similarities between Americans and English Canadians can be found not only in the revolutionary period but well into the nineteenth century. Britain's Lord Durham, who is best known for his report in 1839 recommending the union of Upper and Lower Canada (Ontario and Quebec), believed that English Canadians and Americans shared a strong commitment to individualistic economic enterprise and material progress, and felt that the French of Lower Canada would be best served by assimilating to the same values and forms of social organization (see, e.g., Creighton 1972: 100–2). As discussed in Chapter 2, Alexis de Tocqueville's experiences in North America also led him to conclude that, while French Canadians represented 'the remnant of an old nation', the British population of Canada was not only a 'new people' but was 'identical with that of the United States' (Tocqueville 1840: 448). Another prominent visitor who made comparable remarks was William Seward, who served as President Abraham Lincoln's Secretary of State in the 1860s. During a tour of Canada in 1857, Seward noted that English Canadians were an 'ingenious, enterprising, and ambitious people', and were much like their American counterparts in these respects (Stuart 1988: 218). Other less famous American tourists also commented on the obvious parallels between themselves and English Canadians, often noting that these affinities existed despite attempts to squelch them by senior British officials in the colonies (Stuart 1988: 160; Errington 1994: 21–2; Clark 1968: 223).

TORY VALUES: COMPARING THE ELITE AND THE LARGER POPULATION

The latter observation raises another important issue to consider when trying to understand the nature of English-Canadian society during the period surrounding the Revolution and the loyalist migration. This issue concerns the crucial distinction between the beliefs of the mass of the English-Canadian population and those of elite officialdom, especially if the latter were also British-born. Many researchers have concluded that a relatively small British elite was largely responsible for the impetus to maintain strong ties with the mother country and to remain clearly separate from the United States (e.g., Clark 1968: 223; Brym 1989: 61–3; Adamson 1994: 432; Errington 1994: 23; Granatstein and Hillmer 1991: xiii–xiv; Harris and Warkentin 1974: 113; Wynn 1987: 208–9, 213–14). Moreover, while elite loyalists may have been 'pulled' to the counter-revolutionary side by their commitments to England, many ordinary loyalists were 'pushed' to take sides by those holding sway in their local communities (Bell and Tepperman 1979: 49; also Wynn 1987: 220; Osborne and Swainson 1988: 24; Knowles 1997: 15). Hence, in the same way that we noted the divergences between the American people and their elite leaders when examining the core values of the United States historically, it is equally important to be aware of such differences when discussing the Canadian situation.

Unfortunately, the implications of distinguishing between a pro-British elite and a more neutral, and at times even pro-American, general citizenry in English Canada have not typically been recognized by Lipset. This omission occurs, as well, in the work of writers such as Hartz and Horowitz, who tend not to consider that whatever Tory touch may have existed in English Canada at this time was in all likelihood concentrated in the elite and not in the mass of the population. These same analysts also appear to overlook a second, related distinction, which involves the recognition that loyalism and Toryism are not equivalent ideas or synonymous terms. In other words, while it seems true, by definition, that all Tories would be loyalists, it does not follow that all of those harbouring varying degrees of loyalty to Britain would also embrace Tory or anti-liberal values. On the contrary, true Tory values suggest a traditional aristocratic outlook that would be more common among British members of the elite than within the general population (see, e.g., Upton 1971: 49; Wilson 1971: 146; Christian and Campbell 1983: 25; MacKinnon 1986: 118; Morton 1963: 174–5; McRae 1964: 240–1; Craig 1963: 109–10; Adamson 1994: 432).

The apparent failure to take into account these two key distinctions—between elite leaders and the masses, and between loyalists and Tories—is especially important for explaining why Lipset's conclusions about the historical differences between Canadians and Americans are so different from those drawn by other researchers. We cannot confirm this argument with direct evidence from the mass of the population, because most Canadian and American inhabitants at the time lacked the literacy necessary to leave written indications of their values, beliefs, and behaviours (Bell and Tepperman 1979: 53; Noel 1990: 4; Errington 1994: 9). However, as we did previously in our analysis of the American colonials (recall Shain 1994), it is possible to get a sense of the divergences between the Canadian colonists and their mainly British-born authorities using documents provided by literate but non-elite Canadians. The evidence suggests that most political and military leaders in Canada during this period, including well-known figures such as Lieutenant-Governor John Graves Simcoe, were European-born aristocrats or people of privilege. The records also indicate that these people generally maintained strong beliefs in their British heritage and favoured transplanting Tory ideas to colonial society (Craig 1963: 20–1; Errington 1994: 21–2; Harris and Warkentin 1974: 113; Morton 1961: 25–6; Noel 1990: 31; Wise 1971: 65; Wynn 1987: 208–9; Bell and Tepperman 1979: 81; Wilson 1971: 145). However, the written accounts, though not comprehensive, reveal little to suggest that similar ideas prevailed in the Canadian-born segments of the population. For example, the proposal by Lord Dorchester in 1789, which recommended that the refugees from the American Revolution should be given official designation as 'United Empire Loyalists' (or UELs), was apparently 'greeted with massive indifference' by most colonists in the Canadian territories; this notion seems to have been one of many ideas that 'came from the top' and for which 'popular support was nonexistent' (Upton 1971: 52–3).

Even members of the native-born segment of the Canadian elite, including top business people, religious figures, and intellectuals, often expressed a similar lack of interest regarding the importance of the Empire and attachments to the mother country. The prominent loyalist leader, Richard

Cartwright, once complained that Simcoe 'thinks every existing regulation in England would be proper here', notwithstanding 'the great disparity of the two countries' (see Knowles 1997: 19). The position of such local leaders was that Canada was not and should not be a re-creation of a European-style British society. Some suggest that the native-born elite were themselves 'consciously Anglo-American' and believed that their society was as much American as British (Errington 1994: 20; Osborne and Swainson 1988: 34–5; Knowles 1997: 18). Many of their opinions on business and economics are also quite similar to ideas typically associated with their counterparts in the United States, including a commitment to free enterprise and personal economic independence (Errington 1994: 5–8, 29–30; Noel 1990: 31; Creighton 1972: 94, 99). Such evidence has led some to argue that the prevailing ideas of nineteenth-century English Canadians, especially in regions such as Ontario, were 'liberal in the classic sense', with a stress on 'individual freedom' in economic matters that was basically identical to the outlook that Lipset and others have attributed to the American population at this same time (Harris and Warkentin 1974: 112–14, 157–8, 165; see also Christian and Campbell 1983: 40–1).

Much of the supposed anti-Americanism of the Canadian colonies in this era can also be traced to British-born members of the elite. It appears, in fact, that negative sentiments about Americans rarely resonated with most Canadian colonists, partly because so many had relatives and friends living on the other side of the border. Researchers have noted that, in the revolutionary period and for several decades afterward, the border itself was 'just a line on a map', a 'porous' barrier that could be largely ignored by people who were free to visit kinsmen, engage in commerce, and so on (Simpson 2000: 14–16; see also Thompson and Randall 1994: 16–17; Errington 1994: 94; Harris and Warkentin 1974: 116; Stuart 1988: 18, 31, 53; Wilson 1971: 146; Cross 1971: 162; Craig 1968: 97, 105; Condon 1984: x, 100; Adamson 1994: 432; Laxer 2003: 329–39; Harrison and Friesen 2004: 90). All of these considerations leave the impression of a Canadian colony that had a surprisingly American cast and disposition. Although not completely identical to the United States, English Canada seems clearly to have shared with its southern neighbour a host of basic cultural, social-structural, and institutional features, both during the revolutionary era and for some time afterward.

Perhaps for this reason, some historians argue that the War of 1812, rather than the American Revolution, was more important for pushing Canadians away from their old American identities and affinities, and toward a stronger sense of separation from the United States (e.g., Craig 1968: 109–12; Harrison and Friesen 2004: 89–90). While this appears to be true to some degree, especially for those in the region of Ontario or Upper Canada, even in this later era the break with the United States was neither complete nor precipitous. On the contrary, several researchers have concluded that many English Canadians sustained their sense of connection with their American neighbours and cousins long after the War of 1812 and, in fact, well into the late nineteenth century (e.g., Stuart 1988: 112; Thompson and Randall 1994: 47; Clark 1968: 223).

SUMMARY

In this chapter, we have focused on research dealing with the loyalist migration, and the likely implications of this event for distinguishing the Canadian and American populations around the time of the American Revolution. We have seen that the vast majority of the research and analysis that has been generated on this topic paints a very different picture from that provided by Lipset's origins thesis. There is little or no evidence to support the claim that the loyalists were any more Tory or anti-liberal in their views than were the people who remained in the thirteen colonies throughout this period of history. The more moderate 'Tory touch' arguments of writers such as Hartz and Horowitz also fail to receive clear support, at least as characterizations of the general population. It is only if we focus on certain members of the elite in the Canadian colonies, especially those who were British-born and had aristocratic or privileged class backgrounds, that we find evidence of Tory beliefs and influences. Otherwise, the loyalist refugees, along with the relatively few English colonists who had settled in the Canadian regions prior to the loyalist arrival, seem to have evinced the same 'Anglo-American' values and ways of life as those that were exhibited by the population of the early United States. In other words, although the available evidence is not complete, it appears that a similar mix of local-communalist ideas, coupled with a belief in some limited forms of liberty, legal equality, popular sovereignty, and pluralism, were probably at work in both of these parts of North America during the era of the Revolution and the loyalist exodus.

CHAPTER 6

⁓

CANADIANS AND AMERICANS
HISTORICAL COMPARISONS

To this stage in our historical analysis, we have relied greatly on the accounts of literate local inhabitants and foreign visitors to characterize the American and Canadian populations during the late eighteenth and early nineteenth centuries. These accounts offer a number of important and useful insights into the central ideas, principles, and practices that predominated in the two societies during their early histories. Nevertheless, because such evidence is unavoidably anecdotal and potentially selective, it cannot alone provide a complete or representative basis for understanding and comparing the two peoples. We can, however, extend and supplement the analysis by using other forms of historical evidence. In this chapter, we compare the major background characteristics, institutional forces, and social-structural influences operating in the two societies and their populations. The key factors that we consider in this historical profile are: class structure and economic background, ethnic composition and sources of immigration, religious influences, urbanization patterns, and political organization and political culture.

These elements are integral to what might be called 'the structures of everyday life' (Braudel 1979) of the two societies, and represent major social factors that would have been important for establishing, ingraining, and reinforcing central ideas, beliefs, and values in both populations. If we can demonstrate significant differences between the two peoples with regard to their backgrounds and compositions, then we have a sound basis for concluding, along with Lipset and some of the founding-fragment theorists, that the core principles of the two societies were pushed in divergent directions during their formative stages and afterward. If, on the other hand, we find few or no differences, then we have strong grounds for questioning such claims. A lack of major differences would suggest, instead, that the structures of everyday life of these early Canadians and Americans were highly similar, making it increasingly likely that the deep-structural factors affecting the two societies were also similar during this period of history. In addressing this question, of course, we must attend, as well, to the four sub-societies that, according to the deep-structures perspective, have been fundamental to the historical development of Canada and the United States. For this reason, we also consider the extent to which economic, ethnic, religious, political, and related influences may have contributed to internal differences in the two nations, especially between English Canada and French Canada, and between the northern and southern United States.

CLASS STRUCTURE AND ECONOMIC BACKGROUND

As noted earlier, an analysis of the economic profiles of the loyalist refugees who came north to Canada reveals that most were not more wealthy, more highly educated, or otherwise superior in economic or class terms to their American counterparts. This finding is important for showing that Canada's loyalists were not disproportionately from the privileged classes and, therefore, probably not among those who were most likely to support traditional Tory values.

The same conclusion can be drawn if we expand the comparison to include the general population of Canadians, loyalist or otherwise. Some contend that, during the Revolution and the early decades of the 1800s, British Canada was probably less stratified economically than the United States, parts of which, especially the deep South, still maintained both a large black underclass and the remnants of a landed aristocracy (Gwyn 1985: 19; McPherson 1991: 8; Beard and Beard 1927: 53–4; Fischer 1989: 365–6). Generally, though, the material circumstances of Canadians and Americans in this era were clearly very similar. Most people on both sides of the border lived in ordinary economic circumstances, working in primary resource activities, especially farming, but also lumbering, fishing, trapping, and other forms of extractive enterprise (Wynn 1987: 229–46; Wallot 1971: 99–105; Morton 1963: 234–5; Condon 1984: 2). Many members of both populations were pioneering 'frontier people' (Clark 1959: 231). Few achieved great wealth but, with the exception of American slaves and certain 'pauper immigrants' who came later to both countries from overseas, there were also very few who were extremely poor (Wood 1992: 122, 179, 348; Akenson 1984: 351–2; Galbraith 1985: 43–5; Bell and Tepperman 1979: 49; Clark 1968: 68, 71–2; Craig 1963: 128; McRae 1964: 245; Harris and Warkentin 1974: 117). These patterns suggest that there was little in the relative economic situations and everyday work activities of the two populations that would have promoted divergent values or life perspectives during this period.

Of course, later developments would alter some of the economic or material similarities. In particular, the Canadian colonies eventually fell behind the faster-growing American republic, most notably the northern states, in such areas as overall economic development and general wealth creation. Various factors contributed to this divergence, including American advantages in climate, geography, and the proportion and quality of arable land, all of which provided the United States with greater potential for industrial expansion, product diversity, population and market growth, and so on (Morton 1961: 30; Upton 1971: 46–7; Noel 1990: 36–7; Harrison and Friesen 2004: 93–7). Thus, although Canadian economic development was substantial in the 1800s, especially in the latter decades of the century (Harris and Warkentin 1974: 146–7; Laxer 1985; Brym 1989: 48–9; 1993: 34), the relative gap between the two societies continued to grow. By the second half of the nineteenth century, the United States was fast becoming 'the most thoroughly commercialized nation in the world' (Wood 1992: 311, 358). Indeed, during the half-century following the American Civil War, the United States matched and ultimately surpassed Britain as the world's most powerful economy (Clement 1977: 41–58; Kolko 1984: 1–4, 284; Schlesinger 1964: 164–5; Smith 1994: 65–6; Bryson 1994: 83–4).

These divergent patterns contributed to differences in the class structures and economic realities of Canada and the United States, including a higher average standard of living, but also greater extremes of wealth and poverty, in the southern nation (Gwyn 1995: 62; Davies 2004). Nevertheless, even in the twentieth century, national similarities in economic systems and living standards have clearly outweighed the differences (Lipset 1990: 117–18; Banting and Simeon 1997: 69–70; Thompson and Randall 1994: 301–2), as have similarities in the economic values of the two populations (Nevitte 1996: 115–16, 148–51; Sniderman et al. 1996: 88–9; Perlin 1997: 103–5). These are issues that we consider further in Part III of the analysis. More pertinent for the present discussion, however, is that the historical differences on most economic and class indicators were not large, both at the time of the American Revolution and for several decades afterward. Thus, while value differences may have emerged in later years, because of changing economies and class structures, there is virtually no basis for applying this argument to the period under consideration here.

ETHNIC COMPOSITION AND SOURCES OF IMMIGRATION

Historical patterns of ethnic composition in Canada and the United States are another significant background factor to consider when comparing the cultures, values, and core beliefs of the two nations. In this section, we consider the key features of the early ethnic structures of the two societies. The discussion will focus mainly on the following topics: the special case of French Canada, the major role of British settlement in both Canada and the United

States, and the unique influence of the non-white slave population in defining and distinguishing the American South. As part of this discussion, we also examine the major sources of new immigrants that came to both countries during their formative stages and beyond.

The Special Case of French Canada

In historical terms, perhaps the greatest difference in the ethnic compositions of Canada and the United States has been the much larger proportion of French inhabitants living in Canada.[1] Most of the reasons for this difference stem from events that occurred prior to the era of the American Revolution, especially the Seven Years War, which was fought between England and France from 1756 to 1763. More than a century before this conflict, the French had established permanent colonies in North America (Harris and Warkentin 1974: 19, 25; Craig 1968: 69–71). However, the French military defeat at Quebec City in 1759 ultimately led to the transfer of French-held territory to Britain in 1763, in accordance with the Treaty of Paris (Wynn 1987: 191–3; Harris and Warkentin 1974: 171; Nish 1971: 1; McRae 1964: 228). Prior to this time, the British had also taken control of French Acadia, which included most of present-day Nova Scotia and New Brunswick. In 1755, the English began deporting many French colonists from this region (Wynn 1987: 181–2; Nish 1971: 8–9; Wise 1971: 86–90). Nevertheless, some 65,000 French colonists still lived under British rule at this time, compared with only about 500 English-speaking inhabitants (Nish 1971: 3; Harris and Warkentin 1974: 66; Craig 1968: 81). In spite of little subsequent immigration from France and other French-speaking areas of the world, French-Canadian settlements continued to grow through natural increase (Bell and Tepperman 1979: 43; Houston and Smyth 1990: 6; McRae 1964: 229; Lipset 1990: 182). By 1841, the Quebec region (Lower Canada) alone had a thriving population of approximately 450,000 French-speaking inhabitants, compared with about 200,000 English (Brunet 1973: 42; see also Nish 1971: 3). By 1861, these numbers stood at 850,000 and 260,000, respectively (Harris and Warkentin 1974: 66–7; see also Harrison and Friesen 2004: 93–4).

---

1. The one possible exception to this assertion is the sizeable black population to be found in the southern United States, as a result of the institution of slavery. The number of slaves surpassed the number of whites in some areas. We shall discuss this issue in more detail later in this chapter. The other key ethnic group to note is the aboriginal population in both countries, which, in fact, comprised a diverse range of Indian tribes, Metis, Inuit, and other natives. It is beyond the scope of the present analysis to explore the composition of the native populace. However, in Chapter 9, we consider the general situation of the aboriginal peoples in the two societies.

The research of most analysts supports the claim of Tocqueville and others that French Canada was a distinct society almost from the beginning, with social structures and institutions that were generally quite different from those developing in other parts of North America. Some writers do note that this French distinctiveness was probably not as marked initially as it would be in subsequent years. Especially in the early 1600s, the population of New France enjoyed some of the same autonomy from its Old World parent that the Anglo-Americans experienced. As a result, French Canada was somewhat like the thirteen colonies in certain ways, with the rudiments of its own entrepreneurial business or merchant class, some Protestant (Huguenot) inhabitants, and a segment of the population that held 'semi-liberal' economic and political outlooks (McRae 1964: 220; Stanbridge 1997: 42). The major divergences between the French and English colonists in North America emerged later, most notably after New France was officially designated as a royal province in 1663. From that point onward, French Canada was intended to be 'a deliberate and official projection' of the authoritarian or 'absolutist' form of society operating in France. This meant direct political control by the French crown, an economy based on a quasi-feudal landholding system headed by aristocrats, or 'seigneurs', and a religious system that was dominated by the Roman Catholic Church, and that effectively excluded Protestant minorities (McRae 1964: 221–2, 227; Harris and Warkentin 1974: 32; Stanbridge 1997: 44, 50).

Even under this regime, it appears that the French-Canadian social structure was not an exact replica of the French system in Europe. For example, the relative openness of life in this frontier society meant that French Canada's common people, or 'habitants', exercised more personal freedom than they would have in France. The habitants also tended to be closer in power and social status to the colony's seigneurial elite than would have been the case in the mother country (Rioux 1971: 13–18; McRae 1964: 227–8; Garreau 1981: 368–9).

Nevertheless, there is little doubt that, both before and after the English takeover of the region, French-Canadian society was imbued with a set of core principles that were very different from those operating elsewhere in North America. Although the English regions of the New World, as we have seen, were not yet the bastions of liberalism and individualism that some writers have suggested, there is also little question that the English colonials were generally more likely to be exposed to such ideas as liberty and popular sovereignty than were the French. Consequently, both the American and the English-Canadian populations were guided by precepts that were significantly less collectivist, less authoritarian, less accepting of control by religious and political elites, and more conducive to economic autonomy and material affluence than were those that prevailed in French Canada (Harris and

Warkentin 1974: 62, 127; Burt 1968: 2–5; McRae 1964: 229–30). In all of these ways, in fact, it could be argued that it was really the French-Canadian populace who were infused with the kinds of Tory ideas and beliefs that Lipset and some others have associated with English Canada.

Various historical influences encouraged this French distinctiveness, with its tendencies toward collectivism, anti-liberalism, and respect for hierarchical authority. Among the most important factors were: the fundamental linguistic divide separating the French and English, the growing economic and political control of the French by the British, the isolation of most French Canadians in and around the Quebec region, a somewhat passive and insular French strategy of cultural survival, and the conservatism of the Roman Catholic Church, which dominated French religious life (see, e.g., Falardeau 1960: 28, 45; Harris and Warkentin 1974: 105–6; Lamontagne 1960: 360; Nish 1971: 9; Wrong 1955: 6–7, 26; Milner and Milner 1973: 123; Tremblay 1953: 204; Grabb 1982: 362). Geographic isolation from their European forebears, as well as the virtual end of immigration from France after the English conquest, also meant that French Canadians received only limited exposure to the liberal ideas that later emerged from the French Enlightenment and the French Revolution (Hartz et al. 1964: 17n.; McRae 1964: 225, 233). Under British rule, Quebec also retained the old seigneurial economic system until the 1850s, long after it had been abolished in France. In fact, some vestiges of this system apparently survived into the twentieth century (McRae 1964: 225).

One incident in late 1775, less than a year before the full outbreak of the American Revolution, illustrates the distinctiveness of French Canada as a colonial society. In that year, American forces invaded Quebec and invited the French to form the 'fourteenth colony', by joining in rebellion against Britain (Craig 1968: 88; Moore 1994: 90–1). This was little more than a decade after the official British takeover of New France and offered the French a realistic chance to be free of English control. As events unfolded, however, the opportunity was not seized and the invasion failed. A significant factor in this outcome was the lack of support for the American invaders among most French leaders, particularly the Roman Catholic clergy and the seigneurs. Many members of the French elite favoured continued British rule, which they saw as a means to preserve and protect French culture from destabilizing influences, including the ideas emerging from both the American and the French Revolutions (Rawlyk 1971: 33–4; Craig 1968: 106; Creighton 1972: 98; Bell and Tepperman 1979: 41–3; Lipset 1996: 92).

It is likely, as well, that the French populace generally preferred British rule to the risks and uncertainties of war (Craig 1968: 88). Britain's passing of the Quebec Act in 1774 was of particular importance in this regard. The Quebec Act granted the French full rights to practice the Catholic religion, which many Americans strongly opposed, and also permitted the expansion of French settlements into areas that were highly coveted by the Americans, including large parts of the Ohio wilderness. It has also been pointed out that, under the British, the French people were granted more freedoms than they had ever received under France's kings (see Langguth 1988: 315–16; Garreau 1981: 370–1; Schama 2001: 470; Harrison and Friesen 2004: 23–4, 87–8).

In general, then, the ill-fated American invasion of Quebec suggests that neither the French leadership nor most of the general population found the ideals and goals of the American Revolution to be very compelling. At the same time, however, the failure of the American foray into Quebec was probably not a sign that the French had strong affinities with English values either. Instead, their acceptance of continued British rule mainly reflected the French desire to be left alone, with assurances that their society and culture would be preserved under British auspices (Nish 1971: 12; Rawlyk 1971: 36–40; Stuart 1988: 12–15; Thompson and Randall 1994: 10–13).

The unsuccessful assault on Quebec also provides some interesting illustrations of the shifting alliances that occurred on both the American and the English side during this turbulent period. The American attack was led by a number of notable individuals, including Benedict Arnold, who would later go over to the British side in the Revolution, and thus become the most famous traitor in the history of the United States. Another American leader was Richard Montgomery, who died in the attack. Paradoxically, Montgomery had previously fought for the English at Quebec in 1759, as a member of General James Wolfe's staff in the crucial Battle of the Plains of Abraham, which ultimately won the region of French Canada for the British Empire (Langguth 1988: 316–21).

In summary, the evidence indicates that, in most important respects, French Canada has been, for virtually all of its history, a separate sub-society in the wider North American context, first as a distant and often neglected possession of France, and later as a largely isolated colony subordinated to the British Empire. This sense of separateness continues right up to the present day. Virtually all contemporary observers would agree that French Canada, particularly the province of Quebec, represents a quite distinct and relatively autonomous sub-society within Canadian Confederation (e.g., Rioux 1971; Posgate and McRoberts 1976; Dion 1976).

Early British Settlement in the Canadian and American Colonies

As the previous discussion suggests, French Canada represents a unique element in any historical comparison of the ethnic compositions of Canada and the United States. If we set this special case aside, however, we find a number of significant similarities in the ethnic structures of the two countries, and also in the immigration patterns that would influence the evolution of this structure in later years. Some of these parallels were evident well before the Revolution, and several would continue for decades afterward (Thompson and Randall 1994: 26).

The most telling ethnic similarities in Canadian and American society concern those people who came to North America from the British Isles. Although both early populations comprised various ethnic groups, including a number of Germans, Dutch, and others, the vast majority in each society were of British background—English, Scottish, Irish, or Welsh (Bell and Tepperman 1979: 85–6; Gwyn 1985: 19; Hanna 1902, I: 81–3; Harris and Warkentin 1974: 117–18, 128, 186–7; Rawlyk 1971: 25–6; Shain 1994: 69–70; Wood 1992: 12–14, 110; McPherson 1998: 18). Also, throughout the 1700s and until at least the end of the War of 1812, most Britons who came to Canada and to the United States were either English or Scottish (Jackson 1993: ix–xiv; Errington 1994: 91, 98, 161; Duncan 1976: 72; Clark 1968: 64, 68, 71; Gwyn 1985: 19). As the nineteenth century progressed, the number of Irish immigrants to North America rose to massive proportions, a pattern that once again was common to both societies.

During the first few decades of the revolutionary era, however, the majority of the people in each society had English backgrounds. For example, by 1790, about 60 per cent of the citizens of the new American republic were English (Jackson 1993: x; see also Commons 1907: 24). Although the Canadian evidence for this early period is less complete, it suggests a similar picture. One difference is that there probably were proportionally fewer English and more Scottish in Canada than in the United States at this time (see Harris and Warkentin 1974: 111–12, 166, 172–3, 186–7; Clark 1948: 92; 1968: 65; Osborne and Swainson 1988: 25; see also Galbraith 1985; Bryce 1889, II: 398; McDonald 1988: xxxix).

The similarities in the ethnic compositions of the two societies are not surprising if we consider that, especially during the revolutionary era, most Canadians and Americans came from basically the same pool of inhabitants. That is, as noted previously, the majority of English Canada's population in this period were represented in the 40,000 or so loyalist refugees from the thirteen American colonies. About three-quarters of Canada's loyalists chose to live in the Atlantic region, especially Nova Scotia, where there were long-established economic and kinship ties to the New England states (Wynn 1987: 219; Clark 1968: 49; Thompson and Randall 1994: 15; Stewart 1990). During the 1760s alone, some 5,000 New Englanders had moved to Nova Scotia, making its population about one-half 'Yankee' even prior to the Revolution (Wynn 1987: 218–19; Stuart 1988: 17–18; Thompson and Randall 1994: 10; Craig 1968: 90). Some accounts indicate that most Nova Scotians in this period were actually pro-American, by both 'birth and inclination', and may even have joined the rebellion, if not for the economic hardships involved and the presence of the British naval garrison at Halifax to deter their participation (Bell and Tepperman 1979: 44–5; see also Brebner 1937; Stuart 1988: 18; Thompson and Randall 1994: 13; Harrison and Friesen 2004: 88).

Of course, not everyone in the Atlantic region had American affinities. In particular, the later loyalist refugees who arrived in this area at the end of the Revolution were frequently at odds with the existing Nova Scotian population, over the latter's Yankee sentiments and related problems. Partly for this reason, in 1784, a separate refuge for the loyalists, a 'loyalist province par excellence' (Craig 1968: 97–8), was carved out of the western section of Nova Scotia and renamed New Brunswick (see Condon 1984; Moore 1994; Laxer 2003: 332–3).

On the whole, these observations have at least two important implications. First, they indicate that, for many Canadian settlers, their failure to show active support for the American side in the War of Independence should not be viewed as proof that they harboured either Tory or loyalist values and sentiments. Second, these points suggest, once again, that most of the early inhabitants of both English Canada and the thirteen colonies shared an essential 'Americanness', and that this may have been the overriding 'ethnic' identity of both populations, at least in the initial decades of the revolutionary period.

British Protestantism: The English, Scots, and 'Scotch-Irish'

For the time up to and including the American Revolution, we have seen that, with the exception of the aboriginal and French-Canadian populations, most inhabitants in the two societies were Britons. Another important similarity is that most of the early British settlers, in both the Canadian and American regions, were also Protestants (Harris and Warkentin 1974: 118; Maclean 1976: 101–2; Reid 1976: 121–2; Fischer 1989: 6–7; Wood 1992: 112). This shared Protestant influence has potentially important implications when considering the ethnic structures of the two societies historically, as well as the values and beliefs of the two populations in that period.

The English

First, let us consider the English. As discussed previously, recent historians have argued that, from at least the middle 1600s onward, the average English person was not nearly as docile and obedient as Lipset and others have implied. On the contrary, the English people in this era, both at home and in the colonies, have been portrayed as independent-minded, disrespectful of established authority, and frequently unruly (see, e.g., Wood 1992: 12–15; Macfarlane 1978: 168–73; McClelland 1996: 334). To the extent that this depiction of the English is accurate, there is little question that it is partly attributable to their largely Protestant religious backgrounds. Since the time of Henry VIII, the Anglican Church, or Church of England, had been the predominant English religion, with much of its influence stemming from its ties to the British Crown. Understandably, many English settlers living in North America were themselves Anglican during the period of the Revolution. Nevertheless, the powers of the Church of England were more constrained in the North American colonies than in England itself, with less of the centralization and state support that prevailed in the parent nation (Wood 1992: 18, 111; MacKinnon 1986: 77–8; Langguth 1988: 38–40). Furthermore, in North America, the Anglican Church had to compete with many other denominations. In fact, most of the population in both the English-Canadian and the American regions were not Anglicans, but instead were affiliated with a diverse range of Protestant religions. These included the early Puritans and other 'dissenters' from the Church of England: Methodists, Baptists, Presbyterians, Quakers, and reformed Protestants, among others (Clark 1948: 91–2; 1968: 74–8, 118–21; Lipset 1968: 297; Craig 1963: 6; Noel 1990: 52–3; Osborne and Swainson 1988: 25; Wood 1992: 110–12, 282; Harris and Warkentin 1974: 128; Morton 1963: 194–5; Craig 1968: 120). As was noted previously, some of these Protestant sects could be quite intolerant or exclusionary toward other groups. However, almost all Protestant denominations shared a strong sense of their own rights, especially their freedom to practice religion as they saw fit (Shain 1994: 64, 256; also Clark 1968: 78–9, 121–2; Bryce 1889, II: 312, 555; Hanna 1902, I: 90–3, II: 1–3). What is most significant for the present discussion is that this English-Protestant orientation, with its readiness to dissent from or protest against established religious and secular authority, was evident not only among Americans but in much of the Canadian populace, as well (Clark 1968: 132–4; Adamson 1994: 431–2; see also Grabb, Curtis, and Baer 2001: 102).

The Scottish Protestants

The second major sub-group among the British Protestants who settled in North America included those who came from Scotland. Most of the Scottish colonials espoused the same basic Protestant beliefs as the English. Moreover, like their English counterparts, the Scottish Protestants appear to have played an important role in influencing the cultural heritage of both Canadians and Americans, and in ways that again make the two populations seem far more similar than different. In Canada, for example, Reid (1976: 120–2) has concluded that most early Scots adhered strongly to 'Calvinistic-Presbyterian' religious values (see also Galbraith 1985: 92–3). These values have direct ties to the Protestant ethic, including the belief in a 'divine calling', whereby each individual should work hard to succeed within a chosen life activity. An important related idea is that, while it is acceptable that this life activity should produce wealth and material rewards, it should also be guided by a 'strong sense of responsibility' to contribute to the larger community and the glory of God (Reid 1976: 132–3; also Bellah et al. 1985: 69, 119).

It is interesting that these beliefs, which have been attributed to Canada's Scottish Protestants, not only connect with key elements of the Protestant ethic, but also parallel the 'socially responsible' or 'republican' form of liberty or liberalism that, as was discussed in Chapter 4, many American revolutionary leaders hoped would be the guiding spirit of their new nation (Shain 1994: 157; Bellah et al. 1985: 143; Grabb, Baer, and Curtis 1999; Grabb, Curtis, and Baer 2000; see also Jackson 1993: 72–3, 149). While it now appears unlikely that this version of liberty was a central value among the majority of Americans in the nineteenth century (see Wood 1992: 102–4, 365–7), an intriguing possibility is that, by the middle of the 1800s, this orientation may have been somewhat more evident in Canada than in the United States. This may be true to the extent that the Scottish Calvinists and Presbyterians who allegedly embraced such beliefs constituted a larger proportion of the Canadian than the American population at that time (see Smith 1957: 17–21, Reid 1976: 133; Bryce 1889, II: 398).

Without more evidence, of course, this hypothesis is quite speculative, especially since the support for it is based on the potential influence of just one ethnic group. On the other hand, it has been argued that American Protestants in general moved away from some of the key tenets of both Calvinism and 'Old School' Presbyterianism during the last half of the 1800s, and instead embraced increasingly 'Arminian' doctrines, including a belief in individual 'free will' and 'utilitarianism' (Lipset 1968: 161–2; 1990: 11; Smith 1957: 88–9, 92–3; Wood 1992: 331–2; also Bellah et al. 1985: 142–3, 336). If this shift in emphasis occurred, it could have promoted a more self-interested, as opposed to socially responsible or republican, view of liberty and liberalism in the United States in this later period, a pattern that would be generally consistent with the arguments posed by some American historians (see Wood 1992; Shain 1994). This pattern would also correspond with some of Lipset's claims about the American Creed, but with one crucial exception: it would undermine his origins explanation for the rise of liberalism among Americans, because it would mean that the shift to a more self-focused form of liberalism in the United States did not take place until the latter part of the nineteenth century, and thus would have no direct connection with the founding events of the American Revolution itself.

Regardless of these possible shifts in beliefs, however, the historical evidence suggests that Scottish Protestantism probably had the same impact in shaping Canadian and American values and core principles. Further evidence of this shared influence can be found in the large representation of Scottish Protestants among the leading members of the nineteenth-century capitalist elites of both nations. Some prominent examples of these people include the Carnegies and Rockefellers in the United States and the McGills, Redpaths, and Simpsons in Canada (Hanna 1902, I: 52; MacMillan 1976: 179, 192–3, 196–7; see also Smith 1957: 26). The Scottish influence in big business apparently was especially important for Canada in the 1800s, so much so that, according to at least one well-known Canadian commentator, 'the Scots ran the country' during this time (Berton 1971: 319; see also Craig 1968: 99; Shaw 2003). Here we might also recall that, along with the Scots, the English formed the largest portion of the American and Canadian populations in the first several decades of the nineteenth century, and it was England, after all, that was the centre of the burgeoning capitalist industrial revolution in this same period. Thus, the common English heritage of many Canadians and Americans presumably would also have promoted similarities in their views on such ideas as free enterprise and economic liberalism (see Schlesinger 1964: 164). At any rate, this similarity in economic attitudes seems highly likely among the nations' business leaders, if not the two populations in general.

The 'Scotch-Irish'

Various researchers have identified a third major sub-grouping within the general British Protestant migration to North America during the eighteenth and early nineteenth centuries. That category of people has come to be known as the 'Scotch-Irish'. Particularly in their analysis of the United States, numerous writers have assigned a crucial role to this group (e.g., Hanna 1902; Leyburn 1962; Fitzpatrick 1989; Fischer 1989; Jackson 1993; Nisbett and Cohen 1996; Blethen and Wood 1997a; Chepesiuk 2000; Griffin 2001; Herman 2001). There is some disagreement among researchers about the exact composition of the Scotch-Irish. However, while it is likely that they were rather diverse, and may even have included some people with English Puritan, Dutch Calvinist, and French Huguenot roots, it seems certain that the large majority of the Scotch-Irish were northern Irish Protestants who were originally of Scottish background (Jackson 1993: 9; Dobson 1994: 83; Doyle 1999: 842; Commons 1907: 32–3; Leyburn 1962: 327–8; McDonald 1988: xl–xli; Fischer 1989: 618–21; Blethen 1997: 1–3; Herman 2001: 232).

Thus, the term, Scotch-Irish, is generally used to refer to those people of Presbyterian and other Protestant faiths whose ancestors moved from Scotland to settle in Ulster and adjoining regions of north Ireland, especially during the 1600s. The descendants of these people, who in a sense were both Irish and Scottish, formed a notable part of the British migration to the American colonies, especially from the middle 1700s onward. Although estimates vary, it appears that, by 1790, roughly 15 per cent of the non-aboriginal population of the United States were either Scottish or Scotch-Irish, with perhaps two-thirds of this percentage being Scotch-Irish (Jackson 1993: ix–xiv; Doyle 1999: 842–3, 847; see also Bowen 1995: 472–3; MacLean 1900: 43; Hanna 1902, I: 1; Miller 1985: 157, 197; Wood 1992: 131).

While these figures indicate that the Scotch-Irish were only a minority of the American populace in this period, their formative influence on American values was allegedly far more substantial than their numbers imply. It is possible that some of these allegations have been exaggerated, producing what has been referred to as 'the Scotch-Irish myth' (see, e.g., Miller 1985: 156–7). Even so, many researchers have concluded that this group was a driving force in both the founding events and the subsequent history of the United States. For example, Scotch-Irish officers and soldiers are credited with playing key roles in the major military actions of the American Revolution, and Scotch-Irish political figures are viewed as central to the formulation of the American Declaration of Independence (Hanna 1902, I: 24–5, 31–3; Jackson 1993: 120–9; Blessing 1999: 455; Doyle 1999: 849; Eid 1999: 841). In these respects, the Scotch-Irish have been contrasted with the colonists of exclusively Scottish heritage, who according to some accounts were more likely to support the British in the Revolution (Chepesiuk 2000: 142–3; MacLean 1900: 305). Many post-revolutionary American presidents and military heroes have also been linked to Scotch-Irish ancestors. Just a few of the more famous examples include Andrew Jackson, Ulysses S. Grant, Theodore Roosevelt, and Dwight Eisenhower (Jackson 1993: 148–9; Eid 1999: 839–40, 842; Doyle 1999: 849–50; Hanna 1902, I: 33, 50; II: 185–92; Commons 1907: 32; Herman 2001: 235).

The Scotch-Irish and the Protestant Ethic. In trying to characterize the importance of the Scotch-Irish influence in the economic and social development of the early United States, several analysts have put forward the view that the Scotch-Irish were particularly likely to be imbued with the Protestant ethic, emphasizing such values as hard work, self-reliance, self-discipline, and religious piety in their daily lives (for some discussion, see, e.g., Jackson 1993: 72–3, 148–9; Doyle 1999: 845; Miller 1985: 156–7). This portrayal, of course, is quite consistent with the depictions that we have already seen of other British Protestants, namely those from both Scotland and England. If we could demonstrate that such Scotch-Irish influences existed historically in the United States but not in Canada, then this difference would strengthen the argument that significant elements of the Canadian and American populations were marked by divergent cultural forces, at least with respect to this relatively small but apparently quite influential group. In fact, though, a very similar Scotch-Irish heritage, with close ties to the Protestant ethic, has been identified in Canada, as well.

Before proceeding, we should note that the northern Irish Protestants who landed in Canada from the British Isles are less often referred to as Scotch-Irish than are those who chose to live in the United States. One reason for this may be that most of the contingent that came to Canada arrived in the decades after the Revolution, especially after 1815 and the Napoleonic Wars. By then, the Scotch-Irish name was more closely identified with the earlier arrivals, and especially with those who fought on the American side in the Revolution (see Jackson 1993: 151). Even so, Canadians with these backgrounds have also been referred to as Scotch-Irish in many accounts (e.g., Akenson 1984: 348–9; Harris and Warkentin 1974: 117–18; Hanna 1902, II: 57–8; MacLean 1900: 60; Miller 1985: 161; Rawlyk 1971: 26; Fitzpatrick 1989: 208; Blethen 1997: 1, 13; Wilson 1997: 134–5).

Whatever name they are given, Protestants of Scotch-Irish and Irish background have clearly been a prominent cultural force in Canada. During the 1800s, the Irish formed the single largest group of immigrants to both Canada and the United States (Houston and Smyth 1990: 4–6, 22–6; see also Akenson 1984: 4, 9; 1988: 101; Wynn 1987: 228–9; Harris and Warkentin 1974: 117–18, 184–5). One difference between the countries is that, while the Irish immigrants who entered the United States in the 1800s were mainly Catholics, especially those who settled in the North, most of the Irish who arrived in Canada in the nineteenth century were Protestants (Houston and Smyth 1990: 8, 71–4; Miller 1985: 350, 353; Akenson 1984: 349; 1993: 223, 251). Even so, if we consider the total Irish populations of the two countries, including the native-born and immigrants combined, we find that here, too, the societies were similar. That is, throughout the 1800s, most of the Irish living in both Canada and the United States were Protestants, a pattern that has continued up to the present day (see, e.g., Akenson 1993: 219–20; 2000: 112).

On this point, we should acknowledge that Canada's Irish Protestants were more likely to be Anglican (Church of Ireland), or what some have called 'Anglo-Irish' (Eid 1999: 839), and in this way can be differentiated from their American counterparts, who evinced a stronger Presbyterian influence (Houston and Smyth 1990: 8; Jackson 1993: 121). Nevertheless, there were a large number of Anglicans among the American Irish, as well (Akenson 1985: 64–6; 1988: 100; Blessing 1999: 455). Furthermore, despite such internal differentiation, the similarities in the Protestant religious values guiding the Scotch-Irish in each society are undeniable, as are their common geographic roots in Ulster and adjoining parts of Ireland (see, e.g., Houston and Smyth

1990: 8; Elliott 1988: 123). Probably the major difference is that the Irish-Protestant immigrants to Canada, for obvious reasons, were more likely to express loyalty to the British Crown. Included in this group were members of the Orange Order, a Protestant-sectarian organization formed in the 1790s and named to commemorate the English takeover of Ireland by King William of Orange in the late 1600s (Elliott 1988: 125, 156; Akenson 1984: 170; Houston and Smyth 1990: 7, 144–5; Miller 1985: 86–7; Craig 1963: 229–31; Fitzpatrick 1989: 208–21).

As noted previously, however, the expression of loyalty to Britain should not be equated with the adoption of Tory or anti-liberal values. On the contrary, there is considerable evidence that the loyal Scotch-Irish in Canada frequently opposed both Tory beliefs and the general policies of 'Tory' (i.e., Conservative) governments (see, e.g., Galbraith 1985: 66–70; Akenson 1984: 176–82). In fact, apart from their quite different views on the advantages and disadvantages of British rule, there appears to be little else that clearly separates the outlooks of the Canadian Scotch-Irish from their American counterparts. A very similar Scotch-Irish myth, with its emphasis on economic liberalism, personal ambition, and the Protestant ethic, has been applied in both nations (Houston and Smyth 1990: 5, 7). In addition, although the Scotch-Irish myth is identified more with the United States, and predates most of Canada's Irish-Protestant immigration, these considerations do not undermine its applicability to the Canadian experience. At least one analysis suggests that it was easier for Canada's Scotch-Irish to conform to this myth, because most of their migration occurred later, when such principles as 'laissez-faire', 'individual achievement', and 'material progress' were becoming more widely accepted in both societies (see Harris and Warkentin 1974: 164–5; also Smith 1994: 48–9). This latter point is consistent with research suggesting that such ideas as liberalism and individualism, in their modern meanings, did not become dominant values in North America until several decades after the period of the American Revolution, probably not until the 1860s and beyond (Shain 1994; see also Miller 1985: 156–7; Grabb, Baer, and Curtis 1999; Grabb, Curtis, and Baer 2000). Regardless of the exact time that such values became prevalent in either country, however, there is no clear basis for arguing that the Scotch-Irish influence contributed to any important historical differences in the Canadian and American adoption of such beliefs.

The Scotch-Irish, 'Celtic' Culture, and the American South. Although the Scotch-Irish are frequently characterized as being steeped in the Protestant ethic, a second and contrasting image can also be found in certain discussions of this group. This alternative portrayal is found almost exclusively in analyses that focus on the United States. According to this argument, the American

Scotch-Irish, while often active and adventurous, were not particularly convinced of the virtues of self-discipline, or of doing hard work for its own sake. Some of these accounts go on to assert that the Scotch-Irish were an unusually combative and troublesome people, whose views on freedom apparently gave them license to seize or squat on their neighbours' land, for example (see, e.g., Chepesiuk 2000: 120; Commons 1907: 31; Fischer 1989: 740–1, 754–5; Jackson 1993: 62, 107–8; Nisbett and Cohen 1996: 7–9; Blessing 1999: 455; Doyle 1999: 841; McWhiney 1988: 18; Leyburn 1962: 192–4; Griffin 2001: 101–3, 110–11; Herman 2001: 231).

Of course, either or both of these conflicting images of the Scotch-Irish could be distortions or oversimplifications (see, e.g., Doyle 1999: 845). Moreover, given the incomplete nature of the historical evidence, along with the likelihood that the actual circumstances of the Scotch-Irish were more varied than either of these depictions suggests, we should be cautious about drawing strong inferences on this issue (see Blethen and Wood 1997a). Nevertheless, it may be that these contrasting views at least partly derive from the existence of two relatively distinct groups of Scotch-Irish. In other words, although the Scotch-Irish could be found throughout America in this historical period, there is considerable research suggesting that they coalesced into two more or less distinguishable branches: those who inhabited the northern or northeast regions, especially Pennsylvania and New England; and a larger grouping that lived in the South, particularly along what was then the frontier of the new United States (Jackson 1993: 75–6, 82–92; Chepesiuk 2000: 115–24; Fitzpatrick 1989: 107–11; Blessing 1999: 455, 470; Griffin 2001: 163–5; MacLean 1900: 52–3, 58–60; see also Dobson 1994: 113, 163–4; Commons 1907: 36–7; Doyle 1999: 848–9; Eid 1999: 841; McWhiney 1988: 3, 7–8, 18–19; Blethen 1997: 3, 13; Blethen and Wood 1997b: 215; Fischer 1989: 633–5).

The first of these two branches was smaller in number than the second, in part because so many of the Scotch-Irish immigrants who initially arrived in the North did not stay there. Instead, they moved to the interior and then southward, where land was both cheaper and more abundant. In addition to land considerations, however, another reason why many Scotch-Irish did not remain in the North was that they were often not welcomed by the more established and influential groups already inhabiting those regions, most notably the English Puritans. This seems to have been especially true if the newcomers were not able (or not allowed) to adapt to the prevailing orientations and practices of the existing communities (see, e.g., Jackson 1993: 73; Dobson 1994: 83–4; Blessing 1999: 455; Chepesiuk 2000: 116; Griffin 2001: 101–4; Leyburn 1962: 184–5, 213–19; Commons 1907: 24, 36–7; McDonald 1988: xli–xlii; McWhiney 1988: 29–30). Such tendencies toward exclusion by established groups are consistent with the pattern of local communalism that, as we have already discussed, apparently was widespread in North America in this period (recall Shain 1994; Knowles 1997; Fischer 1989). It is probable that the Scotch-Irish who did put down roots in the North were generally those who successfully adapted to the prevailing economic, social, and cultural forces of that region. In that case, as various writers have suggested, the Scotch-Irish presumably would have tended to live according to the same ideas, stemming from the Protestant ethic, that allegedly guided the English Puritans, Scottish Calvinists, and related sects who predominated in the North at that time. This would, in turn, explain why the Scotch-Irish were apparently as likely as these other groups to engage in and to excel at the kinds of endeavours that were the mainstays of the northern economy, especially independent mixed farming and small-scale business enterprises (Jackson 1993: 148–9, 72–3; Miller 1985: 156–7; see also Eid 1999: 841; Doyle 1999: 845; Leyburn 1962: 236–40, 322; Clement 1977: 41).

This brings us to the second depiction of the Scotch-Irish, which portrays them as a freewheeling, undisciplined, and even truculent people. This perception of the Scotch-Irish has more commonly been attributed to the other major branch of this group, i.e., those who settled primarily in the American South. As noted previously, many of these Scotch-Irish started out as northerners, but over time migrated into the more southern parts of the United States, from Maryland and Virginia to the Carolinas, Tennessee, and Georgia. In these areas, they generally had better opportunities to acquire land, to escape the exclusionary treatment of other groups, and to pursue freely the style of life that they preferred. Over time, their numbers were bolstered somewhat by additional Scotch-Irish, as well as by kindred Irish and Scottish-Protestant immigrants, who came to the American South directly from the British Isles and, in some cases, from the West Indies (Leyburn 1962: 211–12, 241–53, McDonald 1988: xxxix–xl; Blethen and Wood 1997b: 215–17). Evidence provided by McWhiney (1988) and McDonald (1988) indicates that these groups, in combination, produced a southern population that, at least in the formative stages of the United States, was considerably less English and significantly more Irish, Scottish, or 'Celtic' than the northern population (see also Fitzpatrick 1989; Jackson 1993; Nisbett and Cohen 1996; Doyle 1999). More recent research has uncovered a similar pattern, although this work suggests that some of the claims about the magnitude of the Scotch-Irish or Celtic influence in the South may have been exaggerated in earlier accounts (Blethen and Wood 1997b; see also Fischer 1989: 618–21; for some debate, see Johns 1989: 206–7; Johnson 1989: 488–90).

It seems certain, of course, that many of the Scotch-Irish and other so-called Celtic inhabitants of the South would not have conformed to the second depiction noted above. Instead, many would probably have been a lot like their northern counterparts in terms of their economic orientations, religious beliefs, and general outlooks. Nevertheless, it is plausible to infer that, as a group, this southern population was distinct in some important respects. First, it seems likely that a significant amount of the large internal migration to the American South involved a selective process, with people who favoured the open frontier and wilderness of this region being more motivated to leave behind the more confined and settled areas of the North. It is probable, as well, that the Scotch-Irish and other groups who chose the South would have tried to adapt to its existing social structures and institutions. In religious terms, such adaptation seems to have led many Scotch-Irish, most of whom began as Presbyterians, to switch their allegiances to Baptist and Methodist sects and away from 'the strict practices of true-blue Calvinism' (Leyburn 1962: 287; Blethen and Wood 1997b: 219–20; Chepesiuk 2000: 139; Griffin 2001: 164–5; McWhiney 1988: 6–7, 18–19; Doyle 1999: 848). In economic terms, as well, adapting to the southern way of life would have meant that they were less likely than their counterparts in the North to inhabit communities composed of small-scale independent farming or business enterprises. Instead, following the pattern of other southerners, they were more apt to reside in free-standing and isolated homesteads, where many engaged in open-range livestock-grazing, combined with single-crop agriculture and some mixed farming (McWhiney 1988: 51–3, 62–7; Blethen and Wood 1997b: 222–5; Reed 1982: 178–9; Odum 1947: 35–6; Gastil 1975: 7–10; Fischer 1989: 740–3; Nisbett and Cohen 1996: 7–8; Doyle 1999: 848). In addition, although smaller property holdings were the norm in the southern United States, not only for the Scotch-Irish but for the population in general, it nevertheless was far more common in the South than in the North to find large-scale agricultural operations. These enterprises were typically based on major 'staple' crops, such as cotton, tobacco, sugar cane, and rice, and also relied greatly on slave labour for their viability (Reed 1982: 23–4; McWhiney 1988: 51; Thompson 1975: 87, 206–8, 269; Berlin and Morgan 1993: 7–9; Gastil 1975: 179). Such differences in the prevailing economic structures of the North and South may have played a role in promoting and entrenching different values, outlooks, and core beliefs within the two branches of the American Scotch-Irish. Conceivably, such differences, in turn, could have contributed to divergent deep-structural influences in the northern and southern regions of the United States.

It is interesting that, at the time of the Civil War, vaguely similar notions about the ethnic and cultural distinctiveness of the North and South were fostered by certain writers, journalists, and other members of the southern cultural elite. These commentators claimed that southerners, especially the elite class of plantation owners in Virginia and elsewhere, were direct descendants of the aristocratic 'Cavaliers' who fought for England's King Charles I in the 1640s. The Cavaliers were in turn thought to be descended from the Norman barons who arrived in Britain with William the Conqueror in the eleventh century. The image of noble and dashing southern Cavaliers posed by these writers is starkly at odds with their depictions of American northerners, who were represented as the descendants of lowly Saxon 'churls', the common rabble of England (McPherson 1998: 20–1). Such an argument is not identical to the claim of some recent researchers that the South was disproportionately Scotch-Irish or Celtic, but there are rough parallels. This is especially evident in the work of McDonald and McWhiney, who have alleged that the Normans, along with their Norse Viking ancestors, helped to engender the 'Norse-Gaelic' culture, which the Scotch-Irish and other Celtic immigrants supposedly brought with them to America (McDonald 1988: xl–xli; McWhiney 1988: 21; see also Fischer 1989: 207–8, 255–6, 365–6, 416).

The Plantation System, Slavery, and the South

While we have briefly discussed how the differing forms of farming and agricultural production in the North and the South may have affected the American Scotch-Irish, these regional differences in economic organization clearly had repercussions that went well beyond their influence on any single ethnic group. Indeed, many have argued that the greater prevalence in the South of large-scale, slave-based agriculture, or what is generally referred to as the plantation system, was the key factor shaping both the major social institutions and the overall pattern of ethnic stratification in the southern United States. As was discussed in Chapter 3, it was the plantation and its inextricable links with slavery that Tocqueville identified as the defining features of the American South. Since Tocqueville's early observations on this question, a large number of analysts have drawn similar conclusions. It has been argued, for example, that 'whatever is "different", whatever is special, about the South appears to go back to the plantation and to the system of institutions which has grown up around it' (Thompson 1975: 86; see also Odum 1947: 32–6; Reed 1982: 25, 73, 130; Reidy 1992: 6–8, 31–2; Wayne 1983: 3–10; Churchill 1958: 149–51; Bryce 1887: 8).

Some might question such claims, since plantations represented only a minority of the farming establishments that existed in the southern United States in this era. It is also true that most southern whites did not own slaves. Nevertheless, the plantation system did account for a sizeable portion of the southern economy. In 1850, for example, close to one-fifth of all the farms in the American South were classified as plantations according to the US Census; moreover, these were by definition the largest agricultural enterprises, and typically the most affluent as well, with the result that they would have accounted for much more than one-fifth of the South's best farmland

(McWhiney 1988: 51; see also Odum 1947: 35; Leyburn 1962: 221–2, 322–3; Clement 1977: 41; Fischer 1989: 374). It is also significant that, during this same period, close to two-fifths of the total population of the American South were blacks, almost all of whom were slaves. In some southern states, such as South Carolina, more than half of the entire population were slaves. These proportions can be contrasted with those in the North, where, at this same time, blacks accounted for well under one-tenth of the population. In addition, by the middle 1800s, the vast majority of northern blacks lived as free people, although they continued to face significant problems of disadvantage, privation, and discrimination (McWhiney 1988: 51; Tocqueville 1835: 386; Odum and Moore 1938: 536–9; Wesley 1940: 75; Commons 1907: 53–4; Moore 1971: 16–20; Davis 1966: 17; Moore 1994: 28; McPherson 1991: 32; Wood 2002: 56–7; Wilson et al. 1996: 455).

Another point to consider is that the effects of the plantation system and slavery in the southern states were far more pervasive and deep-seated than these proportions by themselves can demonstrate. It has been argued that 'the basic institutions' of the American South, including not only the economic system and local political structure, but also 'the school, the church, the family' and so on, were all shaped by people's regular experience with the plantation way of life, and by their daily reminders of the existence of a black 'underclass' (Thompson 1975: 86, 320, 338–51). Thus, as Tocqueville once suggested, and as subsequent research has shown, these realities of southern society affected the orientations and world views of the slaves, the slaveholders, and the wider population (for a detailed analysis, see Genovese 1974). A number of historical studies confirm Tocqueville's observation that slavery was degrading or debilitating for white southerners in general, leading to idleness and arrogance in some and to guilt and a crisis of conscience for others. When confronted with the cruel and immoral fact of slavery, in a nation that was allegedly committed to universal liberty and equality, many white Americans lived uneasily with the obvious hypocrisy that this situation represented, while others sought to justify or explain away the problem (Newman 1889: 43, 61; Moore 1971: 154; Davis 1966: 3; Thompson 1975: 209–10; Appleby 1984: 102–3).

One means for excusing the treatment of slaves at this time was to portray them as 'heathens', who were not entitled to the same mercy and charity that would be afforded to any Christian (Moore 1971: 85). Although some Americans, especially the Quakers and later some Methodists and Baptists, did see slavery as un-Christian and a 'perversion of Scripture' (Davis 1975: 523; 1966: 307–10; Newby 1978: 74; Fischer 1989: 601–3; Shain 1994: 293), many others maintained that this system of human bondage was actually consistent with Christian religious teachings, and should be seen as a penance that blacks must pay to redeem themselves as sinners before God (Davis 1975: Chapter 11; 1966: Chapter 6; see also Moore 1971: 154; Thompson 1975: 326; Allahar 1993). However, perhaps the most effective mechanism used to justify slavery in America was to argue for and ultimately pass into law the principle that slaves were inherently inferior, and hence not to be regarded as real people. A series of such laws was formally enacted during the period when the American colonies were still British possessions, dating from the middle 1600s to the early 1700s. While many of these statutes were gradually weakened or rescinded in the northern states during and after the Revolution, the laws sanctioning slavery continued to operate in full force in the South until the 1860s, right up to the Civil War (Moore 1971: 20–1, 85–9, 101; Thompson 1975: 209–10, 289–90; Churchill 1958: 160–1; Wood 2002: 128–9).

One of the more peculiar aspects of what came to be known as 'the peculiar institution' of legalized slavery is that, according to a number of social historians, the belief in the racial inferiority of blacks was not the reason behind the introduction of slavery in the Americas. On the contrary, the reverse appears to have been true. That is, according to this body of research, the establishment of slavery as a system of economic production was in a real sense the cause of the existence of racism in the modern world, and perhaps even the basis for the idea of race itself. In other words, several analysts have concluded that the very concept of race, especially the now widely accepted view that people of black and white skin colour constitute distinct racial categories, was not a prevalent idea prior to this time. Instead, it was an artificial device, or social construction, which came into existence as a means to protect the economic interests of plantation owners. For example, Bonilla-Silva has reviewed a range of studies indicating that 'Negro' and 'Black' were among the racial categories that 'were invented in the sixteenth and seventeenth century' by whites, so as 'to justify the conquest and exploitation' of certain groups, who could then be 'defined as natural candidates for slavery' (Bonilla-Silva 1997: 471; see also Cornell and Hartmann 1998: 102–6; Thompson 1975: 209–19; Allen 1994; Roediger 1991, 1994; Todorov 1984; Fischer 1989: 256). Before this period, plantation owners had to rely greatly on the labour of indentured white servants, who came to America under the legal obligation to work for their overseers, but who were free to go once their terms of service were complete. In many cases, these people were then able to start their own homesteads along the expanding frontier to the west, making it increasingly difficult for large landholders to find and to keep the labourers necessary to work their estates (Thompson 1975: 208–9, 291–3; Blessing 1999: 455; Schama 2001: 405–8). Thus, the legal creation through slavery of an officially 'inferior race', which was readily identifiable by the visible marker of skin colour, made it possible for the planting class of the American South to acquire and maintain the large, cheap, and stable source of labour so essential to their pros-perity. Moreover, while it is true that black slaves could certainly be found in other parts of both British and French North America in the colonial period (McRae 1964: 262–3; Davis 1966: 176–9), their significance in other areas simply does not compare with their fundamental importance in shaping and defining the American South.

Although it is beyond the purposes of the present analysis to examine all the different aspects of slavery in North America, it is notable that the system was rather more complex and multi-faceted than is sometimes assumed. For example, along with blacks, Indians and other aboriginal peoples were some-times used as slaves, although far less extensively (McRae 1964: 262–3; Davis 1966: 176–82). At the same time, though, members of some aboriginal tribes, such as the Cherokee in the American South, were known to own black slaves themselves on occasion (Halliburton 1977). Another complicating factor is that slaves often experienced quite different treatment and living conditions, depending on their geographic locations and their owners. It is interesting to note, in particular, that a number of slaves were permitted to engage in 'inde-pendent economic production', and had the right to sell their own crops and other goods in some cases (Berlin and Morgan 1993: 31–8).

In general, however, it seems clear that Tocqueville was correct in his claims about the crucial impact of slavery and the plantation system for distin-guishing the southern United States. Its distinctiveness has led some contem-porary historians to argue that the divisions between North and South were so marked that they represented a clash between two fundamentally different 'nationalisms', and that, as result, the American Civil War was really 'the second American Revolution' (McPherson 1991: 7–8, 25–42; 1998: 18; see also Beard and Beard 1927; Foote 1989; Reed 1982, 1983). Perhaps the only notable point at issue is whether, as Tocqueville's work implies, the South was similar to a feudal society, with a white landed aristocracy that resembled the noble families of Europe, or whether, as Hartz's founding-fragment thesis contends, the South was mainly a liberal society like the rest of English North America, but with an aristocratic 'touch' stemming from the slave-based plantation system (recall Tocqueville 1835; Hartz 1955; Hartz et al. 1964).

Previous commentators have drawn somewhat conflicting conclusions regarding which of these depictions is more accurate. On Tocqueville's side of the argument, it is clear that many of the southern plantations constituted landed estates that closely parallelled those of Europe, with a 'leisure class' that matched the feudal aristocracy in its opulence, idleness, and absolute power. It is also fair to say that, in many respects, southern slaves resembled the class of European serfs, and faced basically the same privations, oppressions, and humiliations in their everyday existence (Cash 1941: 5–8, 74–5; Davis 1966:

155–6; Thompson 1975: 206–8, 338–46; Gastil 1975: 177; Fischer 1989: 253–6, 410–16; Wayne 1983: 3–10; Newby 1978: 41–8; Churchill 1958: 150–7). This way of life, moreover, dominated the South for some two centuries, and was so deeply entrenched that it would take unprecedented events and exertions, including the most bloody and destructive war in the history of the United States, to bring it to an end (McPherson 1991: 16–21, 37–8). Many would argue, in fact, that its influence on the southern states lingers even today (e.g., Reed 1982: 130–1; Gastil 1975: 186). Such considerations lend support to the conclusion that there were real and enduring feudal elements in the deep-structural characteristics of the American South.

On the other side of the argument, it should be pointed out that, especially after the Revolution, the South came to be influenced by some of the same liberal core principles that Tocqueville, Hartz, and others have ascribed to the rest of Anglo-America. Included here are such central English precepts as liberty, equality, and popular sovereignty. The emphasis on economic liberty, for example, may help to explain why the southern states evinced certain features of modern capitalist enterprise in some areas, suggesting that its economy was based on more than just feudal-style plantation agriculture. Nevertheless, the South's level of industrial development never approached that of the North. Moreover, the inescapable truth to confront when discussing principles like liberty and equality in the context of the American South is that such ideas clearly applied only to whites. The same can be said for the concept of popular sovereignty which, of all the ideas that we have identified as English core principles, was easily the most important in the southern United States. Much more than in the North, in fact, people in the South adhered to the belief that each individual state was sovereign, and that the national government should not be allowed to override what was typically referred to as 'states' rights'. Indeed, many southern leaders maintained that the issue of states' rights was the real underlying cause of the Civil War, rather than slavery or other problems. In the southern view, by not allowing each state to make its own decisions on the question of whether or not to abolish slavery, Abraham Lincoln's government was in violation of the states'-rights principle, and thereby made the war between the states both inevitable and justifiable (see, e.g., McPherson 1991: 45–8; Newby 1978: 128–30, 185–8; Churchill 1958: 154–7). We see here as well, though, that the principle of popular sovereignty took on a peculiarly particularistic meaning in the South, since the right of the people of each state to decide their own destiny was once again granted only to whites.

Before concluding, we should note one other possible explanation for the South's historical distinctiveness. This concerns the clear preponderance of evangelical Christian religious groups, especially many Methodists and

Baptists, in this part of the United States (see, e.g., Finke and Stark 1992: 282–8). According to the 'revolutionary ethos' thesis of writers such as Hatch (1989), it was primarily these Baptist and Methodist groups who were the most likely among the American population to embrace such central revolutionary ideas as local autonomy, anti-elitism, and individual freedom, at least for whites. Hence, if true, this thesis would provide an another way of accounting for the apparently greater southern commitment to the kindred ideas of popular sovereignty, states' rights, and personal liberty that we have noted here. Our own view is that the economic and social organization of slavery is the most important factor behind the South's distinctiveness. It is an open question whether this religion-based argument can also provide part of the explanation.[2]

On balance, we suggest that, although the southern United States in this period of history should not be viewed as an exact replica of a European feudal society, there are some key features of the economic and social organization of the American South that probably qualify it as at least quasi-feudal, though with a discernible liberal 'touch' in segments of the white population. Whatever label is chosen for this region, however, it seems indisputable that its distinctive plantation-based way of life, its singular ethnic structure, its reliance on a large underclass of black slaves for its prosperity and continuity, and its perversely narrow conception of such ideas as liberty and popular sovereignty all made the American South a unique entity in North America throughout the early history of the United States.

Ethnic Composition: Some Additional Considerations

So far, our historical analysis of the ethnic composition of Canada and the United States indicates that French Canada and the American South constituted two quite distinct sub-societies. It has also been determined that English Canada and the northern United States, while not identical, were highly similar in their ethnic structures, especially because of shared English, Scottish-Protestant, and related Scotch-Irish or Irish-Protestant influences. These patterns arose in the pre-revolutionary period and appear to have continued at least through the first half of the 1800s.

In the latter part of the nineteenth century, both Canada and the United States experienced other important changes in their ethnic mix. As briefly touched on earlier, one major shift was the growth in Irish-Catholic representation, which occurred in both countries but was especially pronounced in the United States. Also, there were sharp increases in immigration from other

---

2. We thank Mike Carroll, who brought this interpretation to our attention in a personal communication.

European countries. From the 1860s until the end of the century, the number of immigrants entering the United States from places other than Britain greatly increased. For example, the proportion coming to America from Germany was almost as large as that from England, Scotland, and Ireland combined in this period (Bureau of the US Census, Historical Tables 1975; Statistical Abstract of the United States 1899–1900). While Canada also saw a rise in non-British immigration during the latter decades of the nineteenth century, most of Canada's foreign-born population continued to originate from the British Isles (see 1951 Census of Canada, Historical Tables). These subsequent shifts in immigration patterns may have promoted some differences in the core values and cultural influences shaping the two societies. Another consideration is the large number of Canadians who themselves moved to the United States in later years. For example, between 1840 and 1900, more than a million Canadians migrated south of the border. As a result, by the turn of the twentieth century, almost 1.2 million native-born Canadians lived in the United States, compared with a total population in Canada of only about 5.4 million. Canadians were, in fact, the third largest ethnic group in the United States in 1900, after the Irish and the Germans (1951 Census of Canada, Historical Tables; Statistical Abstract of the United States 1910; Simpson 2000: 16–17; Harrison and Friesen 2004: 104). Although the migration of Canadians into the United States during the 1800s and afterward can be largely explained by the superior economic opportunities south of the border (see Thompson and Randall 1994: 52–3; Craig 1968: 136), it is at least conceivable that this movement involved a disproportionate outflow of Canadians who favoured an 'American' value system and way of life (see, e.g., Craig 1963: 253; Simpson 2000: 13–14). If so, the outflow could have contributed to divergences in the belief systems of the two populations. Still, whatever effects these and other subsequent changes in immigration flows had on the cultures of the two countries, the evidence indicates that, apart from the distinctive sub-societies of French Canada and the American South, the ethnic profiles of the two populations were very similar, both for the period of the American Revolution and for many decades afterward.

RELIGION IN CANADA AND THE UNITED STATES

It will be apparent from the foregoing discussion of ethnic composition and immigration that religion represents another key factor to consider when comparing the backgrounds and orientations of Canadians and Americans. However, although the previous section dealt with some important religious influences in both societies, there are a number of other religious issues that should be addressed. Religious involvement is an especially significant topic to consider in the American case, because, as many others have noted, Americans exhibit a greater devotion and commitment to religion than most other peoples of the world, including Canadians (e.g., Lipset 1963b: 150; 1996: 19, 62; Bibby 1987; Bellah et al. 1985; Finke and Stark 1992).

Among the theorists that we have focused on in the present analysis, Lipset is clearly the foremost proponent of the view that religious forces have been pivotal in making the United States an exceptional society in the world. Lipset suggests that personal freedom—to worship one's own God in one's own way—is sacrosanct for Americans, overriding pressures for group constraint or conformity imposed by the church or religious community. To Lipset, the 'Protestant sectarian' nature of American religion is a key indicator of this emphasis on individual choice, and is reflected in the large and varied range of churches in the United States. He contrasts the diversity in American religious organizations with the allegedly more monolithic, authoritarian, and 'state-supported' Catholic, Anglican, Lutheran, and Orthodox churches that he sees as dominant in Canada and most other Christian nations (Lipset 1996: 19, 93; also Lipset 1968: 52–3, 248–51). This alleged difference is said to reflect and promote a greater acceptance of hierarchical authority and collectivist restrictions among Canadians, compared with a strong desire for religious freedom and a distrust of 'statist communitarianism' among Americans (Lipset 1968: 52–3, 248–51; also 1963b: 52–6; 1990:16, 80–2; 1996: 19, 31).

There are, however, several problematic aspects of Lipset's comparison of religion in Canada and the United States. To begin with, the notion that Canada's major religions are 'statist', in the sense of being official arms of the government, is essentially untrue; the historical connections between church and state generally were far less official and direct than this characterization implies (see, e.g., Talman and Young 1934; Christiano 2000: 75–6). Second, even if we adopt Lipset's dubious definition of a statist religion, such a depiction of Canada's religions pertains almost exclusively to French Quebec. There, the Roman Catholic Church has had ties to the state historically (see, e.g., Wallot 1971: 118), and has always been the dominant religious affiliation. In 1871, for example, 86 per cent of Quebecers were Catholics, the great majority of them French-speaking. Using Lipset's definition, the only other major state-related religion in Quebec at that time was Anglicanism, which accounted for another 6 per cent of Quebecers, almost all of whom were British (1871 Census of Canada).

In the mainly English-speaking parts of Canada, however, the patterns were generally quite different. Newfoundland was the only English region in the 1800s where a majority belonged to one or the other of the Catholic and Anglican religions (see, e.g., Wallot 1971: 117; Harris and Warkentin 1974: 220–1; Morton 1963: 194–5; 1951 Census of Canada, Historical Tables). It is true that the percentage of Roman Catholics in English Canada was substantial during the nineteenth century, especially in the Atlantic region, and represented about 23 per cent of the non-Quebec population in 1871. In addition, the proportion of Anglicans increased gradually over time. Still, by 1871, less than 20 per cent of Canadians outside Quebec belonged to the Church of England (1871 Census of Canada; see also Rawlyk 1995: 138). Thus, even if we combine the Anglican and Catholic percentages for 1871, we find that close to 6 out of 10 Canadians outside Quebec were not affiliated with either of these two religions.

Although it never equalled the pre-eminent position of the Roman Catholic Church in Quebec, it is correct that the Anglican Church, as an institution, generally enjoyed considerable influence in parts of English Canada. Also, somewhat in keeping with Lipset's 'statist' label, the Anglican Church did benefit disproportionately from informal government connections. In the revolutionary period some powerful British political figures, including John Graves Simcoe in Ontario (Upper Canada), sought special land grants and other privileges for the Anglican Church (Bell and Tepperman 1979: 81–2; Wynn 1987: 208–9; Myers 1914: 73; Clark 1948: 91; 1968: 169–70; Christian and Campbell 1983: 43; Wise 1971: 64, 84; Careless 1971: 238; Morton 1963: 194; Craig 1963: 16, 19). As the nineteenth century progressed, Anglican Church leaders enhanced their influence through their links to the heads of pro-British Conservative governments in English Canada. The best illustration is the association between the prominent Anglican bishop, John Strachan, and the politicians who formed the so-called 'Family Compact' in Ontario during the 1820s and 1830s (Wynn 1987: 210, 213; Clark 1968: 180–1; Cross 1971: 161–3, 169; also Craig 1963: 106–10; 1971: 174; Smith 1994: 30; Evans 1976: 280–1; McRae 1964: 240–2; Adamson 1994: 441–6).

Nevertheless, it is important to emphasize again that, in analysing the prevailing values and beliefs within a society, a crucial distinction must be made between the ideas and inclinations of the elites and those of the larger population. In other words, while Anglican Church leaders may have enjoyed considerable influence with those at the top of English Canada's political structure, and may have shared Tory values with some of these people in many cases, such elite affinities tell us little about the orientations of the general population.

If we look at the proportion of people who actually belonged to the Church of England historically, we see that Anglicanism was not a dominant religious or cultural force among the wider Canadian populace. We have already noted the relatively small size of the Anglican Church's following in the latter half of the 1800s (see also Harris and Warkentin 1974: 118). In fact, the proportion of Anglicans was even smaller in earlier decades. Consider, for example, that, in Ontario during the 1790s, only 5 per cent of the population was Anglican (Errington 1994: 32; also Osborne and Swainson 1988: 25). As late as 1815, 'all attempts to establish the Church of England in the colony were unsuccessful', with the result that there were only six Anglican clergymen in the entire Ontario region (Errington 1994: 51; also Craig 1963: 55). The evidence reveals that Anglican religious teachings and values had great difficulty taking root in English Canada until well after the revolutionary period, and even then faced serious opposition from large numbers of colonists (Clark 1959: 495; MacKinnon 1986: 78; Morton 1963: 194–5; Craig 1963: 38, 55, 165; McRae 1964: 243; Adamson 1994: 431–2). Many settlers were openly resentful of attempts by top government leaders to impose Anglicanism in their communities (Wise 1971: 67; Wallot 1971: 107; Evans 1976: 273, 276; Talman and Young 1934: 369, 373). Perhaps as a consequence, even some government authorities were reluctant to give special support to Anglicanism, not only in Ontario, but in Nova Scotia and other regions, as well (Errington 1994: 51–2; Wallot 1971: 117). In New Brunswick, the local loyalist elite did seek and receive British government assistance for the Church of England; nevertheless, by 1814, the Anglican Church in that province continued to be an 'ineffective institution', with a rigid and formal style of religious practice that was 'far removed from the needs of the population at large' (Condon 1984: 185–7).

If Anglicanism was not predominant among the English-speaking populace, what religions were? Catholics, as noted earlier, did account for an appreciable portion of the population. However, the majority of English Canadians in the 1800s belonged to a variety of Methodist, Presbyterian, Baptist, and other denominations (Wynn 1987: 216; Clark 1968: 49–50; Harris and Warkentin 1974: 118, 128, 220–1; Monet 1971: 207; Morton 1963: 195, 224; Condon 1984: 186; Craig,1968: 120). Of these broad categories, Methodists formed the largest group until 1881, when they were surpassed by Presbyterians (Reid 1976: 125–6). In other words, most English Canadians, like most Americans, were Protestant sectarians (see especially Clark 1948).

It should be noted that American religion was even more sectarian, since Americans could choose from a wider array of Protestant denominations than Canadians. These choices included hundreds of small and often unusual groups, like the 'Two-Seed-in-the-Spirit' Baptists, for instance (Wood 1992: 333; see also Clark 1968: 127; O'Toole 2000: 45–6). Still, Protestant religious choices in Canada were also numerous and diverse, ranging from Freewill Baptists to Primitive Methodists. The Canadian congregations likewise included many relatively obscure groups, with the 'Newlights' and 'Campbellites' being just two examples (Clark 1968: 118–21; see also Clark 1948: 181–5, 287; Condon 1984: 187; Christiano 2000: 75–6). The popularity of these different Protestant sects shows that most English Canadians basically resembled most Americans, in that they did not favour the so-called 'statist' religions stressed by Lipset, either Anglican or Catholic. Instead, English Canadians often matched their American neighbours in being 'deeply suspicious of any alliance between church and state' (Smith 1994: 47; see also Christian and Campbell 1983: 44–5; Reid 1976: 123).

Another intriguing feature of religion in English Canada during the first several decades of the 1800s was that many of the ministers who headed the different Protestant congregations were itinerant American preachers (Wynn 1987: 216; Clark 1968: 76–7; Errington 1994: 52; Reid 1976: 123; Wallot 1971: 117; Morton 1963: 224; Craig 1963: 55–6; 1968: 120; Adamson 1994: 425). Similarly, as late as the 1850s and beyond, it was not unusual to find Protestant revivalist gatherings in English Canada that attracted hosts of willing participants, and that were led by Methodist and Baptist ministers from the United States (Smith 1957: 67–8, 123). These connections provide additional evidence of the common religious outlooks and influences shared by large numbers of Canadians and Americans in this period.[3]

From its earliest stages, then, religious activity in Canada, with the possible exception of French Quebec, was clearly not statist. Especially outside the elite, there is no basis for claiming that most English Canadians were historically drawn to or influenced by statist religions. Instead, religious choices and beliefs in English Canada were highly variable, as evidenced in the large number of Protestant denominations that persisted in the 1800s and that, to some extent, still exist today (see Bibby 1987: 14–15, 27–8). The historical patterns of religious involvement in English Canada and the United States were not identical, and these patterns probably became more dissimilar with time. One change that arose through the middle decades of the nineteenth century was an erosion of the similarities between American Methodists and other Protestant sectarians, on the one hand, and their counterparts in the Ontario region, on the other hand. However, here again, research indicates that the impetus for this pattern of divergence came not from the general population in this part of Canada, but from the 'policies and practices of the Loyalist, almost exclusively Anglican, political and professional elite' (Adamson 1994:

---

3.   Parallel patterns occurred in education, where there was a similar American influence on the culture and values of Canadians at this time. For example, during the early decades of the nineteenth century, it was commonplace for American teachers and textbooks to be employed in the Ontario school system. It was not until the mid-1800s that any concerted or systematic effort was made to inculcate a more distinctively British or Canadian curriculum (Smith 1994: 254–6; Thompson and Randall 1994: 26–7; Senior and Brown 1987: 216; Craig 1968: 120).

434). Another example of increasing religious dissimilarity between the countries is the larger proportion of Catholics in Canada compared with the United States in more recent years (see Bibby 1987: 220; 1993: 184–6; also Banting and Simeon 1997: 65–7; Clark 1948, 1968, 1975; Gwyn 1985: 180–1). Nevertheless, it is also true that, during the historical period being considered here, running from the time of the American Revolution through the first half of the nineteenth century, Protestant sectarian diversity was a point of similarity in the religious compositions of both societies. This has been largely overlooked by other writers. A similar oversight has been attributed to some Canadian church historians, because of their tendency to concentrate on the larger established churches and to give only 'passing notice' to the many smaller and less prominent denominations that have long existed in Canada (Clark 1968: 117). Such omissions may explain some of the unfounded assumptions about major discrepancies in the religious backgrounds of the English-Canadian and American populations in the revolutionary period. The available evidence suggests many similarities in the patterns of religious affiliation and attendant values in the two societies, both at the time of the Revolution and for many decades afterward.

PATTERNS OF URBANIZATION

To comprehend the everyday lives and experiences of Canadians and Americans historically, another important factor to consider is the process and pace of community growth during the formative years of both societies. It is natural now to imagine the early United States as a thriving and vibrant society that grew rapidly and steadily into a highly urbanized modern nation. The Canadian colonies, in contrast, are typically perceived as far more backward, rural, and undeveloped during this period of history.

In some respects, these contrasting images are accurate. Because of its climatic, geographic, and related economic advantages, the United States from the outset attracted many more settlers, and soon became a more heavily populated country than Canada, especially in the North (Harris and Warkentin 1974: 176). As an illustration, by 1860, the American population was 31.4 million. This number is more than ten times larger than Canada's population of 3.1 million in 1861 and, for that matter, matches Canada's present-day population. Another telling comparison is that, while there were about 5.3 million people living in the United States in 1800, it was not until 1900 that Canada's population equalled this number (Statistical Abstracts of the United States 1899–1900; 1951 Census of Canada, Historical Tables).

Throughout the 1800s, the United States also had more centres of relatively heavy urban concentration than did Canada. For example, four American cities had populations greater than 25,000 in 1800, and this number had risen to 77 by 1870 (Historical Tables of the United States 1975; see also Weber 1967: 20–4). By comparison, Canada had no cities of 25,000 or more in 1800 and only six by 1870 (Harris and Warkentin 1974: 152–3, 216–18; Careless 1971: 230; Weber 1967: 130–2).

Still, it is important to realize that, especially in the first several decades of the nineteenth century, the differences in urbanization between Canada and the United States were matters of degree. Consider, as was discussed in Chapter 4, that only 5 per cent of Americans lived in population centres of 2,500 or more in the revolutionary period and, as late as 1870, this proportion was still only about 25 per cent (Chandler 1977: 17; Shain 1994: 65). During most of the 1800s, then, the United States was, like Canada, a society composed largely of rural homesteads or small towns, and was far from being the metropolitan nation that it became in the twentieth century.

Another point of note is that, although there were undoubted differences in urbanization in the revolutionary period, these differences were not uniform across all regions of the two societies. The higher American levels of urbanization were most obvious in the eastern parts of the continent, and less pronounced in those areas that then formed the western frontiers of the two societies (see Clark 1968: 63–5; 1959: 231). For instance, in the second decade of the nineteenth century, the Niagara region of New York was less populous and less developed economically than the neighbouring Canadian settlements. Buffalo had a population of only 500 by 1810, compared with Toronto's 1,000 and Kingston's 3,000. As well, reversing the pattern of modern times, finished goods and supplies tended to flow from the Canadian to the American side of the border in this region, while raw exports moved the other way (Stuart 1988: 71; Wilson 1971: 145; Wynn 1987: 260–1; Craig 1963: 44). As another illustration, it is interesting to note that, even as late as the 1850s, Chicago, which is now one of the world's largest cities, had a population of less than 30,000, making it somewhat smaller than Toronto and only half the size of Montreal at that time (Census of Canada 1851–52, Volume 1; Statistical View of the United States: Compendium of the Seventh Census 1854).

Such considerations do not negate the fact that the United States was both more populous and more urbanized than Canada, but they do indicate that neither population was particularly urbane or cosmopolitan in the first half of the nineteenth century, even by the standards of the time. On the contrary, in both societies most people lived a rural, agriculturally based, and frequently isolated existence (Wood 1992: 312; Harris and Warkentin 1974: 125–8; Noel 1990: 26–7; Wynn 1987: 245, 258; Duncan 1976: 69; Stuart 1988: 18, 71–2). These similarities are illustrated in Errington's research on Ontario, which indicates that 'there was little to distinguish rural settlements in the backwoods of

Upper Canada from those on the frontiers of New York or the New England states' (Errington 1994: 15; also Craig 1968: 105). Particularly in the first several decades of the 1800s, most people in both societies were farmers and primary labourers, working in remote circumstances, either alone, with their families, or in small groups. Especially in the frontier regions, inhabitants made few visits even to their closest neighbours, because of the distances separating them and the poor roads and means of transportation (see Errington 1994: 15–18; Harris and Warkentin 1974: 119–22, 125; Wilson 1971: 141–2; Wood 1992: 131; Condon 1984: 185; Craig 1963: 50–1).

Later, of course, with improvements in transport and communication, the expansion of commerce, and increasing immigration, larger population centres emerged. Such developments promoted more frequent interaction and a greater sense of local community identity (Clark 1968: 80; Errington 1994: 90; Wood 1992: 315; Shain 1994: 64–5). Local allegiances eventually progressed toward a fuller national vision in each country, although the process apparently took longer in Canada, and encountered more persistent and long-term regional divisiveness (Smith 1994: 154–5, 271–4; Christian and Campbell 1983: 46–8; see also Gwyn 1985, 1995; Perlin 1997: 75–6; Simeon and Willis 1997: 176–8). Still, like the United States, Canada did not remain a rural society. Although America's biggest cities are clearly much larger than their Canadian counterparts, Canada actually surpasses the United States in terms of the percentage of the population that is concentrated in metropolitan areas (Gwyn 1985: 181–2; Adams 2003: 118). During the early to mid-1800s, however, the lives of Canadians were influenced by many of the same forces of rural and small-town 'local communalism' that, as noted previously, were prevalent in the American populace during that period (Shain 1994; see also Pekelis 1950; Appleby 1984, 1992). One possible difference may have been a slower development of shared community values in Canada, where the population was sparser and the potential for both local and individual isolation was that much greater.

POLITICAL CULTURE AND ORGANIZATION

The analysis to this point suggests that the lives of most early Canadians and Americans were conditioned by two rather distinct influences. On the one hand, in the cultural and spiritual spheres of existence, both societies promoted a sense of local communalism, emphasizing conformity to values and beliefs that were collectively held and often religiously based. On the other hand, because a large number of inhabitants in both societies had considerable personal freedom in the economic sphere, including the opportunity to own and to work their own land in many cases, their experiences were often conducive to a sense of economic liberty or independence. In addition, given the isolated and frequently uncertain circumstances of everyday life, people in each society were motivated to develop a sense of self-reliance and self-sufficiency, if only to increase their own physical security and chances for economic survival.

Although we might expect that this mix of communal conformity and individual self-reliance should promote similar sets of values and outlooks in both societies during the revolutionary era and beyond, a few observers have concluded that the orientations of Canadians and Americans moved in quite different directions, especially regarding their beliefs about the role of government. Lipset's analysis is especially likely to emphasize this view, although some of the founding-fragment theorists, particularly Horowitz, also seem to suggest the same idea at times. The crux of this argument is that the early settlement experiences of Canadians made them less likely than Americans to fend for themselves, and more likely to turn to a strong government for help and guidance. Such an interpretation, of course, is consistent with Lipset's more general conclusion, as discussed earlier, that Canada was from the beginning a more government-regulated society, with a more statist set of institutional structures and political culture. The United States, in contrast, is portrayed as a much more decentralized and democratic polity, where individual citizens acted independently and were largely free from government control or intervention.

Lipset contends that at least three factors moved the political organization and political values of the two societies along divergent paths. These factors include: the early impact of the British government's assistance to Canadian colonists during the period immediately following the Revolution; differences in climate and geography between the two societies, which necessitated more state dependence in Canada; and the greater centralization of government power in Canada in the post-revolutionary era. Let us review and assess each of these claims.

British Assistance in Canada after the Revolution

One basis for the argument that Canada has always been a more statist society than the United States concerns the British provision of economic assistance to some Canadian colonials, especially during the period spanning the Revolution and the first few decades of the nineteenth century. British officials at this time did offer forms of aid to loyalists, military veterans, and others, especially in frontier areas. As noted previously, these included opportunities to acquire their own land at little or no cost, as well as free tools, weapons, and other supplies to help in the initial phases of settlement (Errington 1994: 22; Noel 1990: 34; Duncan 1976: 51–2; also Harris and Warkentin 1974: 113–16, 166; Craig 1963: 7–8, 52).

However, several issues should be considered before drawing strong conclusions from these practices. First, despite the impression of pervasive and comprehensive government aid to the Canadian colonists (Lipset 1968: 49; 1990: 17–18), such benefits were by no means granted to everyone (Talman 1946: xxviii–xxx; Knowles 1997: 17–18). Moreover, British help was often given grudgingly, irregularly, belatedly, and indifferently. This was so much the case that, for many inhabitants, the process undermined, rather than strengthened, any feelings of loyalty or gratitude toward British authority (MacKinnon 1986: 67, 70–2; Condon 1984: 38, 170; Craig 1968: 84; Harrison and Friesen 2004: 28). Much of whatever government provisioning did occur was compensation to refugees whose lands and possessions were wrongfully taken during the Revolution, or represented incentives to attract later settlers to the less inviting climes of the Canadian colonies (MacKinnon 1986: 67, 71; Osborne and Swainson 1988: 25–6). Even in subsequent years, the British government's involvement with its Canadian subjects was not sustained and consistent. After the War of 1812, British interest in Canada waned considerably, partly because of Britain's desire to improve relations with the United States (Morton 1963: 273; Craig 1968: 117, 126). Overt British support for and commitment to Canada became weaker and more intermittent. In the 1860s, the British did send troops to Canada because of possible threats posed by the outbreak of the Civil War in the United States. For the most part, however, a prime British concern was to reduce the costs of her colonies, and eventually to encourage Canada's movement toward confederation as a single nation (Gwyn 1985: 24, Errington 1994: 155; Morton 1963: 302, 317–19; Craig 1968: 126, 140). Thus, British assistance to some Canadian inhabitants in the early post-revolutionary period was not the beginning of a long and continuous history of state dependency and government paternalism in Canada. Instead, the norm was that individuals and families, in Canada as in the United States, mainly relied on themselves, not on state support, to meet the needs of their daily existence.[4]

Here we might also note that, although Canadians today do experience more government intervention in their lives than Americans, much of the evidence for greater Canadian statism is of recent origin. For example, as we shall discuss in Part III of our analysis, Canada now has a more elaborate and extensive system of state-sponsored social programs than the United States, but these differences between the two societies did not clearly emerge until the

---

4. Some historians argue that Canada's welfare state really began in the 1920s, with the establishment of veterans' benefits and other programs to support soldiers who had returned from the First World War (e.g., Granatstein and Morton 1989: 251). Interestingly, these writers also note that veterans' pensions were granted to American soldiers about 50 years earlier, after the Civil War.

latter half of the twentieth century. Researchers specifically identify the period during and after World War II as the time when the size of Canada's welfare state began to surpass that of the Americans. These researchers also point out that many of the government programs introduced into Canada in this period, not to mention various laws and regulations passed by Canadian governments, were largely copied from counterparts already established in the United States in previous years. Most notable here are the social programs initiated under President Franklin Roosevelt's New Deal in the 1930s and 1940s (Thompson and Randall 1994: 177; Banting 1997: 282–3; Gwyn 1995: 18–19; Bothwell 1992: 289–92; Gibbins 1982: 14–15, 30–1; Pocklington 1985: 34–5, 264–5).

Climate, Geography, and Political Culture

The second of Lipset's arguments for concluding that Canada has a more statist culture and political organization than the United States has to do with differences in climate and geography. According to this argument, the Canadian environment was so inhospitable that it undermined the capacity and willingness of Canadians to be as self-reliant and independent as Americans. Canada's less forgiving weather and more imposing topography, which led to a smaller population and more scattered communities, allegedly promoted a greater need for and dependence on government paternalism to provide protection and aid (see, e.g., Lipset 1968: 60; 1990: 2, 17–18, 20–1; 1996: 93–4). These factors supposedly reinforced an acquiescence to government control and an acceptance of anti-liberal values that were already engendered in the Canadian populace by the early loyalist and Tory presence.

Once again, however, there are difficulties with this interpretation. First, while the environment in much of Canada was and is more forbidding than that found in most regions of the United States, it is arguable that the difficult conditions of Canada's northern latitudes might actually make those who chose to live there even more rugged and determined individuals than Americans (see, e.g., Clark 1968: 213; Gwyn 1995: 18; Condon 1984: 185). Similarly, the consistently smaller Canadian population historically may have meant that Canada's inhabitants had to be even more self-reliant than their American counterparts, who normally had more local community members to turn to in times of hardship (see Bryce 1887: 26–7).[5]

---

5.   Some analyses of early Canadian literature have identified an aversion to the harshness and isolation of the frontier among Canadians, which is contrasted with the American literary emphasis on the abundance and individual freedom of frontier life. Even here, though, researchers speak of similarities between the Canadian and American orientations, and the 'well-nigh seamless veneer of "Americanness"' that overlays Canadian outlooks (McGregor 1985: 412, 47–52, 425–6; see also McGregor 1988).

It should also be remembered that, while the two nations generally have quite different climates, the vast majority of Canadians, then as now, lived very close to the American border. Thus, most Canadians, from the east coast to the western plains and beyond, shared a rather similar environment with the Americans residing immediately below them (see Clark 1968: 236). This suggests that environmental factors probably had little significance for differentiating Canadians from their American neighbours in the northern tier of states. It also raises the interesting possibility that differences in climate and geography may have promoted appreciable disparities in the life experiences of Canadians and those Americans inhabiting the deep South, although it is perhaps still debatable whether these differences also led to widely divergent views on the virtues of statism.

The previous point raises other potentially significant qualifications of Lipset's claims about Canadian–American differences in this period. There are several good reasons for contending that, at least until the middle of the 1800s, Americans in the northern states probably had more in common with their Canadian neighbours than with their southern countrymen. In addition to the geographic proximity and similar climates experienced by English Canadians and American northerners, we should recall the considerable similarities in ethnic composition linking the American North and English Canada that were noted previously. Furthermore, we should remember the numerous kinship and friendship ties that connected the two populations. We have already discussed that, during the first several decades of the 1800s, even the border between the two countries was not officially established, making it only a vague idea, or 'imaginary line', that carried little meaning for many of those living on either side of it (Stuart 1988: 112; Thompson and Randall 1994: 47; Simpson 2000: 16–17; Adamson 1994: 431–3). The evidence of linkages and affinities between Canadians and northern Americans in this period stands in marked contrast to the situation existing between the northern Americans and their southern compatriots. In fact, as we have seen, from the very founding of the United States, the North and South were separated by major cultural cleavages and structural dissimilarities. Here, as well, climate and geography, along with related differences in industrial development and economic base, may account for many of these dissimilarities.[6]

---

6. Another telling sign of the ties between Canada and the American North, as well as the division between the northern and southern states, was the Canadian reaction to the American Civil War. Although Canada's politicians may have been split on the issue, of the more than 20,000 Canadians who volunteered to serve in this conflict, the overwhelming majority fought on the northern side (Simpson 2000: 12; see also Mayers 2003).

Differences in Political Centralization

The third key element in Lipset's claim for the existence of statism in Canada is that Canadians have always had a more centralized system of government than the United States. This difference allegedly has meant that Canada was marked from the beginning by a more statist political culture than the United States, and that Canadians have always expected and preferred more pervasive government involvement in their lives. The first part of this argument is substantially correct. At least during the nineteenth century, Canada's political structure was more centralized than that found in America, in part because of the recurring Canadian fear of American invasion or boundary encroachment in this period. As many researchers have noted, such concerns also spurred government involvement in Canada's westward expansion, as well as the drive for Confederation in the 1860s and the incorporation of Canada's western provinces in subsequent years (e.g., Lipset 1968: 18–19; also Clark 1968: 214; Gibbins 1982: 24–5; Harris and Warkentin 1974: 249; Thompson and Randall 1994: 44–6; Morton 1963: 327–30; Harrison and Friesen 2004: 97–8). However, while these events demonstrate a more central government role in Canada historically, their significance in promoting different political cultures and values in the two societies cannot be accurately assessed without considering some other key issues.

The major points to note here concern differences in both the timing and the processes involved in establishing the United States and Canada as democratic societies. The American polity began as a loose association of independent states, under the Articles of Confederation of 1781 (Gibbins 1982: 8–9). The United States was then transformed, after the drafting of the American Constitution in the late 1780s, into what has been called the first 'true federal state' (Pocklington 1985: 152). Under this arrangement, the American political system sustained an effective national-level government, while simultaneously preserving a decentralized system of relatively autonomous states (Pocklington 1985: 153; see also Bryce 1889, I: 16–17, 29–34; Brogan 1954: 1–3, 265–6; Creighton 1972: 71). In contrast, during this same period, Canada still comprised a set of diverse British colonies. The individual provinces did have some rights of self-government, however, and, through the first half of the 1800s, gradually established democratic institutions, albeit within the constraints of a colonial framework. This meant that, although provinces remained subject to the central authority of the British monarchy, the Crown's formal power often was sufficiently remote that the colonies enjoyed considerable autonomy in their everyday administration, and also had the power to write their own legislation in many cases (see, e.g., Morton 1963: 209–10, 234–5, 271–2; Waite 1987: 308; Lipset 1990: 13). In 1867, of course, more than 80 years after American independence, Canada was constituted as a democratic country in its own right.[7] While Canada's political structure reflected the influence of British institutions, especially its parliamentary system of democracy, it is notable that the Canadian polity was also a federation, and hence resembled the United States in many ways. In fact, elements of Canada's system of government were consciously modelled after the American example (Gibbins 1982: 26; Pocklington 1985: 152–3; Craig 1968: 142; Harrison and Friesen 2004: 98).

With respect to the centralization of power, there were significant differences between the two federations in this period. In particular, as previously discussed, the American states retained a number of powers, or states' rights, that could not easily be superseded by the national government, whereas the jurisdictions of Canada's provinces were limited by and secondary to federal government authority (Gibbins 1982: 28; Creighton 1972: 70–1; Morton 1963: 327–8; Pocklington 1985: 155; Waite 1987: 326–7; see also Bryce 1889, I: 681–2; 1921: 39–40; Brogan 1954: 265–6, 396). However, while there is little question that, formally and officially, power was more centralized in Canada's national government, the diverse and unwieldy nature of Canadian society, with its sparse and widely scattered population and its pronounced regional, cultural, and linguistic divisions, meant that in practice Canadians were often not subject to centralized authority (Gibbins 1982: 32; Morton 1963: 326; Pocklington 1985: 167–9; Craig 1963: 13–17, 43–4, 107, 141; Harrison and Friesen 2004: 99). These divisions eventually moved Canada toward a less concentrated political system while, paradoxically perhaps, the decentralized system that characterized America's early history changed in the opposite direction, leading to a political structure that today is actually more centralized than the Canadian system (Creighton 1972: 74; Gibbins 1982: 28–9, 42; Pocklington 1985: 156–7, 162, 167–72; Craig 1968: 41).

Here again we see the historical significance of the Civil War, both for the United States and for Canada. After this conflict, the American principles of state autonomy and states' rights, which had been championed far more by the defeated South than by the victorious North, began to erode. Subsequently, American leaders promoted a centralized and truly national system of government, hoping to counteract the divisiveness of state sovereignty and to deter

---

7.   Craig (1968: 127, 147) points out that the Canadian provinces had actually obtained a significant degree of self-government at least 20 years before Confederation itself. However, Canada did not achieve official status as an independent nation until the 1926 Balfour Declaration and the 1931 Statute of Westminster (Gibbins 1982: 24; Cook 1987: 438, 454). Some historians also suggest that it was in the aftermath of World War I that Canadians truly came to see themselves as a people distinct from their British forbears (Granatstein and Morton 1989: 1, 143).

the prospect of civil insurrection in future. In contrast, Canadian leaders in the 1860s, on witnessing the destruction and strife of the American experience, saw one more important reason for starting with a more highly centralized democracy at the national level (Creighton 1972: 128; Gibbins 1982: 12–13; Waite 1987: 321; McPherson 1991: 37–8; Ajzenstat 2003: 71; Harrison and Friesen 2004: 99).[8] Thus, some of the acknowledged early differences in government centralization between the two societies can be attributed, not so much to fundamental national differences in political culture or values, but rather to Canada's not achieving political independence until a later time, and in a different historical context.

Notwithstanding these considerations, however, it is true that, at least until the middle of the nineteenth century, Canada did have a more centralized political structure than the United States. The key question is whether this historical fact reflects major differences in the political values of the two societies. The answer we propose is that it may well indicate divergences in the views of the people in power at the time, i.e., the political elites and other leaders with the capacity to frame the systems of government in both societies. However, it is far less certain that differences in political organization and related elite values also reflected differences in the political preferences or orientations of the two general populations.

It seems certain, first of all, that most people on either side of the border shared a generally low level of sustained interest in politics of any kind. Their main concerns, as we have discussed, were with daily existence and providing a living for themselves and their families (Clark 1959: 212, 213; Craig 1963: 7; 1968: 105; Adamson 1994: 432–3). Thus, unless political issues and events bore directly on these exigencies, the attention paid to political problems in both populations was probably minimal most of the time. As for those who were more deeply concerned with politics, at least those outside the elites, there is little reason to conclude that Canadians and Americans had radically different attitudes and outlooks. On the contrary, numerous historians believe that it was largely the ruling Tory leaderships in various parts of Canada who embraced such ideas as respect for central government authority, while much of the general population favoured reformist, liberal, and 'Whiggish' views similar to those typically associated with American politics (see, e.g., Errington

---

8. As McPherson (1991: viii) notes, it is interesting in the American case that the Civil War years witnessed the first clear shift away from speaking of the United States in the plural, as in 'the United States are a republic', and instead speaking of the United States as a single entity, as in 'the United States is a republic'. This shift in language may also signal the beginnings of the fundamental change toward a more national (rather than a regional or state) identity in American society.

1994: 93–4, 187–8; Wynn 1987: 274–6; Bell and Tepperman 1979: 48–51; Clark 1959: 227; Morton 1963: 174–5; Talman 1946: xxii–xxiii). Likewise, as Ajzenstat has shown, there is good reason to conclude that the Canadian people retained a sense of popular sovereignty, liberty, and legal equality that was similar to that found in the American public during this same period (Ajzenstat 2003: 52–7).

As well, given the isolated rural or small-town circumstances of both populations, most people's political attitudes would have shared a similar focus on local community concerns, which would often be far removed from what was happening at the national or federal level (Craig 1963: 9). It appears, again, that local communalism was a strong influence in each society, and in this case significantly affected both the Canadian and the American political cultures. In other words, the familiar saying that 'all politics is local' was probably especially applicable in this historical period.

Overall, then, there is good reason to believe that, in the revolutionary era and for many decades afterward, the political values and perspectives of most Canadians and Americans were generally similar. In fact, according to one of Canada's foremost historical sociologists, S.D. Clark, this was so much the case that most of the Canadian population in this period wanted either to create a political system parallel to that of the United States, or else to join with their southern neighbours to form one great democratic nation. Clark has contended that 'it was only a small minority of the population, individuals or groups identified with the vested interests of empire or, later, nation, who had any real desire to remain politically separate from their American neighbours' (Clark 1968: 223; also Pocklington 1985: 153). He adds that 'had the [Canadian] people at the time had their way, in 1760, and again in 1775, 1812, and 1838, and possibly even in 1860, the society growing up on the northern half of the Continent would have joined forces politically with the society growing out of the Atlantic sea-board'. Here, as before, then, we confront the question of whether national value differences are best judged by considering the views of the elites or the larger population. The position taken here is that, although differences in elite values have a significant bearing on the problem, it is the ideas and beliefs of the wider populace that should take precedence when comparing the two societies.

To summarize, in this section we have raised several questions and qualifications concerning the suggestion that Canada and the United States had fundamentally different political organizations and political cultures in the period spanning the American Revolution and the first half of the1800s. Our assessment indicates that the Canadian political structure was more centralized and probably somewhat more statist than that of its southern neighbour at this time. However, it is doubtful that these differences can be attributed to state assistance from the British colonial administration in the early part of the period. Second, at least if we compare Canada with the northern American states, there is virtually no basis for concluding that climatic or geographic differences between the two societies generated distinct orientations toward government in the two populations. Such differences seem particularly unlikely given the many similarities in the backgrounds and experiences of Canadians and Americans outlined in earlier sections of Part II. Third, while there were indeed structural differences in statism and government centralization during this period, some were more formal than real and most have changed considerably since then. Finally, the divergences in political institutions and forms of government that did exist seem more likely to reflect differences between the elites, and not between the general populations.

SUMMARY

In this chapter, our goal has been to review the historical evidence pertaining to the major background characteristics, institutions, and social structures that defined the everyday existence of the Canadian and American peoples, especially during the era of the American Revolution and the first half of the nineteenth century. The key purpose was to determine if there were notable differences with respect to these important influences, both between the two societies as a whole and among the four sub-societies that were initially identified in Chapter 2. Overall, the findings lend considerable credence to the view that the principal historical differences shaping Canada and the United States derive largely from the existence of distinct entities within the two nations, rather than from any major divergences between them.

First, in economic terms, both Canada and the United States in this early period were lands inhabited by ordinary people, who were engaged almost exclusively in agricultural and other forms of primary labour or small-scale enterprise. The main economic or class differences between the two countries at that time stemmed from the existence of quasi-feudal sub-societies in both French Canada and the American South, the first of these organized basically along the lines of the seigneurial system of Old World France, and the second based largely on the slave-based plantation mode of production that arose in the New World. Otherwise, any comparison of the two peoples, and especially the comparison of English Canadians with northern Americans, shows that they were very similar in regard to both class background and economic circumstances.

Next we considered the ethnic compositions and sources of immigration of the two nations. Here, as well, we found that, except for the quite distinct French population in and around the Quebec region of Canada, as well as the unique ethnic or racial structure of the American South that arose from the widespread use of black slaves, Canada and the United States were very similar during the historical period in question. In fact, English Canada and the northern United States appear to have been quite similar, with a mixture of English, Scottish, and Irish (or Scotch-Irish) Protestants accounting for the majority of the population in both regions. One acknowledged difference is that Irish Catholics formed a larger segment of immigration to the American states, especially in the North, than was the case in Canada. However, we also saw that, in spite of this difference, the Irish population has been majority-Protestant in both societies since the 1800s. Perhaps the only other ethnic difference of note is the possibility that a particular 'Celtic' influence, involving a mix of Scottish-Protestant, Irish-Protestant, and Scotch-Irish peoples, added an element of ethnic distinctiveness to the American South, although the evidence supporting this hypothesis is not completely definitive.

Third, in regard to religious background, there is again little to separate the two populations historically, other than the unquestioned dominance of Roman Catholicism in French Quebec. If we set Quebec aside, however, it is apparent that, at least until the mid-1800s, both English Canada and the United States as a whole were diverse Christian societies, with most people in each nation adhering to a range of Protestant faiths.

We have also looked briefly at the question of urbanization in the two countries. Here it was determined that, in spite of the obvious and substantial differences in population size between Canada and the United States today, the societies were relatively similar in their early stages. That is, both were predominantly rural in nature, with few large cities and with the vast majority of the population living in the countryside or in small villages and towns. It is only after the middle of the nineteenth century that significant differences in urbanization and city size occur, with much of this occurring in the northern United States.

The last area of comparison we considered was political organization and political culture. We looked in particular at two claims regarding possible differences between Canadian and American society. These claims were that, compared with the United States, Canada has always relied on a more centralized system of governance and political decision-making and, second, that Canada has long been a more statist society, in which the people are heavily dependent on government assistance and social programs for their livelihood. In general, we have found that the first of these claims is true. There is consistent historical evidence to support the view that Canada's political structure was more centralized, although probably more so in theory than in actual practice. However, we also saw that, in recent history, this difference has reversed, with Canada's government being significantly less centralized than its American counterpart. As for the second claim, there is some support for the view that Canada was a more statist society historically, although the impetus came primarily from the political elites of the time and not from the general populace. Moreover, it was not during the early histories of the two nations that statism came to be demonstrably greater in Canada. Instead, any notable differences between Canada and the United States in this regard did not occur until well into the twentieth century, especially in the period after the Second World War.

CONCLUSION TO PART II

In Part II of the analysis, we have reviewed a considerable amount of comparative historical research on Canada and the United States. Although the evidence we have examined is not exhaustive, it is sufficiently extensive and comprehensive to allow us to draw a number of conclusions about the historical similarities and differences between the two nations, especially during the important formative years beginning in the late 1700s and running through the first half of the 1800s. Our conclusions, in turn, provide a basis for judging the relative merits of the major historical perspectives that were presented in Part I, and that have informed much of the foregoing analysis.

Among all of the perspectives that have been considered, Lipset's defining-moments thesis has received the least support. It will be recalled that Lipset perceives fundamental and lasting differences in the core values and guiding principles of Canadians and Americans, especially with regard to such central ideas as liberty, liberalism, and individualism. He also contends that it was the American Revolution that was absolutely crucial for establishing these differences. However, the historical research that we have examined shows, first of all, that liberty was actually a precept that had a similar salience in all of English North America, not just the thirteen colonies. We also found that the idea of liberty was clearly traceable to Old World English roots, and to a time long before the American Revolution. Even so, the evidence we have reviewed also suggests, that, in contrast to both Lipset's analysis and the founding-fragment perspectives of Hartz and others, liberty had a meaning that was far more restricted in its implications during the early years of English North America than it would come to have in the modern era. The contemporary conceptions of liberty did not become prevalent until at least the latter half of the nineteenth century. The same can be said for the idea of liberalism, and especially for the related concept of individualism, which was not even used in the English language until well into the 1800s. With respect to the deep-structures perspective, which we posed as an alternative to both Lipset's thesis and the founding-fragment approaches, the evidence provided in Chapter 4 does support the conclusion that the idea of liberty, in its more restricted sense, and also the core principles of legal equality and popular sovereignty, were relatively widespread in colonial America and the early United States. It is mainly the fourth of the core English principles that we have identified, namely the idea of pluralism, that does not appear to have been broadly adopted or embraced at this time. Instead, the particularistic and frequently intolerant values of small-town community life, which are integral to what Shain has referred to as local communalism, seem clearly to have dominated in early American society. As a result, the prime basis for encouraging, or at least allowing, religious, ethnic, and other forms of pluralism in the late 1700s and early 1800s was what might be called a 'separate but equal' arrangement emerging out of local communalism, in which different groups were often relatively free to establish their own distinct settlements in isolation from one another.

In Chapter 5, we shifted our focus to an examination of the situation in English Canada during the same historical period. In this part of the analysis, we were especially concerned with assessing the existing research on the loyalists, whose migration out of the thirteen colonies in the revolutionary period provides the key basis for the claim found in Lipset's argument, and to a lesser extent in the founding-fragment perspectives, that Canadians and Americans were steeped in divergent value systems. However, we determined that, despite the contention that the loyalist migration was a defining event that forever distinguished the two peoples, most of the evidence suggests otherwise. The available information on the loyalists indicates that, except for their choice not to support the break with Britain, their outlooks and general life experiences were clearly similar to those of their American contemporaries. Indeed, they probably were just as 'American', in the broader meaning of the term, as those who stayed in the thirteen colonies. Even allegiance to Britain, which we most closely associate with the loyalists, was not universal among their number, which included many groups whose reasons for fleeing north to Canada had little to do with loyalism: aboriginals, slaves, religious minorities, and people looking for a new start. We have also found that, even for those who were truly loyal to Britain, it is mistaken simply to equate them with Tories. Especially for the large majority from humble or non-elite backgrounds, there is little reason to believe that they were more committed to Tory or anti-liberal ideas— deference to authority, collectivism, elitism, or statism—than those living in the United States at the time. The available accounts, by the loyalists themselves and by American and other foreign visitors to Canada, indicate that the Canadians and Americans of this period were of like mind on a broad range of concerns, with far more in common than has often been argued or assumed. Both populations apparently also held to similar kinds of local-communalist values, especially in the religious and family spheres of life. At the same time, the two peoples exhibited considerable economic independence, especially because both populations generally had to be self-sufficient and self-reliant in sustaining their everyday material existence.

As outlined in Chapter 6, the same picture emerges from comparative evidence for subsequent years, especially the available information on the key background characteristics, institutional forces, and demographic compositions of the two societies through the first half of the 1800s. During this time, many population shifts and related developments occurred that almost certainly had larger and more significant effects than did the initial loyalist migration. Especially important were the waves of European immigrants that arrived through the early to middle 1800s and beyond. Again, what is most notable about these events is that, at least for the first half of the nineteenth century, they underscore the similarities between the two peoples, rather than their supposed fundamental differences. The key exceptions to this assertion are the long-standing and deeply entrenched sub-society of French Canada and the almost equally distinct American South. Otherwise, we see that, throughout this period, both societies were inhabited by mainly British, Protestant-sectarian, rural or small-town populations, who made their livelihoods through the sweat of their brows, especially in agriculture, but also in other forms of primary labour. Moreover, apart from occasional and irregular economic assistance given to some Canadians by the British colonial administration in the early part of this era, individuals and families in both populations were clearly not wards of the state, but in fact had to fend for themselves most of the time. As for political organization and culture, both countries evolved into democracies, although the Canadian nation-state, which originated decades after the United States, was initially more centralized and more akin to the British parliamentary system than to the American republican form of government. Still, substantial parallels between the Canadian and American democracies have long been evident, since both developed as federations of constituent regions, and the Canadian structure was modelled on the American system in numerous ways. At the level of mass political culture and the political outlooks of the general population, the evidence, though limited, reveals little that distinguishes Canadians from Americans in this period of history. Most people in both societies had minimal direct involvement in political matters, although they tended to share at least a vague sense of themselves as free citizens living under relatively democratic or representative systems. Thus, apart from clear differences between the French and English in Canada, and also major differences between the populations of the American North and South, which eventually contributed to the war between the states, we are left with an image of two peoples and two societies that seem substantially similar in most important respects.

But, if this depiction is accurate, why have social scientists and commentators so often accepted the conventional view that there were major and fundamental Canadian–American differences in the early histories of the two societies? The answer to this question is not simple, but, as some elements of the preceding analysis suggest, it may stem from the power of the myths that have been spun by later writers looking back on this crucial period of history. A tendency exists for after-the-fact myth-making to arise out of many historical accounts, not only about the American Revolution, but about other significant events, as well. Shenkman (1988), in particular, has pointed out the numerous 'legends, lies, and cherished myths' in American history generally, including the Revolutionary War. Here we should also recall Shain's (1994) analysis of the myth of American individualism, and his conclusion that the people of the early United States never were the individualists that some subsequent observers have claimed (see also Grabb, Baer, and Curtis 1999; Grabb, Curtis, and Baer 2000).

In the Canadian accounts of the American Revolution and its aftermath, we have also found some prime examples of myth-making. The most notable illustrations are those involving 'the loyalist myth'. Various researchers have pointed to the ways in which later observers, including Lipset, in particular, have mythologized the loyalists, treating them as the stalwart bearers and defenders of traditional Tory values when, as we have seen, the majority of them were not like this at all (e.g., Bell and Tepperman 1979: 77–82; Thompson and Randall 1994: 16; Gwyn 1985: 17–19, 167; Knowles 1997: 11–13; see also Upton 1971: 52–3; Noel 1990: 50; Craig 1963: 7; Ajzenstat 2003: 2–8, 93–6; Harrison and Friesen 2004: 90–1). Others have likewise discussed the related myths arising from the War of 1812, including the ways that later commentators seriously overstated the strength of support for this conflict in both the Canadian and the American populations (see, e.g., Errington 1994: 92, 102; Stuart 1988: 65–6; Clark 1968: 223: Wilson 1971: 128–9; Craig 1963: 67, 70–5; Harrison and Friesen 2004: 89–91). This creative reworking of our images of early Canada contributes to what has aptly been called the 'catalogue of fables' surrounding other important historical developments, including the rebellions in Upper and Lower Canada in 1837 and Confederation in 1867 (Bell and Tepperman 1979: 78; Craig 1968: 123–4, 144–7; Talman 1946: lx–lxv).

To some degree, of course, it may be inevitable that accounts from an earlier time are rewritten by subsequent generations of researchers and commentators. It is almost in the nature of historical research to proceed in this way, although we hasten to add that this should not excuse the overlooking or selective appreciation of pertinent historical evidence. Perhaps, as well, we should attend to W.I. Thomas's famous theorem, that situations defined as real are real in their consequences (Bell and Tepperman 1979: 63). Thus, it could be argued that, regardless of whether or not there were fundamental differences between the core principles and outlooks of Canadians and Americans during the formative years of their respective societies, as long as we cling to the recurring myth that such differences existed, the impact on our present sense of the two peoples is the same as if the myth were in fact true. It is for this same reason, however, that we find the opposite position more compelling. In our view, it is crucial to question or dispel such myths wherever the historical evidence warrants, because an accurate sense of where Canadians and Americans started is crucial for understanding where they are today. The main purpose of Part III of our analysis is to examine in detail an array of recent evidence bearing on several of the most well-known and most enduring myths that still influence the way we think about the two nations and their peoples. We shall see that, in the present day as well, many of the beliefs that Canadians and Americans have about the two nations and their differences also occupy the realm of myth.

PART III

⁓

ENDURING MYTHS AND CONTEMPORARY REALITIES

INTRODUCTION

Until now, we have concentrated on exploring the historical basis for the emergence of Canada and the United States as distinct societies. In Part I, we began our discussion with a review and assessment of several prominent theoretical perspectives, each of which argues that certain major events from the distant past have been crucial for explaining or understanding the development of the two countries. We also posed an alternative deep-structures approach, which suggests that there are a number of important similarities between the countries, but also argues for the existence of significant regional divisions within each nation. In Part II, we tested the applicability of these theories, using evidence drawn almost exclusively from the early histories of Canada and the United States. Based on our analysis of this evidence, we concluded that several of the most prominent myths about the two societies and their peoples are either largely or completely unfounded. In particular, we have seen that many of the images and perceptions arising around the time of the American Revolution, such as the myth of American individualism and Canada's loyalist myth, receive little or no support. Instead, such widely held beliefs as the idea that Americans have always been more individualistic than Canadians, or that Canadians have always been more loyal to and accepting of established government authority than Americans, have been shown to be fundamentally at variance with the historical record. In keeping with the deep-structures argument, we also determined that the most notable historical differences seemed to arise within, rather than between, the two nations, especially in the divergences between the French and English populations in Canada and between northerners and southerners in the United States.

In the remainder of this volume, our main goal is to build on these historical underpinnings, so as to arrive at a fuller understanding and a more accurate comparison of present-day Canada and the United States. In Part III, we address a series of beliefs and assumptions about the two countries and their citizens in the current era. Of course, since the events of the eighteenth and nineteenth centuries, which were our central focus in Part II, the two nations have undergone significant changes, in their economic structures, forms of political organization, and many of their major social, cultural, and religious institutions (see, e.g., Gwyn 1985, 1995; Thompson and Randall 1994; DePalma 2001; Adams 1997, 2003). As a result, there is no question that both countries and their peoples have moved beyond their early histories, and have been transformed by more recent developments in a number of fundamental ways.

At various stages in the analysis that follows, we discuss some of these major transformations and their implications for shaping Canada, the United States, and the four sub-societies that they subsume. Nevertheless, in spite of these acknowledged alterations to both nations over the past century or more, it is striking just how many present-day beliefs about Canadians and Americans are echoes of the old myths that we discussed in previous chapters. For example, based on their alleged historical differences, including the contrast between Canadian loyalism and American individualism, it has been commonly assumed, as noted in Chapter 1, that Canadians are more polite, respectful, and law-abiding than Americans, while also being more passive, obedient, and submissive to authority. Similarly, there is the belief that Canadians and their government leaders are more in favour than their American counterparts of social assistance to the disadvantaged, with the result that Canadians also have a greater dependency on the state for their livelihood and place a lower value on individual initiative and self-reliance. Further, there is the perception that Canadians are more open and accepting than Americans with respect to ethnic diversity and other cultural differences in their society, so much so that Canadians have a much weaker sense of national unity, identity, and pride. These are the kinds of present-day issues and questions to which we turn in the remainder of this book.

SAMPLES AND DATA SOURCES

The contemporary evidence we present in Part III follows most existing research by comparing the nations as two whole entities. In addition, however, we go beyond previous studies to consider findings on the similarities and differences operating across the four sub-societies that, as we have argued, are the major constituent elements of the two countries.

Researchers in this area have generally assumed that what Canadians and Americans do, say, and think about major social issues are probably the best measures of the two peoples' central values and beliefs. We take a similar approach in much of the analysis presented in Part III, for we devote considerable attention to attitudinal and behavioural data, which have been collected through recent sample surveys of the two populations.

Some of our evidence is based on the Canadian and American waves of the World Values Surveys (WVS) from the early 1990s. These are part of a larger set of international surveys that were conducted by Inglehart and associates, and that involved more than 40 countries. In each society, a nationally-representative sample was interviewed using virtually the same questionnaire (see Inglehart 1997: Appendix 1). Respondents 18 years old or older are included in our analyses. A weight factor was applied to ensure that the samples were representative of the populations in each country. Because of disparities in the number of missing responses for some questions, the working samples varied somewhat across the different analyses that were conducted. In general, however, the weighted working sample for the Americans included about 1,990 cases, with roughly one-third of these respondents residing in the US South. The weighted Canadian sample comprised approximately 1,730 cases, with about one-quarter of these living in Quebec.[1]

For the most part, we have selected measures from the WVS on the basis of two main criteria. First, we have chosen items dealing with topics that feature prominently in previous comparisons of the two nations. Second, we have restricted our analysis primarily to topics for which we could draw on multiple rather than single indicators of the issue in question, so as to enhance the overall reliability of our measures and our findings. In the end, we have included close to 90 different items and composite indices from the WVS, which are presented in 13 separate tables. The exact wordings for each of the items used in the tables are provided in Appendix I. Further details on the procedures that were applied in using the WVS are reported in Appendix II. As will be noted, in some instances we rely on data from other surveys to supplement the WVS results.

In addition to analyzing sample survey data, we also present extensive findings using a large number of published sources that are available from governmental and other agencies. These sources contain a wealth of valuable information that allows us to compare the two nations and their populations on a number of behavioural and social-structural indicators, including religious composition, criminal activity, patterns of government spending, levels

---

1.   We thank Ronald Inglehart and colleagues and the Inter-university Consortium for Political and Social Research, University of Michigan, for making the data from the World Values Surveys available to us. Neither the original investigators nor the disseminating archive bears any responsibility for the analyses conducted here.

of economic inequality, and so on. In combination, these varied sources of evidence enable us not only to conduct an up-to-date analysis of Canada and the United States, but also to provide a comparison that spans a period of several decades, going back to the early 1970s and even earlier in many cases.

RESEARCH QUESTIONS

The research presented in Part III focuses for the most part on five interconnected themes or questions. These questions are among the most central topics involved in previous comparative research on the two societies. First, in Chapter 7, we consider a series of moral issues in Canada and the United States, especially in the areas of religion, moral liberalism–conservatism, and orientations to crime and the law. In exploring this first set of topics, we begin with an analysis of religiosity and religious involvement in both countries. One of the goals in this part of the analysis is to determine the extent to which the populations of the two nations and the four sub-societies have sustained their historical emphasis on the importance of religion in their everyday lives. Next, we compare people's views on family values, marital practices, and sexual morality. We then consider research on crime and the legal system in the two societies, including national differences in rates of homicide and other crimes, as well as Canadian and American attitudes about various forms of criminal behaviour. In somewhat different ways, the responses to questions in these areas may be seen as indicators of the relative commitment of the two peoples and the four sub-populations to certain core principles, including the belief in liberty as opposed to licence, in the rule of law, and in some aspects of pluralism or tolerance of diversity.

The second set of issues, which are addressed in Chapter 8, centre on individualist and collectivist values. Here we examine people's beliefs about the role of the individual and government in society. We begin this chapter with a review of recent evidence on important social-structural indicators, including the amount of state spending in both nations and the levels of economic inequality in the two populations. We then conduct a detailed analysis of the extent to which Canadians and Americans differ in their views on such issues as the value of individual self-reliance versus government assistance, in their levels of self-confidence or assertiveness, and in their attitudes about change. The results of this research should help us to weigh the claims of those who have argued that individualism is more deeply ingrained in the American value system or national consciousness versus those who contend that such differences are either non-existent or greatly exaggerated.

The third area of study, as discussed in Chapter 9, concerns problems of social inclusion and tolerance, most notably Canadian and American attitudes about the rights of different ethnic or cultural minorities, as well as certain 'outgroups'. The findings in this chapter are relevant for determining whether allegedly deep-seated values, such as liberty and pluralism, are equally important for the people living in both nations and the four sub-societies, or instead are more prevalent in some populations than in others.

In Chapter 10, we move to a fourth theme and look at the relative levels of political interest and political action among Canadians and Americans. Here we assess a number of claims, such as the view that Americans are generally more suspicious or sceptical of government institutions than are Canadians, and that Americans are more committed and assertive than Canadians with respect to most dimensions of political life. These findings are pertinent for determining if there are cross-national similarities or differences with regard to some of the core principles and related ideas that were discussed in Parts I and II, including the two peoples' commitments to the concept of popular sovereignty and their views on the role that the individual can and should play in democratic political systems

Finally, in Chapter 11, we consider levels of social involvement and voluntary action, both in the two nations as a whole and in the four sub-societies. The main goal in this chapter is to test the well-known assumption that the United States is the pre-eminent 'nation of joiners', with citizens who are considerably more engaged and active than their Canadian counterparts when it comes to participating in voluntary organizations of various kinds. Here again, some long-standing claims about such core democratic principles as popular sovereignty, political liberty, and freedom of association will be examined in the light of recent evidence.

CHAPTER 7

⬥

MORAL ISSUES

RELIGION, FAMILY VALUES, AND CRIME

RELIGION AND RELIGIOSITY

In our historical comparison of Canada and the United States, one of the central social institutions that we considered was religion. Although it was not possible to quantify the relative power of religion and religious beliefs in the two societies or the four sub-societies historically, the general impression from the evidence we reviewed was that religion almost certainly had a pervasive influence on the lives of most inhabitants in all of these settings. It appears that, in those early times, the main factor that distinguished the various populations was not their comparative levels of religious adherence or involvement. Instead, the primary area of divergence was their chosen religious affiliation. The key finding in this regard was that, during the early development of the two nations, French Canadians were overwhelmingly Roman Catholic, while most English Canadians and most Americans, both northern and southern, followed a number of distinct Protestant faiths. Given this historical pattern, one question to address is whether the long-standing unitary Catholicism of Quebec, as opposed to the relatively diverse Protestantism found in English Canada and the United States, has contributed to important variations in values and outlooks among the four regional populations.

We can begin by examining the religious compositions of the two countries and the four sub-societies in more recent times, using evidence from the WVS for the early 1990s. These and other data on social indicators are reported in Appendix III. Looking first at the two peoples as a whole, we see that Canadians are significantly more likely than Americans to indicate that they are Catholics, at 41 per cent versus 28 per cent, while Americans are more likely to report that they are Protestants (37 per cent versus 28 per cent) or members of 'Other' faiths (10 per cent versus 4 per cent). These findings, in large measure, parallel those reported in other research, both for the 1990s and for more recent years (Bibby 1987: 220; 1993: 23; 2002: 37; Ogmundson

2002: 56; Matyas 2003; Statistical Abstract of the United States 2001: 56, Table 66; Mayer, Kosman, and Keysar 2003).

The higher percentage of Catholics in Canada in the1990s might seem to indicate a change from the historical patterns. However, if we look at the data for the four sub-societies considered separately, it becomes clear that Canada's higher Catholic proportion is really due to the extremely high level of Catholicism in Quebec, where 80 per cent of the respondents embrace this faith. This proportion is very close to the 83 per cent reported for Quebec in the 2001 Census (Canadian Press 2003b). Our results using the WVS also show that, in English Canada by itself, 36 per cent of respondents are Protestant, a level that is virtually identical to the 37 per cent found in the overall American sample. Within the United States, we find that southerners, at 49 per cent, are the most likely to report a Protestant affiliation, while the Protestant proportion in the northern US stands at 32 per cent. Research also indicates that, both historically and in the present day, residents of the American South have been significantly more likely than people in the other regions to belong to the more 'fundamentalist' or conservative Protestant religions, including Baptist and Pentecostal sects, for example (see Finke and Stark 1992: 282–8; Bibby 1993: 23; 2002: 22, 37, 85; Martin, Wilson, and Dillman 1991: 106–7; Reed 1991: 230–1; Putnam 2000: 75–7). Results from the WVS (not shown in the tables) reveal the same pattern, with 15 per cent of respondents from the US South claiming such affiliations in the early 1990s, compared with less than 5 per cent in the US North, about 2 per cent in English Canada, and less than 1 per cent in Quebec. An analysis of more recent survey data from 1996 produces similar results.[1] Overall, then, the findings show that the same general religious compositions that existed historically are still broadly evident in the present day. However, this is not to suggest that there have been no changes in religious composition. For example, recent evidence in both nations indicates a rise in the proportion of people belonging to Muslim, Buddhist, Hindu, and other non-Christian faiths (e.g., Bibby 2002: 21–2, 83–4; Canadian Press 2003b; Statistical Abstract of the United States 2001: 56, Table 66; Mayer, Kosman, and Keysar 2003).

---

1.   The data for 1996, which come from the 'God and Society in North America Survey', are based on a somewhat different definition of fundamentalism than that used in the WVS. The findings from this survey indicate that 34 per cent of respondents from the US South belong to fundamentalist religions, compared with 13 per cent in the US North, 5 per cent in English Canada, and 1 per cent in Quebec. These data were collected as part of the Research Project on Religion and Political Action, University of Notre Dame, Notre Dame, Indiana, in conjunction with the George Rawlyk Research Unit on Religion and Society, Queen's University, Kingston, Ontario.

One other notable comparison regarding religious composition concerns the proportion of people from each of the four sub-populations who state that they have no religious affiliation. Despite some resurgence of religious interest and spirituality in recent years, including a revival of some conservative Protestant faiths in the US South and elsewhere, most research suggests that, for several decades, formal religious involvement has generally declined in both Canada and the United States (e.g., Bibby 1987, 1993, 2002; Clark 2003; Krauss 2003; Putnam 2000: 69–79; Watt 1991: 257–9; Wilson 1982; Wuthnow 1998). In the WVS data, we see that this decline is most pronounced among English Canadians who, at 32 per cent, are the most likely to report 'no religion'. The proportions reporting no religion for the two American groups are slightly lower, at about 25 per cent, while Quebecers, at 12 per cent, are the least likely to say that they have no religious affiliation.[2]

The latter finding might seem to suggest that French Canadians have retained a stronger commitment to their religious beliefs than have other people in the two countries, perhaps because of the powerful collectivist influences of the Roman Catholic Church historically. However, as shown in Table 7.1, additional analyses based on various measures of religiosity reveal that the patterns of religious commitment and involvement among Quebecers and the other three sub-groups are more complex than can be conveyed by looking solely at nominal religious affiliation.

In Table 7.1, the two national samples and the four sub-samples are compared using five different indicators of religious activity and religious beliefs. First, we can see that, for all five of these measures, Americans as a whole evince significantly higher levels of religiosity than do Canadians. That is, compared with Canadians, Americans are more likely to say that they are religious people, to report high levels of attendance at religious services, to say that God is important in their life, to pray regularly, and to rank highly on an eight-item composite scale of conventional religious beliefs. These results are quite consistent with recent comparative studies on religious commitment,

---

2. The percentages of respondents indicating that they have no religion are higher in the WVS samples than in other sources. Census data show, for example, that 12 per cent of Canadians in 1991 and 16 per cent of Canadians in 2001 identified themselves as 'atheists, agnostics, or non-believers' (Matyas 2003). Data from the United States suggest that between 8 per cent and 11 per cent of Americans reported having no religion during this same period (Statistical Abstract of the United States 2001: 56, Table 66). The discrepancies between these figures and the WVS results are probably due to differences in question wording. In the WVS, respondents were asked if they are actual 'members' of a religious denomination, whereas the other sources typically asked about respondents' religious 'preference' or 'identification'.

Table 7.1 Measures of Religious Involvement and Religiosity by Region and Nation

	Region					Nation		
	English Canada	Quebec	US North	US South	Sig[1]	Canada Total	US Total	Sig[1]
1. Religious self-identification (%):								
I am a religious person	68	81	81	86		71	83	
I am not a religious person	30	15	17	13		26	16	
I am a convinced atheist	2	4	1	1	√	3	1	√
2. Frequency of attendance at religious services (% at these levels):								
More than once per week	7	5	11	20		7	14	
Once per week	20	21	30	26		20	29	
Once per month	12	16	14	17		13	15	
Less than once per month	28	39	26	20		31	24	
Never	33	19	20	17		29	19	
3. Importance of God in your life (10 pt. scale[a])	6.80	7.23*	7.71*	8.56*	√√	6.91	7.99	√√
4. How often do you pray outside of services (5 pt. scale[b])	3.44	3.72*	3.97*	4.17*	√	3.51	4.03	√
5. Religious Beliefs Scale (average number of beliefs endorsed from among 8[c]):	5.06	4.44*	5.87*	6.58*	√	4.91	6.10	√

Notes

[1] A check mark (√) indicates that the likelihood ratio chi-square for the overall four-category comparison across regions, or the two-category comparison across nations, is significant at <.05. The asterisk (*) indicates that the category is significantly different from the English Canadian reference group at <.05.

[a] The scale ranged from 1 = 'not at all' to 10 = 'very important'.

[b] The scale ranged from 1 = 'never' to 5 = 'often'.

[c] Respondents were asked whether they believed in God, life after death, a soul, the Devil, Hell, Heaven, sin, and resurrection of the dead.

as well as with early findings going back to at least the 1950s. This research consistently shows that Americans are more religious than almost all other western peoples, including Canadians (e.g., Lipset 1963b: 147–50; 1996: 19, 62; Watt 1991: 257–67; also Bibby 1987, 1993, 2002; Bellah et al. 1985; Finke and Stark 1992; Reimer 1995; Verba, Schlozman, and Brady 1995; Halman, Pettersson, and Verweij 1999; Mazzuca 2002d; Krauss 2003; Ray 2003).

Again, however, if we separate the respondents into the four sub-groups, some other important and interesting patterns emerge. This is especially true with respect to the Quebec sub-sample. In keeping with the previous finding that Quebecers are the least likely to say they have 'no religion', Quebecers are also among the most likely to say 'I am a religious person', with 81 per cent choosing this option. This percentage is slightly lower than the figure for southern Americans (86 per cent), but it is the same as that for northern American respondents, and is considerably higher than the 68 per cent reported for English Canadians.[3] The WVS results also show that Quebecers are similar to people from both the northern and the southern United States, in that they are among the least likely to report that they never attend religious services.

Nevertheless, there are a number of other considerations suggesting that Quebecers actually rank lower than the American groups in overall attendance. First of all, if we consider the other end of the attendance spectrum, we see that the American respondents, especially in the US South, are considerably more likely than either Quebecers or English Canadians to report exceptionally high levels of attendance at religious services. For example, almost half (46 per cent) of the respondents from the US South, and more than 40 per cent of those from the US North, report going to religious services once per week or more, compared with only about one-quarter of the two Canadian sub-groups. We should also be aware that more recent data, from 2001, show a significant decline in the religious attendance of Quebecers since the WVS data were collected in the early 1990s, placing them among the least regular attenders at formal religious services in all of Canada (Clark 2003; Mazzuca 2002d).

The third measure of religiosity in Table 7.1 reveals similar results, with Americans from the southern states being the most likely to say that God is important in their lives, followed by respondents from the northern United States, Quebecers, and lastly English Canadians. Essentially the same pattern emerges using the fourth measure of religiosity, which is a single question

---

3. We should clarify that studies show considerable regional involvement in religious attendance among English Canadians. For example, religious attendance in the Atlantic provinces is generally the highest in the country, while attendance levels for those from British Columbia are typically among the lowest (Clark 2003: 2–3; Bibby 2002: 60; Mazzuca 2002d: 54).

asking how often the respondent prays outside of religious services. Here too we see that the respondents who rank the highest come from the US South, followed by those from the US North, Quebec, and English Canada.

The final indicator in Table 7.1 is an eight-item composite scale that combines each respondent's answers regarding a series of conventional or fundamental religious beliefs. These include their belief in the existence of God, life after death, a soul, the Devil, Hell, Heaven, sin, and resurrection.[4] The results using this summed scale indicate that respondents from the southern United States are clearly the most likely to hold such beliefs, with an average score of 6.58 out of 8.0. Next come those from the US North, with a score of 5.89. Hence, for all of the measures in Table 7.1, the American South shows the highest level of religiosity among all the regions, with the American North typically ranking second (see also Cantril and Cantril 1999: 164; Mazzuca 2002d: 53). One notable difference from the other findings in Table 7.1 is that Quebecers, rather than English Canadians, have the lowest scores on this measure. In other words, although Quebecers rank relatively highly on the other religiosity items, sometimes matching people from the American North, they are the least likely among all the groups to express a belief in these eight conventional or fundamental religious tenets.

This shift in the rank-order of the Quebec respondents could be due to a number of factors. One plausible interpretation is that, while present-day Quebecers still see Christianity (specifically Roman Catholicism) as central to their identity, and so rank relatively highly on the other religiosity items considered in Table 7.1, Quebecers are now far less likely than they would have been historically to adhere to a strict or literal interpretation of Christian religious teachings (see Gagnon 2003a; Martin 2000: 25). In other words, it may be that Quebecers' expressions of religious adherence, as judged by the other indicators in Table 7.1, are mainly signs of their continuing ties to their traditional culture and way of life, rather than their dutiful obedience to official Catholic Church doctrines. This interpretation becomes especially relevant when we consider the next set of issues in this section, which pertain to the general question of moral conservatism.

---

4. We might expect that, for some items included in the composite scale (e.g., those asking about Hell or the Devil) respondents with Hindu and Buddhist religious affiliations would either not answer or else answer in the negative simply because such beliefs are not inherent to their faiths. However, most respondents with these affiliations did answer these items and some did so in the affirmative. Also, there were only 20 people in the Canadian and American samples who belonged to these two religions, in any event. As a result, the inclusion or exclusion of Hindu and Buddhist respondents for the eight-item scale does not alter the findings reported here.

Table 7.2   Liberal–Conservative Attitudes on Family and Sexual Issues by Region and Nation

	Region					Nation		
	English Canada	Quebec	US North	US South	Sig[1]	Canada Total	US Total	Sig[1]
Ratings of the acceptability of the following on a 10 pt. scale:[a]								
1. Married person having an affair	2.35	3.31*	1.98*	1.75*	√	2.58	1.90	√
2. Having sex under legal age of consent	2.56	4.71*	2.38	1.94*	√	3.08	2.23	√
3. Homosexuality	3.84	4.77*	3.36*	2.55*	√	4.07	3.09	√
4. Prostitution	3.37	3.46	2.60*	2.06*	√	3.39	2.42	√
5. Abortion	4.85	5.18*	4.28*	3.50*	√	4.93	4.02	√
6. Divorce	5.54	5.65	5.02*	4.65*	√	5.57	4.89	√
Family and Sexual Issues Index (responses to the 6 items above summed and divided by 6):	3.75	4.48*	3.24*	2.73*	√	3.93	3.07	√
% indicating that they would not want as neighbours:								
1. People with AIDS	21	19	24	37*	√	21	28	√
2. Homosexuals	33	19*	35	44*	√	30	38	√

Notes

[1] A check mark (√) indicates that the likelihood ratio chi-square for the overall four-category comparison across regions, or the two-category comparison across nations, is significant at <.05. The asterisk (*) indicates that the category is significantly different from the English Canadian reference group at <.05.

[a] The scale ranged from 1 = 'never justified' to 10 = 'always justified'.

FAMILY AND SEXUAL VALUES

Table 7.2 presents findings using a number of different items from the WVS, all of which deal in some fashion with the moral views of Canadians and Americans. The first six items ask respondents to rank, on individual 10-point scales, the degree to which they believe that the following activities are acceptable or unacceptable: a married person having an affair, sex under the legal age of consent, homosexuality, prostitution, abortion, and divorce. The other two items in Table 7.2 ask whether respondents would object to having AIDS sufferers or homosexuals as neighbours. These measures provide us with a partial means for assessing the extent to which people in the two nations and the four sub-societies differ in their adherence to conservative or liberal beliefs in the areas of family values and sexuality.

It is notable, first of all, that respondents in both nations and in all four regions generally seem to hold rather conservative or traditional views on most of these issues. On the 10-point scales, the average acceptability scores are usually in the range of 3.0 or less and rarely rise above 5.0. As might be expected, those activities that are illegal, such as prostitution and having sex under the legal age of consent, generate some of the lowest acceptability scores. However, other practices, including homosexuality and having an affair while married, are also rated as highly unacceptable by most respondents. As for the remaining two items in Table 7.2, they too elicit what might be seen as comparatively conservative attitudes. Between one-quarter and more than one-third of respondents are prepared to state that they would not want homosexuals or AIDS patients as neighbours.

If we look at differences between the two nations as a whole, we find that, for all eight dependent measures, Canadians have more liberal, accepting, or permissive attitudes than do Americans. Although few of these differences are truly large, all of them are statistically significant. This outcome may be surprising, at least from the point of view of some of the arguments presented in earlier sections of this volume. Such findings certainly seem inconsistent with Lipset's assertion that Americans have always been more liberal and more individualistic than Canadians, since presumably this difference should mean that Americans are more likely than Canadians to believe that freedom of personal choice and the rights of the individual should override collective or community values on such questions as divorce, abortion, or sexual preference.

In fact, though, Lipset's work on this question has often been equivocal and inconsistent. At certain times, for example, he has said that Canadians do, indeed, show higher levels of what he calls 'moral conservatism' than Americans (1968: 54–5), but, at other times, he speaks of the deeper sense of 'evangelical Protestant moralism' of Americans, which has caused them to hold more traditional beliefs concerning marriage, the family, and sexual freedom (1985: 125; 1986: 126–8). (For further discussion, see Grabb and Curtis 1988; Baer, Grabb, and Johnston 1990a, 1990b, 1990c.)

Although Lipset does not attempt to reconcile his sometimes discrepant assessments of the moral views of Canadians and Americans, his allusion to religious factors, especially the impact of evangelical or conservative Protestantism, does hint at a key explanation for why Americans may be more conservative on sexual, family, and related matters. We have already seen that Americans are not only more religious than Canadians, but also are more likely to be members of conservative or fundamentalist Protestant faiths. Numerous studies have shown that religiosity in general, and a strong commitment to conservative Protestantism in particular, are both associated with more restrictive or conservative views on family, sexual, and other social or moral issues (e.g., Nunn, Crockett, and Williams 1978; Smidt and Penning 1982; Ellison and Musick 1993; DiMaggio, Eans, and Bryson 1996: 729–31; Wuthnow 1998: 107–10; Loftus 2001: 771–5; Hill 2003).

Many of these same studies have also found that, partly because of the much greater prevalence of conservative Protestantism in the American South, people in that region typically have the most traditional beliefs about morality, sexuality, and the family (see also Cantril and Cantril 1999: 148–9; Himmelfarb 1999; Mazzuca 2002b: 95; Adams 2003: 86–8). This pattern is confirmed by the comparison of the four sub-societies in Table 7.2, which reveals that respondents from the southern states consistently express the most restrictive attitudes on each of the dependent measures. Respondents from the American North are slightly less conservative than their southern compatriots, while English Canadians have significantly more liberal views than both of the American sub-groups. However, it turns out that, for virtually all of the items listed in Table 7.2, it is Quebecers who hold the most liberal attitudes. This is the case, even though some of the activities listed, such as abortion and divorce, are officially forbidden by the Roman Catholic Church, which still predominates in Quebec, while such practices are now accepted by at least some of the Protestant faiths that prevail in the other three sub-populations.

How are we to interpret these contemporary findings on moral and sexual attitudes, especially in the light of the historical analysis presented in Part II? First of all, the patterns for the American South seem consistent with the conclusion that, although this sub-society has recently shown clear signs of growing similarity with other parts of North America, especially in the areas of economic development and industrialization, the South's social and cultural institutions probably still retain important elements of that region's conservative past (for some discussion, see, e.g., Marsden et al. 1982; Reed 1986; Himes 1991). We shall address this issue at greater length in subsequent sections of

Part III. Second, the results for English Canada and, less so, the American North, probably signify a somewhat greater commitment to liberal values in these two regions than in previous decades, and certainly suggest more liberalism in comparison with the American South. Nevertheless, the findings also indicate that, in an absolute sense, there is still a relatively traditional or conventional value system in these two sub-populations when it comes to questions of family, morality, and various sexual practices.

The findings from Table 7.2 that may be most surprising are those for the Quebec sub-sample. Given the historical evidence reviewed in Part II, which suggested that early French Canada was marked by religious, political, and social structures that were generally more authoritarian, hierarchical, and collectivist than elsewhere in North America, we might have expected that, even in the present day, the people of Quebec would adopt the least liberal and most traditional views on a variety of issues. However, the evidence clearly belies this expectation, at least with respect to questions of sexual morality and family values.

Before seeking to explain this outcome, we should make the initial observation that our findings for Quebec are not anomalous. On the contrary, they are consistent with a considerable amount of attitudinal and behavioural evidence on family values, gender roles, marital practices, and sexuality in Canada and the United States. Taken together, this previous body of research generally suggests that, in all of these topic areas, Quebecers are the most liberal or least traditional population in the two nations, followed by English Canadians, northern Americans, and southern Americans. This pattern, which has been evident for some two decades or more, covers a wide spectrum of issues. For example, this rank-ordering of the four regions is evident in studies of support for feminism and women's equality (e.g., Baer, Grabb, and Johnston 1990b: 699–702; Lipset 1990: 191–2; Fischer 1989: 893–4; Martin, Wilson, and Dillman 1991: 122–9; Clement and Myles 1994: 161, 219–23; Wu and Baer 1996: 444–6; Pelletier and Guerin 1996; Ornstein and Stevenson 1999: 205; Adams 2003: 51–2).[5] It also holds for beliefs about gay rights and

---

5. Although attitudinal support for gender equality is generally higher in Canada, comparisons involving more objective indicators, such as income, indicate that the two nations are very similar, with the gap between male and female earnings being almost the same for the past several decades (Rosenfeld and Kalleberg 1990; O'Connor, Orloff, and Shaver 1999: 96; Cohn 2000: 14; Tremblay 2000: 327; Lemieux and Mohle 2003: 349–50; Creese and Beagan 2004: 249). For the period from 1990 to 2000, full-time working women had average incomes that were between 70 per cent and 73 per cent of the average for full-time working males in both Canada and the United States. As for regional differences, the most recent figures, for 2000, are 70 per cent in Canada as a whole, 73 per cent in Quebec, and 73 per cent in both American regions (Statistics Canada 2003d; US Census Bureau 2000).

homosexuality (Driedger 1996: 42–3; Sniderman et al. 1996: 103–8; DiMaggio, Eans, and Bryson 1996; Chadwick and Heaton 1999: 160; Wood 1999: 21; Newport 1999; Gallup 2001a; Loftus 2001; Mazzuca 2002a: 1; Tepperman and Curtis 2004: 259–60), for the acceptance of pre-marital heterosexual and homosexual activity among adolescents (Bibby 2001: 90–1; Driedger 2002: 20–2), and for people's views on the permissibility of extra-marital sexual behaviour (Bibby 1995: 76; Branswell 1997: 35; Tervit 1997: A1; Adams 2003: 82). Other areas where this pattern of regional differences has been found include the use of various birth control techniques, including abortion (Le Bourdais and Marcil-Gratton 1996: 421–2; Chadwick and Heaton 1999: 172; Gallup 2001h; Mazzuca 2002b: 95), and levels of cohabitation or common-law marriage (Hobart and Grigel 1992: 321; Lipset 1996: 273; Fournier, Rosenberg, and White 1997: 191–2; Beaujot 2000: 220–2).

Results from the WVS are consistent with the latter studies, with Quebecers, at 12 per cent, being the most likely to enter into common-law relationships, compared with only 6 per cent in English Canada, 4 per cent in the US North, and 3 per cent in the US South. (See Appendix III.) Based on additional findings that are not shown in the tables, we can note, as well, that Quebec respondents in the WVS are the most likely to believe that 'marriage is an outdated institution', with 19 per cent saying 'yes' to this statement, compared with 10 per cent or less in the other regions. This also suggests that Quebecers are more willing to depart from traditional marital and family arrangements than are the other sub-groups in our analysis (see also Adams 2003: 82).

Such findings pose at least two key questions. First, given the historical evidence indicating that French Canada began as a decidedly conservative society, how is it that Quebecers today exhibit the most liberal, tolerant, or permissive views on family and sexual mores? Second, is it possible to reconcile Quebecers' contemporary views on such issues with their moderately high levels of religiosity in recent years? In addressing these questions, and in seeking to understand the situation of present-day Quebec more generally, it is important to discuss some of the momentous changes that have occurred in French Canada in its recent history.

The 'Old' and the 'New' Quebec

Prior to what has been called the 'Quiet Revolution' period of the early 1960s, Quebec was largely an isolated French enclave within Canada, a distinct 'nation within a nation' that, in some respects, was much like it had been for centuries. Its economy was in the hands of a long-established and mainly English-Canadian capitalist elite, who limited the opportunities for French Quebecers to control, or to benefit from, their province's material resources. Even more importantly, perhaps, Quebec was dominated in most other spheres of existence by the Catholic Church, which, in conjunction with a long line of like-minded French-Canadian provincial political leaders, continued to foster a conservative and collectivist way of life that was significantly at odds with the modernizing, secularizing, and liberalizing forces that were shaping English Canada and much of the United States (Rioux 1971; Milner and Milner 1973; Dion 1976; Morris and Lanphier 1977; Garreau 1981; Fournier, Rosenberg, and White 1997; Chadwick et al. 1994; Baum 2000).

For the most part, this 'old' Quebec now stands in stark contrast to the 'new' Quebec that emerged after the 1960s. Although Quebec still remains quite distinct in a number of crucial ways, it has clearly come to resemble the other three sub-societies in several other respects. This is largely because Quebec was eventually subject to many of the same forces for change that English Canada and the United States experienced in earlier decades. To name just a few, these forces included: higher levels of economic growth and development, which helped to promote a general rise in living standards and material well-being; significant demographic changes, especially a decline in fertility rates and family size, which spurred advances in such areas as women's labour-force participation and gender equality; and a revamped and modernized educational system, which enhanced the skill levels and occupational opportunities of many Quebecers, and also promoted changes in the social and moral outlooks of the wider population (Guindon 1978, 1988; Grabb 1982; Grabb and Poole 1988; Beaujot 1991, 2000; McRoberts 1993; Chadwick et al. 1994; Latouche 1995; Trent, Young, and Lachapelle 1995; Young 1995; Fournier, Rosenberg, and White 1997; Breton 1998; DePalma 2001: Chapter 13; Langlois 2003).

Nevertheless, while Quebec's transformation has been similar to that which occurred elsewhere in North America, there is no doubt that the process also differed in some key ways. It seems likely, first of all, that Quebec had greater obstacles to overcome, given the conservative and authoritarian religious and political institutions of the old regime. There is also the French language and cultural heritage, which clearly distinguished Quebec from the three English sub-societies in important ways, and probably slowed French Canada's adaptation to or adoption of important social, political, and economic changes happening elsewhere on the continent. Perhaps the most important difference, however, is that Quebec's transformation came after a much longer 'premodern' period than was experienced in other regions, specifically in English Canada and the northern United States. Therefore, the changes in Quebec took place in a significantly shorter time frame, spanning less than 50 years. For these reasons, Quebec's transition, in many ways, has been the most rapid and fundamental of all the four regions. Quebec's process of development seems particularly remarkable when compared with that of the American South, which during the same 50-year period did not witness such dramatic alterations to its traditional culture and social institutions. This difference is illustrated in our finding that the people of the southern United States have sustained a consistently strong and relatively unquestioning commitment to conservative Christian teachings up to the present time, whereas the adherence of contemporary Quebecers to their old Catholic heritage has become more contingent and conditional.

Another distinctive feature of Quebec's transformation during the latter half of the twentieth century has been its increasing affinity with recent political, cultural, social, and intellectual influences originating from outside North America. The most important of these connections has been with western Europe, especially France. As we discuss later in Part III, these influences are consistent with Quebec's adoption in recent decades of economic and political policies that are more left-leaning or social democratic than those found in the rest of North America (see, e.g., Lemel and Modell 1994: 33–8; Forse and Langlois 1994: 269–301).

These considerations lead us back to the two questions posed earlier: Given its traditional Catholic roots, how did Quebec come to be the most morally liberal sub-society in North America? And how is it possible for Quebecers to hold such views about family values and sexuality, and yet retain a relatively close, if sometimes ambivalent, connection to their religious identity? We suggest that a significant part of the answer to both of these questions can be found in a point touched on earlier. Previously, we speculated that the religiosity that many present-day Quebecers still express and espouse may have more to do with cultural symbols than with religion per se. That is, because of recent historical events and the notable changes in their society since the 1960s, it is possible that Quebecers have rejected many of the formal restrictions that were imposed upon them in the past by official Catholic doctrines or precepts, while at the same time choosing to preserve some allegiance to their religion, as an element of their cherished French-Canadian cultural, linguistic, and ethnic heritage (see also Martin 2000: 25).

Such an interpretation is similar to a view that has been expressed about contemporary Jews in both the United States and Canada. According to this argument, the liberalizing influences that stem from living in an industrialized democratic society, and from being a highly urbanized and educated people, have caused some Jews in North America to abandon or to play down many of the more rigorous strictures of traditional Judaism. Although there is considerable debate over just how widespread this 'secularist' (Freedman 2000: 23, 338–9; Dershowitz 1997: 180, 324–6) or 'non-religious' (Weinfeld 2001: 3, 310) form of Judaism has become, its existence illustrates how, for some people, affiliation with a particular faith can be more a matter of cultural identity or ethnic background than of religion itself.

It is arguable that a parallel process has also taken place for many French Catholics in Quebec, and probably to greater effect (see Gagnon 2003a). Indeed, a case can be made that this shift, from a place that was steeped in traditional family values and sexual conservatism, to one that now fosters the most liberal moral attitudes and behaviours in North America, is part of a more general pattern of fundamental change in Quebec society. If we imagine this shift as something like the swing of a pendulum, it is as if, in Quebec's rush to find its place among the modern nations of the world, its transformation has been so pronounced and far-reaching that it has gone beyond English Canada and the United States. Thus, it has been suggested that Quebec has become, in some ways, not just the most modern region, but in fact the most 'post-modern' sub-society in either country (see Adams 2003: 82, 87–8). We explore this argument further in the concluding chapter of this volume.

CRIME AND THE LAW

We have compared Canadian and American attitudes regarding various marital practices, family values, and sexual preferences, or what is commonly referred to as 'morality'. However, for many social theorists, the idea of morality is a more general concept, subsuming not just marital, familial, or sexual mores, but all of the rules and norms that serve as guides for human conduct in social settings (e.g., Durkheim 1893: 51, 65, 107–10, 135). From this perspective, then, a major component of the morality of any nation is its system of formal laws.

In this section of Chapter 7, we look at morality in Canada and the United States in the broader sense noted above, and consider evidence in the areas of crime and the law. Because, in theory, all democratically constituted countries place a paramount emphasis on the universal rule of law within their borders, we might expect that both Canadians and Americans would be strongly committed to obeying the statutes and regulations devised for them by their appointed or elected lawmakers and government representatives. However, while there is no question that most citizens in the two countries are, in fact, law-abiding, it is also true that some people in each society are quite prepared to deviate from the law and to engage in various types of criminal behaviour.

A considerable body of research has been conducted on crime and the law in both countries (e.g., Hagan 1989a, 1989b, 1991, 1994; Lenton 1989a, 1989b; Gartner 1990; Zimring and Hawkins 1997; Roberts and Stalans 1997; Ouimet 1999; Maxim and Whitehead 1998; LaFree 1999). Some analysts have found evidence in this research that, in their interpretation, demonstrates deep-seated differences in the values and core principles shaping Canada and the

United States. Probably the most influential of the writers to draw such a conclusion is Lipset, whose theory of 'revolution and counterrevolution', of course, was one of the major perspectives that we assessed in Part I. As we saw then, one of Lipset's main contentions is that, beginning with the era of the American Revolution, the United States developed a unique set of founding principles known as the American Creed. Central to this Creed is the belief in a particular form of liberty or liberalism that, in contrast to the Lockian conceptions of Hartz and others, favours a relatively unrestricted commitment to individual freedom. According to Lipset, this has important implications for differentiating both the systems of justice and the patterns of crime in Canada and the United States.

Comparing Justice Systems

Lipset contends that the American belief in largely unbridled liberty has promoted a justice system that, in key respects, differs from that found in Canada and elsewhere. In particular, in contrast to Canada's legal structure, which is said to place primary emphasis on crime control and keeping social order, the American system stresses, above all, the civil liberties and citizenship rights of the individual. It is suggested that protecting these freedoms for everyone, 'including those accused of crime and political dissidents', is so important that Americans would rather let the guilty escape punishment than risk putting an innocent person behind bars (Lipset 1985: 129; see also Lipset 1968: 128–9).

Some analyses of the justice systems of the two countries do indicate that the American and Canadian legal structures have differed along these lines, with the Canadian system putting somewhat greater emphasis on maintaining law and order, as opposed to protecting the civil liberties of the accused (see, e.g., Hagan and Leon 1977; Hagan 1991). Even so, it is clear that, beginning with the early histories of both countries, there have always been substantial affinities between the two systems. As we discussed in Part I, several of the fundamental similarities, including the use of trial by jury, the appointment or election of independent judges, the application of strict rules governing the admissibility of evidence, and so on, can be traced to the shared influence of English Common Law on both legal structures. In addition, there are numerous historical examples of Canadian legal practices that have been derived from American precedents, suggesting again that the systems are in many ways 'remarkably similar' (Bothwell 1992: 287). It is important to be aware, as well, that many of the differences between the systems identified by Lipset and others in earlier studies have dissipated significantly since the institution of the Canadian Charter of Rights and Freedoms in 1982. Hence, for the period covering the 1980s and 1990s, studies of litigation patterns, judicial structures, and the role of the courts in shaping government policy have shown numerous areas of convergence, along with some continuing differences (Kritzer, Vidmar, and Bogart 1991a, 1991b; Cross 1992; Kerans 2000; Manfredi 1997, 2000).

One major difference in the two justice systems is the level of incarceration of convicted criminals. The United States far exceeds other industrialized nations in this respect, with 645 prisoners per 100,000 population as of 1998. Canada's level of 125 per 100,000 is above the median, but is considerably lower than the American level (Roberts et al. 2003: 16; see also Lipset 1996: 46–7; Zimring and Hawkins 1997: 31). On the whole, however, the evidence suggests that, although national differences in legal structures still remain, there is also little doubt, as Lipset himself has observed, that the Canadian justice system has taken major steps to 'Americanize itself', and now bears a relatively close resemblance to that of the United States (Lipset 1990: 225; see also Simpson 2000: 343–6).

Crime in Canada and the United States

When discussing crime in Canada and the United States, Lipset also sees fundamental divergences between the two nations and their populations. Here, as well, he attributes these differences to the distinctively American commitment to personal liberty. While Lipset consistently portrays Canadians as a people who are obedient and respectful toward legal and political authority, he asserts that Americans, because of their unsurpassed love of liberty, distrust any attempt by the state to limit their freedoms. This proclivity is so pronounced that Americans often show a 'lack of respect', even a 'contempt', for the law and its officers (Lipset 1963a: 525–6; 1963b: 307). This makes them different from Canadians, in being more 'willing to tolerate lawlessness', more likely to condone the criminal activity of others, and more apt to break the law themselves (Lipset 1963a: 525–6, 528; see also 1990: 10, 94; 1996: 21, 26, 46, 269–70).

Evidence on Violent versus Non-violent Crimes

It is widely assumed, by both Americans and Canadians, that the United States is a much more crime-ridden society than its northern neighbour. Thus, it may come as a surprise to learn that, on the whole, this presumed difference has been greatly exaggerated. In fact, for some crimes, no such difference exists. It is important, first of all, to make a distinction between violent and non-violent crimes. If we focus on extremely violent offences, particularly homicide, then there is consistent evidence that crime is a more serious problem in the United States than it is in Canada. American homicide rates have been between three and four times higher than Canadian rates for many decades. As an illustration, in 1992 the American rate was 9.3 per 100,000 people in the population, compared with 2.6 in Canada (Ouimet 1999: 399;

see also Zimring and Hawkins 1997: 55; Fedorowycz 1995: 4). By 2001, the American level was still more than three times the Canadian level, although the gap had declined somewhat, and the rates themselves had fallen substantially in both nations, to about 5.6 and 1.8, respectively (Dauvergne 2002: 3).

The recent decline in homicide is important to emphasize, for, as some researchers have found (e.g., Roberts and Stalans 1997: 26–9; Simpson 2000: 109), many people have the mistaken impression, especially from the mass media, that the American homicide rate is not only very high, but also has steadily escalated with time. In fact, the homicide rate in the United States has fluctuated widely over the years. One study has shown that the rate rose from about 1 per 100,000 people in the American population in 1900, to almost 10 per 100,000 in the 1930s, before dropping to approximately 5 per 100,000 in the 1950s and 1960s (Zimring and Hawkins 1997: 57). The common belief today that murder is increasingly rampant in the United States appears to stem mainly from the considerable rise in homicide figures between the 1960s and 1980s. Since then, as described above, the American rate has fallen significantly, and now matches the level of 50 years ago (see also Hagan 1989a: 363–4; 1994: 22–3; Gartner 1990: 99; Zimring and Hawkins 1997: 8; Roberts and Stalans 1997: 26–30; Simpson 2000: 110–11).

Another question to raise about homicide rates is whether they are the best barometers for judging the level of criminality in different societies. Consider the following evidence. There were 554 homicides in Canada in 2001, representing less than 3/100 of one percent of Canada's more than 2.4 million criminal code violations in that year (Savoie 2002: 16). As noted previously, the American homicide rate in 2001 was roughly three times the Canadian level. This means that homicide in the United States accounted for about three times as much crime as it did in Canada for the same year, or approximately 9/100 of one percent of the American total. What this demonstrates is that, in both countries, homicide is an exceptionally rare event, and thus is only a tiny part of the overall crime picture. As a result, the homicide rate is a very poor indicator for determining if there is a difference in the general level of criminality, or in what might be called the 'culture of lawlessness', in the two societies.

Broadening the analysis to include other types of violent crime provides a somewhat better comparison. As with homicide, the rates for other forms of violent crime generally have been declining in both countries since the early 1990s (Simpson 2000: 109, 286; see also US Department of Justice 2002: 66). Nevertheless, it is true that throughout this period the rates for the most serious types of violent crime have been higher in the United States than in Canada. Thus, by 2000, for example, the combined rate for homicide, aggravated assault, and robbery in the United States was 474 incidents per 100,000, as opposed to just 233 in Canada (Gannon 2001: 2; see also Tremblay 1999;

Simpson 2000: 110–11; Dobrin et al. 1996; Ouimet 1999: 399–401; Savoie 2002). However, research also shows that, if we look beyond the extreme or so-called 'lethal' violent crimes, and consider instead the far more numerous and less serious violent offences, such as simple assault, then the American rates are no higher, and in some cases are actually lower, than those reported in Canada, Australia, New Zealand, and elsewhere. (Zimring and Hawkins 1997: 37–9). Consequently, while it is clear that, compared with Canada, American society has more difficulties with extreme forms of violence, much of which stems from the greater availability of firearms in the United States (Zimring and Hawkins 1997; Ouimet 1999), it would be incorrect to conclude that Americans uniformly experience more violent crime. Instead, national differences in violent crime appear to be largely restricted to the rarest and most serious offences. This is not to deny the horrific nature of lethal violent crimes. Neither do we mean to suggest that such egregious incidents do not have a stronger impact than other illegal activities in shaping both the popular consciousness and the perceptions that people have about the United States relative to other countries. Nevertheless, such considerations do underscore the importance of not drawing conclusions about an entire society solely on the basis of very specific, quite rare, and in many ways unrepresentative criminal events (see also Simpson 2000: 95, 136).

If we turn to the research on non-violent crimes, which account for the vast majority of all the criminal cases arising in both countries (Roberts and Stalans 1997: 33; Savoie 2002), it becomes even clearer that the image of the United States as a more lawless place than Canada is overstated, and for some crimes is simply wrong. As an example, for both the early 1990s and more recent years, the rates for non-violent crimes such as burglary and motor-vehicle theft were actually higher in Canada than in the United States (Simpson 2000: 111; see also Ouimet 1999: 399–401). By 2000, the rate per 100,000 for burglary was 954 in Canada and 728 in the United States, while the rate for motor-vehicle theft in the same year was 521 in Canada and 414 in the United States (Gannon 2001: 8; see also Canadian Press 2003a: A2). This pattern does not appear to hold for every type of non-violent crime, since arrest rates for such offences as impaired driving, prostitution, and some drug violations are generally higher in the United States; however, some researchers suggest that 'statistics for these crimes reflect as much the level of police enforcement as the actual behavioural patterns' (Gannon 2001: 9–11). In other words, as exemplified in the recent Canadian government decision to decriminalize such crimes as marijuana possession (see, e.g., Tibbetts 2002; Rodgers 2003; Westhues 2003: 12–13), Canada's justice system has been less stringent in both policing and prosecuting such activities and, partly for that reason, Canada has lower official crime rates for some non-violent offences than does the United States.

There are a number of other methodological issues to take into account when comparing official crime statistics in the two countries. For example, on the one hand, the United States for some time has had more police officers per capita than does Canada (see, e.g., Lipset 1990: 101). This difference could contribute to greater police surveillance in American society and, consequently, to proportionally more arrests and higher official crime rates in the United States. On the other hand, other differences, such as the possibility that Canadians are more likely than Americans to be confident in the police and legal system (see, e.g., Baer et al. 1995: 184–8) and so are more apt to report crimes than are Americans, could lead to higher official rates for some crimes in Canada than would otherwise be the case.

Studies of victimization provide additional support for the conclusion that, except for the most extreme cases, crime levels in the two nations are generally quite similar. Several studies covering the period from the late 1980s to the mid-1990s have found that victimization rates in Canada and the United States are typically very much alike, even for some violent offences (Simpson 2000: 110; Zimring and Hawkins 1997: 35–7; Ouimet 1999: 390; Maxim and Whitehead 1998: 104). More recent results from the 2000 International Crime Survey reveal essentially the same patterns (Besserer 2002). In that year, Canada actually had somewhat higher overall victimization levels than the United States, with 24 per cent of Canadian respondents reporting at least one incident, compared with 21 per cent for the Americans. As might be expected, respondents in the United States were more likely to report being victims of violent crime, although even here the levels were close, at 7 per cent for Americans and 5 per cent for Canadians (Besserer 2002: 13).

Another consideration regarding violent crime is that, in proportional terms, American victims are far more likely to be black than to be white. For example, the homicide rate in the United States, both in the early 1990s and in 2001, was about half as large when cases involving blacks were excluded from the calculation (Zimring and Hawkins 1997: 80; US Department of Justice 2002: 20, 22). This suggests that the Canadian and American rates of violent victimization are even more similar when we restrict the comparison to the white populations in both nations (see also Simpson 2000: 111).

It should also be noted that, on the whole, Canada is closer to the United States in its total violent crime rate than are other developed societies, such as Japan and most of western Europe (Zimring and Hawkins 1997: 8, 53; Simpson 2000: 95). In general, then, the findings do not support the notion that the actual experience of crime is sufficiently dissimilar in the two nations to demonstrate deep-structural differences in the two people's commitments to the rule of law. On the contrary, for the most part, both populations appear to share a pronounced 'culture of lawfulness' in their everyday lives.

Regional Variations: The Violent South and Peaceable Quebec?
We now have a sense of the overall levels of criminality in Canada and the United States. However, we have yet to consider regional variations in crime rates within the two populations. There is sufficient evidence available to arrive at a reasonably complete picture of how the four sub-societies vary when it comes to criminal activity. Generally speaking, the available research suggests a regional rank-ordering for crime that parallels that which we found for sexual and moral conservatism. That is, with a few exceptions, the data suggest that the American South tends to experience the highest levels of criminal behaviour, followed by the rest of the United States, English Canada, and lastly Quebec.

There is no question, first of all, that the southern United States has the highest violent crime rates of all the four sub-societies. This has long been true for homicide (Dobrin et al. 1996: Chapter 1; Nisbett and Cohen 1996: 16; Ouimet 1999: 401), although research indicates that, for some other violent offences, the western United States (which we subsume under the 'American North' in our formulation) once had rates that matched or surpassed those in the American South. By the mid-1990s, however, the South led the rest of the United States for these other violent crimes, as well (Dobrin et al. 1996: 47, 105, 118). As of 2001, the American South's top ranking was even more apparent. In that year, the southern homicide rate was 6.7 per 100,000, or about 20 per cent higher than the overall American average of 5.6. For all violent crimes combined, the South again led all other regions, at 580 per 100,000 compared with 504 for the United States as a whole (US Department of Justice 2002: 66–73). A number of writers have commented on the high rates of violent behaviour in the South, both historically and in the present day. Although some observers dispute the claim (Wilensky 2002: 516–18), several researchers attribute this pattern in part to the 'culture of honour' that was integral to the quasi-feudal way of life of the pre-Civil-War era (Nisbett 1993; Nisbett and Cohen 1996; see also Franklin 1956; Hackney 1969; Cash 1941: 42–3, 73–4; Gastil 1975: 97–116; Fischer 1989: 889–92).[6]

---

6. The practice of duelling to protect a person's reputation from slights or insults can be seen as one prominent illustration of this culture of honour, and is said to be part of a more general tendency for southerners to settle disputes on their own rather than through the police or the courts. Another point to consider is that the only violent offence for which the South does not typically rank first in the United States is forcible rape, which has been somewhat higher in the western and mid-western regions over the years (US Department of Justice 2002: 66–73). This finding of relatively less violence toward women in the South, notwithstanding the significantly greater violence among men in that region, may also be attributable to the lingering sense of honour in the southern states (see, e.g., Nisbett and Cohen 1996; McWhiney 1988).

In any event, today the South surpasses all other American regions, not only with respect to levels of violent crime, but also when it comes to non-violent offences. For example, the South's rate for all property crimes in 2001 was 4,181 per 100,000, compared with the national rate of 3,656. The US West ranked second in total property crime in 2001, with a rate of 3,835 (US Department of Justice 2002: 66–73). One other factor that complicates America's regional crime picture is the role of large urban centres. Some large cities in the northern and western states, such as Los Angeles, Detroit, New York, and Philadelphia, have experienced higher violent crime rates than some of the larger cities in the American South (Gannon 2001: 9). Overall, however, the South generally exhibits higher crime rates than the rest of the United States, whether or not large cities are included in the calculations (Ouimet 1999: 401; see also Dobrin et al. 1996: 18).

While the American South occupies one extreme when comparing crime rates in the four sub-societies, Quebec occupies the opposite pole. There are some exceptions to this general assertion. In particular, data from 2001 (Savoie 2002: 16) reveal that Quebec's homicide rate is 1.9 per 100,000, or a little above the Canadian average of 1.8 for that year. Nevertheless, the same data source shows that, for all violent crimes combined, Quebec has the lowest rate of all the Canadian provinces, at 719 incidents per 100,000, compared with 994 for Canada as a whole. The next lowest violent crime rate is for Prince Edward Island, at 746. In addition, for all criminal code violations, which combine the total for violent and non-violent crimes, Quebec has lower rates than every other province except Newfoundland. Therefore, while there is some variation in crime levels among the nine provinces that form our English Canada sub-group, Quebec clearly has lower crimes rates than does English Canada generally, and thus ranks lowest in crime among the four sub-societies in our analysis. Consequently, although Canada has sometimes been dubbed the 'peaceable kingdom' by some commentators (see, e.g., Kilbourn 1970; Simpson 2000: 95), it appears that Quebec generally has a stronger claim to this title than does English Canada.

As for English Canada's standing relative to the two American sub-societies, it ranks below the American South for all types of crime, and is also lower than the American North for violent crime. However, while there is considerable internal variation in both English Canada and the American North, these two sub-societies are very similar when comparing their overall rates for non-violent offences. Although we do not conduct a detailed comparison of English Canadians and northern Americans, the data on total property crimes provide a good illustration of the similarities between these two regional populations when it comes to non-violent offences. In 2001, the property crime rates for the English-Canadian provinces varied from a low of 2,284 per 100,000 in Newfoundland to a high of 6,451 in British Columbia (Savoie 2002: 16). In the United States, excluding the South, the rates for total property crimes ranged from a low of 2,577 per 100,000 in the 'Northeast' region to a high of 3,835 in the 'West' region (US Department of Justice 2002: 66–73).

Attitudes about Crime

Before concluding our analysis of crime and the law in Canada and the United States, it is important that we briefly consider research on people's attitudes about crime in the two nations. This comparison will provide us with some sense of whether there are important differences in the general perception or consciousness of Canadians and Americans regarding the problem of crime in their respective societies. Is it the case, for example, that Americans are more accepting of or more used to criminal activity in their lives, as writers such as Lipset would have us believe (see also Adams 2003: 52–3)?

First of all, recent studies indicate that fear of crime is generally higher among Americans than among Canadians (e.g., Hung and Bowles 1995: 7; Besserer 2002: 8, 15). This is probably to be expected, given the greater prevalence of serious violent crimes in the United States, as well as their widespread and often sensational exposure by the American media, or by what some have called 'Crime Time News' (Simpson 2000: 109; Roberts and Stalans 1997: 3–5). Perhaps for the same reason, there is also a somewhat greater tendency for Americans to favour harsher treatment of criminals by the justice system; however, it is notable that, on this issue, the differences between Americans and Canadians are often small, and at times are not statistically significant. Survey data covering the last three decades or more show that a clear majority of respondents in both nations believe that the justice system is too lenient with criminals (e.g., Grabb and Curtis 1988: 133; Baer, Grabb, and Johnston 1990b: 701–2; Perlin 1997: 116–17; Besserer 2002: 16–17; Roberts et al. 2003: 27–9). It is clear that, at present, Americans are significantly more in favour than Canadians of invoking the death penalty for convicted murderers than are Canadians, although this was not always the case. Support for the death penalty was almost identical in the two countries throughout the 1980s, and at times was slightly higher in Canada. In general, about two-thirds of both Canadians and Americans favoured capital punishment during this period (Perlin 1997: 117). More recently, however, support has declined to a slim majority in Canada, while still standing at about 65 per cent in the United States, as of 2001 (Gallup 2001e; Mazzuca 2002c: 51–2).

When looking at regional differences in attitudes about crime, we might expect that southern Americans, because of the higher violent and non-violent

Table 7.3   Attitudes on the Acceptability of Economic Crimes by Region and Nation

	Region					Nation		
	English Canada	Quebec	US North	US South	Sig¹	Canada Total	US Total	Sig¹
Ratings of the acceptability of the following on a 10 pt. scale:[a]								
1. Claiming government benefits you are not entitled to	1.89	1.91	2.00	2.08*		1.90	2.03	√
2. Avoiding a fare on public transport	2.24	1.86*	2.21	2.31	√	2.15	2.24	
3. Cheating on tax if you have the chance	2.39	2.44	2.04*	1.94*	√	2.40	2.01	√
4. Buying something you know is stolen	1.84	1.70	1.73	1.61*	√	1.81	1.69	√
Economic Crimes Index (responses to the 4 items summed and divided by 4):	2.08	1.97	1.98	1.98		2.05	1.98	

Notes

¹ A check mark (√) indicates that the likelihood ratio chi-square for the overall four-category comparison across regions, or the two-category comparison across nations, is significant at <.05. The asterisk (*) indicates that the category is significantly different from the English Canadian reference group at <.05.

[a] The scale ranged from 1 = 'never justified' to 10 = 'always justified'.

crime rates in their region, would take the hardest line on the treatment of criminals by the justice system. Following the same argument, it seems plausible that Quebecers, with their low crime rates, would have the most relaxed or lenient views on the punishment of criminals, with English Canadians and northern Americans presumably falling somewhere in between the other two sub-groups. Although there are some exceptions, this pattern does seem to emerge in most recent research.

For example, based on data from the 1990s, one study for the United States found that southerners were consistently more likely than northerners to favour the use of deadly force by the police against criminal perpetrators. This study also showed that southerners were clearly more likely than other Americans to believe that citizens themselves should have the right to punish criminals for purposes of self-defence, and also for protecting their families and personal property (Nisbett and Cohen 1996: 26–30). Other research suggests that southerners are somewhat more supportive than other Americans of 'vigilantism' or 'taking the law into one's own hands' (Zimring 2003: 118, 234–5). Some opinion polls indicate, as well, that support for the death penalty is highest in the American South, although this is not always the case, with patterns varying considerably depending on the wording of the question (Dobrin et al. 1996: 324, 330, 334; Zimring 2003: 229; Jones 2003b: 103). In contrast, present-day Quebecers, along with their political leaders and judicial system in most cases, tend to take the most liberal positions on a range of criminal justice issues. For example, recent Gallup poll data for Canada show that respondents from Quebec are the least likely to agree with the assertion that the federal government is not harsh enough in its treatment of criminals (Gallup 2000b: 3). In addition, although most Quebecers do favour stronger sanctions for young offenders than in the past, they are still the least likely of all Canadians to hold such views (Gallup 2000a: 2–3). Quebecers also show the lowest support in the country for the idea that possession of small amounts of marijuana should be a criminal offense (Gallup 2001b: 2). Finally, except for respondents from the Atlantic provinces, Quebecers are the least in favour of reinstating the death penalty in Canada (Gallup 2001e: 2).

The World Values Surveys provide us with some additional data that can be used to compare attitudes about criminal behaviour in Canada and the United States. In fact, we have already considered two relevant measures from the WVS. These are the items in Table 7.2 that ask respondents to judge the extent to which both prostitution and having sex under the legal age of consent are acceptable behaviours. We saw previously that Canadians were somewhat more likely than Americans to find both of these illegal acts acceptable. We also found that, in judging these activities, Quebecers were the most accepting among all the four sub-groups, followed by English Canadians, northern Americans, and southern Americans. These results are consistent with the general pattern that we have observed to this stage, which is that Quebecers are the most liberal or lenient in their views on criminal behaviour, while Americans from the southern states are the most harsh or restrictive.

Table 7.3 compares Canadian and American attitudes about the acceptability of four additional illegal activities. These items, however, deal with crimes that are economic rather than moral or sexual in nature. The four illegal acts include: claiming undeserved government benefits, avoiding paying a fare on public transport, cheating on the payment of taxes, and buying stolen goods. The results using these four measures suggest much weaker differences than those found for the two sexual offences considered in Table 7.2. Perhaps the most significant finding in Table 7.3 is the low level of acceptability that all respondents express for these four crimes. People in both countries, and in each of the four sub-societies, largely reject these activities, with levels of acceptability usually in the range of 2.0 or less, on a scale from 1 to 10. Moreover, the few statistically significant national or regional differences that show up in the table indicate no consistent pattern. For example, there is a slightly greater tendency for Americans, especially in the South, to say that claiming undeserved government benefits is acceptable. On the other hand, Canadians are marginally more likely than Americans to find cheating on taxes justifiable. In general, however, the differences are so minuscule that, when the responses for the four crimes are summed into a composite index, there are no statistically significant differences for any of the comparisons.

Overall, then, the findings in both Table 7.3 and Table 7.2 suggest that, contrary to the claims of some writers, Americans are not very different from Canadians when deciding whether it is ever appropriate to show disregard or contempt for the law. Where there are differences, specifically in the case of the two moral or sexual offences that we have considered, it is Canadians, not Americans, who find these crimes relatively more acceptable. Thus, while some of the evidence we have reviewed suggests that Americans, especially in the South, are a bit more likely than Canadians, particularly those from Quebec, to be tough on crime, this should not be seen as proof that there are parallel national or regional differences regarding whether or not criminal activity should be engaged in or condoned by the respondents themselves. On the contrary, both Canadians and Americans, and all of the four regional sub-groups, seem to share a strong preference for the rule of law. Even the patterns for the two items dealing with prostitution and under-age sex may well say more about national and regional differences in family values or sexual mores than about differences in attitudes about crime per se.

SUMMARY

To summarize, in this chapter, we have examined the general topic of morality in Canada and the United States, with specific reference to religion and religiosity, family and sexual values, and problems of crime and the law. Overall, the research we have presented reveals that, on the whole, Americans are more traditional or conservative than are Canadians, as judged by their higher levels of religious involvement and commitment, and by their more restrictive views about family life and sexual mores. In addition, although we have found numerous similarities in the two nations' legal systems and in their rates for several types of crime, Americans also appear to have a somewhat greater concern than Canadians with controlling crime and maintaining law and order. Nevertheless, the latter difference is often marginal. In fact, for the large majority of the comparisons that we have conducted in this chapter, the differences are too small to suggest fundamental cleavages between the two countries or their peoples. Instead, with few exceptions, the most important and consistent differences lie, not between the two nations, but in the pronounced splits that we have frequently seen within the two societies. Briefly stated, these internal divisions involve a distinctively more liberal Quebec within Canada and a demonstrably more conservative southern region of the United States. The remaining two sub-societies, i.e., the northern United States and English Canada, tend to stand in between the other two on this conservative–liberal 'morality continuum'. On some of the measures that we have considered, these two sub-populations are quite close to one another, although there is little doubt as well that, to a lesser degree, northern Americans share some of the more traditional or conservative proclivities of their southern compatriots, while English Canadians, also to a lesser degree, have some of the more liberal or permissive tendencies of their fellow citizens in Quebec. In the next chapter, we consider whether a parallel pattern can be discerned when comparing the two nations and the four regions with respect to the general issue of individualism versus collectivism.

CHAPTER 8

꿍

INDIVIDUALISM, COLLECTIVISM, AND THE STATE

One of the pivotal ideas that has informed most of the comparative work on Canada and the United States over the years is the concept of individualism. We have already seen ample evidence of this focus on individualism in Part I of this volume. There we found that virtually all of the leading theorists who have sought to understand or explain the development of the two nations have paid considerable attention to the relative commitment of Canadians and Americans to individualist values and ideals. To varying degrees, the analyses provided by almost all of these writers, from Hartz, McRae, and Horowitz, to Montesquieu, Tocqueville, Churchill, and Dahrendorf, have suggested that the English-speaking peoples of both nations have the same deeply held and long-standing allegiance to individualist principles, as judged by their strong beliefs in such ideas as individual liberty, popular sovereignty, personal freedom of choice, and the equality of all citizens under the law. The one major writer that has taken a different position on this issue is Lipset. As discussed in Part I, Lipset's argument is that a form of self-focused individualism was an important founding principle in the United States. However, he contends that neither this nor any other type of individualism was a force shaping Canadian society during its formative years. Instead, in his view, Canada has always been marked by its prolonged connection to the British Empire and, as a result, has forever been guided by a set of Tory values and institutions that are clearly more collectivist, statist, hierarchical, and elitist than those of its southern neighbour.

In our review and assessment of historical evidence in Part II, we saw that several of these claims about the role of individualism in early North America were significantly overstated. In fact, some arguments, most notably that provided by Lipset, received little or no support. Contrary to the views of many analysts, we found that individualism, at least in the present-day sense of the term, was not embraced by most people living in either society during these early stages. Instead, both populations were similarly influenced by small-town collectivism and local-communalist orientations and beliefs. We did see consistent evidence of a commitment to individual economic independence and self-reliance among Americans and English Canadians in these early times, as well as some signs of what we have called a 'separate but equal' form of pluralism, or the acceptance of the right to be different, regarding such issues as religious preference. This pattern carried on until the latter half of the nineteenth century and beyond. It was only after that time that a broadly Lockian-inspired form of individualism, involving a belief in personal liberty tempered by the recognition of the rights of others, seems to have become the predominant orientation in both the United States and English Canada. As for French Canada, we found that most of the observers whom we reviewed were correct in concluding that the emphasis on collectivism was probably even stronger in Quebec than was the case elsewhere in the two nations. Moreover, as touched on previously in Chapter 7, Quebec appears to have remained a collectivist, hierarchical, and authoritarian society until the important changes that occurred in the latter half of the twentieth century.

Nevertheless, in spite of the substantial historical evidence to the contrary, the assumption still continues among some contemporary commentators that Americans have always been an exceptionally individualistic and self-focused people, while Canadians, despite becoming more individualistic over time, continue to retain more collectivist or communalist values and attitudes than do Americans (e.g., Presthus 1977a: 8–9; Lipset 1990: 38, 110–13; 1996: 261, 267–8; for some discussion, see Truman 1971; Crawford and Curtis 1979; Ferguson 1997: Chapter 11; Adams 2003: Chapter 4). In Chapter 8, we consider several sources of evidence bearing on the general issue of individualism and collectivism in Canada and the United States. Because a central question in this discussion is whether the state should play a prominent part in providing for the needs of individuals in society, we begin by considering comparative data on government spending and other indicators of state activity in the two nations. We also look at data on national differences in economic inequality. One of the main purposes of this chapter, however, is to consider evidence on whether the Canadian people are more likely than Americans to favour or expect collective rather than personal solutions to the problems that they face in their daily existence, particularly through the assistance of government. We then look at whether there is support for the argument that Canadians in the present day are less likely than Americans to voice a belief in such values as individual self-reliance or independence. We also assess whether Canadians are less likely than Americans to exhibit feelings of self-confidence and assertiveness about their personal achievements. In addition to comparing the two countries on such issues, we consider possible differences among the four sub-societies. One question of special interest is whether Quebec's early and prolonged emphasis on hierarchy and collectivism in its major religious, political, and social institutions may have played a role in moving this sub-society in a different direction from the others in recent times. We examine the American South as another special case, and explore the possibility that, in part because of its unique past, the people of this region of the United States have adopted a complex and somewhat contradictory mixture of both collectivism and individualism in their core values and orientations to life.[1]

COLLECTIVISM AND THE ROLE OF THE STATE

At several points in previous chapters, we have considered the role of the state in Canada and the United States. One of our main concerns was the idea of statism, including the contention that Canadian society has long been char-acterized by more extensive government intervention than the United States, especially in offering social and economic aid to its citizens. This claim is the central component in the more general argument made by Lipset and others, which is that Canadians have always been a more collectivist and less individualist people than Americans, expecting and depending on outside assistance from government, rather than seeing the virtues of personal accountability, individual responsibility, and self-reliance (see also Lipset and Marks 2000: 266–9).

We found in Part II that these claims of greater Canadian statism received little support in the historical record. Rather than a long and unbroken history of state dependency and paternalism dating back to the time of the loyalists, the typical pattern in Canada was much the same as that found in the United States, with individuals and families essentially making their own way, fending for themselves without any substantial help from government. It was also determined that, while government now plays a more prominent role in Canada than in the United States, this is a relatively recent development, with most commentators concluding that this difference did not clearly arise until the 1940s or 1950s (recall, e.g., Thompson and Randall 1994: 177; Banting 1997: 282–3; Gwyn 1995: 18–19; Bothwell 1992: 289–92; Gibbins 1982: 14–15, 30–1; Pocklington 1985: 34–5, 264–5; Simpson 2000: 274–5).

---

1. For purposes of this analysis, the ideas of individualism and collectivism are generally treated as opposite ends of the same continuum. We should stress, however, that some researchers disagree on whether or not these two concepts should be understood in this way, since it may be possible to be individualist on some issues but collectivist on others (e.g., Triandis 1973; Triandis, McCusker, and Chui 1990; Schwartz and Bilsky 1990; Vandello and Cohen 1999).

Government Spending in Canada and the United States

If we look at evidence from the contemporary period, we do find support for the conclusion that state involvement is somewhat more pronounced in Canada than in the United States. One of the standard procedures used to judge the relative extent of this involvement is to calculate the amount of government expenditures on various social programs as a percentage of each nation's Gross Domestic Product (GDP), which refers to the value of all goods and services produced in the country in a given year. Applying this approach, one researcher has compared Canada and the United States, along with several other nations, with respect to the level of government spending on 'social protection' for their citizens. The idea of social protection in this context combines a number of state-funded benefits, including old-age pensions, disability pensions, unemployment insurance, and health care. This study, which covered the period from 1960 to 1990, found that Canadian state expenditures on social protection represented about 9.1 per cent of the nation's GDP in 1960, compared with about 7.3 per cent in the United States; by 1990, the gap had widened, with Canada spending 18.8 per cent and the United States 14.6 per cent (O'Connor 1998: 188; see also Card and Freeman 1993: 15–17; Banting 1997: 285–303; Reitz 1998: 206–15; Olsen 2002: 35). Further research has shown that, during this same period, Canada's government funding for education, as well as for such programs as parental or maternity leave, has also been proportionally higher than in the United States (O'Connor 1998: 195; O'Connor, Orloff, and Shaver 1999: 85; Blank and Hanratty 1993).

While the Canadian state is more involved than its American counterpart in providing overall social protection to the population, the pattern for health care by itself has changed significantly in recent years. Whereas in 1970, for example, the Canadian government spent about 5.0 per cent of GDP on health care, compared with only 2.7 per cent in the United States, by 1999, the difference had declined substantially, with the Canadian state spending 6.6 per cent of GDP, as opposed to 6.1 per cent for the United States. A more recent study based on 2001 data shows an even smaller gap, with figures of 7.0 per cent for Canada and 6.7 per cent for the United States (Kennedy and Gonzalez 2003: 4; see also Saunders 2004). None of the above figures includes private-health-care expenses, which are much larger in the US and which, when combined with government expenditures, make the total American health bill far higher than the Canadian health bill, at 13.7 per cent versus 9.5 per cent, as of 1999 (see O'Connor 1998:192; Evans 2000: 27; Statistical Abstract of the United States 2001: 837; Olsen 2002: 48). It is also notable that, in spite of the greater state contribution to health funding in Canada, evidence from 1997 shows that the average amount of health expenses that are not covered by either government or private insurance, and that consequently must be paid for by individual citizens out of their own pockets, stands at 17 per cent of the total in both nations (Evans 2000: 27). In other words, personal responsibility for paying the health bill appears, on average, to be about the same for Canadians as it is for Americans.

A different gauge for comparing the role of the state in each nation is to look at total government spending, not just for social protection and similar social services but for all state activities. Findings based on this measure also suggest higher government involvement in Canada than in the United States over the last several decades. For example, one analysis found that total government spending 'outlays' in Canada represented 40 per cent of GDP in 1978 and 42 per cent in 1998, compared with American figures of 31 per cent in 1978 and 33 per cent in 1998 (Perry 2000: 54–5; see also Calvert 1984: 17; Glatzer and Hauser 2003: 190). More recent data for 2001 show a slight decline in total government outlays since the 1990s for both countries, although Canada's state outlays were still higher, at 38 per cent of GDP versus 30 per cent for the United States (Kennedy and Gonzalez 2003: 2; see also Department of Finance 2002: 62; Adams 2003: 58). Similar differences are evident using other indicators, including the amount of tax revenues collected by government as a percentage of GDP (Perry 2000: 57; Department of Finance 2002: 64–5; see also Emes and Walker 1999: Chapter 8).

There clearly are some areas of state expenditure where the United States surpasses Canada. The obvious case is military and defence spending, which represents about 4.0 per cent of GDP in the United States, compared with only 1.2 per cent in Canada, as of 2001 (Kennedy and Gonzalez 2003: 4; see also CIA 2003; Thomas 2000: 389). In addition, American government expenditures tend to be proportionally higher for roads, environmental protection, agricultural subsidies, publicly financed research, and universities (Simpson 2000: 77–8). However, such spending is probably not relevant for gauging national differences in what is usually meant by statism, since, with few exceptions, these programs do not redistribute funds to disadvantaged groups or otherwise contribute to the social-welfare 'safety net'. In the case of taxation, most comparisons show that, although total taxation is higher in Canada, the differences are sometimes small, and occasionally are even reversed, depending on the income bracket that is being compared, and on the state, province, or municipality that is being considered (Simpson 2000: 160–71; Dakin 2003). In general, though, we can see that the contemporary Canadian state does provide more services to the public than its American counterpart, while also spending proportionally more of the national wealth and collecting proportionally more taxes from its citizens.

While the data reveal that, in recent decades, Canadians have experienced a more activist and proprietary government than have Americans, it is worth noting that Canada is not unusually statist, especially when we expand the comparison to include other nations. Such analyses reveal that Canada generally falls in the middle range among developed societies in regard to most indicators of state intervention or involvement. For example, data for 2001 from the Organization for Economic Cooperation and Development (OECD) indicate that, using total government outlays as a percentage of GDP, Canada was only slightly above the average for the 27 industrialized countries included in the comparison (OECD 2003: Annex Table 26). Moreover, when judged by rank-order, Canada was actually below the median, standing 18th out of the 27 nations (see also O'Connor 1998: 191; Glatzer and Hauser 2003: 190–1). Among the countries that ranked ahead of Canada on this measure were a number of relatively left-liberal or social-democratic European nations, including Sweden, Denmark, and Finland (see also Statistical Abstract of the United States 2001: 837, 846; Lipset and Marks 2000: 281). These comparisons explain why, for most researchers working in this area, the Canadian government's approach to social policy and social welfare is typically referred to as a 'liberal welfare regime', one that is closer to that of the United States than to the 'social democratic welfare regime' found in other nations (Olsen 2002: 70–5; Banting 1997: 309; O'Connor 1998: 180–7; 1999: 9–19; see also Esping-Andersen 1990; Reitz 1998: 206–15; Glatzer and Hauser 2003: 191).

Another means for assessing Canada's level of statism relative to the United States and other countries is the 'economic freedom' index, which is calculated annually by Canada's Fraser Institute. The countries that rank highest on the index have a combination of traits, including relatively low levels of government spending and taxation, as well as free market business practices and the legal protection of individual property rights under the rule of law. In 2001, out of 123 nations, the United States ranked third (after Hong Kong and Singapore), while Canada stood sixth (just behind New Zealand and Britain) (Perkel 2003). This is a further indication that, although it is somewhat more statist than the United States, Canada is very close to its American neighbour when considered in the larger international context.

Regional Differences in Collectivism and Statism: Quebec and the US South

We have determined that, by most standard indicators of government activity, Canada is a more statist society than is the United States. The next question that we should address, however, is whether there are variations within the two countries that complicate this basic national difference. In most of the analyses that have been presented in Part III so far, the internal variations involving the four constituent regions have been more substantial than the divergences between the two countries themselves. For the most part, we have also seen a strikingly consistent pattern, in which Quebec and the US South occupy opposite ends of whatever continuum we consider, with English Canada and the US North falling somewhere in between. It turns out that the evidence on the role of the state in the four sub-societies again suggests a similar ordering, with Quebec ranking as the most statist region in the two countries, the American South the least statist, and English Canada and the American North once more located in the middle.

State Intervention in Quebec

In Quebec, the clear emergence of statism can be traced to the 1960s and the period of the Quiet Revolution. Prior to this time, as was noted previously in Chapter 7, members of the provincial political elite, although enjoying considerable influence themselves, generally accommodated their policies and actions to the pre-eminent power of Quebec's religious leadership. Since the 1960s, however, Quebec has witnessed a pronounced shift away from what might be termed the 'hierarchical' collectivism embodied in the authoritarian institutions and conservative principles of the Catholic Church (see, e.g, Presthus 1973: 22–4). In its place, there has developed a system based on a more state-sponsored or 'egalitarian' collectivism, combining aspects of traditional Quebecois nationalism with social-democratic economic principles. It has been suggested that the Quebec people's long familiarity with the old collectivism centred in the Catholic Church helped to ease the way for their acceptance of this new egalitarian collectivism centred in the state (Christian and Campbell 1983: 36; see also Lipset 1990: 147–8; 1996: 93–4). Some writers have argued, in fact, that this shift was eventually encouraged by the Catholic Church itself, which in more recent years has come to embrace the 'modern values of democracy' and to support government policies to promote more social welfare and 'social justice' for the Quebec population (Seljak 2000: 145; see also Baum 2000).

This more statist system has also been nurtured by a series of activist Quebec governments, especially those led by the Parti Quebecois (PQ), which headed the province for most of the last 25 years of the twentieth century. The PQ's political agenda has concentrated mainly on promoting Quebec's status as a distinct national collective. This goal has been pursued through regulations to ensure that French is the only official language in the society, through the expansion of provincial cultural and social institutions designed to be wholly separate from those of the federal government, and through repeated efforts to establish Quebec as an independent country. However, in addition to mobilizing state power for these nationalist purposes, the Parti Quebecois, in many instances, has also fostered a social-democratic or quasi-socialist style of collectivism. In particular, PQ governments have generally sought to level economic differences among individuals and groups in the province, by increasing taxation on high-income earners, expanding state ownership and control of the Quebec economy, and redistributing income to the disadvantaged through an array of social-welfare programs.

While analysts disagree on whether these activities make the PQ a truly social-democratic political party (e.g., McRoberts 1993: 253–6; Lipset and Marks 2000: 19, 57), there is no question that such programs and priorities resemble those favoured by the statist social democracies of northern and western Europe (e.g., Langlois et al. 1992: 292; Forse and Langlois 1994: 288; Clement and Myles 1994: 223, 252; Fournier, Rosenberg, and White 1997: Chapter 1; Iton 2000: 146). This statist orientation is apparent if we consider government spending under Parti Quebecois administrations over the years. Data for the 1970s and 1980s suggest that, for most of this period, Quebec's spending as a proportion of GDP was substantially greater than that for English Canada as a whole (Langlois et al. 1992: 301; Perry 2000: 56; see also Fournier, Rosenberg, and White 1997: 276). This pattern has continued in recent times. For example, one study from 1998/99 showed that Quebec ranked higher than all other provinces in overall government spending per capita (Emes and Walker 1999: Chapter 8). Other findings derived from Statistics Canada's CANSIM data base reveal that, as of 2002, Quebec's combined provincial and local government expenditures were higher than those for English Canada, at 33 per cent of provincial GDP compared with 26 per cent for the other provinces combined (Statistics Canada 2003a).[2] The same pattern occurs in the case of taxes, where Quebec has long had the highest general levels of taxation in the country. As of 1998/1999, for example, Quebec ranked ahead of all other provinces in its overall rate of taxation (Emes and Walker 1999: Chapter 8; see also Perry 2000: 58–60; Panetta 2003). Generally, then, we find consistent evidence that Quebec is a more statist region than English Canada, and has been for several decades. It is possible that both taxation rates and government spending could decline in Quebec in the future, given the replacement of the PQ regime by Jean Charest's Liberals in April of 2003.

---

2.   If the Atlantic provinces are considered separately, and not included under the broad 'English Canada' category, their government expenditures as a percentage of provincial GDP are actually slightly higher than those for Quebec, at about 34 per cent, as of 2002. It should also be noted that the figures reported here are calculated from a base that is different from that for the OECD data reported earlier in this chapter. Therefore, the exact percentages shown here are not directly comparable to the earlier figures.

However, Quebec's Liberal administrations over the years have also tended to favour policies of relatively high taxation and state intervention.

Collectivism and the State in the South

We saw in Part II that the histories of Quebec and the American South share some common elements. In particular, we found that, in their early stages, both of these sub-societies could be distinguished from the rest of Canada and the United States by their collectivist or quasi-feudal modes of social organization, the first stemming from the old French seigneurial economy and the hierarchical institutions of the Catholic Church, and the second arising from the economy of slavery and the clearly defined racial hierarchy associated with that system. In addition to these similarities, some observers have identified other historical parallels between French Quebec and the US South, including their crucial military defeats at the hands of outside forces, their subsequent economic and political subordination to these forces within their respective countries, and, until recently, their long-standing social and cultural isolation from the other sub-societies of North America (e.g., Baer, Grabb, and Johnston 1993: 28–9; see also Garreau 1981: 376–7; McPherson 1998; Marchand 2001).

However, in spite of these and other historical commonalities, we have found in Part III that, in many ways, Quebec and the southern United States are really quite different from each other. These clear divergences, which we have already seen in such areas as religion, sexual morality, and criminal activity, are also apparent if we consider issues related to the role of the state. In fact, most research indicates that, in relative terms, the American South ranks as the polar opposite to Quebec, with the least statist political structure among all of the four sub-societies.

Previous studies, going back to the 1960s, have determined that the American South has tended to be the region of the United States with the lowest levels of government involvement in, or support for, funding initiatives to subsidize the health, education, welfare, or general 'social well-being' of the population (e.g., Smith 1973: 100; Gastil 1975: 93–7; Streib 1991: 86–7; Luebke 1991: 238–9, 251–3; Draper 1993; Banting 1997: 278–9). Recent evidence reveals a similar pattern. For example, data from 1998 indicate that every one of the southern states ranks below the US national average in terms of total per capita expenditures by state and local governments (Statistical Abstract of the United States 2001: 272). With occasional exceptions for individual states, the same low rankings for the American South also occur for a range of other measures of state involvement. These include per capita funding for public elementary and high schools (as of 2000), average weekly state unemployment insurance payments (as of 1999), and per capita state taxation rates (as of 1999) (Statistical Abstract of the United States 2001: 154, 350,

279). The only major category of state funding for which the South surpasses the rest of the United States is for expenditures on state prisons. Data from 1996, for example, show that the large majority of southern states spend more per prison inmate than do their counterparts elsewhere, a finding that might be expected given the significantly higher crimes rates in the American South (Statistical Abstract of the United States 2001: 201).

In general, then, the American South is a society in which government plays a relatively small part in the lives of its citizens, at least in comparison with the situation in the rest of the United States and Canada. The differences in the role of government in the American South and Quebec seem especially notable, given some of the historical parallels between these two regions that we have noted. However, whereas Quebec's old collectivist roots would eventually lead to its adoption of a new state-sponsored and more social-democratic form of collectivism, with the most interventionist government of all the four sub-societies, the collectivist elements in the history of the American South have taken this region in a rather different direction.

The explanation for the southern approach to statism is probably multi-faceted. However, we suggest again that the principal reason can be traced to the institution of slavery, and the unusual marriage of seemingly incompatible collectivist and individualist influences that this system engendered in that part of the United States. As writers since the time of Tocqueville have asserted, slavery established a unique culture and way of life in the American South, one that combined aspects of a feudal-style collectivism, especially the designation of people's fundamental rights solely on the basis of inherited group affiliation, based on skin colour, with such powerfully individualistic precepts as the belief in personal liberty for all people, but only if the people were white. The southern view of liberty, as well as the kindred idea of popular sovereignty, was also manifested in the principle of state autonomy or states' rights, which, as we have discussed previously, was far more deeply entrenched in the South than in the rest of the United States.

According to a number of researchers, this joining together of essentially contradictory collectivist and individualist values has led to a distinctive set of institutions and orientations in the South. It has been suggested, for example, that many parts of the southern United States have always been marked by 'extremely individualistic and anti-government attitudes', especially in cases where federal authorities are concerned (Gastil 1975: 55, 57, 64, 187; see also Cash 1941: 31, 42–3). At the same time, however, the population of the South is also said to be guided by strong collectivist forces, which complicate and interact with their individualism and anti-statism (Elazar 1966: 93; Reed 1982: 170–2; Vandello and Cohen 1999: 280–1). It is argued that these forces tie certain social groups closely together, but also draw clear lines of separation between one group and another. Reed (1991: 228), for example, contends that this brand of collectivism involves 'firm and fixed boundaries between categories', which set apart local people from strangers, family members from non-family members, men from women, and whites from other racial or ethnic groups. We have previously discussed research indicating that, among our four regional sub-groups, southern Americans express the most conservative and exclusionary attitudes about the roles and rights of women in society. We have found similar tendencies in southerners' attitudes about gay rights and homosexuality. To anticipate some of the research reported in the next chapter, this general pattern also occurs with respect to southern views about racial, ethnic, and other minorities.

In several respects, this generally more rigid and exclusionary form of collectivism in the South is quite close to the idea of local communalism that, as we discussed in Part II, apparently predominated in the United States and English Canada in the era of the American Revolution (recall Shain 1994; Knowles 1997). In other words, it is as if the American South, more than any of the other regions of North America being considered in our analysis, has held on to key elements of its distant past, including a unique mix of both parochial localism or small-town collectivism, on the one hand, and an isolated or atomized individualism and anti-statism, on the other hand (see Reed 1982: 170–2; 1983: 70–1; 1992: 145–6; Glenn 1967: 176; Cash 1941: 88, 110–11; Glenn and Simmons 1967: 192; Garreau 1981: 161; Ellison and Musick 1993: 389–92).[3]

The Structure of Economic Inequality in Canada and the United States

Apart from looking at such indicators as government spending and taxation to assess state intervention in Canada and the United States, another potential gauge of statism is the extent of economic inequality that exists in the two nations. Although government intervention is, of course, not the only factor that determines the degree of inequality in a country, most analysts would agree that the state in contemporary countries usually plays an important role in this regard. This is certainly the view of Lipset, who, as we have discussed

---

3.   Another alleged feature of this southern approach to life, or what some have called 'Southernness' (Gastil 1975: 101, 108–16), is referred to by Reed (1991: 231–2) as 'anti-institutionalism'. Here, as well, we find an ambivalent combination of individualist and collectivist values, such that southerners are said to be less apt to engage in certain forms of collective action, including involvement in formal organizations or voluntary associations, because of a desire to be left alone within their own clearly defined and delineated social groupings. We discuss this issue in more detail in Chapter 11.

previously, believes that Canada is a more statist nation than the United States and, as a result, has developed a conception of equality and inequality that is different from the view which prevails in American society. In particular, Lipset's analysis suggests that Canadian governments have long favoured reducing economic disparities and promoting more equality of material condition in the population, even if such practices mean some restrictions on the opportunities for individuals to achieve great personal success. In contrast, American governments are supposedly more accepting of economic inequalities among the populace, as long as everyone is given the same opportunity to succeed, because this approach allows for more personal freedom and the pursuit of individual excellence (Lipset 1990: 8–9, 13–16; 1996: 19–23, 26, 72–3).

Such arguments imply that economic inequality should be significantly higher in the United States than in Canada. It turns out that the general patterns are broadly similar in the two nations. However, there is some evidence of greater inequality in the American population, especially at the low and high extremes of the economic hierarchy. For example, an analysis based on income data from 1995 found that the top quintile (the top 20 per cent) of American income earners received about 42 per cent of the total income earned, while the bottom 20 per cent received about 5 per cent. The corresponding figures for Canada were close to these numbers, at 40 per cent and 6 per cent (Urmetzer and Guppy 1999: 62). Studies based on data from earlier decades reveal comparable outcomes, suggesting that the basic Canadian and American income distributions have been similar since at least the 1950s (e.g., Glatzer and Hauser 2003: 200–1; Urmetzer and Guppy 2004: 78. Lipset 1963b: 322). On the other hand, subsequent findings suggest that the national difference in income inequality may be greater than that found in previous research. It should be noted that this more recent evidence involves calculation procedures that derive from the Luxembourg Income Study, and are different from those used in previous analyses. Therefore, the changes from earlier studies may be partly the result of applying an alternative methodological approach. Nevertheless, according to these data, by the early 2000s, the figures for the top and bottom quintiles in the United States were 46 per cent and 5 per cent, compared with 39 per cent and 8 per cent in Canada (Urmetzer and Guppy 2004: 81; see also Brym 2002: 7).[4]

---

4. Another recent analysis has determined that income distributions in Canada and the United States have been very similar, specifically with respect to the share of income going to the top 10 per cent of income earners. The study concluded that the Canadian and American patterns have parallelled one another for some eight decades, covering the period from 1920 to 2000, and have diverged from those found in other industrialized nations, including France and Japan (Saez and Veall 2003).

Another standard index for assessing income inequality is the Gini coefficient. This coefficient varies from 0 to 1.0, such that the higher the score, the more unequal is the distribution of income among the population in question. One recent study calculated Gini coefficients for Canada and the United States for three different years—1974, 1985, and 1997—and found the following patterns. Rounded to two decimal points, the Canadian and American coefficients were, respectively, .41 and .44 in 1974, .43 and .45 in 1985, and .42 and .47 in 1997 (Wolfson and Murphy 2000: Table 4; see also Card and Freeman 1993: 6; Blackburn and Bloom 1993: 247–8; Reitz 1998: 152; Glatzer and Hauser 2003: 193, 196). These results indicate that economic inequality was, indeed, higher in the United States than in Canada, and for all three years. However, as with most of the research that has looked at income quintiles, the differences are not large.

The Wolfson and Murphy study also considered regional variations in economic inequality. Given the regional differences in state expenditure that we discussed previously in this chapter, we might expect that Quebec, because of its more interventionist government, would tend to have the lowest level of income inequality of our four regional sub-societies, while the American South, with its lower commitment to state spending, would have the highest level of income inequality. Depending on the year, there is some evidence to support these expectations. Quebec has the lowest Gini coefficient of all the regions for two of the three years under consideration (1985 and 1997) and also has the second lowest for 1974. The American South has the highest coefficient for two of the years (1974 and 1985), but was essentially equal to the overall American average for 1997. Here again the differences across the regions, while notable, are relatively modest. As an illustration, the 1997 Gini coefficient was .403 for Quebec, compared with .418 for Canada as a whole, .464 for the American South, and .466 for the United States as a whole (Wolfson and Murphy 2000: Table 4).

One factor that helps to explain some of the national and the regional variations in economic inequality is 'union density', or the proportion of the paid labour force that is unionized. Research indicates that unionization tends to reduce wage inequality in both countries, but even more so in the Canadian case (Lemieux 1993: 95). Although union density in Canada has leveled off over the past three decades, and has actually declined somewhat since the mid-1990s (Banting and Simeon 1997: 40; Reitz 1998: 161–2; Brym 2004: 64), the Canadian figure is still much higher than the American level (Riddell 1993: 113–14; see also Banting 1997: 275; Conley 2004: 50). It is partly for this reason that the Gini coefficient of inequality is lower in the two Canadian regions, and especially in Quebec, which has generally maintained the highest union density of all the four sub-societies (Lemieux 1993: 101; Card and

Freeman 1993: 6; Reitz 1998: 181–3). Union membership levels are consistently the lowest in the American South, where, with the exception of West Virginia, every state was below the national average as of 2000 (Statistical Abstract of the United States 2001: 412).

The fact that Canadian unionization levels have been higher than those in the United States over the years could in itself be seen as evidence that collectivism is more highly valued or accepted in Canada. However, while this might hold with respect to elite values, and is certainly consistent with the idea that Canada's state leaders have been more favourable or responsive to the union movement than their American counterparts, research going back as far as the 1940s shows that the Canadian and American populations are not significantly different in this respect, and in fact 'have very similar attitudes toward unions' (Riddell 1993: 139–40; see also Baer, Grabb, and Johnston 1990b: 704–6; 1993: 20–1; Gallup 1996; Gillespie 1999: 29–30). With respect to regional differences, it is consistent with the evidence on union density that research shows Quebecers to be more supportive of unions than other North Americans, with American southerners (along with Canadians from the Prairie provinces) being the least in favour (Baer, Grabb, and Johnston 1993: 20–1).

In all events, it is primarily at the very top and the very bottom of the economic hierarchies in the two nations, among the wealthy few and the genuinely poor, that we find the most appreciable Canadian–American differences in levels of economic inequality. Recent research on the concentration of wealth, which includes not only wages or earned income but also any accumulated assets (minus debts), suggests that, as of the late 1990s, the top 1 per cent of the American population held approximately 35 per cent of the wealth in their society, compared with 25 per cent in Canada. Both of these proportions are higher than those in social-democratic countries like Sweden, for example, where the figure is about 20 per cent (Davies 2004: 89–90; also D'Souza 2000: 66; Kennickell 2000; Glatzer and Hauser 2003: 210). At the other end of the economic hierarchy, there is evidence of higher poverty rates in the United States than in Canada. Such comparisons should be made with some caution, because of the variable definitions of poverty that are used by different researchers. Thus, one analysis based on data from 2001 found poverty rates of 17 per cent in the United States and 10 per cent in Canada (Jackson 2003: 25). However, statistics calculated by the US government indicate that the American level for 1999 was 11.8 per cent, which is only slightly higher than the Canadian level for this period (Statistical Abstract of the United States 2001: 443). The latter pattern is closer to that found in several other studies (see, e.g., Blank and Hanratty 1993: 203–5; D'Souza 2000: 75–6; Glatzer and Hauser 2003: 206). On the whole, though, the evidence is consistent with the conclusion that there is greater economic inequality in the United

States than in Canada, with this difference being concentrated mainly in the extreme ends of the distribution.

It could be remarked that, while there may be more economic inequality in the United States for some groups, there is also a generally higher standard of living, as measured by such indicators as average income or GDP per capita (Simpson 2000: 78, 151; Statistical Abstract of the United States 2001: 840). However, averages can sometimes mask extreme differences. Therefore, it is an open question whether these indicators show that most Americans are materially better off than are most Canadians, in spite of living in a more unequal society. Another consideration is that national differences on these measures can be partly a function of fluctuating currency rates, with the apparent gap in living standards at times artificially increasing or decreasing, depending on the rise and fall of the American dollar compared with the Canadian dollar.

ATTITUDES ABOUT INDIVIDUALISM, STATISM, AND COLLECTIVISM

The findings we have presented on levels of government spending, taxation, and other indicators of statism in Canada and the United States lead us to the next key question: Are there parallel differences in the 'cultures' of statism or individualism in the two nations? In other words, because the Canadian people have generally experienced more interventionist governments than the American population over the past half-century, should we expect that Canadians, particularly those from Quebec, will be more likely than Americans, especially those from the South, to express support for greater state involvement in their lives, and less likely than Americans to embrace such individualist beliefs as self-reliance and personal responsibility? In the previous discussion of statism in the US South, we noted that some researchers and commentators have perceived such differences in outlooks when comparing southern Americans with northern Americans. In this section, we take a more systematic look at the issue. Our main goal in the analysis that follows is to determine if there is consistent evidence of systematic differences, across the two nations and the four sub-societies, in people's policy preferences, attitudes, and values regarding individualism, statism, and collectivism.

Views on Individualism and the State

Table 8.1 compares Canadian and American responses to a set of eight attitude items from the World Values Surveys. Each of these items deals with some aspect of the role of the individual versus the state (or the collectivity) in society. One of the first findings to note in Table 8.1 is that the majority of both Canadians and Americans express ideas that are relatively more individualist

Table 8.1   Eight Measures of Individual/Self Orientation versus Statism/Collectivism Orientation by Region and Nation

	Region					Nation		
	English Canada	Quebec	US North	US South	Sig[1]	Canada Total	US Total	Sig[1]
1. Have greater incentive for individual effort versus make incomes more equal[a]	7.03	5.99*	6.72*	6.73*	√	6.77	6.72	
2. Individuals should take more responsibility to provide for themselves versus the state should take responsibility[a]	6.95	7.28*	7.54*	7.51*	√	7.03	7.53	√
3. Unemployed people should take any available job versus unemployed should be able to refuse a job[a]	6.23	5.99	6.41	6.21		6.17	6.34	
4. Competition is good, stimulates hard work and new ideas versus competition is harmful[a]	7.84	8.04	7.87	7.66		7.89	7.80	
5. Hard work produces a better life versus hard work doesn't lead to success[a]	7.36	6.71*	7.54	7.46	√	7.20	7.51	√
6. There should be more private business ownership versus there should be more government business ownership[a]	7.60	7.59	7.83*	7.60	√	7.60	7.76	√
7. Wealth can grow so there's enough for all versus wealth accumulation can only come at other people's expense[a]	6.75	7.62*	6.28*	6.13*	√	6.97	6.23	√
8. We are more likely to have a healthy economy if the government lets individuals be free to do as they wish[b]	3.24	2.58*	3.16*	3.14*	√	3.08	3.15	√

Notes

[1] A check mark (√) indicates that the likelihood ratio chi-square for the overall four-category comparison across regions, or the two-category comparison across nations, is significant at <.05. The asterisk (*) indicates that the category is significantly different from the English Canadian reference group at <.05.

[a] The scale ranged from 1 = 'agree completely with the second statement' to 10 = 'agree completely with the first statement'.

[b] The scale ranged from 1 = 'disagree completely' to 5 = 'agree completely'.

than statist, with the average scores of the two national samples falling toward the individualist side of the continuum for each of the seven 10-point scales, and for the single 5-point item. It is also notable that the differences between Canadians and Americans are generally quite small on all eight measures. In fact, on four of the items, there are no statistically significant differences between the two samples. Specifically, Canadians and Americans are equally likely to say: that there should be more incentives for individual effort rather than an equalization of people's incomes; that unemployed people should be obliged to take any available job rather than remain idle; that competition is a good rather than a harmful force in society; and that individual freedom from government is good for the economy.

On the other four items in Table 8.1, we do find differences between the two national samples that, while relatively minor, are statistically significant. Americans are somewhat more likely than Canadians to believe: that individuals should take more responsibility to provide for themselves rather than rely on state assistance; that hard work leads to success; that private business ownership should be increased rather than government business ownership; and that a person's wealth can only grow at the expense of others, as opposed to accumulating in a way that provides for everyone. The first three of these outcomes are consistent with the prediction that, compared with Canadians, Americans tend to espouse more individualist beliefs, and less collectivist or statist attitudes. The remaining item, dealing with wealth accumulation, might appear at first to be inconsistent with the others, since it could be interpreted as evidence that Americans have a less favourable view than Canadians about the virtues of personal wealth accumulation, given the negative effects that such accumulation has on other people. However, an alternative interpretation, and one suggesting that this outcome may actually be consistent with the other findings, is that Americans are merely stating their stronger belief that material success naturally entails a focus on the self, and that, in this competitive 'dog-eat-dog' world, personal wealth generally must come at the expense of others.

Table 8.1 also compares responses across the four regional sub-groups. Here, too, the overall pattern is one of generally small differences, with most people leaning toward an individualist orientation in all four sub-samples. However, the results reveal a couple of interesting patterns. In particular, we find some modest support for the conclusion that Quebecers, who have been subject to the most statist government of the four sub-groups, also tend to express the most collectivist or pro-statist attitudes. Although the results are certainly mixed, this outcome occurs for three of the eight questions, i.e., those dealing with individual income incentives (item 1), the value of hard work (item 5), and individual economic freedom (item 8). This pattern also exists for the question about wealth accumulation (item 7) if, as touched on earlier, Quebecers' relatively low support for the idea that wealth must come at others' expense, and their relatively high support for the belief that wealth can grow so there is enough for all, is interpreted as a collectivist rather than an individualist sentiment.

Because of the history of smaller governments in the US South, it might be predicted that the respondents from this region would voice the most individualist and anti-statist attitudes. However, the findings in Table 8.1 provide little or no support for this prediction. It is true that southerners are among the most likely to favour individual responsibility over state responsibility (item 2), although on this issue they are no different from their northern American compatriots. Southerners are also the most likely to believe that wealth accumulation can only come at others' expense, which again could be interpreted as a self-focused or anti-collectivist belief. Otherwise, however, there is nothing here to suggest that people from the American South are unusually anti-statist or exceptionally pro-individualist.

In summary, then, apart from a few modest tendencies, as mentioned above, this battery of items reveals no notable national or regional differences in individualist, statist, and collectivist attitudes. The weakness of these findings may be unexpected, given the distinct approaches to state intervention and government spending that, as we have seen, have operated in Canada and the United States for the past several decades. On the other hand, because these national differences in state involvement are far from large, the lack of major differences in people's opinions about individualism and the state may be less surprising. The weak patterns shown in Table 8.1 are even more understandable if we consider, as was suggested in the historical analysis in Part II, that policy differences between the two countries probably stem more from ideological differences that have existed at the elite level over the years, and not from fundamental value differences between the two populations themselves (see Presthus 1973, 1977a, 1977b).

Individualism and Values for Children
The WVS contains a second set of measures that allow us to gauge Canadian and American views about individualism and collectivism, this time from a somewhat different perspective. These items ask respondents to consider a checklist of qualities that could be taught to children in the home, and to choose the qualities that, in their opinion, are the most important for children to learn. There are five qualities on the list that, in various ways, may be interpreted as evidence of individualist values or orientations. As shown in Table 8.2, these five qualities are: 'independence', 'hard work', a 'feeling of responsibility', 'determination, perseverance', and 'unselfishness'.

Table 8.2   Views on Which Qualities Should Be Encouraged in Children by Region and Nation

	Region					Nation		
	English Canada	Quebec	US North	US South	Sig[1]	Canada Total	US Total	Sig[1]
% of respondents citing the following characteristics:								
1. Independence	49	28*	52	54	√	44	53	√
2. Hard Work	33	43*	47*	51*	√	35	49	√
3. Feeling of Responsibility	71	86*	73	67*	√	75	71	√
4. Determination, Perseverance	34	49*	35	37	√	38	36	
5. Unselfishness	42	43	40	31*	√	42	37	√

Notes

[1] A check mark (√) indicates that the likelihood ratio chi-square for the overall four-category comparison across regions, or the two-category comparison across nations, is significant at <.05. The asterisk (*) indicates that the category is significantly different from the English Canadian reference group at <.05.

As with the findings in Table 8.1, the results in Table 8.2 indicate only minor national and regional differences. Once more, however, there are some statistically significant outcomes that can be noted. First, if we compare the two national samples, we find significant differences on four of the five measures. Americans are more likely than Canadians to value independence (53 per cent versus 44 per cent) and hard work (49 per cent versus 35 per cent), while Canadians are slightly more likely than Americans to mention responsibility (75 per cent versus 71 per cent) and unselfishness (42 per cent versus 37 per cent). There is no significant difference between the two samples on the value of determination or perseverance (38 per cent versus 36 per cent).

Although it would be foolhardy to make any strong claims about these relatively weak patterns, we can cautiously suggest one possible interpretation. The stronger American emphasis on 'independence' and 'hard work' fits with the notion that Americans place more importance on those individualist values that pertain to the self alone, while the stronger Canadian emphasis on 'responsibility' and 'unselfishness' could imply that the Canadian conception of individualism entails a greater sense of each person's obligation to other individuals. In other words, the patterns in Table 8.2 may be consistent with the conclusion that Americans are apt to favour a more self-focused or 'self-oriented' brand of individualism in their children, whereas Canadians prefer a form of individualism that is more socially responsible or 'socially oriented' in its implications. This possible difference between Canadians and Americans is akin to a distinction that Durkheim once drew between 'egoism', or narrowly self-interested individualism, and genuine 'individualism', which for him entailed a real interdependence among individuals, in which people are free to pursue their own goals and interests while at the same time recognizing their obligations and responsibilities to others (Durkheim 1893: 172–3; see also Baer et al. 1995: 302; Grabb 2002: 81–2). Although tentative at best, this hypothesis may gain some credence if we consider that a similar pattern was found in research using data from the previous waves of the WVS, which were conducted in the 1980s (Baer et al. 1995; see also Archibald 1978: 235–7). Nevertheless, we should also be aware that the differences between Americans and Canadians found in this earlier study were much weaker and less consistent if English and French Canadians were considered separately (see Baer et al. 1995: 307).

The latter observation points to the need to go beyond the national samples on these items, and to conduct a comparison involving the four sub-groups. We can see in Table 8.2 that such a comparison produces a highly mixed pattern, raising doubts that there are consistent and easily interpretable regional differences in regard to these five child-rearing values. Consider, for example, the two so-called 'self-oriented' values of independence and hard work. Using the four-way comparison, we now see that Americans value independence more than French Canadians, but do not rate it more highly than English Canadians. At the same time, Americans mention hard work more than English Canadians, but not more than French Canadians. Similar complexities arise if we reconsider the two so-called 'socially oriented' values of responsibility and unselfishness, using the four-region delineation. Now we find that French Canadians still rate responsibility more highly than both American groups, but English Canadians do not. As well, neither of the Canadian groups ranks unselfishness more highly than do people from the US North, although both Canadian groups rank this value more highly than do people from the US South. In short, then, the general pattern of findings for the four sub-groups in Table 8.2 does not lend itself to any definitive conclusions. Even more than the comparisons involving Canadians and Americans as a whole, the results based on the four sub-societies fail to reveal clear differences in attitudes about individualism, at least as this principle relates to qualities that people would like to see instilled in children.[5]

Self-Confidence and Personal Assertiveness

There is a third set of measures in the WVS that provide additional insight into Canadian and American perspectives on the general question of individualism. In this case, respondents were asked to consider a list of eight statements and to identify any statement that, in their opinion, applied to them personally (see Table 8.3). The eight items comprise a variety of self-descriptions, such as whether the respondents: enjoy convincing others of their opinions, like to assume responsibility, serve as role models for others, expect to be successful, are good at getting what they want, are rarely unsure about their actions, and so on. These measures delve into the topic of individualism in a way that is different from that of the previous items we have considered. In this case, we are able to assess how self-confident or assertive Canadians and Americans are about their personal abilities and individual accomplishments.

It is a common stereotype that Americans are unusually self-assured and bold individuals, with considerably more confidence about themselves (and their nation) than the other peoples of the world; at the same time, it is also assumed by many people that Canadians are typically quite unlike Americans in this respect, with a much more modest or guarded sense of their own aptitudes and personal efficacy (e.g., Naegele 1961: 22–32; Lipset 1963b: Chapter 7; 1990: Chapter 3; 1996: Chapter 2; for some discussion, see Ferguson 1997:

---

5. Although they are not reported in tables, two other items from the WVS may be relevant for assessing individualism and collectivism. These items also produce mixed results. One asked respondents to say if 'freedom' (i.e., being able to live 'without hindrance') is more or less important than 'equality' (a situation in which 'nobody is underprivileged' and 'social class differences are not so strong'). Most people from both nations chose freedom over equality, but Americans were more likely to do so. The percentages that opted for freedom were: 62 per cent for English Canada, 59 per cent for Quebec, 70 per cent for the US North, and 72 per cent for the US South. This pattern is consistent with the conclusion that Americans, especially southerners, may be slightly more individualist than Canadians, most notably those from Quebec. On the other hand, a second question, dealing with whether it is fair for a worker (a hypothetical secretary) to be paid more money than less 'efficient' and less 'reliable' co-workers, showed no differences. More than 80 per cent of the respondents in both countries, and in all four regions, said that the more efficient and reliable secretary should receive higher pay. This suggests that all of the groups are about equally likely to believe economic inequality is fair, if it is based on individual performance and effort.

Table 8.3 Eight Measures of Self-Confidence and Personal Assertiveness by Region and Nation

% agreeing with the following statement:	Region					Nation		
	English Canada	Quebec	US North	US South	Sig[1]	Canada Total	US Total	Sig[1]
1. I enjoy convincing others	26	27	26	27		26	27	
2. I often serve as a role model	22	14*	23	23	√	20	23	√
3. People envy my possessions	10	11	10	9		11	10	
4. I like to assume responsibility	63	70*	62	58	√	65	61	√
5. I am rarely unsure of myself	39	29*	41	38	√	36	40	√
6. I often give others advice	44	37*	43	46	√	42	44	
7. I count on being successful	60	72*	60	61	√	63	60	
8. I am good at getting what I want	25	35*	26	26	√	27	26	

Notes

[1] A check mark (√) indicates that the likelihood ratio chi-square for the overall four-category comparison across regions, or the two-category comparison across nations, is significant at <.05. The asterisk (*) indicates that the category is significantly different from the English Canadian reference group at <.05.

Chapter 11; Simpson 2000: 338–63; Adams 2003: Chapter 4). However, the results from Table 8.3 give us little or no reason to accept these familiar characterizations of the two populations. The findings show that there are significant Canadian–American differences on only three of the eight measures. In addition, all three of these differences are very small, and only two of them are in the expected direction: Americans are slightly more likely than Canadians to say that they often serve as role models (23 per cent versus 20 per cent) and are slightly more apt to say that they like to assume responsibility (65 per cent versus 61 per cent). Canadians, on the other hand, are marginally more likely than Americans to indicate that they are rarely unsure of themselves in the things that they do (40 per cent versus 36 per cent).

If we consider the results for the four sub-societies in Table 8.3, we again find virtually no support for the view that Americans, whether they live in the South or the North, are appreciably more self-confident or self-assertive than English Canadians or Quebecers. First of all, there are no comparisons in which either of the two American groups is significantly different from the English Canadian sub-sample. Second, although we do find several statistically significant differences involving the Quebec respondents, the outcomes are inconsistent. For example, Quebecers are the least likely of all the four groups to state that they serve as role models, are rarely unsure of themselves, and often give others advice. However, at the same time, Quebecers are the most likely to say that they like to assume responsibility, usually count on succeeding, and are good at getting what they want. In combination, these results offer no basis for contending that Canadians, from either region of the country, are less self-confident or assertive than their counterparts south of the border.

Attitudes about Change in Canada and the United States

Table 8.4 summarizes responses to three attitude questions from the WVS, each of which deals with different aspects of change in society. These items ask respondents to place themselves on 10-point scales between contrasting statements about their 'outlook on life'. The questions ask: (1) is it better to be 'cautious about making major changes in life', or is it true that 'you will never achieve much unless you act boldly?'; (2) are the best ideas those 'that have stood the test of time', or is it the case that 'new ideas are generally better than old ones?'; and (3) when life changes occur, do they lead a person to 'worry about the difficulties they may cause', or should they be welcomed because of 'the possibility that something new is beginning?'.

Although these items do not deal directly with the question of individualism or collectivism, we include them in this section of the analysis because they are pertinent to the overall assessment of how Canadians and Americans feel about individual action or activism in life. As was touched on

Table 8.4 Attitudes about Change by Region and Nation

	Region					Nation		
	English Canada	Quebec	US North	US South	Sig[1]	Canada Total	US Total	Sig[1]
1. Being cautious about major change versus acting boldly to achieve goals (10 pt. scale[a])	5.69	6.57*	5.82	5.92	√	5.91	5.85	√
2. Ideas that have stood the test of time are generally best versus new ideas are generally better than old ones (10 pt. scale[a])	5.64	5.84	6.03*	6.32*	√	5.69	6.13	√
3. Changes in life may cause difficulties versus changes are welcome as a new beginning (10 pt. scale[a])	4.50	4.60	5.04*	5.14*	√	4.53	5.07	√

Notes

[1] A check mark (√) indicates that the likelihood ratio chi-square for the overall four-category comparison across regions, or the two-category comparison across nations, is significant at <.05. The asterisk (*) indicates that the category is significantly different from the English Canadian reference group at <.05.

[a] The scale ranged from 1 = 'agree completely with the second statement' to 10 = 'agree completely with the first statement'.

in our description of the findings from Table 8.3, it is commonly assumed that Canadians are less self-assertive and less self-confident than their southern neighbours. This suggests that Canadians should not be as favourably disposed as Americans to taking risky or bold steps in their daily existence. If this is true, we should find that Canadians will have an aversion to change, especially if it happens rapidly and without careful consideration.

However, as might be expected given the findings already reported in Table 8.3, the results in Table 8.4 offer no support for the claim that Canadians are more fearful or cautious about change than are Americans. On the contrary, although the differences are small, on two of the three items the results go in the opposite direction, with Canadians being significantly more likely to prefer new ideas over old ideas (item 1), and also to welcome change rather than see it as a source of difficulty (item 2). On the third item, dealing with whether it is better to be cautious or bold about change, there is no Canadian–American difference. If we compare the four regional sub-samples in Table 8.4, a similar overall pattern obtains. For all three items, English Canadians express greater support for change than either of the two American groups. In addition, although Quebecers rank as the most cautious of the four sub-samples on item 1, on the other two questions they are less cautious than both American sub-samples, and no different from the English Canadian sub-sample. Thus, the general picture is one in which Canadians are, if anything, somewhat more receptive to change than are Americans.[6]

Other Attitude Research

One aspect of this discussion that we have not yet considered is how our findings fit with previous studies of individualism and related values in the two nations. Although there is a limited amount of systematic research that has directly compared Canada and the United States on this question, and almost none that has considered the four constituent sub-societies, the available evidence is generally very consistent with the findings reported here. While a detailed assessment of this work is beyond the scope of the present analysis, we can note some key illustrations.

First of all, one review of public-opinion research, which covered the period from the 1970s to the early 1990s, concluded that both Canadians and Americans embrace 'the individualist idea of equality of opportunity', although this review also determined that, compared with Americans, Canadians

---

6. In an analysis of attitudes about political change, Nevitte (1996: 100–1) found, similarly, that Canadians were either no different from Americans or else slightly more receptive than Americans to the idea of political change in their society.

(especially Quebecers) were somewhat more supportive of certain state-sponsored policies to increase opportunities for the unemployed and other disadvantaged groups (Perlin 1997: 89, 113–14, 123–4). On the latter point, however, more recent survey findings collected in the early 2000s have led one researcher to conclude that Canadians have less appetite than they once did for 'old-style interventionist government' (Gregg 2003: 29–30). Moreover, data for the late 1990s indicate that American support for such government programs is on the increase, and is now closer to the Canadian level than in the past (Cantril and Cantril 1999: 1; see also Glatzer and Hauser 2003: 212). Another review, which looked at research for the last three decades on the value of 'equal opportunity for individual achievement', found virtually the same high levels of commitment among Canadians and Americans to the belief that every individual should have, and usually does have, a more or less equal chance to succeed in life (Curtis and Grabb 2004).

Related studies covering the 1980s and 1990s have shown that Canadians and Americans give almost identical rankings to individualist values, such as 'hard work', 'ambition', and 'natural ability', and, along with educational attainment, see these factors as the prime reasons for why people get ahead in the world (Pammett 1996: 70–3; see also Li 1988: 5; Inkeles 1997: 379; Maclean's 1998). There is some evidence that French Canadians may be less likely than English Canadians to believe that individual qualities like hard work and ability really do lead to success, especially when compared with the effects of group affiliations, such as race or religion (Johnstone 1969; Perlin 1997: 113–14; Curtis and Grabb 2004: 401). However, other findings suggest that, perhaps in spite of this difference, French Canadians express a stronger desire for individual striving and achievement than do English Canadians (Baer and Curtis 1984, 1988). Additional research indicates that Canadians and Americans are very similar in their views about the positive effects of individual competition for achieving personal excellence (Sniderman et al. 1996: 97–102; Perlin 1997: 113). Other studies show that the two populations share an equal preference for occupations that encourage individual initiative (Hampden-Turner and Trompenaars 1993; Lipset 1996: 294) and for jobs that allow individuals to work longer hours if they desire (Stier and Lewin-Epstein 2003: 312–15). Based on an analysis of recent opinion-poll data, one researcher has concluded that Canadians now may actually be more individualist than Americans, at least in the sense of believing in individual autonomy or freedom from conformity to externally imposed rules (Adams 2003: 54–5, 115–17, 122–4; see also Bibby 1990: 90–7). Overall, then, these studies support the conclusion that any differences between Canadians and Americans on issues pertaining to individualism and collectivism are minimal and often inconsistent.

SUMMARY

To summarize, it should be clear from the results presented in this chapter that, when we closely compare Canadian and American beliefs about individualism, statism, and collectivism, we find patterns that are markedly different from those that have been suggested by Lipset and other commentators. Although the evidence does indicate that Canadians have experienced moderately higher levels of state intervention than have Americans in recent years, along with somewhat lower levels of economic inequality, we have found, at best, only minor and mixed support for the notion that this has made Canadians different from Americans with respect to their views about the virtues of government assistance. For the most part, we have seen that Canadians are as committed to the values of individual self-reliance and personal responsibility as are Americans. Furthermore, we have uncovered no evidence to suggest that, compared with Americans, Canadians are less individualist in their attitudes about child-rearing values, are less self-confident and assertive about their accomplishments, or are less accepting of change. Instead, we have identified only a few statistically significant differences, and many of these operate in the opposite direction to that which Lipset and some other writers would predict. The comparisons of the four sub-societies on these issues have also revealed differences that are minor, frequently inconsistent, and often non-significant. When coupled with our brief review of other research on this question, the results presented here make it apparent that the long-standing view of Americans as appreciably more individualist, or less collectivist, than Canadians is in need of serious reconsideration. Indeed, depending on exactly what is meant by the terms, individualism and collectivism, the claim would seem to be essentially incorrect.

≈

SOCIAL INCLUSION AND TOLERANCE TOWARD MINORITIES

In Chapter 9, we turn our attention to the crucial issue of social inclusion and tolerance toward ethnic and other minority groups. This topic is of central concern to us, for a number of reasons. First of all, it stands at the very heart of the image that many Canadians and Americans have about their societies, as places of fairness, justice, and equal opportunity for all people. In addition, the questions of inclusion and tolerance lead us directly back to a consideration of the core ideals, or deep-structural principles, that we have suggested are inherent to the value systems of both nations. Especially relevant to the present discussion is the belief that, in a democratic society, everyone should enjoy individual liberty, equality under the rule of law, and pluralism, or what we have called the basic right to be different.

We have seen that historically the two nations often have not lived up to these high principles. Perhaps the most obvious example of the early failure to realize such lofty goals is the prolonged existence of slavery in the United States, especially in the South. In the other regions of the two societies, we have also found historical examples of exclusion or intolerance, particularly on the basis of religious affiliation. Our conclusion in Part II was that, in the initial development of both countries, some forms of pluralism and diversity did arise. However, these instances occurred in a kind of 'separate but equal' arrangement, whereby different groups were relatively free to practice their religion and to preserve their own culture and values, but mainly in segregated community enclaves. Other illustrations could easily be added to these historical examples of exclusion or intolerance, most notably the treatment of aboriginal peoples in both nations throughout their respective histories (Ponting 1986; Frideres 1988; Fleras and Elliott 1992; Strickland 1997; McIlwraith 2001; Wishart 2001; Wynn 2001; White, Beamon, and Maxim 2003; Hall 2003), as well as the discrimination against Chinese, Japanese, and other Asian minorities during much of the nineteenth and twentieth centuries (Li 1988, 1996, 1998; Ujimoto and Hirabayashi 1980; Ramcharan 1982; Marger 1999: 265, 292; Hurst 2001: 104; Harrison and Friesen 2004: 104–6).

Nevertheless, since the early years of the two nations, important changes have occurred in both the patterns of ethnic composition and the material conditions of ethnic minorities. These changes have been spurred by major historical developments and social forces, some of which we have discussed in previous chapters. First, in the case of the United States, there were the cataclysmic events of the Civil War and the abolition of slavery, which enabled the American people to embrace, with somewhat greater conviction, their cherished beliefs about individual liberty and freedom for all.[1] Second, there was the unprecedented influx, particularly after the early 1800s, of millions of immigrants, who originated primarily from Europe in the early stages, but who would come in later years from a host of non-European societies. The arrival of these new peoples was a key factor in the westward expansion of both countries, and greatly enhanced the religious, cultural, and ethnic diversity of the two nations. Moreover, to the extent that many newcomers had the chance to own their own land or otherwise improve their economic circumstances, these developments also added to both the perception and the reality of Canada and the United States as lands of freedom and opportunity. On the other hand, as we discuss later in this chapter, such events, while benefiting many Canadians and Americans, often did so at the cost of untold damage and long-term injustice for the aboriginal peoples.

The main question for us to address at this stage is whether and to what extent these historical occurrences have led, in the contemporary period, to differences in the kinds of pluralism and acceptance of diversity that both nations are said to foster and embrace. Our discussion of this question concentrates on four central topics or issues. We begin with a look at the 'mosaic' versus 'melting pot' metaphors that have been applied in most comparisons of ethnicity in Canada and the United States, and their implications for our perceptions of cultural pluralism in the two societies. Next we examine major patterns of immigration and racial composition, as gauges of the relative degrees of ethnic diversity in both countries. We then consider research on socioeconomic attainment, in order to identify any differences in the success

---

1.   The timing of the end of slavery was somewhat different for the United States and Canada. Although some northern states banned slavery in the early 1800s, it was not officially abolished throughout the United States until 1865, at the end of the Civil War. By that time, slavery had already been eliminated in Canada for more than 30 years, as part of the general outlawing of slave-holding in all of the British Empire in 1833. In fact, there is some basis for arguing that slavery was prohibited in parts of Canada as early as 1793, when John Graves Simcoe declared that the practice of owning slaves was no longer permitted in the region of Upper Canada (Ontario) (Riddell 1920: 51; Schlesinger 1964: 169; Moore 1971: 20–1, 85–9, 101; Errington 1994: 134; Martis 2001: 160–1; Archives of Ontario 2002).

rates or opportunity levels of ethnic and cultural minorities in Canada and the United States. Finally, we review contemporary research on various attitudinal indicators of discrimination and prejudice against minority groups in the two nations. Throughout, we also consider the available evidence about inclusion and tolerance in the four regional sub-societies.

MOSAIC AND MELTING POT

When discussing the topic of ethnicity in Canada and the United States, almost all writers draw on a now familiar distinction, between the Canadian cultural 'mosaic', on the one hand, and the American 'melting pot', on the other hand (e.g., Porter 1965, 1967, 1975, 1979; Driedger 1978; Li 1988; Reitz and Breton 1994; Curtis and Helmes-Hayes 1998). Although this distinction is something of a truism, these terms effectively capture the rather different approaches that the two societies are perceived to take when it comes to questions of ethnic pluralism and diversity. Thus, it is commonly assumed that, over the years, Canadian society has typically encouraged 'multiculturalism', or the idea that virtually all minority-group members are free to maintain ethnic, racial, or cultural identities that are separate from their Canadian identity. In contrast, the United States is portrayed as a society where ethnic pluralism is accepted, but where most people ultimately become 'blended' together by their common and overriding American identity.

The image of diverse individuals being melded together in the great American melting pot has some obvious parallels with Lipset's view that the people of the United States are imbued with a unified commitment to 'Americanism', or the American Creed (recall Lipset 1963b: 178; 1979: 25; 1996: 31; also Myrdal 1944). This perception of the country has been popular since before the turn of the twentieth century, and is central to the notion that the United States is a nation of immigrants that was created by people from many different backgrounds, but is also a society in which almost everyone eventually chooses to conform or assimilate to the majority American culture.

Although the idea of the melting pot has predominated in much of the thinking about ethnicity and culture in the United States, it has never been presented as a formal goal or policy of the American government. In contrast, Canada's image as a multicultural mosaic has been both a popular metaphor used by commentators and intellectuals to describe the Canadian experience, and also an official policy of the Canadian state. There are numerous examples of the formal entrenchment of multiculturalism in Canada in recent decades, including the Official Languages Act of 1969 and the Charter of Rights and Freedoms of 1982. However, the best illustration is probably the Multiculturalism Act of 1988, which made Canada the first nation in the world to grant official statutory powers and legal protections to distinct cultural minorities (Merelman 1991: 31, 107, 218; Breton 1998: 93–6; Fleras and Elliott 2002: 67–8).

Several possible explanations have been offered for the greater promotion of multiculturalism in Canada compared with the United States. Certain writers, most notably Lipset, have said that the formal establishment and greater acceptance of ethnic pluralism in Canada is due to fundamental national differences in values. Lipset sees such initiatives as proof that Canadians are guided by more elitist and particularist values, which supposedly place a higher priority on the needs of ethnic collectivities and other special interest groups, rather than on individual rights and freedoms (Lipset 1985: 151–2; 1986: 142–3; see also Clark 1950; Naegele 1961; Porter 1979: 99; Merelman 1991: 218). However, some have suggested that this is a peculiar position for Lipset to take. In particular, given his own thesis that Americans have an unparalleled love of individual liberty and equal opportunity, presumably it should be the United States, rather than Canada, where pluralism and tolerance of individual differences should truly flourish (see Baer, Grabb, and Johnston 1990a, 1990b, 1990c).

A more plausible explanation for the different approaches to ethnic diversity in the two nations is the dual ethnic and linguistic character of Canada's founding peoples. Various scholars have suggested that Canada's origins as both a French and an English nation have meant that, from the outset, Canadians have shown at least some acceptance of the concept of ethnic pluralism. Canada's bilingual and bicultural reality, it is argued, has made it easier for additional minority groups to avoid assimilation into the majority culture because, with two dominant cultures instead of one, Canada already had a 'built-in tolerance for the perpetuation of ethnic identities' (Hiller 2000: 169; see also Palmer 1976; Weinfeld 1981: 86; 1990: 89; Lipset 1990: 37–8; Merelman 1991: 31).

There are also some compelling economic and political explanations for Canada's ethnic pluralism. In particular, it is clear that, very early on, the Canadian government saw advantages in encouraging high levels of immigration, both to increase population growth and economic development, and to settle the western half of the nation, which was under threat of possible American incursions in the period after Confederation (Clement 1977: 3, 50). It is true that some of the initial waves of immigration did not produce a great deal of ethnic diversity, because Canadian political leaders favoured the entry of British, American, and northern or western European peoples, who were culturally similar to the predominant English and French inhabitants of the country, and who would most readily assimilate to the prevailing Canadian way of life (Reitz 1980: 5; Beaujot 1991: 102–10). However, in later years, once again as a spur to further growth and development, the right of entry to Canada was increasingly granted to immigrants with far more diverse and distinct backgrounds, including eastern and southern Europeans, Asians, Africans, Latin Americans, and others (Beaujot and McQuillan 1982; Beaujot 1991; Li 2003; Boyd and Vickers 2004). Ultimately, then, the immigration process itself added greatly to Canada's ethnic pluralism.

PATTERNS OF IMMIGRATION AND RACIAL COMPOSITION

We have discussed the contrasting perceptions that have developed about the nature of both immigration and ethnicity in Canada and the United States. However, we have yet to look at specific evidence on the actual patterns of immigration and ethnic composition in the two societies. One of the first findings to note in this regard is that, while there is truth in Emma Lazarus's famous words about the welcoming of foreign peoples to America's shores, Canada has long been even more open to new immigrants than has the United States.[2] For example, as far back as 1871, 17 per cent of Canada's population was foreign-born, compared with 14 per cent in the United States. Although the American proportion surpassed the Canadian level for a brief period between 1891 and 1901, in every Census since then the Canadian percentage has been larger, and the gap has tended to grow with time (Bell and Tepperman 1979: 92; see also Reitz 1998; Li 2003). By 2001, 18.4 per cent of the Canadian population was foreign-born, a proportion that ranks as one of the highest in the world. By comparison, the American proportion, as of 2000, stood at 11.5 per cent (Statistics Canada 2003b; Maclean's 2003a: 13; Statistical Abstract of the United States 2001: 45). Calculations based on data circa 2000 show that, among the four sub-regions of the two nations, English Canada had the highest proportion of foreign-born, at about 21 per cent, followed by the American North at 13 per cent, Quebec at 10 per cent, and the American South at 8 per cent (see Statistics Canada 2003b; Schmidley 2003; Statistical Abstract of the United States 2001: 45). Although the proportion of foreign-born people has been on the rise in the American South and Quebec in recent years, these figures reflect the long-standing tendency for most new immigrants to choose English Canada and the American North as their place of residence (see, e.g., Cash 1941: 96; Gastil 1975:174–5; Garreau 1981: 130–1; Statistical Abstract of the United States 2001: 12; Beaujot 1991: 120–1; Statistics Canada 2003b). To get a fuller sense of the extent of ethnic pluralism in Canada and the

---

2.   Emma Lazarus composed the lines of poetry that are engraved at the base of the Statue of Liberty: 'Give me your tired, your poor, your huddled masses yearning to breathe free, the wretched refuse of your teeming shore. Send these, the homeless, tempest-tossed, to me. I lift my light beside the golden door.'

United States, it is also helpful to look at racial composition. Focusing first on the foreign-born, we find that, mainly because of more open government policies in recent decades, the racial backgrounds of new immigrants to both countries have become increasingly diverse over time. For example, Li (2003: 32) has shown that, whereas the large majority of Canada's immigrants came from Europe before the 1960s, since 1979 almost 8 out of every 10 immigrants have been non-Europeans, with more than half coming from Asia alone. The vast majority of these people would have been of non-white or 'visible-minority' origin. The term visible minority is used by Statistics Canada to subsume a number of different ethnic groups. Among those included in this category are people who identify themselves as Asian, South Asian, West Asian, Chinese, Arab, Filipino, Lebanese, Vietnamese, Caribbean, African, and Latin, Central, or South American. Statistics Canada treats aboriginals as a separate category.

In the United States, during roughly the same period (1981 to 1998), an even larger proportion of immigrants (88 per cent) were non-European (Statistical Abstract of the United States 2001: 11; see also Card and Freeman 1993: 15; Reitz 1998: 10–11). Here, too, it seems certain that most of these immigrants were non-white, although the racial composition of non-European immigrants in the United States is somewhat more ambiguous than is the case in Canada. That is, while most of Canada's non-European immigrants are Asians, and so can more readily be identified as having visible-minority status, more than half of America's non-European immigrants come from Mexico, Central America, or South America. In US government tabulations, individuals from these areas are considered to be of 'Hispanic' origin, but this category includes persons 'of any race', and so combines substantial numbers of both whites and non-whites (Statistical Abstract of the United States 2001: 12).

Recent research on the citizenship levels of Canadian versus American immigrants provides further food for thought on which nation, or which set of government policies, is more pluralist. An analysis based on Census data from 1990 and 1991 has shown that 'immigrants living in Canada are on average much more likely to be citizens than their counterparts in the United States', with a key reason being that Canadian government agencies are more likely than those in the United States to encourage immigrants to apply for citizenship (Bloemraad 2002: 193). The data in this study also suggest that the tendency for citizenship levels to be higher among Canadian than among American eligible immigrants is especially strong for those from non-European or visible-minority backgrounds (see Bloemraad 2002: 200). These findings could be interpreted in a number of ways. For example, the national differences could be seen as evidence that, through the citizenship mechanism, the Canadian state more actively promotes the assimilation of immigrants than does the American government. On the other hand, the results could also be viewed as support for the claim that Canada is a more tolerant, and in that sense more pluralist, society when it comes to welcoming new immigrants as citizens, particularly those of non-European origin.

In the total population, both foreign-born and native-born combined, the percentage of non-whites in the United States is higher than in Canada. However, this is primarily because, since the era of slavery, there have always been many more native-born blacks in the United States. As of 2000, for example, about 18 per cent of the American population was non-white, including about 13 per cent who were black. By comparison, as of 2001, the visible-minority proportion in Canada stood at 13.4 per cent (Statistical Abstract of the United States 2001: 13; Statistics Canada 2003c). The American South has proportionally more blacks than the North, but the North has proportionally more people from Asian and other non-white backgrounds. Overall, the percentage of non-whites in the South is higher, at approximately 21 per cent, compared with about 17 per cent in the North (see Statistical Abstract of the United States 2001: 26–7; Humes and McKinnon 2000; McKinnon 2001; see also Reitz 1998). In the case of the two Canadian regions, 15.5 per cent of English Canada's population was non-white as of 2001, which is very close to the proportion for the American North, while the percentage of non-whites in Quebec was 7 per cent, which is the lowest of all the four sub-societies (Statistics Canada 2003c; Treble and Wickens 2003: 31).

Overall, the substantially higher proportion of foreign-born people living in Canada, especially outside Quebec, may provide the strongest support for the view that, in keeping with its mosaic image, Canada is a more culturally diverse nation than is the United States. In addition, although the American population has a higher proportion of non-whites, given that the majority of them are native-born blacks, it could be claimed that, on the race dimension, as well, Canada has been shaped by a stronger impetus toward ethnic pluralism than its southern neighbour. And, as noted previously, there is the bilingual nature of Canadian society, which some observers also perceive as evidence of greater cultural diversity in Canada and which, notwithstanding the use of such languages as Spanish in the United States, seems to have no real American counterpart. Thus, although there are arguments on either side of this question, it is for all of these reasons that some analysts see Canada as a more 'pluralistic' and more 'multi-hued' nation than the United States (Siddiqui 2001a, 2001b; Ibbitson 2004).

Such considerations, when coupled with the Canadian government's official initiatives to promote multiculturalism, also help to account for the common assumption that Canadian society is not only more pluralist but also more inclusive and tolerant toward minorities than is the United States.

However, some of Canada's pre-eminent experts on the topic of ethnicity and race have concluded that, when it comes to the actual treatment and experience of minorities in the two societies, most of the alleged distinctions between the Canadian mosaic and the American melting pot have been overstated, amounting mainly to 'rhetoric in prose and poetry' (Porter 1979: 144), or to an 'illusion of difference' (Reitz and Breton 1994). Thus, we need to assess these supposed national differences in ethnic pluralism and tolerance, using more direct measures. It is to this task that we now turn.

SOCIOECONOMIC ATTAINMENTS OF IMMIGRANTS AND ETHNIC MINORITIES

One of the best gauges of how well or how poorly different ethnic groups are treated in Canada and the United States is to look at their levels of socioeconomic attainment. Assuming most people in both societies are granted more or less the same opportunities to succeed, we should find that, on average, people from minority ethnic or racial backgrounds are able to achieve levels of education, income, and occupational status that are similar to those of other groups.

In the case of Canada, early research by Porter showed that, in spite of the nation's mosaic image, many non-British ethnic groups, including French Canadians, actually faced serious socioeconomic disadvantages. Thus, in comparing Canada and the United States, Porter ultimately concluded that Canada's mosaic was 'vertical' in nature, with a clear hierarchy of inequality among ethnic groups that, in some ways, was not greatly different from the American structure. That is, although the patterns in the United States were not precisely the same, with native-born blacks having a more prominent place among America's disadvantaged groups, significant problems of blocked opportunity for minorities were obviously present in both nations (Porter 1965: Chapter 3; 1975; 1979: Chapter 6).

In the most detailed and extensive analysis of this question in recent years, Reitz and Breton found that the incorporation of different ethnic groups has been more complete in Canadian than in American society, since Canada's minorities have done somewhat better than their American counterparts in terms of employment, earnings, and occupational status (Reitz and Breton 1994: 90, 123–4). The authors suggest, however, that this has occurred largely because so much of Canada's non-white population is composed of recent immigrants who, mainly as a result of Canadian immigration policies, arrive with better average education and skill levels than those of the native-born population (see also Breton 1998: 61; Borjas 1993: 26–36; Ogmundson 2002: 57). In related research, Reitz has compared the socioeconomic circumstances of recent immigrants to Canada, the United States, and Australia. This analysis revealed that immigrants in Canada had more success in the job market than those in either the United States or Australia. Once again, however, a key reason was that Canada's immigrants tended to be more highly educated than the host population (Reitz 1998: Chapter 4).[3]

Several studies from the 1980s and 1990s have shown that, although racial minorities in Canada generally have higher levels of schooling than other Canadians, on average they tend to earn lower incomes and to work at jobs with lower occupational statuses (e.g., Li 1988; Hou and Balakrishnan 1996; Pendakur and Pendakur 1998, 2001; Lian and Matthews 1998; Gee and Prus 2000). Similar patterns have been found in both early and recent analyses of the relationship between education and success among American racial minorities (e.g., Niemonen 2002: 95–7; Wilson 1999: 16–18, 55; Wright 1979: 227–8). These results suggest again that the situations in the two countries are broadly similar.

Other recent evidence shows that, with some notable exceptions, there is a continuing gap in the socioeconomic attainments of whites and non-whites in each country. For example, in the United States, as of 2000, the median family incomes of both blacks and Hispanics were only 62 per cent of the median for whites; however, one exception in these American data were people from Asian backgrounds who, as a group, reported median family incomes that were 10 per cent higher than those for whites (Statistical Abstract of the United States 2001: 40; see also Rossides 1997: 489; Beeghley 2000: 108–9). In Canada, a study based on data from the 1996 Public Use Sample showed similar patterns. This analysis looked at education, income, and occupational status for 28 self-identified ethnic categories. The findings revealed that many ethnic groups, including those who identified themselves as Jewish, Dutch, and Balkan, for example, did very well, ranking ahead of the British and the French, Canada's two so-called 'founding' or 'charter' groups, on all three dimensions (Grabb 2004). However, for most of the 11 visible minorities in this study, as well as for the aboriginal respondents, the patterns were different. Here the analysis found that, even though more than half of these 12 groups were above the Canadian median for education, slightly less than half were above the median for occupational status, and only one group ('Other Asians') was above the median for family income. Aboriginals were the most disadvantaged of all, with an average family income that was about 57 per cent of the Canadian average in 1996. Other groups with low incomes relative to the Canadian average

---

3.   Reitz (1998: 161–3) also concluded that greater union strength in Canada compared with the United States could be another reason why immigrants do relatively better in Canadian society.

included Africans, at 59 per cent, and Caribbeans, at 66 per cent (Grabb 2004). It should also be noted that research in both countries suggests the gap between visible minorities and others may have increased somewhat over the past decade (e.g., Reitz 1998; Pendakur and Pendakur 2001; Stuhr 2003).

One mitigating factor to consider is that the socioeconomic disadvantages among Canada's visible minorities are substantially reduced if we focus on those who are Canadian-born, as opposed to those who are new immigrants. For example, another analysis using the Public Use Sample database, which looked only at full-time workers aged 25 to 64 in both 1991 and 1996, found that Canadian-born visible minorities, when combined into a single group, had the same average incomes as did Canadian-born whites. This study also showed that, except for aboriginals, foreign-born visible minorities were the only groups who earned less than Canadian-born whites in both years (Kunz, Milan, and Schetagne 2000: 24). The overall patterns were similar in Quebec, except that the incomes for foreign-born visible minorities were slightly below the provincial average. This study also determined that foreign-born whites actually earned about 6 per cent to 8 per cent more than native-born whites in the two years, suggesting that it is the combination of being non-white and foreign-born, and not being foreign-born per se, that leads to income disadvantages. There are undoubtedly several reasons for these outcomes, including the failure of employers and governing agencies to give full recognition to the educational credentials of some immigrants. On the other hand, recent research suggests that, if new immigrants, both white and non-white, are able to acquire Canadian educational qualifications, over time their incomes and occupational attainments converge with those of their native-born counterparts (Wanner and Ambrose 2003: 37–9; see also Wanner 2003a, 2003b). It is also likely that native-born Canadians, whether they are from white or visible-minority backgrounds, would usually have the advantage of being more fluent in one or both of the two official languages, and would be more assimilated to the prevailing Canadian value system than their foreign-born compatriots.

Studies of Job Discrimination

Such considerations, of course, do not negate the possibility that Canada's visible minorities, both foreign-born and native-born, may also be confronted with discrimination and unequal opportunity in their attempts to achieve socioeconomic success. In fact, there is evidence to suggest that Canada has many of the same problems in this area as does the United States. One useful means for assessing this question is to look at research on job discrimination. Several different analyses of job discrimination have been conducted in the two nations over the years, using basically the same 'field experiment' approach (see Henry and Ginsberg 1985; Henry 1989, 2004; Turner, Fix, and

Struyk 1991). In all of these analyses, researchers arranged for black and white actors to answer job advertisements that were posted in newspapers in major cities, with the purpose of seeing if the actors would receive differential treatment in the hiring process on the basis of their race. Each of these experiments, along with a similar study conducted in Great Britain (see Reitz 1988), produced almost identical results. Although there was no sign of preferential hiring practices in roughly three-quarters of the cases, in the other instances there was evidence that the black applicants faced some form of discriminatory behaviour on the part of prospective employers. As with the research on socioeconomic attainment, then, the results of these studies suggest that some ethnic minorities in Canada and the United States have been exposed to similar problems of discrimination and inequity in the job market.

There is another piece of evidence about ethnic or racial discrimination that may be relevant for judging national differences. Although it did not ask specifically about jobs, one self-report question in a 1989 Maclean's/Decima sample survey of both countries asked: 'Have you ever been a victim of racial or ethnic discrimination?' The study showed that 18 per cent of American respondents, but only 11 per cent of Canadian respondents said 'yes' to this question. The regional breakdowns were 11 per cent in English Canada, 9 per cent in Quebec, and 18 per cent in both American regions. Although this result suggests that there may be slightly more general discrimination in the United States than in Canada, we must obviously be cautious in drawing conclusions here, because the evidence comes from only one attitude item and the national difference is rather small.

There are no comparable data for the United States, but recent findings from Canada's Ethnic Diversity Survey of 2002 indicate that perceived discrimination levels for the general Canadian population may be lower in Canada than in the past. In this study, 7 per cent of the overall sample reported that, in the previous five years, they had 'sometimes' or 'often' been discriminated against or treated unfairly because of their 'ethno-cultural characteristics'. It is notable, however, that the level of discrimination reported by visible minorities was substantially higher, at 20 per cent (Statistics Canada 2003h: 23).

Overall, then, it seems appropriate for Reitz and Breton to take the view that, despite the higher success rates of racial minorities in Canada compared with the United States, this does not mean that there is a substantially lower incidence of prejudice or discrimination in Canadian society (Reitz and Breton 1994: 123–4; Reitz 1998: 37–41).

The Special Case of Aboriginals

The situation of aboriginal or First Nations peoples in both Canada and the United States provides an especially clear example of how poorly some minority groups have been treated in the two nations. Despite the fact that the plight of aboriginals has been a serious policy issue in North America for many decades, long-standing problems of injustice and inequality continue to this day (Abella 1984; Cairns 2000; White, Beamon, and Maxim 2003; Hall 2003). We have already seen recent evidence on the low levels of socioeconomic attainment among Canadian aboriginals (see also Gee and Prus 2000; Maxim et al. 2001; Menzies 2004; Harrison and Friesen 2004: 228–30). This pattern also occurs in the United States, although there is evidence that, in the specific case of educational attainment, the Native situation in America is perhaps somewhat better than it is in Canada (Strickland 1997: 52–3; Carney 1999: Chapter 7; Marger 1999: 287–8; Beeghley 2000: 109; see also Statistical Abstract of the United States 2001: 175; Grabb 2004). On the other hand, perhaps in keeping with the more statist tendencies of the Canadian government compared with its American counterpart, research shows that per capita state funding of aboriginals in such areas as education and economic development is considerably higher in Canada than in the United States (Frideres 1998: 169). In general, however, it appears that problems of higher poverty, lower life expectancy, and generally poorer life chances are quite similar for Native peoples in both societies, and that the sources of these difficulties can be traced to the same process of dislocation of the Native populations in each country, beginning with the historical encroachment of European nations into North America centuries ago (Strickland 1997; Frideres 1998; Menzies 2004; Fleras and Elliott 1992, 2003: Chapter 7).

Some have gone so far as to argue that, again in contrast to the image of Canada as the more pluralist and tolerant of the two nations, the United States may provide more in the way of legal rights to aboriginals. According to this view, the aboriginal policy in the United States was based on the principle 'that Indian tribes constitute nations with residual sovereign powers', whereas in Canada the 'government has never defined aboriginal peoples as having a nationhood status with an inherent right to self-determining autonomy' (Fleras and Maaka 2004: 50–1; Gwyn 1995: 235). As a result, American aboriginals have used the courts to protect previously established statutory rights, while the Canadian First Nations have had to rely on the courts to achieve recognition of such rights, including the right to self-government.

There is some debate on both sides of this question, with others contending that the aboriginal situation in Canada is more advantageous. For example, it has been asserted that Canadian First Nations peoples form a larger proportion of the population, are more concentrated in certain political districts, and have a more sustained relationship with the federal government, all of which may give them more political influence than aboriginals in the United States (Brock 2000: 340–1; see also Frideres 1998; Cairns 2000; White,

Beamon, and Maxim 2003; Hall 2003). In general, however, while analysts may disagree on this issue, they all concur that Canada and the United States share many of the same problems in regard to the tolerance, inclusion, and opportunities that are afforded to aboriginal peoples.

COMPARATIVE RESEARCH ON ATTITUDES TOWARD MINORITIES

The evidence on patterns of immigration, ethnic and racial composition, and the socioeconomic attainments of minorities probably provide us with the most objective or direct indicators for comparing ethnic relations in Canada and the United States. However, another useful means for assessing cultural pluralism and ethnic tolerance in the two societies is to consider the attitudes and opinions of the Canadian and American peoples themselves. A number of sample surveys in both societies have collected evidence that provides us with a reasonably good sense of the relative levels of social inclusion and tolerance of minorities in the two populations. Here we will focus specifically on research dealing with three issues that have been the subjects of multiple studies in the two societies. These are support for immigration, attitudes about interracial marriage, and expressions of anti-Semitism. Finally, we complete our assessment of attitudinal evidence by presenting additional findings from the WVS, which compare the views of Canadians, Americans, and the four regional sub-samples on the acceptability of having ethnic minorities and other distinct social groups as neighbours.

Views on Immigrants and Immigration

Existing comparative research provides a somewhat mixed picture concerning which of the two nations has a more supportive view of immigrants and immigration. On the one hand, there are numerous studies, based on data from national surveys spanning the early 1980s to the early 2000s, which show that Canadians are consistently more in favour than Americans of increasing immigration to their country (Harvey 1996; Espenshade and Hempstead 1996: 546; Perlin 1997: 144–5; Simon and Lynch 1999: 461; Wood 1999: 21; Gallup 2001d; Jones 2003c). On the other hand, there is some evidence that Canadians are more likely than Americans to believe new immigrants should blend in with the dominant culture, rather than hold onto their distinct ethnic identities. For example, Reitz and Breton analyzed national data from the 1989 Maclean's/Decima survey, and found that only 34 per cent of Canadian respondents thought new immigrants should be 'encouraged to maintain their distinctive culture or ways', compared with 47 per cent of Americans (Reitz and Breton 1994: 28; see also Perlin 1997: 145; Brym 1989: 105; Wood 1993:

26; Sniderman et al. 1996: 111). However, using a different question, a national survey from 1997 in the United States found that only 38 per cent of Americans believed newcomers should 'live by their own traditions', with 54 per cent saying that they should 'make an effort to fit into the mainstream' (Cantril and Cantril 1999: 181–2). Generally, then, while the results show that Canadians are more in favour of immigrants being admitted to their society than are Americans, it is not clear whether Canadians or Americans are more open to the idea of new immigrants retaining their distinct culture and values.

As for research that compares the four regions on the issue of immigration, little published work is available. One study that used data from the Canadian Charter of Rights survey of 1987 found that Quebecers were somewhat more likely to believe that 'people who come to Canada should try harder to be like other Canadians', at 76 per cent versus 60 per cent for English Canadians (Sniderman et al. 1992: 23; see also Sniderman et al. 1996: 111). However, our own re-analysis of the 1989 Maclean's/Decima item used by Reitz and Breton, with results broken down into the four regions, shows no real internal differences in either country. The findings (which are not shown in the tables) indicate that 36 per cent of English Canadians and 35 per cent of Quebecers believe immigrants should be encouraged to maintain their distinctive ways, compared with 49 per cent of northern Americans and 46 per cent of southern Americans. Another study of the two American regions, based on 1997 national survey data, found no significant difference between southerners and northerners in the proportion who believed that immigrants should try to fit in (Cantril and Cantril 1999: 145). On the other hand, Espenshade and Hempstead (1999: 548–9) reported on national data from the early 1990s that showed a tendency for southerners to be less positive toward immigration than other Americans, especially those living in New England and the Northeast. In addition, although he does not present the findings, Adams asserts in a summary of his own recent survey research that people from the American South are more 'xenophobic' than their northern compatriots. By this he means that southerners are more apt to worry about immigration as a threat to the 'purity of the country', and also voice a stronger preference for newcomers to 'set aside their cultural backgrounds and blend into the American melting pot' (Adams 2003: 86, 167). Thus, there are some grounds for concluding that, of the four regional sub-groups, southern Americans are the least supportive of immigration. Otherwise, however, the existing evidence is rather sparse and inconsistent, making it difficult to draw strong conclusions about regional differences.

Interracial Marriage

The analysis of attitudes about interracial marriage in Canada and the United States provides another means for assessing the state of ethnic relations in the two countries. It is worth remarking, however, that there are at least two ways to interpret the findings in this area of study. First, higher support for inter-marriage could be a sign that respondents are more tolerant of cultural differ-ences, and not concerned about maintaining clear segregation or 'social distance' between ethnic or racial groups (Reitz and Breton 1994: 73). While this is perhaps the more plausible interpretation, a second possibility is that intermarriage is mainly a mechanism for encouraging cultural 'blending' and the 'weakening' of distinct ethnic identities (Reitz and Breton 1994: 51, 54). Consequently, engaging in or expressing favourable attitudes about interracial marriage, especially on the part of the dominant or majority group in a society, could be interpreted as proof of that group's preference for assimilating ethnic minorities, rather than encouraging them to remain distinct.

In either event, there is consistent evidence that Canadians have more positive views about interracial marriage than do Americans. For example, one analysis, which was based on cross-national data from several surveys covering the period 1968 to 1983, found significantly higher levels of opposition to interracial marriage in the United States than in Canada, while also showing that the level of opposition had declined markedly in both countries over time (Lambert and Curtis 1988: 345). In the latter study, American opposition fell from 72 per cent in 1968 to 50 per cent in 1983, whereas opposition in Canada went from 53 per cent to 21 per cent in the same period (see also Bibby 1990: 52; 1995: 54). Using more recent data from the 1989 Maclean's/Decima poll, Reitz and Breton found evidence suggesting that oppo-sition to interracial marriage had continued to drop in both nations, but that Americans were still less supportive. In this study, 32 per cent of American respondents said that they would be 'unhappy' if one of their children married someone from a different racial background, compared with only 13 per cent of Canadians (Reitz and Breton 1994: 81; also Perlin 1997: 144). Another sign of the stronger opposition to interracial marriage in the United States is that, as recently as 1988, 25 per cent of Americans thought that black-white marriages should be illegal (Reitz and Breton 1994: 81). More recent data indi-cate that, by 1996, this proportion had fallen to about 11 per cent (Mitchell 1998: 194–5). Overall, the evidence is consistent with Reitz and Breton's conclusion that, while 'the social distance between the majority and racial minorities has declined in both countries, it has consistently been smaller in Canada, especially in relation to intermarriage' (1994: 88–9).

With regard to differences across the four sub-regions of Canada and the United States, the evidence, while limited, suggests a fairly consistent pattern in which support for (or lack of opposition to) interracial marriage is highest in Quebec, with English Canada a relatively close second, the American North next, and the American South a distant fourth. In the case of English and

French Canada, the Lambert and Curtis (1988: 345) study noted above found that English-Canadian opposition dropped from 60 per cent in 1968 to 24 per cent in 1983, but that French opposition was lower throughout this period, falling from 38 per cent in 1968 to just 11 per cent in 1983. Our own re-analysis of the 1989 Maclean's/Decima poll data, with the findings broken down into the four regions (the results are not reported in tables), indicates that the percentage of respondents who would be 'unhappy' if their child married someone of a different race was almost the same in the two Canadian groups, at about 13 per cent for English Canadians and about 15 per cent for Quebecers, but stood at 28 per cent for northern Americans and 42 per cent for southern Americans.

There are no comparable American data, but 'The New Canada' survey of 2003 shows generally similar results for Quebec and Canada to those reported in earlier studies. This survey, which over-sampled people aged 18 to 30 and included some 2,000 respondents, was prepared jointly by the Canadian Centre for Research and Information on Canada (CRIC) and by Toronto's Globe and Mail newspaper (see Globe and Mail 2003). One item in the study revealed that 11 per cent of Quebecers, compared with 12 per cent of Canadians as a whole, would be either 'uncomfortable' or 'very uncomfortable' if 'a close relative, like your sister or daughter, was going to marry someone who is black'. Another question, which asked if it would be 'a bad idea for people of different races to marry one another', found that 14 per cent of Quebecers, compared with 10 per cent of Canadians as a whole, agreed with this statement.

More current American research on attitudes about interracial marriage is not available, although one recent study has found that the proportion of Americans who think 'it is all right for blacks and whites to date each other' rose from less than 50 per cent in 1987 to almost 80 per cent in 2003 (Parker 2003: 9). There is also evidence from the United States for the late 1990s that considers actual rates of intermarriage, and that is consistent with the attitudinal patterns we have noted. Romano (2003: 58–9) reports that marital unions between races have increased over time in American society, but are still less evident in the southern states, where interracial marriage was generally illegal until the 1950s (Romano 2003: 58–9). Another recent study has shown that some minorities, including Asians and Hispanics, have higher levels of intermarriage with other groups than would be predicted given their proportion of the population, but that the rates of black–white marriages are lower than would be expected on this basis (Qian, 1999; see also Romano 2003: 3; Statistical Abstract of the United States 2001: 47). Therefore, the lower support for interracial marriage in the United States, especially in the South, may stem more from opposition to black–white marriages specifically, rather than from a rejection of interracial unions in general.

Anti-Semitic Attitudes in Canada and the United States

Another important issue to consider when assessing levels of tolerance and social inclusion is anti-Semitism. This topic is too large to be examined in detail in the present analysis. However, there is some comparable evidence on anti-Semitic attitudes in Canada and the United States that provides us with an additional basis for judging national and regional differences in support for cultural diversity and ethnic pluralism. As was briefly discussed in our analysis of ethnic differences in socioeconomic attainment, Jews rank among the most successful groups in all of Canada, a status that they have also achieved in the United States (see, e.g., Lipset 1996: Chapter 5; Dershowitz 1997; Rossides 1997: 489; Marger 1999: 257; Weinfeld 2001; Grabb 2004). Nevertheless, while Jews provide a prime example of how some religious or ethnic minorities are able to do extremely well in both countries, there is a body of research showing that the Jewish population at times has faced serious problems of prejudice and discrimination.

The work of Reitz and Breton once again serves as a good starting point for our discussion. Their review of behavioural evidence, such as the number of anti-Semitic incidents reported to different agencies in each country, as well as attitudinal studies measuring the acceptance of anti-Semitic stereotypes, led them to conclude that the level of prejudice and discrimination toward Jewish people was quite similar in Canada and the United States (Reitz and Breton 1994: 71–2, 130). Although some other analysts hint at small national differences, these writers are also of the view that the two populations are alike on this issue. The general conclusion has been that overt anti-Semitism is now relatively rare in the two societies, and that, according to recent sample survey findings, most Canadians and Americans have positive attitudes toward Jews (Martire and Clark 1982; Brym and Lenton 1991; Sniderman et al. 1992, 1993; Lipset 1996: 166–8; Weinfeld 1990: 90; 2001: 336–8, 425–6). In addition, as we have discussed, it is clear that Jewish people in both countries have had a similar opportunity to attain high socioeconomic standing. In all of these ways, then, the evidence leads to the conclusion that there are no strong Canadian–American differences in ethnic tolerance or support for cultural diversity, at least as judged by the situation of the Jewish minority in each country.

If we move to a comparison of the four sub-societies, we do find some evidence of differences in people's attitudes and orientations to Jews. First of all, early studies based on data collected prior to the 1970s found a greater prevalence of anti-Semitism in the American South than in the North, particularly in rural areas (Glenn and Simmons 1967: 185–6; Quinley and Glock 1979: 29–30; Dinnerstein 1987: 73–6; see also Lipset 1996: 165–6). Subsequent evidence from the 1980s finds a similar, though weaker, pattern (Martire and Clark 1982: 36–7). These findings are dated, but are consistent with more recent research suggesting that the South is generally a region where there is relatively less tolerance or openness regarding ethnic, racial, and other cultural differences (Ellison and Musick 1993; Weakliem and Biggert 1999: 876; Cantril and Cantril 1999: 145).

Within Canada, studies have found that there is a regional division on the question of attitudes toward the Jewish minority, with Quebecers generally being more likely to express negative views about Jews than are English Canadians (e.g., Brym and Lenton 1991; Sniderman et al. 1992, 1993; see also Reitz and Breton 1994: 71–2). The findings from these studies are consistent, but the interpretations of their meaning have been quite varied. The most compelling interpretations, in our view, centre on factors that we have discussed previously, especially the influence of Quebec's conservative religious and political elite prior to the time of the Quiet Revolution. There is little question that, although anti-Semitic viewpoints could be found in all parts of Canada during its early development as a nation, Quebec's Catholic Church hierarchy, along with various political officials, journalists, and other opinion leaders, once played a particularly prominent role in promoting anti-Jewish beliefs in parts of the Quebec population (Langlais and Rome 1991: Chapter 3; Delisle 1993; Weinfeld 2001: 324–31). In addition, it is clear that, at least until recently, Quebecers have had long-standing and deeply held concerns about cultural survival, going back to the time of Confederation. Over the years, these concerns over preserving their own society and collective identity have been an impetus for Quebecers to expect some degree of conformity to their culture on the part of Jews and other minorities. As various writers have noted, these forces in combination probably go a long way toward explaining why Quebecers at times have expressed more guarded, suspicious, or otherwise negative views about some ethnic groups in their society, including the Jewish minority (Curtis and Lambert 1976; Lambert and Curtis 1983; Berry, Kalin, and Taylor 1977: 219; Sniderman et al. 1993; Reitz and Breton 1994: 72).

Still, even when such considerations are taken into account, these findings seem inconsistent with other research that we have presented. For example, we have seen that Quebecers, for many years now, have tended to express more tolerant views than both English Canadians and Americans on the question of interracial marriage. Moreover, we should also recall the research discussed in Chapter 7, which showed that Quebecers are more supportive, positive, or accepting than all of the other regional sub-groups in their opinions about such issues as gender equality, gay rights, sexual freedom, and the trend toward common-law marriages and non-traditional families. In the next segment of this chapter, we assess some additional evidence suggesting that problems of anti-Jewish attitudes in Quebec may be mainly a thing of the past. These data also allow us to broaden the discussion of tolerance and social inclusion in the two countries, by looking at people's views about a larger and more varied array of ethnic and other minorities.

Having Minorities as Neighbours

The WVS surveys include a set of items that provide us with another basis for comparing tolerance and social inclusion in Canada and the United States. These measures (see Table 9.1) are part of a general question, in which respondents are asked to look at a list of 14 'various groups of people', and to indicate any category that they 'would not like to have as neighbours'. This battery of items deals with a less intimate form of social contact between peoples than does the research on intergroup marriage discussed previously. However, these additional indicators serve as further evidence for assessing whether Canadians and Americans have different ideas about the social distance that they would like to maintain from ethnic and other minorities.

The first five categories listed in Table 9.1 can be broadly considered as ethnic (including racial and religious) groupings, and so are the most directly pertinent to our analysis of ethnic tolerance among Canadians and Americans. These items refer to: 'people of a different race', 'Muslims', 'immigrants', 'Jews', and 'Hindus'. In addition, Table 9.1 shows the results for the other nine groups listed in the survey question, as well as an average score for all 14 items combined. The remaining nine groups are: 'people with a criminal record', 'heavy drinkers', 'emotionally unstable people', 'drug addicts', 'people with AIDS', 'homosexuals', 'left-wing extremists', 'right-wing extremists', and, finally, 'people with large families'. The questions asking about AIDS sufferers and homosexuals were also considered in Table 7.3, where we discussed the issue of family values and sexuality. Although these items do not deal specifically with ethnic minorities, the results for these other groups are also instructive. The answers to these questions help us to determine if there are national differences in tolerance in general, by considering a diverse range of other distinct minorities or 'outgroups'.

Attitudes about Five Ethnic Minorities

If we focus, first of all, on the five ethnic categories, we can see that the large majority of both Canadians and Americans show no indication of rejecting any of the groups as their neighbours. On this basis, then, the degree of ethnic tolerance and inclusion appears to be very high in Canada and the United States. As for relative differences between the two nations, we find that Canadians are somewhat more inclusive than Americans when asked about Muslims, immigrants, and people of a different race, but are not significantly different from Americans with regard to Jews, and are slightly less inclusive

Table 9.1 Social Groups That Respondents Do Not Want as Neighbours by Region and Nation

	Region				Nation		
	English Canada	Quebec	US North	US South	Sig[1]	Canada Total	US Total	Sig[1]
% mentioning the following groups as among those they would not like as neighbours:								
1. People of a different race	4	6	9*	12*	√	5	10	√
2. Muslims	10	11	15*	13	√	10	14	√
3. Immigrants	6	5	9*	14*	√	6	10	√
4. Jews	5	8*	4	8*	√	6	5	√
5. Hindus	10	11	7*	10	√	10	8	√
6. People with a criminal record	43	42	47*	55*	√	42	50	√
7. Heavy drinkers	56	51	59	62*	√	55	60	√
8. Emotionally unstable people	32	21*	42*	44*	√	30	43	√
9. Drug addicts	66	55*	78*	80*	√	63	79	√
10. People with AIDS	21	19	24	37*	√	21	28	√
11. Homosexuals	33	19*	35	44*	√	30	38	√
12. Left-wing extremists	30	19*	30	31	√	27	30	√
13. Right-wing extremists	26	20*	28	29	√	25	29	√
14. People with large families	7	5	8	11*	√	6	9	√
Average number of groups opposed	3.48	2.92*	3.93*	4.50*	√	3.34	4.12	√

Notes

[1] A check mark (√) indicates that the likelihood ratio chi-square for the overall four-category comparison across regions, or the two-category comparison across nations, is significant at <.05. The asterisk (*) indicates that the category is significantly different from the English Canadian reference group at <.05.

than Americans in the case of Hindus. In all instances, however, the differences are small, amounting to five percentage points or less.

The 'God and Society in North America Survey', which was conducted in 1996, also found that Americans had somewhat more negative attitudes toward Muslims than did Canadians (Harvey 1996). Unfortunately, in the aftermath of the attack on the World Trade Center in September of 2001, it is plausible to assume that people's views about Muslims in both nations will have become less positive and more exclusionary than those reported here.

When we compare the results for the five ethnic minorities across the four sub-societies, we again find that only a small minority of respondents express negative attitudes toward any of the groups, and we also see very little in the way of regional differences. In three of the five comparisons, those involving Muslims, immigrants, and people of a different race, both northern Americans and southern Americans are slightly less inclusive than the English-Canadian reference group. In one instance, the question about Hindus, people from the American North are marginally more inclusive than English Canadians. Finally, when asked about Jews, both Quebecers and southern Americans are slightly less inclusive than either English Canadians or northern Americans. The latter finding is consistent with the research on anti-Semitism reviewed earlier. However, the differences are very small, and suggest that negative sentiments toward Jews in both of these regions are minimal. Overall, there is little evidence of notable differences in attitudes about ethnic minorities across the four regions.

Attitudes about Nine Other Minorities and Outgroups

The other nine items in Table 9.1 show a substantially different pattern from that found for the five ethnic groups. First, except for the question about people with large families, the levels of exclusion are all much higher than those for any of the five ethnic minorities. Second, we see a much clearer tendency for Canadians to hold more inclusive attitudes than Americans when it comes to having these nine groups as neighbours. In fact, in every case, Canadians express a significantly greater willingness than Americans to accept such people in their neighbourhoods.

In the regional comparisons, there are several important findings. The most notable may be that Quebec respondents consistently exhibit the most tolerant attitudes of all the four regional sub-groups. In fact, in each case, they are the least likely to reject the nine target groups as neighbours. In addition, in five of the comparisons—those for emotionally unstable people, drug addicts, AIDS sufferers, homosexuals, and both left-wing and right-wing extremists—Quebecers are significantly more inclusive than English Canadians, who show the second most tolerant attitudes of the four regional sub-groups. English Canadians, in turn, are significantly more accepting than northern Americans in three cases, but are no different from northern Americans in the other six comparisons. Finally, as we would predict given previous research, respondents from the American South are the least inclusive or accepting. Southerners express the highest levels of exclusion for every one of the nine outgroups, and also have an average score on the composite index that is the highest of the four regional sub-samples.

In summary, then, these findings from the WVS reveal a modest tendency for Canadians to be more tolerant and inclusive of the five ethnic minorities than are Americans, with differences across the four regions that are small and somewhat mixed. However, the comparisons involving the nine other distinct groups reveal a consistent pattern, with Canadians, especially Quebecers, being more tolerant and accepting than both American groups, and with people from the American South ranking as the least inclusive of all.

SUMMARY

In this chapter, we have considered a large body of research on the question of social inclusion and ethnic tolerance. We have been especially interested in comparing the relative commitment to cultural pluralism in Canada and the United States, as judged by a variety of social-structural, behavioural, and attitudinal indicators.

In keeping with the arguments of some writers, we have found that the two countries are similar in a number of important ways. On the positive side, there is little doubt that, compared with most other nations, Canada and the United States offer relatively more open and free economic and political environments for their populations, with opportunities for material well-being and 'the pursuit of happiness' that are among the best in the world. On the negative side, however, it is apparent that the two countries also share some of the same harsh realities, including the fact that individual opportunities and freedoms are not equally available to everyone, especially many non-whites and new non-white immigrants. In addition, both societies have done a similarly inadequate job of eliminating the inequities and injustices faced by their aboriginal peoples. Finally, the populations of both countries appear to evince roughly the same, though also relatively low, levels of anti-Semitic behaviour and attitudes.

In several respects, our reading of the comparative evidence on cultural pluralism is that, as Reitz and Breton have argued, there are signs of 'both a tolerance for diversity and a bias toward assimilation' in each nation (1994: 10). Even so, the existence for the past several decades of an official multi-cultural policy in Canadian society, as well as a consistently higher level of immigration, especially by members of visible-minority groups, would appear to make Canada a more ethnically diverse and, in that sense, a more pluralist nation than the United States. We also suggest that there are some differences in levels of social inclusion and tolerance in the two societies. In particular, the evidence indicates a continuing tendency for Americans to be more exclusionary than Canadians in regard to interracial marriage. In addition, Americans also appear to be less receptive than Canadians to having certain outgroups or distinct minorities sharing their neighbourhoods with them. Lastly, while there clearly are significant examples of racism in each nation, it is difficult to identify an issue in Canadian society that quite compares with the problems faced by native-born blacks in the United States.

As with other topics that we have considered in this analysis, some of the most important differences that we have found have been those operating within the two countries, especially with regard to Quebec and the American South. We have seen that Quebecers tend to express the greatest support for interracial marriage and also exhibit the highest levels of acceptance when asked about having various minorities and outgroups in their neighbourhoods. These results are consistent with our findings in Chapter 7, which showed that Quebecers have the most liberal or tolerant attitudes on issues such as gender equality and gay rights. The one discordant element we have found in this section of the analysis is the indication that Quebecers have more negative attitudes toward Jews than do other Canadians. Even this tendency, however, may now have largely dissipated, considering the more recent evidence on attitudes about neighbours presented here. The other notable regional difference concerns the American South, which again stands out as the most traditional or intolerant of the four sub-societies in much of the evidence dealing with ethnic minorities, just as it did on the issues of family and sexuality that we considered in Chapter 7.

In short, then, we see divergences between the two societies that are sufficiently great to make us disagree with the assertion that there are no meaningful differences between Canada and the United States on the question of social inclusion and tolerance of ethnic and other minorities. However, to borrow from Reitz and Breton, we do believe that most claims of truly large differences between the two peoples are almost certainly illusions.

CHAPTER 10

≈

POLITICAL ATTITUDES AND POLITICAL ACTION

One of the most important elements in any comparative analysis of Canada and the United States is an assessment of political attitudes and political action in the two populations. These areas of study, which form the main focus in Chapter 10, are usually considered by social and political scientists under the general rubric of 'political culture'. This term basically refers to a society's political 'climate', as judged by the ways that people think about, participate in, and relate to the system of government and politics in their society (see, e.g., Almond and Verba 1963; Elazar 1966; Bailyn 1967; Presthus 1977a, 1977b; Inglehart 1977, 1990, 1997; Bell and Tepperman 1979; Gibbins 1982; Nevitte 1996; Putnam 2000).

Because both Canada and the United States are well-established and stable democracies, with long-standing shared English influences, it is plausible to expect that they would have quite similar political cultures. This is certainly the expectation that would be derived from the deep-structures perspective that was outlined in Part I. It will be recalled that, according to this perspective, English-speaking democracies such as Canada and the United States are very much alike when it comes to their commitment to a set of common core principles, including individual liberty, popular sovereignty, legal equality, and pluralism. If the two nations do indeed have the same strong allegiance to these ideals, we should expect that this commonality will be apparent in their political systems, with both fostering such ideas as the right and responsibility of individuals to participate as equal citizens in the political process, and the right of all people to express and to act on any dissenting views that they might have about their government and its operation.

However, while virtually all observers agree that there are such parallels in the Canadian and American political cultures, some prominent writers have pointed mainly to what they see as substantial national differences. Not surprisingly, perhaps, Lipset has been one of the major contributors to this discussion. Following the same line of argument that we saw in his delineation of the American Creed in Chapter 2, Lipset asserts that the American 'republican' approach to democratic politics is quite different from the Canadian approach. In particular, he contends that the system in the United States is more broadly based, egalitarian, and pluralist, with an emphasis on populist or mass decision-making, a distrust of centralized government authority, and a reliance on a set of 'checks and balances' that divides power among the legislature (the Senate and Congress), the courts or judiciary, and the executive branch (the Presidency), and so limits the influence of any one part of the system. The Canadian political structure, while it resembles the American system in several ways, including the separation of powers among the legislature (the Senate and House of Commons), the judiciary, and the executive (the Prime Minister and the Cabinet), is seen by Lipset as being closer to the British parliamentary form. In his view, this means that Canada's version of democracy generally grants far less influence to the wider population and has fewer checks and balances, particularly on the activities of the executive. As a result, political power in Canada is said to be more elite-based, more centralized, and more highly concentrated within a small group of top leaders, especially the Prime Minister and his senior Cabinet members (see, e.g., Lipset 1968: 44, 49; 1985: 142; 1990: 49–52; 1996: 39–46).

Most researchers working in this area agree that there are these kinds of formal differences between the two political structures; however, many of these analysts also remark that the Canadian form of government is not purely British and includes many elements that were purposely adopted from the American model (e.g., Presthus 1973: 310; 1977a, 1977b; Gibbins 1982: 26; Pocklington 1985: 152–3; Merelman 1991: 11, 27; Simeon and Willis 1997: 153–5, 168–71; Smith 2000: 243–4). It is also the case that, like the Canadian system, the American political system was itself significantly influenced by the British form of government and by many British policy precedents, including the granting of voting rights to women and the development of numerous social-welfare and humanitarian reforms (see, e.g., Schlesinger 1964: 156–70). In addition, observers have generally concluded that power within the Canadian system is now much more decentralized than it once was, with the devolution of more authority to the provinces after Confederation, as discussed in Part II, and also with the growing power of the judiciary after the adoption of the Charter of Rights and Freedoms in 1982 (e.g., Gibbins 1982: 26–9; Pocklington 1985: 152–7, 167–72; Lipset 1990: 194–5; Sniderman et al. 1996: 159–62, 168–9; Simeon and Willis 1997: 172–81; Manfredi 1997, 2000).

Nevertheless, given that there are in fact continuing structural differences between these two modes of government, a central question to be addressed in this chapter is whether and to what extent such divergences have generated distinctive political cultures in Canada and the United States, especially as reflected in the political outlooks and actions of the two national populations and the four regional sub-groups. Because there is a large literature on the general study of politics in both countries, we will limit our discussion of this question to research that pertains to the major themes which have been emphasized throughout this volume. We are especially concerned with the common view that, because their political system is supposedly more centralized and elitist, Canadians have come to be consistently more passive and compliant than Americans, both in their orientation to government authority and in their level of personal involvement in the political process. This viewpoint closely parallels other alleged differences between the two peoples that we have considered in previous chapters, including the claim that Canadians are more reliant on and accepting of state economic and social assistance than are Americans. This argument is also broadly consistent with the assumption, which we discussed in our analysis of crime in the two countries, that Canadians are more law-abiding, peaceable, and accepting of legal authority than are Americans. In varying ways, all of these perceptions and assumptions suggest that, compared with the American population, the Canadian people are more passive, obedient, deferential, and trusting in their relationship to those who have political and legal authority over them.

Although we have already seen in previous sections that the portrayal of Canadians as more dependent and more docile is either seriously overstated or essentially incorrect, we have not looked at evidence on whether Canadians may have such proclivities in the specific areas of political attitudes and political action. Hence, in this part of the analysis, we test the general hypothesis or assumption that Canadians are more passive and deferential than Americans, this time with a focus on political outlooks and behaviour. Our evidence is based on two sets of interrelated measures. First, we look at data on whether Canadians are less likely than Americans to show an interest in or engagement with politics, as judged by their expressed attitudes, and also by behavioural indicators such as voting activity and participation in various forms of political protest or civil dissent. Second, we present evidence dealing with levels of political trust and confidence in governmental or state-controlled organizations, in order to determine if it is true, as some have argued, that Canadians have a greater acceptance of, respect for, and faith in the actions of their political leaders than do Americans. As part of this comparison, we also look briefly at levels of general trust and feelings of national pride or patriotism. In all cases, we test for any significant variations in both political attitudes and political actions across the four regional sub-groups. As part of our overall assessment, we discuss, as well, the fit of our findings with those in the larger literature on political culture in the two nations.

POLITICAL INTEREST AND POLITICAL BEHAVIOUR

Students of Canadian and American politics generally concur that one of the hallmarks of an effective democracy is a high level of citizen interest in and engagement with the political process. Even so, there are some who have argued the opposite view. Lipset, in particular, has suggested that widespread political apathy in the population may well be preferable to political activism, for it is 'evidence of the electorate's basic satisfaction with the way things are going' (Lipset 1981: 227). However, the predominant sentiment among most researchers working on this question is that regular and extensive political participation is essential for a genuinely pluralist and democratic society (see, e.g., MacIver 1947; Lane 1959; Dahl 1963, 1967; Hamilton 1972; Inglehart 1997; Putnam 2000). There has been some concern that the United States and other democratic nations may be witnessing a decline in both political activity and civic participation in recent years (see especially Putnam 2000). Nevertheless, a number of researchers studying Canada, the United States, and various other nations have found that levels of political interest and civic involvement have generally been increasing, or remaining stable, and that this has been true since at least the 1980s (e.g., Dalton 1984; Nevitte 1996: 51–4; Inglehart 1997: 308–15; Paxton 1999; Rotolo 1999; Curtis, Baer, and Grabb 2001; Curtis, Grabb, Perks, and Chui 2004).

The main question of concern to us here is whether levels of political interest and involvement differ substantially for Canadians and Americans, and for the four regional sub-groups. If it is true, as Lipset and some others have claimed, that Canadians are more passive and deferential than Americans toward government authority, this difference should presumably mean that Canadians will be less inclined toward political activism. As for variations among the four sub-societies, the prediction is less clear. On the one hand, it seems consistent with Lipset's perspective to expect that Quebecers, who live under the most interventionist government of all the four regional sub-groups, would be the most accepting of existing power arrangements and the least apt to engage in political activity to alter those arrangements. By the same argument, we would then expect people from the American South to be the most active, with English Canadians and northern Americans in between. On the other hand, given the alleged tendency for people from the southern United States to have the most anti-statist attitudes, as well as the most anti-institutionalist orientations toward formal organizations and collective action, it is conceivable that respondents from the American South may be the most likely to turn away from politics and government, and hence would be the least interested in following or participating in the political process.

Self-Reports of Political Interest and Activity

One means for assessing national and regional differences in people's political interest and activity is to look at self-reports. Table 10.1 presents some relevant evidence from the WVS, using three measures: a 4-point scale of the respondent's expressed political interest; a 4-point scale of how important politics is in the respondent's life; and a 3-category measure of how often the respondent discusses politics with friends.

We can note first that none of the results in Table 10.1 shows a high level of political engagement in the two nations or the four sub-societies. Instead, only a modest level of political interest is expressed by all of the groups, with scores falling close to the middle on the 4-point scales, and with no more than 20 per cent of respondents, in any of the samples, saying that they frequently discuss politics with friends.

If we compare the two national samples, we find that, on both the political-interest scale and the political-importance scale, there are no statistically significant differences between Canadians and Americans. For the question about discussing politics with friends, we do find a difference, but it indicates that Canadians, not Americans, are somewhat more likely to say that they engage in such discussions. Based on these results, then, it is clear that, contrary to the assumptions of some writers, Canadians are neither more passive about politics, nor more disengaged from the workings of the political system, than are Americans.

As for variations across the four regional sub-groups, here too the differences are small, although there are two minor patterns of note. First, Quebecers seem to rank toward the lower end on political interest, in that they report the lowest scores on both of the 4-point scales, while standing somewhere in the middle of the four sub-groups on the question of discussing politics with friends. Second, respondents from the American South are also closer to the lower end of the continuum. While they are just as likely as both English Canadians and northern Americans to say that politics is important, southerners are significantly lower than both English Canadians and northern Americans on the political-interest item, and are also the most likely of all the four sub-samples to say that they never discuss politics with friends. Taken together, these results provide some weak support for the prediction that both Quebecers and southerners, perhaps for different reasons, are less engaged with politics in their respective societies.

Self-Reports of Political Protest and Civil Dissent

Another useful gauge of political interest and activism is the extent to which people take part in various types of political protest or civil dissent. Table 10.2 presents findings based on five items from the WVS, in which respondents

Table 10.1 Political Interest by Region and Nation

	Region					Nation		
	English Canada	Quebec	US North	US South	Sig[1]	Canada Total	US Total	Sig[1]
1. How interested would you say you are in politics (4 pt. scale[a])	2.67	2.48*	2.63	2.59*	√	2.63	2.62	
2. How important is politics in your life (4 pt. scale[b])	2.51	2.42*	2.56	2.52		2.49	2.55	
3. How often do you discuss politics with friends (%):								
Frequently	20	17	14	14		19	14	
Occasionally	56	57	58	53		56	56	
Never	25	26	28	34	√	25	30	√

Notes

[1] A check mark (√) indicates that the likelihood ratio chi-square for the overall four-category comparison across regions, or the two-category comparison across nations, is significant at <.05. The asterisk (*) indicates that the category is significantly different from the English Canadian reference group at <.05.

[a] The scale ranged from 1 = 'not at all interested' to 4 = 'very interested'.

[b] The scale ranged from 1 = 'not at all important' to 4 = 'very important'.

Table 10.2 Political Protest and Civil Dissent by Region and Nation

	Region					Nation		
	English Canada	Quebec	US North	US South	Sig[1]	Canada Total	US Total	Sig[1]
% saying they 'have done' or 'might do':								
1. Signing a petition								
Have done	77	76	75	63		77	71	
Might do	14	19	19	27		15	21	
Never do	9	6	7	10	√	8	8	√
2. Joining a boycott								
Have done	21	26	20	14		22	18	
Might do	45	38	45	49		43	47	
Never do	34	36	35	37	√	34	36	√
3. Attending lawful demonstrations								
Have done	17	32	16	14		21	16	
Might do	44	38	45	49		43	46	
Never do	38	30	39	37	√	36	38	√
4. Joining unofficial strikes								
Have done	5	12	4	4		7	4	
Might do	29	27	33	32		28	32	
Never do	66	62	63	64	√	65	63	√

	Region					Nation		
	English Canada	Quebec	US North	US South	Sig[1]	Canada Total	US Total	Sig[1]
5. Occupying buildings								
Have done	2	8	2	2		3	2	
Might do	19	25	17	22		21	19	
Never do	79	68	81	76	√	76	79	√
Civil Dissent Index (count of the 'have done' responses on the 5 items)	1.21	1.48*	1.13*	.94*	√	1.27	1.07	√

Notes

[1] A check mark (√) indicates that the likelihood ratio chi-square for the overall four-category comparison across regions, or the two-category comparison across nations, is significant at <.05. The asterisk (*) indicates that the category is significantly different from the English Canadian reference group at <.05.

could report whether they 'have done' or 'might do' different types of 'political action'. These actions ranged from legal and relatively moderate forms of protest—signing petitions, joining boycotts, and going to lawful demonstrations—to the more extreme activities of joining unofficial strikes and occupying buildings.

We can see from Table 10.2 that all of the groups of respondents are far more likely to pursue legal forms of political protest (especially signing petitions) than they are to engage in extreme and potentially illegal actions, such as unofficial strikes and the occupation of buildings. The minuscule levels of involvement in the latter two activities are consistent with previous findings considered in Chapter 7, which showed that the vast majority of people, both Canadian and American, reject illegal behaviour and have respect for the rule of law.

However, Table 10.2 does reveal that there are some differences in the willingness of the two national samples and the four regional sub-samples to engage in protest activity. First, when we compare Canadians and Americans as a whole, we find small but statistically significant differences for all five types of protest, and also for the overall index of civil dissent, which combines the 'have done' responses on all five items. The crucial outcome here is that, in every instance, it is Canadians, rather than Americans, who are more likely to participate in political protest or dissent. This finding runs completely counter to any claims that, compared with Americans, Canadians are more passive about political issues, or more likely to accept the status quo.

Other notable patterns emerge when we consider the four sub-societies. In these comparisons, we see that people from the southern United States are generally the least likely to be active in the various types of protest. Southerners receive the lowest score of all four groups on the overall civil-dissent index (.94), and also have the smallest percentages of 'have done' responses for each of the five individual items considered separately. This outcome is basically consistent with the findings on political interest that were shown in Table 10.1, and support the idea that, compared with other people, southerners do, indeed, adopt a more anti-institutionalist or anti-collectivist stance when it comes to political action (see Milbrath 1965: 21–2, 63). However, in contrast to the findings in Table 10.1, which showed that Quebecers were similar to southerners in expressing low levels of political interest, this time it is northern Americans who report the next lowest level of political activism. Respondents from the American North, who have a score of 1.13 on the overall civil-dissent index, are significantly below both English Canadians and Quebecers in this respect. In fact, Quebecers have the highest level of protest activity among all four sub-samples, with a score of 1.48 on the civil-dissent index. In other words, then, while it appears that Quebecers are slightly below the norm in their expressions of political interest, as shown in Table 10.1, here we see that they are significantly more involved than the other regional sub-groups in promoting their political views and interests through actual protest behaviour.

Voting in Canada and the United States

A final indicator of political interest and political action that we should consider is voting. Over the years, voting activity has been almost universally employed by political and social scientists as a key barometer for assessing the level of citizens' involvement in the democratic process. As we saw with the other measures of political interest discussed earlier in this chapter, Lipset is one of the few writers to take a contrary view. According to this alternative interpretation, low voter turnouts may really show that democracy is working, since the choice not to vote is proof that people are relatively content with their society and feel no need to change it through the ballot box (Lipset 1981: 227). Elsewhere, Lipset adds that, in the specific case of the United States at least, the act of not voting is also a sign of individualism and 'disdain of authority'; in other words, non-voting provides yet another example of the famous American aversion to obeying the dictates of others, including those political leaders who insist that all citizens must go to the polls at election time (Lipset 1996: 21).[1]

Although such counter-intuitive interpretations of voting and non-voting are probably unconvincing to most of the researchers studying this question, there is no doubt that Lipset is correct about there being relatively low voter turnouts in American society today. For example, one study of international election data, covering the period from 1960 to 1995, found that the United States ranked 35th out of 37 countries, with an average turnout of 54 per cent among eligible voters (Martinez 2000: 213). In recent American presidential elections, the voting rates have been even lower, at 49 per cent in 1996 and 52 per cent in 2000. For the election of senators and congressmen, the figures were 46 per cent in 1996 and 48 per cent in 2000 (Statistical Abstract of the United States 2001: 253; Martinez 2000: 214). By comparison, Canada has

---

1. An analysis of historical voting patterns raises serious doubts about Lipset's notion that low voter turnouts in the United States are a sign of American individualism and disdain for political authority. For example, for most of the nineteenth century, voting rates in American presidential elections were quite high, never falling below 70 per cent and often surpassing 80 per cent (Lane 1959: 20; also Putnam 2000: 32). Therefore, unless this is seen as evidence that Americans were less individualistic and more respectful of political authority throughout the early development of the United States, a conclusion that is completely at odds with Lipset's own origins thesis, then it is difficult to see how low voting rates can be interpreted in this way.

had higher voting levels than the United States for many decades, with an average rate of 76 per cent for the period from 1960 to 1995, for example (Martinez 2000: 213).

There are some cautionary notes to make when assessing these results. First, Martinez suggests that the gap between the Canadian and American voting levels may be overstated somewhat because of different measurement procedures in the two countries; in particular, the Canadian percentage is calculated as a proportion of only those who are enumerated or registered to vote, whereas the American level is calculated as a proportion of the total population who are 18 years old or older. Second, the Canadian voting rate, like the American rate, was still well below the median for other societies, placing Canada 25th out of 37 nations, and behind such leading countries as Iceland, New Zealand, Denmark, and Germany (Martinez 2000: 213–16; see also Studlar 2001: 302–5). Finally, voter turnout in Canada, as in the United States, has been declining in recent years, falling from about 75 per cent in the 1988 federal election to just 61 per cent in the 2000 federal election (Elections Canada 2003). Nevertheless, on balance the evidence indicates that Canadians are significantly more likely to exercise their democratic right to vote than are Americans. Hence, here again we see no support for the assumption that Canadians are somehow less involved or less interested in politics than the people of the United States.

As for variations in voting across the four sub-societies, the data show, first of all, that Quebec matches or exceeds the rest of Canada in overall voter turnout. One early analysis of federal elections between the 1930s and the 1970s found voting rates in Quebec of around 74 per cent, which compared favourably with the figures for English Canada during that time (Presthus 1973: 57). Evidence for federal elections since 1988 reveals that, in recent years, Quebec voting levels have typically surpassed the rates for the rest of Canada as a whole (Elections Canada 2003; see also Dyck 1996: 646; Studlar 2001: 306–7). Given Quebec's unique status as a distinct 'nation' within the larger Canadian nation, voting behaviour in provincial elections is also relevant. Here, as well, the evidence indicates that Quebec's voter turnouts are generally higher than those for provincial elections in the rest of Canada as a whole, again suggesting that Quebecers are among the most politically active people in North America (Dyck 1996: 646; Studlar 2001: 306–7; Canadian Council on Social Development 1996).

In the case of the two American regions, the evidence reveals a long history of low voter turnouts in the South. One study has shown that, for every presidential election between 1820 and 1996, voting levels in the South were below those in the North. During some of this period, the lower voter turnout in the American South was partly due to the disenfranchisement of southern

Table 10.3 Political Trust and Confidence in Political Institutions by Region and Nation

	Region					Nation		
	English Canada	Quebec	US North	US South	Sig[1]	Canada Total	US Total	Sig[1]
1. Our government should be more open to the public (5 pt. scale[a])	1.61	1.71*	1.88*	1.95*	✓	1.63	1.90	✓
2. If an unjust law were passed by government, I could do nothing about it (5 pt. scale[b])	3.20	2.95*	3.44*	3.27	✓	3.14	3.38	✓
3. How much do you trust the government in Ottawa/Washington (4 pt. scale[c])	1.93	2.07*	2.34*	2.42*	✓	1.97	2.37	✓
How much confidence do you have in (4 pt. scale[d]):								
1. The legal system	2.59	2.55	2.58	2.65		2.58	2.60	✓
2. The police	3.12	2.88*	2.90*	2.97*	✓	3.06	2.93	✓
3. Parliament/Congress	2.29	2.46*	2.39*	2.46*	✓	2.33	2.41	✓
4. The civil service	2.45	2.60*	2.66*	2.73*	✓	2.49	2.69	✓
5. The Canadian/American political system	2.28	2.43*	2.59*	2.65*	✓	2.31	2.61	✓
Political Confidence Index (responses to the 5 items above summed and divided by 5):	2.54	2.59	2.63*	2.69*	✓	2.55	2.65	✓

Notes

[1] A check mark (√) indicates that the likelihood ratio chi-square for the overall four-category comparison across regions, or the two-category comparison across nations, is significant at <.05. The asterisk (*) indicates that the category is significantly different from the English Canadian reference group at <.05.

[a] The scale ranged from 1 = 'agree completely' to 5 = 'disagree completely'.
[b] The scale ranged from 1 = 'agree completely' to 5 = 'disagree completely'.
[c] The scale ranged from 1 = 'almost never' to 4 = 'almost always'.
[d] The scale ranged from 1 = 'not at all' to 4 = 'a great deal'.

blacks, through such technical obstacles as literacy tests and poll taxes, and also through fraud and violence (Putnam 2000: 33). Still, although the gap between the North and the South has declined substantially in recent decades, the northern turnout was still about 10 per cent higher as of the 1996 election (Putnam 2000: 32; see also Lane 1959: 341; Milbrath 1965: 58; Gastil 1975: 69). Results from the 2000 presidential election also show that, except for Virginia and Louisiana, all of the southern states were below the national voting average, even though in that election both major candidates, George W. Bush and Al Gore, were southerners themselves (Statistical Abstract of the United States 2001: 253). We can see from the voting data, then, that the people of the American South appear once again to be the least engaged and the least involved in politics of all the four regional sub-populations.

POLITICAL TRUST AND CONFIDENCE IN GOVERNMENT

So far in Chapter 10, we have found that Canadians are generally more active and involved in political life than their American counterparts. These findings clearly run counter to the assumptions of those commentators who have portrayed Canadians as more passive and accepting than Americans in their approach to government and politics. Our next task is to consider a similar assumption about differences in the political cultures of Canada and the United States. In this case, the premise is that, in relating to their government leaders, Canadians have always been a more respectful and deferential people than Americans, with a stronger faith in the capacity and willingness of their political officials to do what is best for the population.

In many respects, this argument is consistent with some of the historical assessments that we reviewed in previous chapters. It closely parallels Lipset's assertion that Canada began as a society of loyalist refugees, who readily put their trust in an elitist and hierarchical government to provide for their general welfare. We found in Part II that this historical argument is essentially erroneous. Nevertheless, Lipset's views on this issue have continued to influence the thinking of various analysts, a number of whom still accept the idea that, for centuries, the Canadian people have shown a deep sense of deference toward their political and other elites (e.g., Presthus 1973: 61; 1977a: 9; Merelman 1991: 27).

Some other writers, while maintaining that Canadians at one time were unusually trusting and respectful toward their leaders, have concluded that the situation is different today, with the Canadian people shifting from 'deference to defiance' in their dealings with those in power (Newman 1995; Adams 2003: 5–6; Gregg 2003: 29). In fact, there is a growing body of research indicating that deference to political leaders and other authority figures has been declining during the contemporary period, both in Canada and in other nations (see, e.g., Nevitte 1996, 2000; Inglehart 1997: 274–5; Perlin 1997: 99–101; Kanji and Nevitte 2000; Adams 2003: 52, 74–6). A few of these studies have determined, as well, that Canadians are now less trusting of their political elites than are Americans (see also Centre for Research and Information on Canada 2002). What is less widely recognized, however, is that this finding is not new. On the contrary, there is evidence that, compared with Americans, Canadians have shown less respect and trust toward their political leaders for more than two decades, and probably longer (Baer, Grabb, and Johnston 1990a, 1990b, 1990c; Baer et al. 1995; see also Presthus 1977b: 28–32, 39–40).

Table 10.3 presents additional findings that confirm this pattern, using two different categories of items from the WVS. The first set includes three measures of trust in government, while the second set is a battery of five questions asking about people's confidence in certain government or state institutions, along with an index combining the answers to these five questions. The table shows small but statistically significant differences on all but one of the items, with Americans generally expressing more trust and more confidence than Canadians in their political system and state-related organizations. The only exceptions to this statement are that Americans have less positive views about the police than do Canadians, and do not differ from Canadians when it comes to confidence in their legal system. In other words, the findings are almost completely at variance with the assumption that Canadians are more trusting, deferential, or accepting in their views about government or related political and legal institutions.

The comparisons involving the four sub-samples also show some notable patterns. Again, except for the question on the legal system, there are small but statistically significant inter-group differences on each of the items. Although not all of the questions produce the same rank-ordering of the four regional sub-groups, English Canadians usually express the lowest levels of trust and confidence, the one major exception being their high level of trust in the police. Quebecers rank second-lowest in the majority of cases. The most unexpected outcome in Table 10.3, especially given the allegedly anti-statist and anti-institutionalist heritage of the American South, is that respondents from the southern United States generally exhibit the most positive views about government. Southerners have the highest scores on two of the three political trust items, and on four of the five confidence measures. Therefore, while we have found in previous tables that American southerners tend to evince the lowest levels of political interest and political activism of all the four regional sub-samples, at the same time they are the most trusting and positive about their political system. In other words, the American South may be the closest approximation to Lipset's notion of the ideal democratic society, as a place where people are relatively passive or apathetic about politics, but are also comparatively content with and trusting of their government leaders and the workings of the political structure.

FEELINGS OF INTERPERSONAL TRUST AND NATIONAL PRIDE

One final topic that should be briefly addressed before concluding our comparison of the Canadian and American political cultures is interpersonal trust and national pride in the two societies. We have already determined that Americans are more trusting of and confident in their political system and government leaders than are Canadians. These outcomes are unexpected, at least if we proceed from the well-known premise that Americans have an enduring tradition of being suspicious and even disdainful of state authority. Such findings also raise questions about a related premise. Here we refer to the idea that, because of their populist tendencies stemming from the time of the Revolution, the American people have an unusually strong belief in themselves. In other words, while it is commonly argued that Americans have always been sceptical about whether their political leaders can be counted on to preserve their country's founding principles, the other side of this argument is that Americans have no difficulty putting their faith in 'We, the People of the United States' to accomplish this goal (Lipset 1996: 43). This famous phrase, of course, is from the preamble to the American Constitution (see, e.g., Gibbins 1982: 21–2).

The view that the people can and should be trusted in this way is closely linked to the deep-structural principle of popular sovereignty, the belief that any democratic society must be based on government of the people, by the people, and for the people. The key question to address here is whether, as we have argued, this is a fundamental value in both Canada and the United States or whether, as Lipset has suggested, it is more strongly and deeply felt in the American population. If the latter argument holds true, presumably we should find that Americans express a higher degree of trust in their fellow citizens than do Canadians, and also a more pronounced sense of patriotism or love of country.

Table 10.4 presents findings from the WVS that allow us to test these predictions. The table includes three items, two of which deal with respondents' feelings of trust regarding other people in their society, and a third that simply asks, 'how proud are you to be American/Canadian'. The results indicate that, for the most part, Americans and Canadians are really very close in their levels of both patriotism and trust in the people. Table 10.4 shows that the American sample has a slightly higher score on national pride, at 3.73 on the 4-point scale, versus 3.53 for the Canadian sample. On the other hand,

Table 10.4 Measure of General Trust and National Pride by Region and Nation

	Region					Nation		
	English Canada	Quebec	US North	US South	Sig[1]	Canada Total	US Total	Sig[1]
1. How much do you trust the Canadian/American people (5 pt. scale[a])	4.05	3.96*	3.86*	3.91*	√	4.03	3.87	√
2. Generally would you say most people can be trusted or you can't be too careful in dealing with people (% agreeing with the first statement)	58	37*	53*	44*	√	52	50	
3. National pride scale (4 pt. scale[b])	3.64	3.20*	3.70*	3.79*	√	3.53	3.73	√

Notes

[1] A check mark (√) indicates that the likelihood ratio chi-square for the overall four-category comparison across regions, or the two-category comparison across nations, is significant at <.05. The asterisk (*) indicates that the category is significantly different from the English Canadian reference group at <.05.

[a] The scale ranged from 1 = 'do not trust them at all' to 5 = 'trust them completely'.

[b] The scale ranged from 1 = 'not at all proud' to 4 = 'very proud'.

Canadians are slightly more trusting of their fellow citizens, with a score of 4.03 out of 5, compared with 3.87 for the American sample. The third item, which asks about interpersonal trust in a somewhat different way, shows no significant difference, with only about half of the respondents in both countries agreeing that 'most people can be trusted'. These findings are all broadly similar to those reported in recent Canadian and American research on both patriotism (Gallup 2001c; Gallup 2003; Burkholder 2003; Lunman 2003) and interpersonal trust (Moon, Lovrich, and Pierce 2000).

There is at least one study that suggests a possible difference in the meaning of patriotism for Canadians and Americans. This analysis relied on representative national survey data for the early 1990s, which were provided by the Carleton University Survey Centre, as part of the International Social Survey Program. The analysis showed that Canadians and Americans were very similar on a number of questions, including one in which 35 per cent of both Canadians and Americans said that they felt 'very close' to their country. However, when respondents were asked if 'people should support their country even if the country is in the wrong', Americans were substantially more likely to agree, with 32 per cent accepting this statement, compared with 16 per cent of Canadians. On this item, then, which taps what might be termed a more unconditional or even 'blind' form of patriotism, there appears to be a notable difference between the nations (see Literary Review of Canada 1998).

Moving to a comparison of the four sub-societies in Table 10.4, we find some small but statistically significant differences. Perhaps because of their perception of English dominance nationally, or because of their relatively stronger Quebec identity, Quebecers express less pride in being Canadian than do respondents in the rest of the country (see also Gallup 2001c). The two American sub-samples report somewhat higher levels of national pride than both of the Canadian groups, with people from the American South ranking highest of all. The finding that national pride is highest in the American South is consistent with recent evidence reported by Adams (2003: 86). On the other hand, it is English Canadians who rank at the top on both of the trust questions. In general, however, the patterns indicate relatively minor differences regarding questions of trust in people and pride in country, suggesting again that the political cultures of the two nations and the four regions are not as distinct from each other as is sometimes assumed.

SUMMARY

In Chapter 10, we have considered a variety of evidence comparing the political cultures of Canada and the United States. In general, we have found only modest differences between the two peoples. Moreover, where there are differences, they reveal that several of the most familiar and widely accepted assumptions about politics in the two countries are either incorrect or subject to serious qualification. Contrary to the claims of various observers, Canadians are more interested and more active in the political arena than are Americans. In addition, notwithstanding the arguments of some prominent writers, Canadians are actually less trusting, less accepting, and less deferential than Americans toward their government leaders and institutions. Finally, in contrast to certain popular perceptions, the two peoples differ very little on questions of national pride and interpersonal trust, although Americans are slightly more patriotic in their stated opinions, and Canadians have somewhat more faith in their fellow citizens.

With regard to regional differences in political culture, perhaps the most consistent finding is that the people of the American South tend to be distinct from the other sub-groups, in that they combine a relatively low level of political interest and activism with a comparatively high level of political trust, confidence in government, and patriotism. There is also some indication that Quebecers are more active politically than the other sub-groups, especially as measured by protest activity and voter turnout. Otherwise, however, the four sub-societies seem to be quite similar in their general approach to and involvement with the political structure.

CHAPTER 11

≫

VOLUNTARY-ASSOCIATION INVOLVEMENT AND ACTIVITY

Chapter 11 is the final section of our contemporary analysis of Canada and the United States. In this chapter, we explore available evidence on how frequently people in the two nations, and in the four component regions, join and participate in voluntary associations. This question is important for our discussion, because of the long-standing belief that Americans comprise 'a nation of joiners' (Schlesinger 1944; Hausknecht 1962), and clearly surpass Canadians and people from other societies in this regard. Thus, in much the same way that certain writers, as noted in Chapter 10, have portrayed Americans as more active in the political sphere than Canadians, some observers have also contended that similar national differences exist in what has been called the 'parapolitics' of local organizations and community associations.

PREVIOUS RESEARCH

While a good deal of the recent American literature on voluntary-association participation mentions the idea that Americans have higher involvement levels than any other peoples, this view is a truly venerable one, going back at least as far as two early foreign observers: Alexis de Tocqueville and Max Weber. Based on their general observations of the United States compared with European societies, each of these scholars argued that Americans were higher in association activity. As we saw in Chapter 4, Tocqueville felt that, during his time, no other nation was as successful as the United States in promoting the ideas of free association and popular sovereignty, although he also believed that these tendencies were evident among English North Americans generally, because of their common English heritage (Tocqueville 1835: 29, 42, 58, 198–9, 201; see also Wood 1992: 329; Ryan 1999: 581). Weber's view, expressed some 80 years after Tocqueville's observation, was that the United States was 'the association-land par excellence' (Weber 1911: 53; see also Wright and Hyman 1958: 286; Schlesinger 1944).

Several scholars have extended this comparative assessment to recent times. In both the 1980s and the 1990s Lipset contended that, compared with other peoples, 'Americans are more likely to take part in voluntary efforts to achieve particular goals', and are less disposed to rely on the state for such purposes (Lipset 1985: 141; 1990: 148; 1996: 277). Drucker is another recent observer to make such a claim, asserting that 'outside the English-speaking countries there is not much of a voluntary tradition' and that 'the modern state in Europe and Japan has been openly hostile to anything that smacks of voluntarism' (1994: 76).

Increasingly, however, studies using directly comparable national data have raised serious questions about how highly Americans actually rank on voluntarism compared with other peoples (e.g., Curtis 1971; Curtis, Grabb, and Baer 1992; Curtis, Baer, and Grabb 2001; Hallenstvedt 1974; Putnam 1995: 74; 2000: Chapter 3; Wuthnow 1991: 289–90). A close examination of the few studies that have been based on cross-national comparative data reveals a rather different picture from that suggested by Lipset and Drucker. Three previous studies have used national sample surveys that included both Canada and the United States. The first of these analyses, based on data from the 1950s and 1960s, found that Canadians were the most likely among six national populations to belong to at least one association, although Americans ranked about the same as Canadians when union membership was excluded (Curtis 1971). Apart from Canada and the United States, the other countries were Britain, Germany, Italy, and Mexico. Unions were excluded in some of the analyses because union affiliations are sometimes mandatory for holding particular jobs, and so are not always truly voluntary.

The other two cross-national studies looked at data for 15 nations from the 1980s, and for 33 nations from the 1990s (Curtis, Grabb, and Baer 1992; Curtis, Baer, and Grabb 2001). These analyses found that Americans ranked among the highest in association involvement, especially when religious organizations were included in the count of memberships. However, people from several nations, including the Netherlands, Sweden, Norway, Canada, and others, either rivaled or surpassed the American sample in association involvement (see also Hallenstvedt 1974). This was particularly true when religious organizations were excluded from the analysis, and when active memberships, as opposed to purely nominal or inactive memberships, were considered.

There is also good evidence to conclude that levels of voluntary-association activity in both the United States and Canada have been quite stable over time. Contrary to those who have argued that there has been a decline in such activity over the past two decades (e.g., Putnam 1995, 2000), several studies covering the period from the mid-1970s to the mid-1990s have uncovered no clear evidence of a drop in voluntary-association membership in the United

States, Canada, and a range of other nations (Paxton 1999; Rotolo 1999; Baer, Curtis, and Grabb 2001). There are, however, discrepant Canadian and American patterns in the specific case of trade-union affiliations, with American levels on the decline and Canadian levels relatively stable, at least until the mid-1990s (Reitz 1998: 161–2; Banting and Simeon 1997: 40; Brym 2004: 64). In addition, as noted in Chapter 7, formal religious membership also has shown a general decline in both countries for several decades, although there is some indication of a recent resurgence for certain sects (recall Bibby 1987, 1993, 2002; Clark 2003; Krauss 2003; Putnam 2000: 69–79).

As several reviews of the literature have concluded, little attention has been given to developing theories that would explain cross-national differences in association involvement (e.g., Curtis, Grabb, and Baer 1992: 149; Knoke 1986: 17–18; Pugliese 1986: Chapter 2; Smith 1975: 264). The lack of theory on this issue may be due to the widespread acceptance of the well-known 'American exceptionalism' thesis. This argument has emphasized the uniqueness of American society, and so has offered no clear rationale for looking past the basic claim that the United States is qualitatively different from all other nations. Probably the principal contemporary proponent of this thesis is Lipset. He sees the high level of associational activity in the United States as consistent with the distinctive American value system, which places a top priority on individual participation in community affairs. This interpretation, of course, is wholly consistent with Lipset's assertion that there is a unique 'American Creed', which we have discussed previously. If this argument is correct, we should expect to find that Americans are higher in associational involvement than either English Canadians or Quebecers. However, given the contrary findings from other studies that we have already noted, there are considerable grounds for questioning this hypothesis from the outset.

With respect to variations across the four sub-societies, very little research has been done that examines regional differences in association activity within Canada and the United States. In his general comparisons of Canada and the United States, Lipset occasionally acknowledges the importance of distinguishing between French and English Canada (e.g., Lipset 1985: 159; 1990: 196–7), but he does not do so with respect to the question of voluntary-association activity. The French–English distinction may be crucial for a complete understanding of similarities and differences in voluntarism in the two countries, since previous research, based on data from the 1980s, suggests that French Canadians are less likely than English Canadians to join voluntary organizations of various kinds (Curtis et al. 1989a, 1989b; Grabb and Curtis 1992). This research also shows that, if only English Canadians and Americans are considered, Lipset's contention that levels of voluntarism are higher in the United States than in Canada is not supported. Such comparisons indicate that English Canadians are about as likely as Americans to join various types of voluntary organizations, with the only major exception being a higher level of American involvement in churches and religious associations.

Additional research based on the 1997 Canadian National Survey of Giving, Volunteering, and Participating also reveals that rates of voluntary-association participation are higher in English Canada than in French Canada (Caldwell and Reed 2000). This research identifies the different religious heritages of Catholic Quebec and Protestant English Canada as one central reason, an observation that fits with previous studies showing that Catholics tend to be less involved with voluntary associations than are Protestants (see, e.g., Lipset 1996; Curtis, Baer, and Grabb 2001). Caldwell and Reed suggest, as well, that Quebec's declining level of religious attendance may be a crucial factor, because religious activities, whether for Catholics or non-Catholics, are conducive to the teaching and promotion of voluntarism (see also Reed and Selbee 2000; Selbee and Reed 2001). On the other hand, some research comparing French and English Canadians has not found significant differences for certain measures of voluntary activity. Using data from the WVS for the 1990s, Curtis and Grabb (2002: 170–1) determined that French-Canadian levels of voluntary-association membership were about the same as those for English Canadians, if religious or church-related organizations were not counted in the comparison; this also held true for comparisons that involved organizations promoting 'new social movements', including environmental groups and women's groups, for example (see also Curtis and White 1992).

The lack of complete consistency in the results from these previous analyses suggests the need to reconsider the issue of cross-national differences in associational activity, this time paying closer heed to the distinction between Quebec and English Canada. For similar reasons, it is important also to take into account the division between the northern and southern United States. As discussed previously in Part III, there is some basis for predicting that people from the American South will be less likely to participate in voluntary organizations. Here we refer to the argument that, compared with other people, southerners are generally more 'anti-institutionalist', preferring to be left to their own devices as independent individuals or families, and not being highly involved in outside organizations or related community activities (Reed 1991: 231–2; 1983: 70–1).

In Chapter 10, we discussed the lower degree of southern activism and engagement in the area of politics, as judged by research showing that southerners tend to exhibit higher levels of political apathy and passivity, to vote less in elections, and to evince lower levels of political interest and protest activity. However, perhaps the most compelling support for the hypothesis

that southerners rank relatively low in voluntary activity and social involvement comes from Reed's work with Marsden, Kennedy, and Stinson (Marsden
et al. 1982). Based on data from a large national survey conducted in the
1970s, this analysis looked at leisure-time activities across the southern and
northern United States. Several measures were employed, including multiple
indicators of social, cultural, and other types of activity that were grouped into
nine different categories. Southerners were found to be less active than northerners in every one of the nine categories, although the differences were not
significant in three of these categories when statistical controls for certain background factors, such as age and education, were taken into account. These
outcomes led the researchers to identify a distinctive culture or style in the
American South, a 'southern manner' that tended to be 'unstructured' and
'unorganized', 'more centered around home, family, and church, and less tied
to formally organized forms of activity than is the leisure of non-southerners'
(Marsden et al. 1982: 1044). Reed's later analysis of survey data from the 1980s
led him to draw the same conclusion (Reed 1986: 91–100; 1991: 232–5; see
also Elazar 1966: 93; Grantham 1994: 157, 315; Vandello and Cohen 1999:
280–2; Putnam 2000: 292–4).

RESULTS FROM THE WORLD VALUES SURVEYS

The results in Table 11.1 compare association involvement in the two nations
and the four regions, using data from the WVS. The findings are based on the
average number of voluntary memberships reported by the respondents, using
a list of 16 types of association. The figures in the upper half of the table
include any reported memberships, while the figures in the lower half include
only those memberships for which the respondent played an active role in, or
did actual work for, the organization. In both halves of the table, the results
are presented in four different ways: (1) for all 16 types of association; (2)
for 14 types, i.e., with both trade unions and religious organizations excluded;
(3) for trade unions only; and (4) for religious organizations only. The reasons
for doing separate analyses that both include and exclude unions and religious
associations have to do with the exceptional nature of these two types of organizations, as noted earlier. In the case of unions, there is the question of whether
they are really compulsory memberships for many jobs, and so should not be
counted when assessing levels of voluntarism. In the case of religious organizations, we have seen that church-group involvement features prominently,
and varies considerably, in previous research on differences involving Canada,
the United States, and the four component regions. For these reasons, it is
important to look at the results with unions and religious organizations considered both separately and as part of the overall count of memberships.

Table 11.1 Measures of Affiliation with and Activity in Voluntary Associations by Region and Nation

	Region					Nation		
	English Canada	Quebec	US North	US South	Sig[1]	Canada Total	US Total	Sig[1]
Sum of affiliations in 16 different organizations[a]	1.72	1.56	2.04*	1.75	√	1.68	1.94	√
Sum of affiliations in 14 different organizations (excluding unions and religious organizations)	1.32	1.28	1.47	1.21	√	1.31	1.39	
Respondent belongs to:								
1. Trade union (%)	11	14	11	4*	√	12	8	√
2. Religious or church organization (%)	28	15*	46*	50*	√	25	47	√
Sum of working memberships in 16 different organizations[a]	1.01	.81*	1.05	.88	√	.96	.99	
Sum of working memberships in 14 different organizations (excluding unions and religious organizations)	.80	.67	.75	.57*	√	.77	.69	
Respondent belongs to:								
1. Trade union (%)	3	5	2	1*	√	4	2	√
2. Religious or church organization (%)	17	10*	27*	29*	√	16	28	√

Notes

[1] A check mark (√) indicates that the likelihood ratio chi-square for the overall four-category comparison across regions, or the two-category comparison across nations, is significant at <.05. The asterisk (*) indicates that the category is significantly different from the English Canadian reference group at <.05.

[a] Respondents were asked separately about 'membership in' and 'work for' each of these 16 types of voluntary organizations: charities and social welfare, churches or religious, education or arts, trade unions, political parties or groups, community action, human rights, conservation or environmental, animal welfare, youth work, sport and recreation, professional, women's, peace, health, and 'others'.

The first row of Table 11.1 shows that, as Lipset and some others have argued, Americans are somewhat more likely to join voluntary organizations than are Canadians. The American respondents averaged nearly two association affiliations (1.94), compared with an average of 1.68 for Canadians. The second row of the table indicates, however, that there is no significant national difference when unions and religion-related associations are excluded from the list of memberships, with averages of 1.39 for the United States and 1.31 for Canada. These results replicate the findings in various studies by Curtis and colleagues, based on data going back as far as the 1960s (Curtis et al. 1989a, 1989b; Curtis, Grabb, and Baer 1992; Curtis, Baer, and Grabb 2001). The next two rows of the table present results for religious associations and unions taken separately. These findings make it clear that the reason why the results in the first two rows of the table show different patterns is that Americans participate in churches and religion-related associations much more than do Canadians. The American rate of involvement in religious associations is almost twice as high as the Canadian level, at 47 per cent versus 25 per cent. The rates of involvement in trade unions are closer, but are still significantly different. As we would expect from previous research, there are greater levels of union involvement for Canadians (12 per cent) than for Americans (8 per cent).

Moving to the bottom half of Table 11.1, we see that, when we restrict the comparison to working or active memberships only, the two nations do not differ at all. The average number of active memberships in Canada and the United States is about one per person, with means of .96 and .99, respectively. There is also no significant difference when unions and church-related associations are excluded, with a mean of .77 for Canada and .69 for the United States.

It appears, then, that Americans and Canadians do not differ significantly in their involvement with voluntary associations, with the major exception being that Americans join religious associations more than do Canadians. Moreover, even when religious memberships are included in the comparison, there are no significant national differences if only truly active organizational involvements are considered. The latter outcome reflects the fact that Americans are more likely than Canadians to be nominal members of organizations, but are not more likely to do actual work with the organizations that they join.

Table 11.1 also shows the results when the four regions are compared. The findings reveal some tendency for people from the American North to have the highest scores on most of the measures of association involvement, although in a number of cases the differences between their scores and those of the other groups are not statistically significant. Northerners are clearly the highest on total memberships, with an average of 2.04 memberships per person. Except for their southern compatriots, northerners are also significantly higher than the other regional sub-groups on the measures of religious-organization membership. Apart from these differences, however, the levels for the northern Americans are generally not significantly different from those of the other groups, most notably the English-Canadian reference group. This is especially true when only active or working memberships are considered. In keeping with expectations, Americans from the South tend to have the lowest scores on the various measures, with the exception that they match or surpass American northerners on both total and active religious-association memberships.

One finding that may not be expected, given some previous analyses, is that English Canadians are not significantly higher than Quebecers in total association memberships. This is true whether unions and church-related associations are included (1.72 versus 1.56) or excluded (1.32 versus 1.28). English Canadians are higher than Quebecers with respect to overall active or working memberships (1.01 versus .81). In addition, English Canadians surpass Quebec respondents when it comes to religion-related organizational involvements, with an English-Canadian level that is almost twice as high, both for total memberships (28 per cent versus 15 per cent) and for active memberships considered separately (17 per cent versus 10 per cent). On all the remaining measures, however, the results indicate no notable differences between Quebecers and English Canadians.[1]

Summary

As we have seen for many of the other dependent measures considered in Part III, there is little difference between Canadians and Americans in voluntary-association activity. The key national difference we have found in this chapter is that Americans are much more likely to belong to religious organizations than are Canadians, while Canadians are rather more likely to belong to unions than are Americans. Once again, however, the four-region comparisons we have considered reveal more notable results, and require us to revise some of the conclusions that we would draw had we looked at the Canadian and American patterns alone. Although the absolute differences across the four regions

---

1.   The 1996 'God and Society in North America Survey', which we have referred to previously in Part III, shows patterns that are roughly similar to those reported here using the WVS. There are some exceptions, however, perhaps because the two surveys employ different question wordings and provide different answer choices. As with the WVS, the 1996 data indicate that respondents from the American North rank highest in involvement, but this difference is more clear and consistent than it appears in Table 11.1. Also, Quebecers stand out as much lower than the other groups in the 1996 survey, and generally are the lowest in involvement among the four regional sub-samples.

are often small, we have found that people from the American North show some signs of being highest in voluntary-association activity, at least for total memberships. However, this is not true for active memberships or when religion-related organizations are excluded from the comparisons. In those cases, English Canadians are no different from the northern Americans. The scores for the Quebec respondents usually place them third in association involvement among the four groups, although in most cases the French are not significantly different from either the English Canadians or the northern Americans. The main exception to this assertion is the low level of religious membership in Quebec. Finally, as we might expect given its characterization in the literature, the American South usually falls toward the low end in membership levels, with the key proviso that people from this region rank ahead of all the other regional groups on religion-related organizational memberships.

CONCLUSION TO PART III

Our main purpose in Part III of this volume has been to extend, into the contemporary period, the theoretical and historical analyses that were presented in Parts I and II. We have presented and assessed a diverse array of recent evidence comparing Canada and the United States, and also the four constituent sub-societies that were identified in Part I. Our focus has been on five main themes or topic areas that have dominated much of the literature on the two nations over the years. These topics include: (1) the general question of moral issues, as indicated by research in the areas of religion and religiosity, family and sexual values, and matters of crime and the law; (2) the comparative evaluation of individualist versus collectivist values, as well as the role of the state in the development of these values in both countries; (3) the problem of social inclusion or exclusion, especially as it relates to the tolerance and opportunities that are afforded to ethnic and other minority groups; (4) the question of political culture, with particular concern for the levels of political interest and activism, and of trust and confidence in government, within the two populations; and (5) involvement in the parapolitics of democracy, as judged by research on the voluntary-association memberships and organizational activities of Canadians and Americans.

Comparing the Two Nations

We have found some differences between the two societies, several of which are of long standing. The most consistent and most marked are those that we have outlined under the general rubric of moral issues in Chapter 7. Here we determined that Americans are more religious than Canadians according to virtually all measures, and are more conservative on various questions dealing with family values and sexuality. In this part of the analysis, we learned that Americans continue to experience much higher homicide rates than Canadians, although we also noted that such crimes are extremely rare events in both societies and that, otherwise, Canadian and American levels of criminality have tended to be far more similar than many commentators have assumed. The general populations of both countries clearly place the same high priority on the rule of law.

Apart from the relatively consistent and substantial Canadian–American differences on certain moral issues, the pattern throughout most of our analyses in Part III has been one of small differences between Canada and the United States and, in many cases, no national differences at all. First of all, we saw in Chapter 8 that Canadians are about as individualistic in their attitudes and outlooks as Americans, and in some cases are somewhat more so, depending on how the idea of individualism is defined. The almost identical commitment to individualistic values among Canadians and Americans has been sustained, in spite of the relatively higher level of state involvement in Canada that we have found in the present day, and the greater impetus toward collectivism that this larger government role is alleged to promote in the Canadian population.

When we examined the existing evidence on social inclusion and ethnic tolerance in Chapter 9, we did find one explicit sign of greater Canadian statism, in Canada's official government policy on multiculturalism. Whether because of this state policy or for other reasons, we also found that Canada is notably different from the United States with respect to the size of its foreign-born population and, in that sense, Canada is a more pluralist 'nation of immigrants' than its southern neighbour. Still, much of the other evidence on inclusion and tolerance revealed rather small differences. It is true that Canadians are somewhat less concerned than Americans about maintaining social distance between themselves and different minorities, as indicated by Canadians' more tolerant attitudes about racial intermarriage, and about having certain designated minorities or outgroups as neighbours. However, many of the differences in the latter comparison were, again, quite small. Furthermore, on several other questions about ethnic groups, we saw considerable national similarities. In particular, some ethnic minorities are clearly able to achieve great success, but their opportunities to do so in either society are generally not equal to those of other people, especially if the minority groups in question are both non-white and foreign-born. All in all, then, the evidence suggests that Canadian society is probably somewhat more pluralist, tolerant, and inclusive than American society in its treatment of ethnic and other minorities, but the differences are rarely substantial.

Similarly, our analysis of evidence on political culture in Chapter 10 showed only modest national differences, although the findings also refuted many of the most widely accepted claims about politics in Canada and the United States. Contrary to what numerous writers and commentators have assumed, Canadians are more interested and active in political life than are Americans, if only moderately so, and are also less trusting or respectful toward their government and political leaders. In Chapter 11, we saw a similar pattern with respect to several popular conceptions about voluntarism in the two societies. Here we found that, again in contrast to what various commentators and pundits have argued, Canadians are not very different from Americans in their levels of voluntary-association membership. In fact, except for the stronger American tendency to join religious organizations, and the somewhat higher level of union membership in Canada, there are no real differences of note in the levels of voluntary activity in the two national populations.

Comparing the Four Regional Sub-societies

In Parts I and II of our analysis, we developed the argument that Canada and the United States are best understood as comprising four relatively distinct regional entities, or sub-societies, which have roots in the distant past. We suggested that, because of the enduring influences of certain core values, or deep-structural principles, which are traceable to their common English or British heritage, the people, social structures, and social institutions of English Canada and the northern United States retained many affinities that, while not making them identical, have meant that these two regions of North America share a number of important similarities. As part of this argument, we also put forth the view that, for a variety of historical reasons, the other two sub-societies, Quebec and the American South, have tended to exist as regional enclaves that are different from both English Canada and the northern United States.

In our contemporary comparisons in Part III, we have found that the four regions are, indeed, often distinctive, and on a diverse set of issues. In addition, although there are some clear exceptions, the four sub-societies frequently array themselves in a consistent pattern or order. This pattern is one in which Quebec occupies one end of the continuum in question, the American South stands at the other end, and the other two regions fall relatively close to one another and between the two extremes. This ordering is especially clear in the findings on moral issues, where we saw that Quebecers are consistently the most liberal or tolerant, with southern Americans being the least liberal or tolerant, and English Canadians and northern Americans occupying the middle range.

This same general pattern is evident in many of our other comparisons. To summarize the most prominent instances, these include: regional crime rates, which are generally lowest in Quebec and highest in the South; people's views on how harshly criminals should be treated, which are typically the most lenient in Quebec and the most punitive in the South; overall levels of government spending, which are highest in Quebec and lowest in the South; support for labour unions, which appears to be highest in Quebec and lowest in the South; tolerance of interracial marriages and having different outgroups as neighbours, which is generally highest in Quebec and lowest in the South; forms of political participation, such as voting and protest activity, which tend to be highest in Quebec and lowest in the South; and feelings of national pride, which are lowest in Quebec and highest in the South.

We suggest that, in combination, these outcomes demonstrate a number of important truths about Canada and the United States. First, there is a clear basis for analyzing Quebec and the American South as separate regional sub-societies, given the consistent patterns of differences that operate across a host of quite varied issues and that distinguish these regions, not only from each other, but also from English Canada and the American North. Second, the results make it readily apparent that, when Quebec and the American South are considered separately, English Canada and the American North are often found to be very similar to one another. Third, on the whole, there is a strong case to be made that the differences among the four regional sub-societies are both more substantial and more consistent than the differences that we have found comparing the two nations alone. In our view, all of these considerations underscore the important theoretical and empirical gains that derive from going beyond the comparison of the two countries, and looking for the intriguing and significant differences that frequently exist within them.

We move now to the concluding chapter, where we explore and discuss the larger meaning of the national and regional patterns that we have found in our analysis of Canada and the United States, both past and present. We also comment on and speculate about several ongoing debates and unresolved questions, many of which stem from both the old and the new myths that have been generated about the two societies and their peoples.

CHAPTER 12

✍

CONCLUSION

We have completed our exploration of the major myths that have arisen, and that in many cases still endure, concerning the nature of Canada and the United States. In previous chapters, we identified and discussed the most prominent theoretical perspectives that have been formulated in conjunction with many of these myths, and that have been put forward to explain how and why the two nations emerged and developed as they did. We also reviewed and assessed a considerable volume of historical and contemporary evidence bearing on these major theories. In this concluding chapter, one of our prime goals is to highlight the main findings and the key implications of the research presented in earlier chapters. In doing so, we also consider what our analysis tells us, not only about the old myths and interpretations that have been provided about Canada and the United States, but also about some of the new images and impressions that recent observers have offered in characterizing the two nations and their peoples.

Our initial task in this chapter is to assess the relative fit of our findings with the deep-structures approach, which we have suggested as an alternative to the founding-fragment and revolutionary-origins perspectives of previous writers. We then address a series of interrelated issues or questions that we believe should be considered in any thorough comparative analysis of Canada and the United States. The first of these questions concerns how many distinct 'nations' or sub-societies can or should be identified and delineated within the two countries, especially in light of the research that has been presented in this volume. Second, there is the issue of whether comparisons of Canada and the United States should concentrate on the elite level or the mass level when trying to draw inferences about both societies. A third question centres on the relative merits of focusing primarily on the most extreme events, attitudes, and behaviours, as opposed to the most prevalent or most typical, when seeking to understand the two societies and their populations. We then conclude the analysis by looking toward the future, and assessing a number of competing hypotheses about the direction or directions that Canada and the United States may be going as they move forward through the twenty-first century.

DEEP STRUCTURES REVISITED

We began our comparative analysis of Canada and the United States by explicating the founding-fragment and origins perspectives, which represent the two most prominent theoretical approaches in the literature on the establishment of the two nations, going back more than two centuries ago. We then posed another perspective, the so-called deep-structures approach, as an alternative to these earlier theses. The main thrust of the deep-structures formulation is that the English regions of North America, particularly the sub-societies that now form English Canada and the northern United States, were imbued historically with a similar set of core values, or deep-structural principles, that are traceable to their common origins as colonies of Britain. We suggested that four of these principles were especially significant: liberty, legal equality, popular sovereignty, and pluralism. In our view, over time the relatively stronger commitment to these precepts in English Canada and the American North, compared with the other parts of North America, was crucial for shaping, in kindred ways, the political, economic, legal, and other social structures of these two regions. Until the last few decades of the twentieth century, the wider prevalence of such principles in English Canada and the American North, as well as the greater acceptance of such ideas among their populations, had a sustained impact in distinguishing these two sub-societies from both Quebec and the southern United States. The distinctiveness of Quebec in this regard stems largely from its French and Catholic origins, which promoted an alternative set of core values in its population and its major social structures historically, and which has contributed to Quebec's unique status in the contemporary period, as well. As for the American South, our interpretation is that this region did not embrace the four deep-structural ideals to the same degree as the rest of English North America, primarily because of the fundamental incompatibility between these principles and the realities of the slave-based form of economic and social organization that dominated the South historically. Moreover, notwithstanding the significant changes that have occurred in the southern United States in more recent years, we argue that these early influences have had some lingering consequences for this sub-society to the present day.

At various points in previous chapters, we have discussed how the deep-structures view is clearly at variance with much of Lipset's origins or defining-moments perspective, especially his claim that the events of the American

Revolution have forever made the Canadian and American peoples substantially different from one another. Our position is that most of Lipset's argument is fundamentally incorrect. However, we have seen that the deep-structures approach does have some elements in common with the founding-fragment arguments of Hartz, Horowitz, and especially McRae. The most significant parallel between our approach and those offered by the three founding-fragment theorists is that these perspectives all acknowledge the shared influence of English values, social structures, and modes of conduct in the early development of the United States and English Canada. Some additional parallels are that, to varying degrees, the founding-fragment approaches concur with our views about the distinctiveness of French Canada, and, in Hartz's version at least, there is also some recognition of the separate nature of the American South.

However, as was outlined in detail in Part I, there are a number of important differences between the founding-fragment approaches and the deep-structures view. One of the main discrepancies is that the deep-structures formulation largely rejects the suggestion, made especially by Hartz and Horowitz, that the loyalist migration at the time of the Revolution brought a special and enduring Tory touch to Canada that has always made it different from the United States. Another notable area of disagreement is that the deep-structures perspective gives much more consideration to events that took place both well before and long after the period of the Revolution, and sees these developments as of pivotal importance for understanding the current state of the two nations and their constituent sub-societies. In addition, we suggest that the deep-structures approach has the advantage of being far more explicit than the founding-fragment arguments in delineating the major dimensions, or core principles, along which the two nations, and the four sub-societies, can be compared and contrasted over time. A central question to ask ourselves now is whether the deep-structures approach represents an improvement on previous perspectives in helping us to characterize or account for the nature of Canada and the United States, both past and present.

Reconsidering the Historical Evidence

In addressing this key question, we can start by briefly reconsidering the historical evidence that was presented in Part II. This research revealed that, particularly in comparison with Lipset's thesis, but also in relation to the founding-fragment perspectives, the deep-structures view provides an appreciably more accurate depiction of what actually happened in the two societies during the crucial period surrounding the American Revolution. This seems especially clear with regard to understanding the impact of the loyalist migration on both societies. Here we found that, in contrast to the arguments made by Lipset, Hartz, and others, the loyalists and other English-Canadian settlers of that era were, in terms of both social backgrounds and probable world views, largely indistinguishable from their counterparts in the thirteen colonies. We have also seen evidence to indicate that the deep-structures approach does a better job than previous perspectives of helping us to see how, until well into the twentieth century, French Quebec and the American South remained separate and distinct from English Canada and the northern United States.

Undoubtedly, an important qualification or caveat to note when assessing the utility or applicability of the deep-structures view, especially in the historical case, is to distinguish between the four core principles that we have identified and the extent to which they were actually put into practice by any of the early sub-societies. This is particularly true for the value of pluralism, or the basic right of individuals to be different. As we have seen, the evidence on religious tolerance, but probably even more so on the treatment of blacks, aboriginals, and other non-whites in this era, makes it apparent that, historically, pluralism was not genuinely fostered or embraced by many members of the general population or the elite leadership in either nation. On the other hand, it also seems clear that, with the passage of time, not only pluralism, but also liberty, legal equality, and popular sovereignty, would eventually become more than just high-sounding words or unattainable ideals for growing numbers of people in the two countries.

Although no region can claim complete success in implementing these core values, our review of the historical research suggests that the movement toward some degree of tolerance and acceptance of racial, religious, and other cultural diversity, as well as personal freedom under the rule of law, probably occurred first and to greater effect in the English-Canadian population. This conclusion is based on such considerations as the relatively early abolition of slavery in English Canada and the allowance from the outset of diverse, though separate, religious communities in this part of North America. The American North, especially after the end of slavery, would come next in the movement toward the attainment of the four deep-structural values, with Quebec and the American South remaining relatively different in this respect until the modern era.

Reconsidering the Recent Evidence

This brings us to an assessment of how well the deep-structures approach comports with the Canadian–American experience of recent times. Our presentation of contemporary research in Part III provides convincing evidence that, while such core precepts as pluralism and equality continue to defy complete realization in either nation in the present day, both peoples and both societies have, nevertheless, come much closer than they once were to accepting and promoting these central values. We have seen, for example, that the large majority of the population in each country, and also in the four regions, express no objections to sharing their neighbourhoods with a diversity of religious, ethnic, and racial minorities. In addition, although studies indicate that there are still individuals in both societies who engage in job discrimination based on race, or who oppose such principles as gender equality and gay rights, the research suggests that, in these areas as well, most Canadians and most Americans no longer hold with intolerant or inequitable behaviours and attitudes.

However, while it is apparent that, over the past century or more, there has been a general increase in the extent to which both societies have come to embrace and to implement the four deep-structural principles, our findings also make it clear that this transformation has not happened to the same degree or at the same pace everywhere. First, in comparing the two nations as a whole, most of the recent research that we have assessed, covering the past three decades or more, indicates a number of Canadian–American differences that, though usually minor, are still worthy of note. The largest differences between the two peoples centre mainly on moral issues, most notably the higher levels of religiosity and sexual or moral conservatism in the United States, as well as the more frequent American experience with lethal violent crime. We have also found some smaller but relatively consistent differences in regard to both ethnic relations and politics. Here we have seen that, in comparison with Americans, Canadians tend to evince somewhat higher levels of ethnic or racial tolerance. Moreover, and in contrast to many prevailing assumptions, we have also found that Canadians exhibit moderately greater political activism than Americans, mixed with less trust in government.

For the most part, though, such national differences are consistently outstripped by more substantial regional variations on a large and diverse set of issues. In general, we have determined that distinguishing among the four major constituent sub-societies reveals some striking patterns that would have been overlooked had we only conducted the two-nations comparisons found in most previous research. First of all, in keeping with the deep-structures argument, our results indicate that English Canadians and people from the American North are, indeed, quite similar to one another. This similarity only becomes truly apparent when the American South and Quebec, which are the two most distinctive of the four regions, are factored out of the comparison. Although northern Americans are certainly different from English Canadians in some areas, most notably in their approach to religious and moral issues, these two sub-groups usually exhibit much the same attitudes, orientations, and behaviours, whether the topic is child-rearing values, feelings about economic crime, experience with many non-violent crimes, the acceptance of individualist beliefs, levels of self-confidence and assertiveness, participation in various forms of civil dissent, or involvement in voluntary-association activity. Therefore, even as these two regions have changed over time, absorbing an increasing number of immigrants from all over the world in the past 200 years, we can still find good evidence to support the view that both English Canada and the northern United States continue to represent two kindred, if somewhat distinct, branches from the same Old English tree.

A second major finding in our regional comparisons, and one that is also consistent with the deep-structures perspective, is that, right up to the present day, the American South stands apart from both Canada and the rest of the United States. In particular, the South is the most conservative, traditional, and insular sub-society with respect to issues ranging from religion and morality to tolerance of ethnic and cultural differences. The American South is also the region that, along with having the highest crime rates in either nation, combines the lowest levels of statism, government spending, and political activism with the highest levels of trust in government and patriotism. Thus, although there is little question that the South has witnessed substantial economic, political, demographic, and cultural changes in recent decades, and is no longer as distinct from the rest of North America as it once was, the research we have reviewed indicates that this region still represents a separate sub-society. We can still see, in this part of the United States, the residual effects of two incompatible sets of influences, which combine certain core English principles, like liberty and popular sovereignty, on the one hand, with remnants of the slave-based and highly particularistic old South, on the other hand. This combination of sometimes contradictory cultural and social forces has encouraged a way of life that, even today, involves a complex and paradoxical mix of collectivism and individualism, and of anti-statism and deference to political authority.

Finally, we come to our contemporary findings for Quebec. The historical research on Quebec that was presented in Part II is wholly consistent with the deep-structures perspective. That evidence shows that the old Quebec was a unique sub-society all its own, with linguistic, religious, economic, and political influences that were clearly very different from those operating in either English Canada or the United States. However, on first consideration, at least, the more recent findings provided in Part III might seem to call into question the utility of the deep-structures view for understanding the new Quebec. After all, while Quebec once was the conservative, authoritarian, and hierarchical society suggested by the deep-structures argument, we have seen that, on a number of issues, its people now generally rank as the most liberal, permissive, or tolerant population in North America. More specifically, our research has shown that, along with being the least committed of all the four sub-groups to conventional religious beliefs, Quebecers are the most open to a host of non-traditional ideas, principles, and practices. This is evident in their relatively more supportive stances on women's equality, gay rights, alternative forms of sexuality, same-sex marital unions, and interracial marriages, as well as their generally more liberal approach to criminal justice.

As already suggested in our discussion of Quebec in Part III, we do not believe that these recent findings contradict the basic deep-structures argument. Instead, the contemporary results can more plausibly be interpreted as evidence of what can occur when a distinct set of decidedly conservative and traditional deep-structural values, which have been essential for shaping and entrenching a particular form of society for centuries, are both rapidly and belatedly called into question or undermined by popular exposure to other more compelling social forces and cultural influences. In other words, for us, the changes that occurred during and after Quebec's Quiet Revolution, as outlined in Part III, are primarily the result of a concerted desire among a new generation of Quebecers to shift away from the hierarchical collectivism found in the old authoritarian religious and political institutions of that society, and toward a different system. The new form of society that emerged out of this 'defining moment' in Quebec history is still marked by several elements of the old system. These elements include the strong commitment to Quebecois nationalism, the ongoing concern for the collective survival of Quebec society and culture, and the continued protection of the French language. In addition, however, we have argued that the new Quebec has taken on other characteristics that, in many respects, resemble the more social-democratic or egalitarian collectivism of certain northern- and western-European societies, such as the Netherlands or Sweden. One example, as noted in Part III, is Quebec's acceptance of civil marital unions between same-sex couples. The passage of Bill 84 by the Quebec government in July of 2002 made it the second political jurisdiction, after the Netherlands, to give legal recognition to same-sex civil unions (CAUT 2002; Tepperman and Curtis 2004: 259). Since then, Belgium has also granted such recognition (Lyons 2003), while Massachusetts and some other American jurisdictions have passed similar laws or are contemplating their creation.

Recently, a different characterization has been offered to denote the changes that have occurred in Quebec since the 1960s. Adams has asserted that these developments are proof of Quebec's emergence as the most 'post-modern' region of Canada, and indeed of all North America (Adams 2003: 82). In this formulation, the post-modern label is apparently meant to convey the notion that Quebecers are more comfortable than other North Americans with incorporating into their society people with 'flexible roles and identities', including a diversity of ethnic allegiances, sub-cultural affiliations, and sexual lifestyles (Adams 2003: 6). It has also been argued that Canada is in general a more post-modern society than the United States, and may well be the world's first post-modern nation-state (Gwyn 1995: 1, 243–53; Adams 2003: 6, 143; see also Fulford 1993: 118; Hutcheon 1988: vii–x).

Given the currency of this term among some journalists and academics, it may be tempting to apply the idea of post-modernism to describe the important transformations that have occurred in Quebec, and that we have outlined, over the past several decades. However, for several reasons, we would not do so. First, as some of the writers who employ this label have themselves asserted, 'post-modernism can be applied to just about anything', and hence can mean whatever the person using the idea wants it to mean (Gwyn 1995: 243–4). Second, present-day Quebec has some important traits that are clearly not congruent with prevailing definitions and conceptions of post-modernism (see Abercrombie, Hill, and Turner 2000: 272–3). For example, Quebec's comparatively more statist political system and more extensive social-welfare regime are normally seen by theorists writing on this subject as features of a 'modern' rather than a post-modern society. In addition, as noted above, there is the intense Quebec nationalism and strong sense of Quebecois identity that have long marked the general population, and that again are typically thought to be inconsistent with a post-modern society or culture. Furthermore, although Quebec has clearly become more ethnically diverse in recent years, it still stands as one of the most culturally homogeneous regions of North America, with the lowest percentage of non-whites and the second-lowest proportion of foreign-born among our four sub-societies. These characteristics are also not in keeping with the heterogeneous and polyglot image that is usually associated with the concept of post-modernism (see Gwyn 1995: 245–6, 253).

The degree of cultural and ethnic homogeneity in Quebec is especially pronounced outside of Montreal, which, as of the 2001 Census, accounted for more than 92 per cent of the province's visible minorities and 88 per cent of its foreign-born population (Statistics Canada 2003f, 2003g). These figures might seem to suggest that Montreal, if not the province of Quebec, may be the centre of post-modernity, or at least cultural diversity, in Canada. However, relative to Canada as a whole, Montreal is right at the national average for visible minorities (13.6 per cent) and foreign-born residents (18.4 per cent). A number of cities in English Canada surpass Montreal on either or both of these dimensions. For example, with respect to the proportion of residents who are visible minorities, Vancouver (37 per cent), Toronto (37 per cent), Calgary (18 per cent), and Edmonton (15 per cent) are higher than Montreal. On percent foreign-born, Toronto (44 per cent), Vancouver (38 per cent), Hamilton (24 per cent), Windsor (22 per cent), Kitchener (22 per cent), Calgary (21 per cent), London (19 per cent), and Victoria (19 per cent) are higher than Montreal.

For all of these reasons, we believe that it is more appropriate to comprehend the shifts in social structures and values within Quebec without calling
them post-modern, as fashionable and as current as this concept may be at
the present time. We suggest instead that, given its affinities with such nations
as Sweden, the Netherlands, and France, today's Quebec may be more accurately described as the most social-democratic, and perhaps the most 'European', sub-society of North America.[1]

HOW MANY 'NATIONS' ARE THERE?

One notable difference between the contemporary findings and the historical patterns that we have uncovered in this analysis concerns the number of
distinct regions or internal 'nations' that can be identified within the two countries. Although we have argued, based on the deep-structures approach, that
Canada and the United States are now best understood as comprising four
major sub-societies, we also believe, as noted in Parts II and III, that the two
countries were basically composed of just three distinct areas in their beginning stages. These regions were Quebec, the American South, and a third entity
that combined English Canada and the American North. This argument raises
the question of how to account for the apparent shift from a three-regions to
a four-regions configuration over time. In other words, how is it that English
Canada and the northern United States, while still being similar today, exhibit
more differences now than they did during their early histories?

It seems certain that a number of explanations lie behind this change. We
have previously discussed or alluded to several factors that have probably
contributed to some more recent divergences between English Canada and
the American North. These factors include the somewhat different patterns of

---

1. It has been suggested that, apart from their obvious historical and linguistic ties, France
   and Quebec also foster a broadly similar perspective on the rights of individual citizens,
   and in this way are distinct from the English-speaking democracies. Some of this speculation is connected to France's recent legislation banning from public educational institutions all religious symbols, including the head scarf, or hijab, worn by Muslim school girls
   and the large crucifixes worn by some Christian students. Some French commentators see
   such restrictions as a way to protect citizens from the intrusion of religion into public life,
   while also guarding against 'an excess of individualism, that philosophy so revered by
   Americans' (Coq 2004). Although no such legal restrictions have been imposed in Quebec,
   similar views about the display of religious symbols have been voiced by Quebecers, with
   some observers arguing that this reflects that province's 'secularism', 'nationalism', and
   'links to France' (Khan 2003). Gagnon (2003b) has argued further that such an approach
   is rather different from 'the British tradition of absolute tolerance' of religious expression
   in the public sphere (see also Gagnon 2004).

economic development, population growth, immigration flow, westward expansion, religious affiliation, and ethnic or racial composition that emerged in the two regions after their early colonial days. In addition, however, we speculate that another crucial factor has been the influence of the other two regions—Quebec and the American South—in 'pulling' English Canada and the American North away from each other to some degree, over the longer term. In the Canadian case, this pattern may be most evident in the efforts of the nation's political leaders to accommodate Quebecers' generally more liberal orientations when formulating government policy, especially in recent decades. For example, it would appear that Quebec's influence has helped to foster a more lenient Canadian approach to the treatment of young offenders, to the decriminalization of marijuana, and to other criminal-justice issues than would otherwise be the case (Gallup 2000b; Maclean's 2003b: 34). It is also likely that the views of Quebecers have promoted greater federal support for the legal recognition of same-sex marriages and, as a result, may have partially swayed the opinions of other Canadians in this regard (Gallup 2001a; Maclean's 2003b: 34). Another example is Canada's decision not to take part in the 2003 invasion of Iraq, a choice that probably was influenced by Quebecers' relatively greater opposition to this action, and to what has been called the 'war on terror' in Afghanistan and other parts of the world (Leger 2003; Gallup 2001f, 2001g, 2002a, 2002b; Maclean's 2003b: 34).

In similar fashion, we believe that many US government policies have been guided by the need to take into account the typically more conservative attitudes and priorities of the people and the leaders of the American South. This pattern is evident in everything from the failed attempt to enshrine equal rights for women in the American Constitution during the 1970s, to the ongoing resistance to sanctioning same-sex marriages and other gay rights initiatives in recent years (see, e.g., Fischer 1989: 892–6; Newport 1999; Loftus 2001; Mazzuca 2002a; Newport 2003: 46). On issues of national security and the use of military force, here too we find the North and the South pulling in different directions. For example, a study completed by the Pew Research Center in November of 2003, which was based on a sample of some 80,000 Americans, found that the United States was 'deeply divided' along regional lines, with people living in the southern states being consistently more 'hawkish' on national-security issues, as well as more religious and 'socially conservative', than those residing elsewhere in the country (Dionne 2003; see also McCarthy 2003; Canadian Press 2003c). The tendency for people from the South to be more supportive than other Americans of military and national-defence programs is of long standing, going back to at least the 1960s (see, e.g., Sharkansky 1978: 33; Ladd and Hadley 1975: 170–1; Gibbins 1982: 172–3). In all of these ways, then, it appears to us that, for reasons of political expediency or the need to balance conflicting regional interests and values, the traditional beliefs and preferences in the southern United States have sometimes placed constraints on America's political and social agenda. We believe that, as a result, the rest of the United States has been less liberal, and hence less like English Canada, than it otherwise would be.

Especially in our analysis of the recent situation, we have devoted much of our attention to assessing the relative value of applying the four-regions model, as opposed to the conventional two-nations approach, for understanding the nature of Canada and the United States. As our findings consistently have shown, a perspective that distinguishes four separate regions or sub-societies is demonstrably superior to the two-nations perspective that has been employed by most of the researchers who have studied this topic. Indeed, the assumption that there are two and only two identifiable societies, although conforming to the political map of North America, probably leads to the least satisfactory assessment of both the historical development and the contemporary circumstances of either country. The truth of this assertion seems especially apparent when we consider that, for many of our measures, English Canadians and northern Americans, despite residing on opposite sides of the official national boundary, share more in common with each other than they do with their fellow citizens from Quebec and the American South. The distinctiveness of the latter two populations, both from one another and from the other two sub-groups, is in many respects the most important single finding that we have presented in this book. This finding would be completely obscured by a two-nations approach.

Nevertheless, a natural question to raise is whether the four-regions model is itself completely adequate to the task of depicting and understanding the social and cultural realities of Canada and the United States. There are certainly precedents for arguing that a more detailed regional breakdown of both countries can produce fruitful insights. Studies going back as far as the early research of Odum (1936, 1947; Odum and Moore 1938), as well as more recent work by Gastil (1975), Garreau (1981), Gibbins (1982), Matthews (1983), Brym (1986), Adams (2003), and others, all suggest the possible advantages that can derive from looking for additional regional sub-divisions in each nation. At several points in the present analysis, we ourselves have reported some notable internal variations within the four regional sub-societies. This is especially true for English Canada and the American North. As an illustration, we noted in Part III that residents of the Atlantic provinces are much higher on measures of religiosity, and much lower on levels of criminal activity, than the other people whom we have included in the broad 'English Canada' category, particularly those living in British Columbia. Similarly, within what we have called the American North in the present analysis, we saw important differences between the Western and Northeastern populations with respect to both violent and non-violent crime rates (see also Himmelfarb 1999).

It is possible that additional internal differences would be found if our data sources had allowed us to use a more elaborate geographic sub-division of the two countries. It would be a major task to engage in the kinds of long-term historical and contemporary analysis that we have presented here, given the added complexities of dealing with even more regions, as well as the likely difficulties in acquiring the sources of data and documentary evidence necessary for such an investigation. We also anticipate that further research of this type would extend and build upon, rather than negate, the four-nations pattern that we have shown in our research. Nevertheless, where the available sources permit, it would be a worthwhile goal to pursue such analyses in subsequent comparisons of the two societies, for it remains an interesting empirical question to determine if there are other significant and enduring regional entities that can be identified in each of the two countries.

Before setting aside the issue of how many sub-societies there are in Canada and the United States, we should also note the potential explanatory value of looking, not only for geographic groupings, but also for the possible ethnic and racial 'nations within' (see Fleras and Elliott 1992). Perhaps the best illustration of this point is the aboriginal population in both countries. If we apply the deep-structures perspective to this group, it becomes clear that, throughout their histories, the aboriginal peoples in each society have existed under and lived by sets of core values and principles that generally are fundamentally different from the English or European-based world views that have characterized most non-native North Americans. In fact, the incompatibility of these divergent value systems is probably one major reason behind the long-term subordination, exploitation, and isolation of the native population in the two countries. Although we should keep in mind, of course, that aboriginals are themselves far from being a homogeneous population, it would be an important extension of the present analysis to determine just how distinctive an aboriginal or First-Nations sub-society would be with respect to the sorts of values, outlooks, and behaviours that we have considered in our comparisons of Canadians and Americans. In a similar fashion, the analysis of the United States could also be extended to consider both blacks and Hispanics as distinct communities. Each of these groups now accounts for more than 12 per cent of the American population, and both could be studied as potentially separate elements within the larger mix of 'nations' or sub-groups that American society comprises. Finally, we might note the possibility of studying the foreign-born peoples in each country as potential sub-societies of their own, although the considerable internal diversity of these populations would, as in the case of the aboriginal peoples, make such an analysis a complex and challenging task.

ELITES AND MASSES

In the historical analysis provided in Part II, we noted on a number of occasions that, when making comparisons of Canada and the United States, it is important to distinguish between evidence that deals with the political and other elite leaders, on the one hand, and findings that pertain to the two general populations, on the other hand. Over the years, the failure of some researchers to draw this distinction, both in their historical analyses and in contemporary research, has led to considerable confusion and misunderstanding about how and to what extent Canadians and Americans are truly similar to or different from one another.

Our historical research has shown that, if there were notable Canadian–American differences in orientations and outlooks during the early years of the two societies, these differences were concentrated almost exclusively at the elite level, and did not apply to the two peoples as a whole. This is perhaps best illustrated by the situation of the loyalists during the Revolutionary era. While we found good reason to conclude that loyalist political and religious leaders, especially those who were British-born, adhered to Tory principles that were at odds with those of their American counterparts, we also determined that the mass of Canadian settlers who were called loyalists actually lived according to values and beliefs that were similar to those of the general American population. Another historical example that we noted in Part II involved the political structures of the two nations during the latter half of the 1800s. At that time, Canada's political elite favoured a more centralized national government, while the American leadership preferred a system of relatively autonomous states. However, we found that this difference at the elite level had little impact on the Canadian and American populace, most of whom apparently had little interest in national political questions, were mainly concerned with local issues, and shared generally similar political viewpoints.

It is also possible to find more recent illustrations of the significant gap that can occur between elite beliefs or priorities and those of the general population. In fact, one Canadian study has concluded that there has been a 'recurrent tendency' for the policy initiatives of government leaders 'to run counter to majority public opinion' (Ornstein and Stevenson 1999: 179; see also Ornstein 1985, 1986). A present-day illustration of this pattern concerns the issue of same-sex marriage, which has been endorsed by the heads of Canada's highest courts and by most of the nation's political leaders, but which, as of the early 2000s, was supported by only a minority of the Canadian people

(Gallup 2001a; Gatehouse 2003).

One of the most enduring and prominent examples of the discrepancies that arise between elite views and popular opinions is the question of capital punishment. Most of Canada's political elite has long been opposed to capital punishment. This is reflected in the federal government's formal abolition of the death penalty in 1976, and in the fact that Canada's criminal-justice system unofficially stopped the use of execution as early as 1962. In contrast, in American society, where capital punishment is under the purview of individual states, the death penalty is still upheld and applied by government leaders in 38 of the 50 state jurisdictions (United States Mission to the European Union 2002). And yet, this substantial Canadian–American difference at the elite level has not been evident when comparing the two populations. We should note that support for the death penalty among Canadians and Americans has varied over time, and is partly a function of how questions are worded in different sample surveys. For example, in May of 2003, 53 per cent of Americans supported the death penalty for murder, if respondents were also given the option of choosing life imprisonment as the punishment; however, support rose to 74 per cent in questions where the option of life imprisonment was not mentioned (Jones 2003a: 28). As discussed in Chapter 7, Americans are, at the present time, more supportive of capital punishment than are Canadians. However, numerous opinion polls covering the late 1970s to the early 2000s have shown that the two people's views have been similar, and at times identical, with a clear majority of both populations in favour of the death penalty throughout most of this period (see, e.g., Perlin 1997: 117; Dobrin et al. 1996: Chapter 5; Amnesty International Canada 1996; Gallup 2001e: 2; Mazzuca 2002c; Jones 2003b: 103). Such examples make it apparent, then, that we can arrive at quite discrepant verdicts about the similarities and differences between the two societies, depending on whether we focus on the elite level or the mass level when drawing our comparisons.

This is not to say, of course, that the values of the people and those of their leaders are completely unrelated, since there is reason to believe that elite preferences and outlooks can and do 'trickle down' to the general population in some cases. For instance, support for capital punishment is lower in Canada today than it was when the death penalty was first abolished (Gallup 2001e: 2). This pattern suggests that, over time, the views of the Canadian population may have been influenced by those of their political leadership. Another example concerns Canada's multiculturalism policy, which was supported by a significantly larger proportion of the Canadian people in the 1990s than when the federal government first introduced the policy in the early 1970s (see, e.g., Canadian Ethnic Studies Association 1992: 4). Even so, there is no question that what the people value and what their elites espouse will not always, or even usually, correspond. This makes it absolutely essential for researchers to attend to the problem of moving back and forth between the elite and mass levels of analysis, and to avoid drawing conclusions about one level based on evidence from the other.

As we have discussed previously, writers continue to disagree on which level of analysis is more relevant or more telling for understanding the core values and guiding principles of a nation. Our view is that, especially over the longer term, the beliefs and outlooks that inhere among the wider population are typically a more accurate representation of a society's prevailing values than are the views of national leaders. One reason is that, particularly in the political sphere, leaders come and go, and usually change far more rapidly than do the values of the populations themselves. Hence, whatever similarities or differences there are between the elites in both nations can also come and go relatively quickly, leading to significant alterations in government policy that may have little or nothing to do with the fundamental beliefs of the two peoples.

There is no doubt, for example, that there were important and deep-seated differences between the policies and priorities fostered by the American administration of President George W. Bush, and those favoured by the Canadian government of Prime Minister Jean Chrétien during the early 2000s. However, it is not at all clear that these differences between leaders were indicative of similarly deep divisions between the Canadian and American peoples. We need only recall the governments of Bill Clinton and Jean Chrétien, just a few years previously, to find a time when the elite leaderships of the two countries were linked by many shared beliefs, alliances, and allegiances. It seems highly unlikely that the values of the two populations radically changed in this brief period, simply because the political leaderships revealed major disagreements. Likewise, should the administration of Canada's new Prime Minister, Paul Martin, introduce policies that are closely compatible with those of the American government (see Russo 2004; Janigan 2004), this by itself should not be seen as proof that the two peoples have suddenly become identical to one another. In short, we believe that it should always be an open and empirical question whether patterns at the elite level are congruent with patterns operating at the mass level in either society.

Of course, some might argue that, because the governments in both nations are elected by the people, such changes in political leadership over time are indeed indicative of value shifts within the two populations. Nevertheless, while there may be some truth in this contention, we should remember that governments in Canada and the United States are rarely put into power by a majority of eligible voters. In Canada, multiple political parties must compete with each other at the ballot box, with the result that successful candidates usually receive significantly less than half of the votes. A minority of the population typically decides the outcomes of American elections, as well, in part because, as we have seen, voter turnouts in the United States are consistently lower than they are in Canada. Even without taking voter turnout into account, however, American elections can often be won by garnering less than 50 per cent of the ballots that are cast. A good example is the 2000 Presidential election, in which George W. Bush was the victor, despite the fact that his opponent, Al Gore, actually received slightly more of the popular vote. It is particularly difficult to see the latter outcome as evidence that major value changes have occurred at the mass level in the United States in recent years. It also occurs to us that, had Gore won what was an extremely close electoral race, far fewer journalists and other observers would now be speculating about, or even noting the existence of, important value differences between the Canadian and American peoples.

NATIONAL DIFFERENCES: COMPARING THE EXTREMES

Just as analysts should be aware of the elite–mass distinction in their discussions of Canada and the United States, we believe it is also crucial that researchers differentiate between extreme or rare events, on the one hand, and prevalent or typical occurrences, on the other hand, when conducting studies of both countries. The failure to take this issue into account can lead to widely divergent and even contradictory conclusions about how the two societies compare with one another.

A prime illustration of this point is the question of political deference, and whether Americans are more or less respectful of their politicians than are Canadians. In the histories of the two nations, it is certainly more common to find occasions when citizens in the United States have demonstrated extreme disrespect, distrust, or outright hatred toward their government or its leaders. A graphic and relatively recent example was the 1995 bombing by right-wing terrorists of federal government offices in Oklahoma City, Oklahoma. The long history of American presidential assassinations, which has no real counterpart in the Canadian experience, provides several additional and quite familiar illustrations of the unbridled enmity that citizens of the United States have had toward their leading politicians over the years.

It is here, however, that we must ask what this difference really tells us about the two societies. There is little doubt, first of all, that these alarming and horrific incidents have left lasting impressions on the popular psyche of Americans, and have also engendered enduring perceptions among Canadians and other outside observers concerning the nature of the United States. In this sense, at least, such occurrences probably have served as 'defining moments' for the American nation. Nevertheless, we should remind ourselves that, although such incidents have been less common in Canada's past, they have also been very rare in the United States, and so are not representative of the everyday lives, personal experiences, and fundamental values of the American people as a whole. Instead, such events are rooted in the extremism of a small minority, who apparently are so antagonistic toward state authority that they have been more willing than any comparable group in Canada to resort to outrageous acts against their political system or its leaders. These actions are far too infrequent to demonstrate that Americans have a greater dislike of their politicians or form of government than do Canadians. On the contrary, as we saw in Chapter 10, the evidence at the level of the general population shows that it is Canadians, and not Americans, who have been more distrustful and disrespectful of their political leaders over the last several decades.

A similar argument can be applied to other examples of extreme behaviour and rare events in the United States, including the higher level of lethal violent crime, which we have discussed elsewhere in this book. That is, given that the vast majority of people in both nations do not commit such crimes, the higher rates in the United States, while they may say a great deal about the tendencies of a narrow segment of the American populace, say very little about differences between Americans and Canadians in general.

Nonetheless, having argued that extremist behaviour in the United States originates with a relatively small number of individuals, it is difficult to deny that, in some ways, the United States is indeed a nation with more extremes and contrasts than is Canada. The historical fact of American slavery, for example, has contributed to problems of racial strife and injustice that seem to be much more intense and deeply rooted than those that have existed in Canada. The violent upheaval and terrible destruction wrought by the American Civil War also have no obvious parallels in Canada's past. Structurally, as well, the United States is often a place of stark contrasts, where immense wealth exists alongside miserable poverty, and where world-renowned universities co-exist beside ghetto schools and rampant illiteracy. By comparison, Canada is a society in which such differences, though present, are usually less pronounced. As we have discussed, most evidence indicates that the gap between the rich and the poor in Canada is not as large as it is in the United States. Moreover, while Canada's educational institutions may lack the international reputation of the best American schools, Canadian schools rarely resemble the worst of American education either, occupying instead a solid middle ground in terms of both eminence and quality (Srebrnik 2000: 166–9; Grabb and Curtis 2002: 50; Ogmundson 2002: 57).

**Figure 12.1 Hypothetical Depiction of the Distribution of a
Characteristic in the Canadian and American Populations**

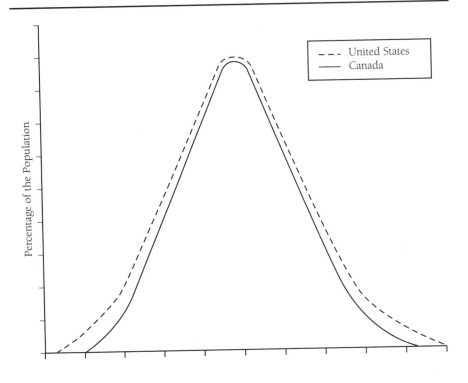

Figure 12.1 offers one way of envisioning the impact that extreme cases may have in characterizing and distinguishing the two societies. This figure shows two approximately normal curves, each of which represents the manner in which various attitudes, behaviours, and other social characteristics are sometimes distributed within a population. In this hypothetical depiction, the curves overlap quite closely, except for discrepancies in the tails, which comprise the two extremities of the phenomenon in question. For example, the curves might represent the distribution of wealth versus poverty within two different populations. The high point in the middle of each curve indicates that most people have something close to the average level of wealth or material well-being in each society, while the declining slopes of the curves on either side represent the smaller percentages of individuals in both countries that fall toward the wealthy extreme, on the one hand, and the poor or low-income extreme, on the other hand.

Although this depiction certainly does not apply to every comparison that might be drawn between Canada and the United States, it can be useful for understanding how and to what extent extreme cases play a role in distinguishing the two societies and their peoples. The large overlap in the middle of the two curves captures the great similarities that most Canadians and Americans share on a large number of issues, including many of the attitudes, behaviours, and social indicators that we have examined in our analysis. At the same time, however, the lack of complete overlap in the tails of the curves indicates where the two populations may differ.

In some instances, as in the case of wealth and poverty, Americans are more apt to occupy both extremes than are Canadians, since there are proportionally more wealthy and more poor people in the United States than in Canada. This is the basic image that is shown in Figure 12.1. For other variables, though, the national differences could be mainly concentrated in just one of the tails. An illustration might be recent attitudes about interracial marriage, with Americans being more likely than Canadians to be extremely opposed to such marriages, but not being more likely than Canadians to be extremely in favour. Yet another pattern is one in which there is an average difference between the two populations that is relatively slight, and that is almost completely the result of having a larger difference in one of the tails of the distribution than in the other. Although we do not have data that show this outcome, we can imagine the possibility, for example, that Americans are, on average, slightly more individualist than Canadians on a scale of individualist versus statist values, but that this difference occurs mainly because the Canadian distribution has a larger proportion of people concentrated in the extreme statist tail than does the American distribution, but differs very little, or not at all, at the individualist end of the continuum.

It obviously follows from such examples that each population varies internally on all manner of values, beliefs, and behaviours and that, in many if not most comparisons, the majority of Canadians and Americans overlap with each other, and so are not very different. Thus, there are people in both countries who are racist and those who are not, people who are statist and those who are not, people who are religious and those who are not, people who are poor and those who are not, and so forth.

At the same time, however, we do have the impression that, at either or both of the extremes of such phenomena, the American distributions occasionally outstretch those found in Canada. This should be seen as a tentative observation, both because the evidence of greater American extremism is not conclusive, and because the reasons for its apparent occurrence are not entirely clear. Nevertheless, to the extent that the tendency for more extreme outcomes does exist in the United States, we may cautiously trace it in part to the relatively greater latitude that contemporary American social structures and institutions either permit or encourage when it comes to self-interested or self-focused kinds of beliefs and behaviours. In other words, whether by design or neglect, it may be that American society simply allows more room than Canadian society for both the 'highs' and the 'lows' of various phenomena to operate within its broad social milieu. On the one hand, for example, this can promote economic prosperity or individual excellence that goes beyond what Canadians can generally aspire to or achieve. Still, on the other hand, this tendency can also abide the kinds of gratuitous poverty or ruthless competitiveness that Canadians are less likely to experience or to witness (see Reitz 1998: 181–3).

We should stress again that it is easy to exaggerate just how different Canada and the United States are in these and other respects. As suggested in previous chapters, such exaggerations are, in our view, a significant weakness in some of the previous comparative analyses that have been conducted on the two countries. Nevertheless, we agree with those commentators who, while arguing that there are many similarities between Canadians and Americans, have also concluded that Canada is in some respects a moderately 'nicer', 'kinder', or 'gentler' version of its southern neighbour (Gwyn 1985: 187; 1995: 256–7; Ferguson 1997: 110; Simpson 2000: 79). There are other recent observers, however, who take a different view of this comparative question, and whose work is part of an ongoing debate about the current state and future direction of both countries. We consider this debate and a number of related issues in the concluding section of this chapter.

PAST, PRESENT, AND FUTURE: CONVERGENCE, DIVERGENCE, OR BOTH?

One of the central themes underlying both our own analysis and most other studies of Canada and the United States concerns the direction, or 'trajectory', of social change that has occurred in the two societies since their early histories. Implicitly or explicitly, almost every past or current observer has contributed in some way or another to the continuing discussion of whether, over time, the two countries have become more or less similar to one another.

As we noted in Part I, Tocqueville long ago concluded that, while French Canadians were very different from other North Americans, English Canadians were 'identical' with the people of the United States, even after the years of conflict and divisiveness that surrounded the American Revolution. He offered this assessment in the 1830s, more than a half-century after the American colonies declared their independence from the British Empire. His first-hand observations suggest that, at least among the English-speaking population, the two societies were both very much alike and also moving along similar paths during that historic era. In 1889, more than six decades after Tocqueville's analysis, the noted British historian, Lord Bryce, also remarked on the shared characteristics that he saw in his direct encounters with Canadians and Americans. In his view, 'it need hardly be said that there is little difference between the populations' (Bryce 1889, II: 398). At about the same time, yet another famous traveller to North America, Friedrich Engels, confirmed Bryce's considered opinion on this question. During a visit to Montreal in 1888, Engels wrote that Canada and the United States were not only similar but were becoming increasingly so. His belief was that, because of its many commonalities with the United States, Canada 'is half-annexed already socially' and that, for economic and other reasons, the two countries should soon 'abolish this ridiculous boundary line' between them (Engels 1888: 204).

Among leading contemporary researchers, Lipset has been the one observer who most strongly disagrees with the views of writers such as Tocqueville, Bryce, and Engels. Lipset has also been the most explicit in arguing that Canada and the United States have always been, and continue to be, distinctly different nations. Thus, while acknowledging that both societies have witnessed major social-structural and cultural transformations since their early histories, Lipset maintains that these changes have not brought the two peoples closer together in terms of values, behaviours, and world views. Instead, Canada and the United States have moved like two ships sailing on parallel courses, or two trains running on 'parallel railway tracks'; as a result, even though 'they are far from where they started', it is also clear that 'the gap between them remains' (Lipset 1990: 37, 213; 1986: 146). Nevertheless, in spite of these strong assertions, even Lipset conceded many years ago that the 'two societies are probably as close to each other culturally as any two in the world' (Lipset 1979: 40). Such concessions seem almost contradictory, given Lipset's other claims about the significant and lasting differences between Canada and the United States. On the other hand, these comments are helpful in demonstrating the difficulties that writers can sometimes face when they honestly believe that there are many important distinctions between Canadians and Americans, but have trouble providing consistent evidence to support their case.

Although debates over the trajectories of Canada and the United States have their own unique elements, this issue is also part of a larger discussion in the literature concerning the processes of social change that are occurring in other nations. Some observers have commented on the possibility that we may be seeing a general movement toward value convergence, not only in North America, but in much of the world. It has even been speculated that this shift may ultimately lead to what Giddens has called 'universal values' that are 'shared by almost everyone' (Giddens 1994: 20–1). This argument stems partly from the theory that the international community is currently experiencing a widespread trend toward more and more 'globalization', with an increase in the need for economic connections, political affinities, and cultural ties among many of the world's nation-states (see, e.g., Dogan and Pelassy 1984; Kohn 1989; Giddens 1990, 1994; Inglehart 1990; Nevitte 1996; Carroll 2004).

Some writers, however, believe that a single global value system is at best a distant possibility. Particularly since the tragedy of September 11, 2001, and the conflicts among nations that have followed in its aftermath, there has been a real concern in some circles that the world may actually be moving in the opposite direction. Indeed, although it is an open question whether recent events signal an imminent 'clash of civilizations' (Huntington 1996), at times there seems to be ample evidence that major rifts still exist, and may be growing, in the value systems and institutions that characterize many societies in the current era (see, e.g., Siddiqui 2003; Parker 2003).

Nevertheless, the work of a large number of researchers supports the conclusion that there has in fact been a trend toward more common or more compatible value systems and forms of social organization among countries, especially if we confine the comparison to various industrialized nations, or to what have been called the 'rich democracies' (Wilensky 2002). Here we include liberal democracies, such as Canada and the United States, but also Britain, Australia, New Zealand, and, to varying degrees, the social-democratic nations of northern and western Europe. Numerous studies, spanning the period from the 1960s to the present, reveal that in general terms these societies have been undergoing similar transformations. For the most part, these changes have comprised a mixture of both increasing convergence and parallel transitions, and have involved an extensive range of economic, political, social, and cultural variables (see, e.g., Hofstede 1980; Nevitte and Gibbins 1990; Nevitte, Basanez, and Inglehart 1992; Lemel and Modell 1994; Inglehart 1990, 1997; Inglehart, Nevitte, and Basanez 1996; Inglehart and Baker 2000; Inkeles 1997, 1998; Kanji and Nevitte 2000; Wilensky 2002; Carroll 2004; for some discussion, see Grabb 1994: 130–1; 1998: 261–3; Baer et al. 1996: 325–6; Parker 2003). The pattern of change is certainly not uniformly convergent, and entails some signs of both divergence and continuing distinctiveness among countries, including internal divisions such as that between English Canada and Quebec, for example. However, the bulk of the evidence clearly indicates a similar and broadly convergent trajectory of social change for these nations.

As might be expected, most of these same studies also reveal close and generally increasing similarities between Canada and the United States during the past four or more decades. It is undoubtedly on the basis of such research that some contemporary writers dismiss Lipset's now familiar contention that Canada and the United States are still moving along paths that are as separate from each other today as they were in the late 1700s. In this regard, one commentator has essentially echoed the views of Tocqueville, Bryce, and Engels from more than a century ago. He has stated conclusively that 'Canadian society has never been more similar to that of the United States' and that 'the two countries are becoming more alike' as time goes on (Simpson 2000: 6).

We might assume that this would be the position taken by most observers of the two societies these days, although many of these observers would probably also maintain that Canada and the United States still have numerous 'small differences that matter' (Card and Freeman 1993; see also Maclean's 2003b: 32). However, at least one recent analyst explicitly rejects this assessment, arguing that it is yet another myth about the two nations, 'the myth of converging values' (Adams 2003: 2–3; see also Adams 2004). On the contrary, Adams sees a long-term trend toward significant and increasing divergence in the value patterns of Canada and the United States.

Given the large body of contrary research findings noted above, as well as a good deal of the historical and contemporary evidence that we have reviewed, this is a bold position to take. The empirical basis for this alternative viewpoint comes from three representative sample surveys conducted in 1992, 1996, and 2000. Many of the comparative findings from these data, such as Americans' relatively more conservative attitudes on moral and religious issues, conform closely to the research that we have presented in this volume. Unfortunately, however, while some of this work can be seen as a valiant corrective to any sweeping assumption that Canadians and Americans are now simply one and the same, Adams's analysis involves a number of significant difficulties. These problems seriously undermine any claim that we are now seeing a new Canadian value system that is becoming substantially divergent from its American counterpart.

First of all, most of the arguments that are posed by Adams are premised on the belief that the Lipset thesis is a correct and accurate depiction of both original and enduring differences in the values and institutions of Canada and the United States. On this point, we would simply remark that, if there is one misconception about the two peoples that our entire analysis should have put to rest by now, it is this one.

Second, Adams's analysis poses a number of methodological difficulties. While the data he provides are useful for updating some of the previous survey research that has been conducted on the two countries, the argument for diverging patterns of values in Canada and the United States relies heavily on comparisons of what appear to be a few key attitude questions. Moreover, even for some of these measures, the degree to which the evidence shows a growing gap in the two populations' attitudes and opinions is on the order of only 10 percentage points or less (see, e.g., Adams 2003: 42, 51, 54, 57,

76). Another especially unfortunate feature of this research is that the method-ological techniques which are applied are often unexplained or obscurely described. The analysis is neither explicit nor transparent in regard to how most measures were devised, especially the construction of the composite scales. As a result, it is frequently not possible from the published work to decipher the exact meaning and main implications of the findings.

Third, and perhaps most important, the time frame of Adams's analysis, which covers less than 10 years, is simply too short to draw strong and defin-itive conclusions about whether or not the two societies are now launched on distinct and increasingly different value trajectories. As Inkeles has argued, for example, when researchers are looking for patterns of convergence or divergence, 'short spans, say of a decade or less, are likely to be particularly misleading'; this is because 'they frequently reflect historically fleeting sentiments, or short-term adjustments to special conditions, such as war or depression', and yet 'are often interpreted in sweeping terms as representing dramatic shifts in long-term direction' (Inkeles 1998: 49). Schlesinger makes a related argument in his classic analysis of the 'tides of national politics' in the United States. He urges social scientists to take note of the political and social cycles that have consistently and regularly marked American history for more than 200 years, especially the 'alternating process of conservatism and liberalism' in American democracy (Schlesinger 1964: 102). Subsequently, Schlesinger's son has provided evidence in support of this argument, while also predicting correctly that the United States would see a move toward greater conservatism in the first decade of the twenty-first century (Schlesinger 1986: 47; see also Klapp 1978). Ajzenstat has recently offered a parallel assessment with regard to Canada, suggesting that Canadian politics has long involved 'an ongoing debate, a back-and-forth' between a more individualist liberal-democratic vision and a more left-leaning 'communitarian' approach (Ajzenstat 2003: 8 [emphasis in the original]; see also Ajzenstat and Smith 1995). As some of our previous discus-sion suggests, it is possible that such swings may be less extreme or dramatic in Canada than those that have occurred in the United States at times (see also Gwyn 2003). Nevertheless, all of these analyses indicate the importance of being aware that what looks like a major change of course in the political or social direction of a society may often amount to little more than a relatively short-lived trend that is soon reversed.

We believe that, taken together, the insights of these writers help put into proper perspective the patterns indicated by Adams's recent research. Hence, even if we set aside the lack of transparency and other problems associated with his analysis, and agree that there has been some value divergence between Canada and the United States over the past decade, it is not at all evident that this short-term shift marks the beginning of a sustained and increasing gap in values and beliefs in the two nations. Instead, we argue that this movement is best interpreted as one stage in a long-standing and continuing pattern. Although the pattern varies somewhat, depending on the issue at hand, we suggest that it is relatively consistent and has been basic to the relationship between the societies for more than two centuries. In essence, it involves a general underlying similarity between the nations, which nonetheless is regularly marked by periods of both convergence and divergence.

While it is well beyond our purposes here to demonstrate this long-term trend in detail, a few illustrations can be noted. To begin with, we have already discussed how slavery was first abolished in all of Canada, and in the British Empire generally, in the 1830s, but that the United States eventually came to agree with Canada on this issue in the 1860s. Another historical example concerns the American experiment with the total prohibition of alcohol consumption in the 1920s and early 1930s. Canadians had witnessed alcohol bans prior to this period, but the bans were typically less restrictive and were not consistently applied in all provinces or regions. Because of little public support for these restrictions in either nation, prohibition was eventually repealed, first in Canada and then in the United States. Thus, here we have another case in which Canada and the United States converged on an important question, after a period of some divergence. Additional instances can be found in the relationship between the nations in World War I, and again in World War II. During these momentous times, both the American government and the American people eventually aligned themselves with their Canadian and allied counterparts, after originally remaining neutral and aloof from the conflict in each case. And, as we have previously discussed, in the 1930s and 1940s the United States led the way in the development of social-welfare policies and programs that served as models for similar initiatives in Canada a few years later. Since that period, as we have shown, the nations have diverged again to some extent, with Canada's level of welfare expenditures now surpassing that of the United States, but still being closer to the American level than to those of the European social democracies.

We can also see this pattern, in which the two nations tend to diverge or converge around a generally similar trajectory, in recent surveys of Canadian and American attitudes. For example, we should recall from Part III that Canadians and Americans have been relatively close to one another over the past several decades on such questions as political trust and support for the death penalty, but have alternated back and forth at times, with one population ranking somewhat higher on these issues in certain periods, but the other population ranking higher during other periods (see, e.g., Perlin 1997: 99–101, 117). Similar findings emerge from various opinion surveys conducted by the Pew Research Center during the early 2000s. Based on this evidence, Andrew

Kohut, the director of the Center, has concluded that Canadians and Americans have diverged of late, most notably since the 2003 war in Iraq. However, he also finds that the national differences are often confined to specific issues (e.g., concerns about terrorism), that most of the differences are only modest, and that, as our research also suggests, the key differences are mainly between Canadians and people from the American South, rather than Americans in general (McCarthy 2003; Canadian Press 2003c).

On occasion, Adams seems to concur with our view that the two countries and their peoples have oscillated over time with respect to their basic similarities and differences, for he also notes that there have been trends toward both divergence and convergence in the historical relationship between Canada and the United States (e.g., Adams 2003: 140–1). However, his approach differs considerably from ours, in that he accepts Lipset's erroneous interpretation that the two societies began as fundamentally different entities at the time of the American Revolution, and he also believes that the brief period since the early 1990s is the beginning of a new and long-term period of increasing divergence between the nations. Based on past experience, our argument is that, in the future, Canada and the United States are almost certain to swing back toward a more convergent pattern on the major issues that confront the nations, although both societies are also likely to oscillate yet again after that. In all of these shifts, however, our view is that the two countries are unlikely to move fundamentally and irretrievably apart, and that a major reason for this is their shared deep-structural principles and their attendant institutional and social-structural commonalities.

To reiterate, then, we conclude that, setting aside the important internal differences that we have identified using the four-nations model, Canadian society and American society have always been substantially similar, though not identical. Throughout their histories, both nations have experienced periods of significant social, political, and economic change that during some stages have made them more similar, but that in other periods have made them more distinct. This long-term pattern, which combines alternating phases of greater or lesser distinctiveness with continuing and underlying allegiances and affinities, is likely to carry on for the foreseeable future, and certainly well into the twenty-first century.

Considering all of the evidence and analyses that have been reviewed and assessed in this book, we believe that it is extremely difficult to conclude otherwise. Besides, in addition to these considerations, we must acknowledge all the other important forces of congruence and alliance that can be named. First, there is the English language. As Tocqueville anticipated long ago, the use of the same language by most Canadians and Americans has always been one of the most powerful and deeply rooted linkages between the two societies, even though it has also been a source of some division within Canada itself. The English language, in turn, has made it inevitable that Canada will continue to share and to be influenced by American popular culture, which for decades has pervaded Canadian tastes in everything from movies and music, to books and television, to food and fashion. Then, of course, there are our close economic linkages, which have meant that, for many years now, more than 80 per cent of Canada's exported goods have gone to the United States, while more than 70 per cent of Canada's imported goods have come from south of the border (Statistics Canada 2003e; Simpson 2000: 6; see also Carroll 2004: Chapter 6).

One final factor to consider when discussing the ties between the two nations is America's unquestioned pre-eminence in the world over the past half-century or more, not only as the most influential player in the global economy, but also as the most powerful political and military force on the planet. It is true that, in recent years, the power of the United States has at times been a significant source of disagreement and divergence between Canadians and Americans. This can be seen in our current disputes over free-trade issues and, perhaps more so, our differences over military and foreign-policy matters. Nevertheless, in the longer term even the latter concerns are likely to re-affirm the linkages between the two countries, because of our shared geography, our similar interests in national or homeland security (see *Maclean's* 2003b: 32), and, ultimately, our kindred core principles. Paradoxically, as Richard Gwyn has contended, it may even be that our commonalities have been one reason behind our recent disagreements, 'that our tensions have been caused by that fact that we're too alike' (Gwyn 2004). Gwyn's position here is that Canada and the United States agree on the importance of fostering such fundamental principles as 'human rights, democracy, gender equality, [and] ethnic tolerance', but currently disagree about how and to what extent these ideals can be realized, both at home and abroad.

Of course, regardless of whatever evidence exists to the contrary, there are people in both countries who will hold fast to the old myths, including the conviction that the two populations have always been, and remain, very different from each other. As touched on at various points in our analysis, one reason for this enduring illusion is the impact that certain politicians, journalists, intellectuals, and academics have had in cultivating the image of Canada and the United States as two quite distinct societies. Especially in Canada, this definition of the situation by some of the nation's leading opinion-makers has taken on a life of its own, becoming a familiar, even comforting, element in the popular folklore, an often-repeated assumption that has influenced the way that Canadians think about themselves and their American neighbours. Another contributing factor in this process has been the desire among the Canadian populace not to be rendered invisible, both to Americans, who generally show far less interest in and knowledge about Canadians than the other way around, and to observers elsewhere in the world, who can all too easily overlook Canada's separate existence and identity, and vaguely lump the two nations together. These considerations may help to explain why some Canadians make concerted efforts to highlight, and at times exaggerate, their distinctiveness from Americans.

In the end, though, notwithstanding our acknowledged differences, the many similarities between the two societies and the two peoples are undeniable. It is for this reason that writers such as James Laxer can emphasize the notable disagreements between the nations but at the same time assert that their 'shared heritage . . . is enormous', and that they are, 'if not sisters, then at least cousins' (Laxer 2003: 315). Indeed, whether we like it or not, most of the bonds that have linked Canada and the United States together over the years remain much as they have been since the beginning. Moreover, it is clear to us that these fundamental ties and affinities are destined to continue, whether in the best of times or in the worst.

APPENDIX I

~

WORDINGS OF THE
WORLD VALUES SURVEY
QUESTIONS USED IN PART III

Table 7.1   Measures of Religious Involvement and Religiosity by Region and Nation

1. Independently of whether you go to church or not, would you say you are a religious person, not a religious person, or a convinced atheist?

2. Apart from weddings, funerals, and christenings, about how often do you attend religious services these days?

3. How important is God in your life?

4. How often do you pray to God outside of religious services?

5. Which if any, of the following do you believe in?

   A. God
   B. Life after death
   C. A soul
   D. The Devil
   E. Hell
   F. Heaven
   G. Sin
   H. Resurrection of the dead

Table 7.2   Liberal–Conservative Attitudes on Family and Sexual Issues by Region and Nation

Please tell me for each of the following statements whether you think it can always be justified, never be justified, or something in between.

1. Married men/women having an affair.

2. Sex under the legal age of consent
3. Homosexuality
4. Prostitution
5. Abortion
6. Divorce

On this list are various groups of people. Could you please sort out any that you would not like to have as neighbours?

1. People with AIDS
2. Homosexuals

Table 7.3   Attitudes on the Acceptability of Economic Crimes by Region and Nation

Please tell me for each of the following statements whether you think it can always be justified, never be justified, or something in between.

1. Claiming government benefits you are not entitled to
2. Avoiding a fare on public transit
3. Cheating on tax if you have the chance
4. Buying something you knew was stolen

Table 8.1   Eight Measures of Individual/Self Orientation versus Statism/Collectivism Orientation by Region and Nation

Now I'd like you to tell me your views on various issues. For each pair of contrasting issues . . . how would you place your views on this scale?

1. Incomes should be made equal versus there should be greater incentive for individual effort.
2. Individuals should take more responsibility for providing for themselves versus the state should take more responsibility to ensure that everyone is provided for.
3. People who are unemployed should have to take any job available or lose their unemployment benefits versus people who are unemployed should have the right to refuse a job they do not want.
4. Competition is good. It stimulates people to work hard and develop new ideas versus competition is harmful. It brings out the worst in people.
5. In the long run, hard work usually brings a better life versus hard work doesn't generally bring success—it's more a matter of luck and connections.

6. Private ownership of business and industry should be increased versus government ownership of business and industry should be increased.
7. People can only accumulate wealth at the expense of others versus wealth can grow, so there's enough for everyone.

I am going to read out some statements about government and the economy. For each one, could you tell me how much you agree or disagree?

8. We are more likely to have a healthy economy if the government allows more freedom for individuals to do as they wish.

Table 8.2 Views on Which Qualities Should Be Encouraged in Children by Region and Nation

Here is a list of qualities which children can be encouraged to learn at home. Which, if any, do you consider to be especially important?

1. Independence
2. Hard Work
3. Feeling of Responsibility
4. Determination, Perseverance
5. Unselfishness

Table 8.3 Eight Measures of Self-Confidence and Personal Assertiveness by Region and Nation

A variety of characteristics are listed here. Could you look at them and select those which apply to you?

1. I enjoy convincing others of my opinion
2. I often notice that I serve as a model for others
3. I own many things others envy me for
4. I like to assume responsibility
5. I am rarely unsure about how I should behave
6. I often give others advice
7. I usually count on being successful in everything that I do
8. I am good at getting what I want

Table 8.4 Attitudes about Change by Region and Nation

Now I want to ask you some questions about your outlook on life. Using the scale listed, could you tell me where you would place your own view?

1. One should be cautious about making major changes in life versus you will never achieve much unless you act boldly
2. Ideas that have stood the test of time are generally best versus new ideas are generally better than old ones
3. When changes occur in my life, I worry about the difficulties they may cause versus when changes occur in my life, I welcome the possibility that something new is beginning

Table 9.1   Social Groups that Respondents Do Not Want as Neighbours by Region and Nation

On this list are various groups of people. Could you please sort out any that you would not like to have as neighbours?

1. People of a different race
2. Muslims
3. Immigrants
4. Jews
5. Hindus
6. People with a criminal record
7. Heavy drinkers
8. People with large families
9. Emotionally unstable people
10. Drug addicts
11. People who have AIDS
12. Right wing extremists
13. Left wing extremists
14. People with large families

Table 10.1 Political Interest by Region and Nation

1. How interested would you say you are in politics?

2. How important is politics in your life?

3. When you get together with friends, would you say you discuss politics frequently, occasionally, or never?

Table 10.2 Political Protest and Civil Dissent by Region and Nation

I am going to read out some different forms of political action that people can take, and I'd like you to tell me, for each one, whether you have actually done any of these things, whether you might do it, or would never, under any circumstances, do it.

1. Signing a petition
2. Joining in boycotts
3. Attending lawful demonstrations
4. Joining unofficial strikes
5. Occupying buildings or factories

Table 10.3 Political Trust and Confidence in Political Institutions by Region and Nation

I am going to read out some statements about government and the economy. For each one, could you tell me how much you agree or disagree?

1. Our government should be made much more open to the public.
2. If an unjust law were passed by government, I could do nothing about it.
3. How much do you trust the government in Washington/Ottawa to do what is right? Do you trust it almost always, most of the time, only some of the time, or almost never?

Please . . . tell me, for each item listed, how much confidence you have in them. Is it a great deal, quite a lot, or none at all?

1. The legal system
2. The police
3. Parliament/Congress
4. Civil service
5. The Canadian/American political system

Table 10.4 Measures of General Trust and National Pride by Region and Nation

1. Generally speaking, would you say that most people can be trusted or that you can't be too careful in dealing with people?

2. I now want to ask you how much you trust various groups of people . . . could you tell me how much you trust the Canadian/American people in general?

3. How proud are you to be American/Canadian?

Table 11.1 Measures of Affiliations with and Activity in Community Voluntary Associations by Region and Nation

Please look carefully at the following list of voluntary organizations and activities and say (a) which, if any do you belong to? (b) which, if any are you currently doing unpaid work for?

The exact wordings for each are: (1) social welfare services for elderly, handicapped, or deprived people; (2) churches or religious organizations; (3) education, arts, music, or cultural activities; (4) trade unions; (5) political parties or groups; (6) local community action (concerning poverty, employment, housing, and racial equality); (7) human rights or Third World development; (8) conservation, environment, or ecology; (9) professional associations; (10) youth work (scouts, guides, youth clubs, etc.); (11) sports or recreation; (12) women's groups; (13) the peace movement; (14) animal rights; (15) voluntary organizations concerned with health; and (16) 'other groups'.

Appendix II

❧

Procedures for Analyzing the World Values Survey Items Used in Part III

The Categorization of Region

In the analyses based on the WVS, we report the results in tabular form, both for the Canadian–American comparisons and for the comparisons involving the four regions or sub-societies. For the analysis of the WVS items in Part III, the procedures used to categorize the four sub-societies require some clarification. First, for the two Canadian regions, all Quebec respondents are treated as one category, while everyone else is grouped into a second category labelled 'English Canada'. This approach raises the question of whether it would have been preferable to divide the Canadian sample on the basis of language rather than region. The latter strategy would have meant placing any English-speaking respondents from Quebec in the English Canada grouping, and combining the French speakers in all ten provinces into a second, 'French Canada' grouping.

Although we considered such a procedure, in the end we chose to distinguish the two sub-societies on regional rather than linguistic grounds. One reason for this choice was our belief that the notion of distinct sub-societies entails at least a general sense of a common geographic location for each group. Second, Quebec is probably a more meaningful category for our purposes, because most residents of this province see themselves as Quebecois, and not as French Canadians. Another more practical consideration was that there were no French respondents from outside Quebec in the WVS sample, and only 32 English speakers from Quebec. Some preliminary analyses, which are not reported here, did show that the few English respondents from Quebec generally resemble other English Canadians more than they do French Quebecers in their attitudes and behaviours. However, the number of English Quebecer was so small that their inclusion or exclusion in either sub-sample proved to have a negligible effect on the patterns of results, in any case. For all these reasons, we divided the Canadian respondents into two groups, distinguishing between those from Quebec and those from the rest of the country.

Another approach would have been to conduct an analysis using additional categories, by further sub-dividing English Canada along regional lines. This analysis might have involved, for example, distinguishing among the Atlantic region, Ontario, the Prairie region, and British Columbia. We did not adopt this strategy, in part because our main purpose in the present analysis was to test the applicability of the four-sub-societies model. It should also be noted that using a more complex regional breakdown was problematic in the present instance because of sample size limitations. In addition, although it is fair to say that the identification of more complex regional sub-societies within Canada is an interesting possibility for future research, we might note that some previous research has not revealed definitive regional splits along these lines. For example, one of the only sociological studies in Canada to attempt a rigorous analysis of this question found that none of these internal differences within English Canada was of much salience. Based on a relatively large and diverse set of indicators, this study concluded that, in Canada, the distinction between Quebec and the rest of the country was the only truly significant regional division (Baer, Grabb, and Johnston 1993; see also Adams 2003: Chapter 3).

When categorizing the two American sub-societies, we were constrained by the final set of regional codes that were applied in the WVS data. Rather than sort respondents into each of the 50 American states, the WVS in the United States relies instead on a set of ten regional categories that are similar to those used in the National Opinion Research Center's General Social Surveys. Seven of these categories were combined to produce our 'US North' grouping: New England, the Middle Atlantic States, the East North Central region, the West North Central region, the Rocky Mountain states, the Northwest region, and California. The second American sub-society, the 'US South', comprised the remaining three regions: East South Central, West South Central, and the South Atlantic. The resulting classification captures the North–South distinction well, except for the inclusion of a few northern states, most notably Delaware and Maryland, in the South Atlantic category. Even so, the vast majority of the states in the South Atlantic region are clearly southern in terms of both geography and historical traditions. All but a few of these states, for example, were on the Confederate side during the Civil War. Therefore, we chose to include the South Atlantic region as part of our US South category. It might also be noted that any errors generated by this minor misclassification of a few states should have a conservative impact on our findings with respect to judging the distinctiveness of the two American sub-societies. In other words, the differences identified using this categorization should, if anything, underestimate the actual differences between the southern and northern American sub-samples.

The South Atlantic region includes Delaware, Maryland, West Virginia, Virginia, the District of Columbia, North Carolina, South Carolina, Georgia, and Florida. The East South Central region combines Kentucky, Tennessee, Alabama, and Mississippi. The West South Central area subsumes Arkansas, Oklahoma, Louisiana, and Texas. All other regions were grouped together to form what we refer to as the US North. As with the Canadian data, we chose not to consider more detailed regional sub-divisions—such as a split between east and west—in the US. This decision was made because of sample size restrictions, because of our primary interest in testing the four-sub-societies model, and because of previous research showing that the North–South division is the major distinction in the United States (Marsden et al. 1982; Reed 1986, 1991; Baer, Grabb, and Johnston 1993).

MULTIVARIATE ANALYSES

For all of the dependent measures taken from the WVS, both bivariate analyses and analyses with multivariate controls were conducted. We are grateful to Doug Baer for his work on the multivariate analyses. The mulitvariate analyses take into account the possible effects of the following nine variables: community size, occupational status, religious affiliation, marital status, race, nativity (foreign versus native-born), gender, education, and age. For a number of reasons, we do not report the multivariate findings. First, because the bivariate findings are themselves quite extensive, we have sought to keep the presentation of results as clear and concise as possible. Second, it is debatable whether controls should be applied in assessing the comparative findings, since this procedure could be seen as effectively subtracting the very structural and related differences across nations and regions that we wished to identify. Finally, except for a few isolated instances, the controls have virtually no effect on the bivariate patterns. The one effect that might be noted is a blurring of some of the regional distinctiveness on some measures with controls, especially in the case of Quebec.

APPENDIX III

❧

VARIOUS SOCIAL INDICATORS BY REGION AND NATION

	Region					Nation		
	English Canada	Quebec	US North	US South	Sig[1]	Canada Total	US Total	Sig[1]
1. Religious denomination (%)								
Roman Catholic	29	80	33	17		41	28	
Protestant	36	4	32	49		28	37	
Other	4	5	10	9		4	10	
No religion	32	12	26	25	√	27	25	√
2. Marital status (%)								
Married	60	56	62	56		58	60	
Common law	6	12	3	4		8	3	
Divorced	4	5	7	9		4	7	
Separated	3	2	2	3		3	3	
Widowed	7	7	8	10		7	9	
Single, never married	21	19	19	18	√	20	18	√
3. Community size (%)								
Under 10,000	33	31	21	30		32	24	
10,000–100,000	16	11	44	42		15	44	
100,000–500,000	13	8	16	15		12	16	
500,000+	38	51	18	14	√	41	17	√

	Region					Nation		
	English Canada	Quebec	US North	US South	Sig[1]	Canada Total	US Total	Sig[1]
4. Nativity (%)								
Foreign-born	20	9	8	4		17	7	
Native-born	80	91	92	96	√	83	93	√
5. Race (%)								
White	92	89	86	75		92	83	
Black	1	2	8	19		1	11	
Other	7	9	6	7	√	7	6	√
6. Number of children								
Percentage with none	29	32	28	28		30	28	
Average number	2.59	2.65	2.71	2.69		2.60	2.70	
7. Occupation (%)								
Large employer	2	4	5	4		3	4	
Small employer	9	6	6	7		8	6	
Professional	16	18	21	17		17	20	
Non-manual middle	8	8	13	9		8	12	
Non-manual junior	11	15	7	6		12	7	
Foreman/super	4	2	4	4		3	4	
Skilled manual	7	5	14	19		7	16	
Semi-skilled manual	15	12	10	11		14	10	
Unskilled manual	16	18	8	9		17	8	
Housewife	5	6	4	4		5	4	
Other	6	6	8	11	√	6	9	√

Notes

[1] A check mark (√) indicates that the likelihood ratio chi-square for the overall four-category comparison across regions, or the two-category comparison across nations, is significant at <.05.

REFERENCES

Abella, Rosalie Silberman. 1984. Equality in Employment: A Royal Commission Report. Ottawa: Minister of Supplies and Services.

Abercrombie, Nicholas, Stephen Hill, and Bryan Turner. 1980. The Dominant Ideology Thesis. London: Allen and Unwin.

———, eds. 2000. The Penguin Dictionary of Sociology, 4th edn. London: Penguin Books.

Adams, Michael. 1997. Sex in the Snow. Toronto: Viking.

———. 2003. Fire and Ice: The Myth of Value Convergence in Canada and the United States. Toronto: Penguin Canada.

———. 2004. 'Continental Drift'. The Walrus, vol. 1, 4 (April/May): 62–71.

Adamson, Christopher. 1994. 'God's continent divided: politics and religion in Upper Canada and the northern and western United States, 1775 to 1841'. Comparative Studies in Society and History 36, 3 (July): 417–46.

Ajzenstat, Janet. 2003. The Once and Future Democracy: An Essay in Political Thought. Montreal and Kingston: McGill-Queen's University Press.

Ajzenstat, Janet and Peter J. Smith, eds. 1995. Canada's Origins: Liberal, Tory, or Republican? Ottawa: Carleton University Press.

Akenson, Donald Harman. 1984. The Irish in Ontario: A Study in Rural History. Montreal and Kingston: McGill-Queen's University Press.

———. 1985. Being Had: Historians, Evidence, and the Irish in North America. Don Mills, ON: P.D. Meany Publishers.

———. 1988. Small Differences: Irish Catholics and Irish Protestants, 1815–1922. Montreal and Kingston: McGill-Queen's University Press.

———. 1993. The Irish Diaspora: A Primer. Toronto: P.D. Meany Publishers.

———. 2000. 'Irish migration to North America, 1800–1920', pp. 111–38 in Andy Bielenberg, ed., The Irish Diaspora. Harrow, Essex, England: Pearson Education Limited.

Allahar, Anton. 1993. 'When blacks first became worth less'. International Journal of Comparative Sociology 34: 39–55.

Allen, Theodore W. 1994. The Invention of the White Race, vol. 1 of Racial Oppression and Social Control. London: Verso.

Almond, Gabriel and Sidney Verba. 1963. The Civic Culture: Political Attitudes and Democracy in Five Nations. Boston: Little Brown.

Althusser, Louis. 1972. Politics and History: Montesquieu, Rousseau, Hegel, and Marx. Translated by Ben Brewster. London: New Left Books.

———. 1974. Essays in Self-Criticism. London: New Left Books.

Amnesty International Canada. 1996. 'The death penalty in Canada: twenty years of abolition'. http://www.amnesty.ca/deathpenalty/canada.htm, accessed 11 August 2003.

Appleby, Joyce. 1974. Materialism and Morality in the American Past: 1600–1860. Reading, MA: Addison-Wesley Publishing Company.

———. 1984. Capitalism and a New Social Order: The Republican Vision of the 1790s. New York: New York University Press.

———. 1992. Liberalism and Republicanism in the Historical Imagination. Cambridge, MA: Harvard University Press.

Archibald, Peter. 1978. Social Psychology as Political Economy. Toronto: McGraw-Hill Ryerson.

Archives of Ontario. 2002. 'Freedom from slavery'. Queen's Printer for Ontario. http://wwww.archives.gov.on.ca/english/exhibits/humnrits/slavery.htm, accessed June 2003.

Baer, Douglas and James Curtis. 1984. 'French Canadian–English Canadian value differences: national survey findings'. Canadian Journal of Sociology 9, 4: 405–28.

———. 1988. 'Differences in the achievement values of French Canadians and English Canadians', pp. 476–84 in James Curtis, Edward Grabb, Neil Guppy, and Sid Gilbert, eds, Social Inequality in Canada: Patterns, Problems, Policies, 1st edn. Scarborough, ON: Prentice-Hall Canada.

Baer, Douglas, James Curtis, and Edward Grabb. 2001. 'Has voluntary association activity declined? Cross-national analyses for fifteen countries'. Canadian Review of Sociology and Anthropology 38, 3 (August): 249–74.

Baer, Douglas, James Curtis, Edward Grabb, and William Johnston. 1995. 'Respect for authority in Canada, the United States, Great Britain, and Australia'. Sociological Focus 28, 2 (May): 177–95.

———. 1996. 'What values do people prefer in children? A comparative analysis of survey evidence from fifteen countries', pp. 299–328 in Clive Seligman, James Olson, and Mark Zanna, eds, Values: The Ontario Symposium on Personality and Social Psychology, vol. 8. Hillsdale, NJ: Erlbaum.

Baer, Douglas, Edward Grabb, and William Johnston. 1990a. 'Reassessing differences in Canadian and American values', pp. 86–97 in James Curtis and Lorne Tepperman, eds, Images of Canada: The Sociological Tradition. Scarborough, ON: Prentice-Hall Canada.

———. 1990b. 'The values of Canadians and Americans: a critical analysis and reassessment'. Social Forces 68, 3 (March): 693–713.

———. 1990c. 'The values of Canadians and Americans: a rejoinder'. Social Forces 69, 1 (September): 273–7.

———. 1993. 'National character, regional culture, and the values of Canadians and Americans'. Canadian Review of Sociology and Anthropology 30, 1 (February): 13–36.

Bailyn, Bernard. 1967. The Origins of American Politics. New York: Vintage Books.

———. 1992. The Ideological Origins of the American Revolution. Cambridge, MA: The Belknap Press of Harvard University Press.

Banting, Keith. 1997. 'The social policy divide: the welfare state in Canada and the United States', pp. 267–309 in Keith Banting, George Hoberg, and Richard Simeon, eds, Degrees of Freedom: Canada and the United States in a Changing World. Montreal and Kingston: McGill-Queen's University Press.

Banting, Keith and Richard Simeon. 1997. 'Changing economies, changing societies', pp. 23–70 in Keith Banting, George Hoberg, and Richard Simeon, eds, Degrees of Freedom: Canada and the United States in a Changing World. Montreal and Kingston: McGill-Queen's University Press.

Bartlett, John. 1968. Bartlett's Familiar Quotations, 14th edn. Boston: Little, Brown and Company.

Baum, Gregory. 2000. 'Catholicism and secularization in Quebec', pp. 149–65 in David Lyon and Marguerite Van Die, eds, Rethinking Church, State, and Modernity: Canada between Europe and America. Toronto: University of Toronto Press.

Beard, Charles and Mary R. Beard. 1927. The Rise of American Civilization, vol. II. New York: Macmillan.

Beaujot, Roderic. 1991. Population Change in Canada. Toronto: McClelland and Stewart.

———. 2000. 'Les deux transitions démographiques du Quebec, 1860–1996'. Cahiers québecois de demographie 29, 2 (automne): 201–30.

Beaujot, Roderic and Kevin McQuillan. 1982. Growth and Dualism: The Demographic Development of Canadian Society. Toronto: Gage.

Beeghley, Leonard. 2000. The Structure of Social Stratification in the United States, 3rd edn. Boston: Allyn and Bacon.

Bell, David. 1992. The Roots of Disunity: A Study of Canadian Political Culture, rev. edn. Toronto: Oxford University Press.

Bell, David and Lorne Tepperman. 1979. The Roots of Disunity: A Look at Canadian Political Culture. Toronto: McClelland and Stewart.

Bellah, Robert, R. Madsen, W. Sullivan, A. Swidler, and S. Tipton. 1985. Habits of the Heart. Berkeley: University of California Press.

Bender, Thomas. 1978. Community and Social Change in America. New Brunswick, NJ: Rutgers University Press.

Bendix, Reinhard. 1960. Max Weber: An Intellectual Portrait. Garden City, NY: Anchor Books.

Berlin, Ira and Philip D. Morgan. 1993. 'Introduction', pp. 1–45 in Ira Berlin and Philip D. Morgan, eds, Cultivation and Culture: Labor and the Shaping of Slave Life in the Americas. Charlottesville and London: University Press of Virginia.

Berry, John, Rudolf Kalin, and Donald Taylor. 1977. Multiculturalism and Ethnic Attitudes in Canada. Ottawa: Ministry of Supply and Services.

Berton, Pierre. 1971. The National Dream. Toronto: McClelland and Stewart.

Besserer, Sandra. 2002. 'Criminal victimization: an international perspective'. Juristat 22, 4. Catalogue 85-002. Ottawa: Statistics Canada.

Bhaskar. Roy. 1978. A Realist Theory of Science. Sussex, UK: Harvester Press.

———. 1979. The Possibility of Naturalism. New York: Humanities Press.

Bibby, Reginald. 1987. Fragmented Gods. Toronto: Irwin.

———. 1990. Mosaic Madness. Toronto: Stoddart.

———. 1993. Unknown Gods. Toronto: Stoddart.

———. 1995. The Bibby Report: Social Trends, Canadian Style. Toronto: Stoddart.

———. 2001. Canada's Teens. Toronto: Stoddart.

———. 2002. Restless Gods. Toronto: Stoddart.

Blackburn, McKinley and David Bloom. 1993. 'The distribution of family income: measuring and explaining changes in the 1980s for Canada and the United States', pp. 233–65 in David Card and Richard Freeman, eds, Small Differences That Matter. Chicago and London: University of Chicago Press.

Blank, Rebecca and Maria Hanratty. 1993. 'Responding to need: a comparison of social safety nets in Canada and the United States', pp. 191–231 in David Card and Richard Freeman, eds, Small Differences That Matter. Chicago and London: University of Chicago Press.

Blessing, Patrick J. 1999. 'The Irish in America', pp. 453–70 in Michael Glazier, ed., The Encyclopedia of the Irish in America. Notre Dame, IN: University of Notre Dame Press.

Blethen, H. Tyler. 1997. 'Introduction', pp. 1–14 in H. Tyler Blethen and Curtis W. Wood, Jr, eds, Ulster and North America: Transatlantic Perspectives on the Scotch-Irish. Tuscaloosa and London: University of Alabama Press.

Blethen, H. Tyler and Curtis W. Wood, Jr, eds. 1997a. Ulster and North America: Transatlantic Perspectives on the Scotch-Irish. Tuscaloosa and London: University of Alabama Press.

———. 1997b. 'Scotch-Irish frontier society in southwestern North Carolina, 1780–1840', pp. 213–26 in H. Tyler Blethen and Curtis W. Wood, Jr, eds, Ulster and North America: Transatlantic Perspectives on the Scotch-Irish. Tuscaloosa and London: University of Alabama Press.

Bloemraad, Irene. 2002. 'The North American naturalization gap: an institutional approach to citizenship acquisition in the United States and Canada'. International Migration Review 36, 1 (Spring): 193–228.

Bonilla-Silva, Eduardo. 1997. 'Rethinking racism: toward a structural interpretation'. American Sociological Review 62, 3 (June): 465–80.

Borjas, George. 1993. 'Immigration policy, national origin, and immigrant skills: a comparison of Canada and the United States', pp. 45–67 in David Card and Richard Freeman, eds, Small Differences That Matter. Chicago and London: University of Chicago Press.

Bothwell, Robert. 1992. 'More than kin, and less than kind', pp. 285–94 in Stephen Randall,

Herman Konrad, and Sheldon Silverman, eds, North America Without Borders? Integrating Canada, the United States, and Mexico. Calgary: University of Calgary Press.

Bowen, Desmond. 1995. History and the Shaping of Irish Protestantism. New York: Peter Lang Publishers.

Boyd, Monica and Michael Vickers. 2004. 'The ebb and flow of immigration', pp. 258–72 in James Curtis, Edward Grabb, and Neil Guppy, eds, Social Inequality in Canada: Patterns, Problems, Policies, 4th edn. Scarborough, ON: Pearson Education Canada.

Bradley, A.G. 1968. The Making of Canada. London: Constable.

Branswell, Brenda. 1997. 'A distinctly hedonistic society'. Maclean's, 29 December, p. 35.

Braudel, Fernand. 1979. The Structures of Everyday Life: The Limits of the Possible, vol. 1: Civilization and Capitalism, 15th–18th Century. New York: Harper and Row.

Breay, Claire. 2002. Magna Carta. Toronto: University of Toronto Press.

Brebner, J.B. 1937 [1969]. The Neutral Yankees of Nova Scotia. Toronto: McClelland and Stewart.

Breton, Raymond. 1998. 'Ethnicity and race in social organization: recent developments in Canadian society', pp. 60–115 in Rick Helmes-Hayes and James Curtis, eds, The Vertical Mosaic Revisited. Toronto: University of Toronto Press.

Brewer, John. 1989. The Sinews of Power: War, Money, and the English State, 1688–1783. London: Unwin Hyman.

Briggs, Robin. 1977. Early Modern France, 1560–1715. Oxford: Oxford University Press.

Brock, Kathy. 2000. 'Finding answers in difference: Canadian and American aboriginal policy compared', pp. 338–58 in David M. Thomas, ed., Canada and the United States: Differences that Count, 2nd edn. Peterborough, ON: Broadview Press.

Brogan, D.W. 1954. Politics in America. New York: Harper and Brothers.

Brunet, Michel. 1973. 'The historical background of Quebec's challenge to Canadian unity', pp. 39–51 in Dale C. Thomson, ed., Quebec Society and Politics: Views from the Inside. Toronto: McClelland and Stewart.

Bryce, James. 1887. The Predictions of Hamilton and de Tocqueville. Baltimore: Johns Hopkins University Press.

———. 1889. The American Commonwealth, 2 vols. London: Macmillan.

———. 1921a. Canada: An Actual Democracy. Toronto: Macmillan of Canada.

———. 1921b. Modern Democracies, 2 vols. New York: Macmillan.

Brym, Robert, ed. 1986. Regionalism in Canada. Toronto: Irwin.

——— with Bonnie Fox. 1989. From Culture to Power: The Sociology of English Canada. Toronto: Oxford University Press.

———. 1993. 'The Canadian capitalist class', pp. 31–48 in James Curtis, Edward Grabb, and Neil Guppy, eds, Social Inequality in Canada: Patterns, Problems, Policies, 2nd edn. Scarborough, ON: Prentice-Hall Canada.

———. 2002. 'Canadian sociology: an introduction to the upper thirteen'. The American Sociologist 33, 1 (Spring): 5–11.

———. 2004. 'Affluence, power, and strikes in Canada, 1973–2000', pp. 55–67 in James Curtis, Edward Grabb, and Neil Guppy, eds, Social Inequality in Canada: Patterns, Problems, Policies, 4th edn. Scarborough, ON: Pearson Education Canada.

Brym, Robert and Rhonda Lenton. 1991. 'The distribution of anti-Semitism in Canada in 1984'. Canadian Journal of Sociology 16, 4 (Fall): 411–18.

Bryson, Bill. 1994. Made in America: An Informal History of the English Language in the United States. New York: William Morrow and Company.

Burkholder, Richard. 2003. 'Proud Canadians assess global role and image'. The Gallup Poll Tuesday Briefing, 11 March, pp. 9–11.

Burt, A.L. 1968. The Old Province of Quebec, vol. I. Ottawa: Carleton University Press.

Cairns, Alan C. 2000. Citizens Plus: Aboriginal Peoples and the Canadian State. Vancouver: University of British Columbia Press.

Caldwell, Gary and Paul Reed. 2000. 'Civic participation in Canada: is Quebec different?' Inroads 8: 215–22.

Calvert, John. 1984. Government, Limited. Ottawa: The Canadian Centre for Policy Alternatives.

Canadian Council on Social Development. 1996. 'Voter turnout in 1988 and 1993 federal elections and in provincial elections circa 1990'. http://www.ccsd.ca/facts.html, accessed 17 June 2003.

Canadian Ethnic Studies Association. 1992. CESA Bulletin 19, 2 (Autumn): 1–5.

Canadian Press. 2003a. 'Thefts: Canadian rate 26% higher than in US'. The London Free Press, 9 January, p. A2.

———. 2003b. 'A nation of faith-shifters'. The London Free Press, 17 May, p. F7.

———. 2003c. 'Canadians, Americans not drifting apart, analyst says'. The Kitchener-Waterloo Record, 10 December, p. A5.

Cantril, Albert and Susan Davis Cantril. 1999. Reading Mixed Signals: Ambivalence in American Public Opinion about Government. Washington, DC: Woodrow Wilson Center Press.

Card, David and Richard Freeman. 1993. 'Introduction', pp. 1–20 in David Card and Richard Freeman, eds, Small Differences That Matter. Chicago and London: University of Chicago Press.

Careless, J.M.S. 1971. 'The 1850s', pp. 226–48 in J.M.S. Careless, ed., Colonists and Canadiens, 1760–1867. Toronto: Macmillan.

Carney, Cary Michael. 1999. Native American Education in the United States. New Brunswick, NJ and London: Transaction Publishers.

Carroll, Michael P. 2001. 'Culture', pp. 41–68 in J.J. Teevan and W.E. Hewitt, eds, Introduction to Sociology: A Canadian Focus. Toronto: Pearson Education Canada.

Carroll, William. 2004. Corporate Power in a Globalizing World. Toronto: Oxford University Press.

Cash, Wilbur Joseph. 1941. The Mind of the South. New York: Alfred A. Knopf.

CAUT. 2002. 'Quebec's Bill 84 to allow same-sex civil unions'. Canadian Association of University Teachers Bulletin, vol. 49, 6 (June).

Centre for Research and Information on Canada. 2002. Canada–US Federalism Survey, April. http://www.cucweb.ca/pdf/ border/border_graphs_june2002.pdf, accessed June 2003.

Chadwick, Bruce, Madeleine Gauthier, Louis Hormant, and Barbara Worndl. 1994. 'Trends in religion and secularization', pp. 173–214 in Simon Langlois, Theodore Caplow, Henri Mendras, and Wolfgang Glatzer, Convergence or Divergence? Comparing Recent Social Trends in Industrial Societies. Montreal and Kingston: McGill-Queen's University Press.

Chadwick, Bruce and Tim Heaton, eds. 1999. Statistical Handbook on the American Family, 2nd edn. Phoenix: The Oryx Press.

Chandler, Alfred Dupont, Jr. 1977. The Visible Hand. Cambridge, MA: Harvard University Press.

Chepesiuk, Ron. 2000. The Scotch-Irish: From the North of Ireland to the Making of America. Jefferson, NC and London: McFarland and Company.

Chevalier, Michel. 1839 [1969]. Society, Manners, and Politics in the United States. New York: Franklin Publishers.

Chomsky, Noam. 1965. Aspects of the Theory of Syntax. Cambridge, MA: MIT Press.

———. 1973. Cognitive Sociology. New York: The Free Press.

Christian, William and Colin Campbell. 1983. Political Parties and Ideologies in Canada, 2nd end. Toronto: McGraw-Hill Ryerson.

Christiano, Kevin. 2000. 'Church and state in institutional flux: Canada and the United States', pp. 69–89 in David Lyon and Marguerite Van Die, eds, Rethinking Church, State, and Modernity: Canada between Europe and America. Toronto: University of Toronto Press.

Churchill, Sir Winston. 1947 [1970]. Speech to the House of Commons (11 November 1947), p. 78 in Kay Halle, ed., Winston Churchill on America and Britain. New York: Walker and Company.

———. 1956a. The Birth of Britain, vol. 1 of A History of the English-Speaking Peoples. Toronto: McClelland and Stewart.

———. 1956b. The New World, vol. 2 of A History of the English-Speaking Peoples. Toronto: McClelland and Stewart.

———. 1957. The Age of Revolution, vol. 3 of A History of the English-Speaking Peoples. Toronto: McClelland and Stewart.

————. 1958. The Great Democracies, vol. 4 of A History of the English-Speaking Peoples. Toronto: McClelland and Stewart.

————. 1998. Churchill Speaks, 1897–1963: Collected Speeches in Peace and War. Edited by Robert Rhodes James. New York: Barnes and Noble.

————. 1999. The Great Republic: A History of America. Edited by Winston S. Churchill. New York: Random House.

CIA. 2003. The World Factbook 2002. http://www.odci.gov/cia/publications/factbook/geos/us.html, accessed 16 June.

Clark, S.D. 1948. Church and Sect in Canada. Toronto: University of Toronto Press.

————. 1950. 'The Canadian community', pp. 375–89 in George Brown, ed., Canada. Berkeley: University of California Press.

————. 1959. Movements of Political Protest in Canada. Toronto: University of Toronto Press.

————. 1968. The Developing Canadian Community, 2nd edn. Toronto: University of Toronto Press.

————. 1975. 'The post Second World War Canadian society'. Canadian Review of Sociology and Anthropology 12, 1: 25–32.

Clark, Samuel. 1995. State and Status: The Rise of the State and Aristocratic Power in Western Europe. Montreal and Kingston: McGill-Queen's University Press.

Clark, Warren. 2003. 'Pockets of belief: religious attendance patterns in Canada'. Canadian Social Trends 68 (Spring): 2–5.

Clement, Wallace. 1977. Continental Corporate Power: Economic Linkages between Canada and the United States. Toronto: McClelland and Stewart.

Clement, Wallace and John Myles. 1994. Relations of Ruling: Class and Gender in Postindustrial Societies. Montreal and Kingston: McGill-Queen's University Press.

Cohn, Samuel. 2000. Race, Gender, and Discrimination at Work. Boulder, CO: Westview Press.

Collins, Randall. 1988. Theoretical Sociology. San Diego: Harcourt Brace Jovanovich.

————. 1992. Sociological Insight: An Introduction to Non-Obvious Sociology. New York and Oxford: Oxford University Press.

Commons, John R. 1907. Races and Immigrants in America. New York: Macmillan.

Comninel, George. 2000. 'English feudalism and the origins of capitalism'. Journal of Peasant Studies 27, 4: 1–53.

Condon, Ann Gorman. 1984. The Envy of the American States: The Loyalist Dream for New Brunswick. Fredericton, NB: New Ireland Press.

Conley, James. 2004. 'Working-class formation in Canada', pp. 38–54 in James Curtis, Edward Grabb, and Neil Guppy, eds, Social Inequality in Canada: Patterns, Problems, Policies, 4th edn. Scarborough, ON: Pearson Education Canada.

Cook, Ramsay. 1987. 'The triumphs and trials of materialism, 1900–1945', pp. 375–466 in Craig Brown, ed., The Illustrated History of Canada. Toronto: Lester and Orpen Dennys.

Coq, Guy. 2004. 'Scarves and symbols'. The New York Times, 30 January.

Cornell, Stephen and Douglas Hartmann. 1998. Ethnicity and Race: Making Identities in a Changing World. Thousand Oaks and London: Pine Forge Press.

Corrigan, Philip and Derek Sayer. 1985. The Great Arch: English State Formation as Cultural Revolution. Oxford: Basil Blackwell.

Craig, Gerald M. 1963. Upper Canada: The Formative Years. Toronto: McClelland and Stewart.

————. 1968. The United States and Canada. Cambridge, MA: Harvard University Press.

————. 1971. 'The 1830s', pp. 173–99 in J.M.S. Careless, ed., Colonists and Canadiens. Toronto: Macmillan.

Crawford, Craig and James Curtis. 1979. 'English-Canadian–American differences in value orientation'. Studies in Comparative International Development 14: 23–44.

Creese, Gillian and Brenda Beagan. 2004. 'Gender at work: strategies for equality in neo-liberal times', pp. 245–57 in James Curtis, Edward Grabb, and Neil Guppy, eds, Social Inequality in Canada: Patterns, Problems, Policies, 4th edn. Scarborough, ON: Pearson Education Canada.

Creighton, Donald. 1972. Towards the Discovery of Canada. Toronto: Macmillan of Canada.

Cross, Michael. 1971. 'The 1820s', pp. 149–172 in J.M.S. Careless, ed., Colonists and Canadiens. Toronto: Macmillan.

———. 1992. 'Towards a definition of North American culture', pp. 303–6 in Stephen Randall, Herman Konrad, and Sheldon Silverman, eds, North America Without Borders? Integrating Canada, the United States, and Mexico. Calgary: University of Calgary Press.

Curtis, James. 1971. 'Voluntary associations joining: a cross-national comparative note'. American Sociological Review 36: 872–80.

Curtis, James, Douglas Baer, and Edward Grabb. 2001. 'Nations of joiners: explaining voluntary association membership in democratic societies'. American Sociological Review 66 (December): 783–805.

Curtis, James and Edward Grabb. 2002. 'Involvement in the organizational base of new social movements in English Canada and French Canada', pp. 164–81 in Douglas Baer, ed., Political Sociology: Canadian Perspectives. Toronto: Oxford University Press.

———. 2004. 'Social status and beliefs about what's important for getting ahead', pp. 393–409 in James Curtis, Edward Grabb, and Neil Guppy, eds, Social Inequality in Canada: Patterns, Problems, Policies, 4th edn. Scarborough, ON: Pearson Education Canada.

Curtis, James, Edward Grabb, and Douglas Baer. 1992. 'Voluntary association membership in fifteen countries: a comparative analysis'. American Sociological Review 57, 2: 139–52.

Curtis, James, Edward Grabb, Thomas Perks, and Tina Chui. 2004. 'Political involvement, civic engagement, and social inequality', pp. 431–49 in James Curtis, Edward Grabb, and Neil Guppy, eds, Social Inequality in Canada: Patterns, Problems, Policies, 4th edn. Scarborough, ON: Pearson Education Canada.

Curtis, James and Rick Helmes-Hayes, eds. 1998. The Vertical Mosaic Revisited. Toronto: University of Toronto Press.

Curtis, James and Ronald Lambert. 1976. 'Educational status and reactions to social and political heterogeneity'. Canadian Review of Sociology and Anthropology 13, 2 (May): 189–203.

Curtis, James, Ronald Lambert, Steven Brown, and Barry Kay. 1989a. 'Affiliating with voluntary associations: Canadian–American comparisons'. Canadian Journal of Sociology 14, 2: 143–62.

———. 1989b. 'On Lipset's measure of voluntary association differences between Canada and the United States'. Canadian Journal of Sociology 14, 3: 383–9.

Curtis, James and Lorne Tepperman. 1990. 'Introduction', pp. 1–17 in James Curtis and Lorne Tepperman, eds, Images of Canada: The Sociological Tradition. Scarborough, ON: Prentice-Hall Canada.

Curtis, James and Philip White. 1992. 'Toward a better understanding of the sport practices of Anglophone and Francophone Canadians'. Sociology of Sport Journal 9, 4: 403–22.

Dahl, Robert. 1963. Modern Political Analysis. Englewood Cliffs, NJ: Prentice-Hall.

———. 1967. Pluralist Democracy in the United States: Conflict and Consensus. Chicago: Rand-McNally.

Dahrendorf, Ralf. 1979. Life Chances. London: Weidenfeld and Nicolson.

———. 1988. The Modern Social Conflict: An Essay on Politics and Liberty. London: Weidenfeld and Nicolson.

———. 1997. After 1989: Morals, Revolution, and Civil Society. Houndmills, Basingstoke and London: Macmillan Press.

Dakin, Audrey. 2003. 'Exploding the myth of lower taxes in the US'. The London Free Press, 30 June, p. D5.

Dalton, Russell. 1984. Electoral Change in Advanced Industrial Democracies: Realignment or Dealignment? Princeton: Princeton University Press.

Dauvergne, Mia. 2002. 'Homicide in Canada, 2001'. Juristat 22, 7. Catalogue 85-002. Ottawa: Statistics Canada.

Davies, James B. 2004. 'The distribution of wealth and economic inequality', pp. 85–98 in James Curtis, Edward Grabb, and Neil Guppy, eds, Social Inequality in Canada: Patterns, Problems, Policies, 4th edn. Scarborough, ON: Pearson Education Canada.

Davis, David Brion. 1966. The Problem of Slavery in Western Culture. Ithaca, NY: Cornell University Press.

———. 1975. The Problem of Slavery in the Age of Revolution, 1772–1823. Ithaca, NY: Cornell University Press.

Delisle, Esther. 1993. The Traitor and the Jew. Montreal and Toronto: Robert Davies Publishing.

DePalma, Anthony. 2001. Here: A Biography of the New American Continent. New York: Public Affairs.

Department of Finance. 2002. Fiscal Reference Tables. Ottawa: Department of Finance, October.

Dershowitz, Alan M. 1997. The Vanishing American Jew: In Search of Jewish Identity for the Next Century. New York: Simon and Schuster.

Diggins, John P. 1984. The Lost Soul of American Politics: Virtue, Self-Interest, and the Foundations of Liberalism. New York: Basic Books.

DiMaggio, Paul, John Eans, and Bethany Bryson. 1996. 'Have Americans' social attitudes become more polarized?' American Journal of Sociology 102, 3 (November): 690–755.

Dinnerstein, Leonard. 1987. Uneasy at Home: Anti-Semitism and the Jewish American Experience. New York: Columbia University Press.

Dion, Leon. 1976. Quebec: The Unfinished Revolution. Montreal and London: McGill-Queen's University Press.

Dionne, E.J., Jr. 2003. 'One nation deeply divided'. The Washington Post, 2 November, p. A31.

Dobrin, Adam, Brian Wiersma, Colin Loftin, and David McDowall, eds. 1996. Statistical Handbook on Violence in America. Phoenix: The Oryx Press.

Dobson, David. 1994. Scottish Emigration to Colonial America, 1607–1785. Athens, GA and London: The University of Georgia Press.

Dogan, Mattei and Dominique Pelassy. 1984. How to Compare Nations. Chatham, NJ: Chatham House Publishers.

Doyle, David N. 1999. 'Scots Irish or Scotch-Irish', pp. 842–51 in Michael Glazier, ed., The Encyclopedia of the Irish in America. Notre Dame, IN: University of Notre Dame Press.

Draper, Alan. 1993. 'Be careful what you wish for . . . : American liberals and the South'. Southern Studies: An Interdisciplinary Journal of the South 4: 309–23.

Driedger, Leo, ed. 1978. The Canadian Ethnic Mosaic. Toronto: McClelland and Stewart.

Driedger, Sharon Doyle. 1996. 'The edge of tolerance'. Maclean's, 30 December, pp. 42–3.

———. 2002. 'What parents don't know'. Maclean's, 30 September, pp. 20–6.

Drucker, Peter. 1994. 'The age of social transformation'. Atlantic Monthly 274: 53–80.

D'Souza, Dinesh. 2000. The Virtue of Prosperity. New York: The Free Press.

Duncan, K.J. 1976. 'Patterns of settlement in the east', pp. 49–75 in W. Stanford Reid, ed., The Scottish Tradition in Canada. Toronto: McClelland and Stewart.

Durkheim, Emile. 1893 [1964]. The Division of Labor in Society, 1st edn. New York: The Free Press.

———. 1895 [1964]. The Rules of Sociological Method. New York: The Free Press.

Dyck, Perry. 1996. Provincial Politics in Canada: Towards the Turn of the Century. Scarborough, ON: Prentice-Hall Canada.

Dyck, Rand. 2002. Canadian Politics: Concise Edition. Scarborough, ON: Nelson.

Eid, Leroy V. 1999. 'Scotch-Irish and American Politics', pp. 839–42 in Michael Glazier, ed., The Encyclopedia of the Irish in America. Notre Dame, IN: University of Notre Dame Press.

Elazar, Daniel. 1966. American Federalism: A View from the States. New York: Crowell.

Elections Canada. 2003. 'Federal general elections, by electors, ballots cast, and voter participation'. http://www.statcan.ca/english/Pgdb/govt09c.htm, accessed 17 June.

Elliott, Bruce. 1988. Irish Migrants in the Canadas: A New Approach. Montreal and Kingston: McGill-Queen's University Press.

Ellison, Christopher G. and Marc A. Musick. 1993. 'Southern intolerance: a fundamentalist effect?' Social Forces 72, 2: 379–98.

Emes, Joel and Michael Walker. 1999. Tax Facts 11. Vancouver: The Fraser Institute.

Engels, Friedrich. 1888. 'Engels to Sorge', p. 204 in Karl Marx and Friedrich Engels, Letters to Americans, 1848–1895. New York: International Publishers.

Errington, Jane. 1994. The Lion, the Eagle, and Upper Canada. Montreal and Kingston: McGill-Queen's University Press.

Espenshade, Thomas and Katherine Hempstead. 1996. 'Contemporary American attitudes toward US Immigration'. International Migration Review 30, 2 (Summer): 455–67.

Esping-Andersen, Gosta. 1990. The Three Worlds of Welfare Capitalism. Princeton: Princeton University Press.

Evans, A. Margaret MacLaren. 1976. 'The Scot as politician', pp. 273–301 in W. Stanford Reid, ed., The Scottish Tradition in Canada. Toronto: McClelland and Stewart.

Evans, Robert G. 2000. 'Two systems in restraint: contrasting experiences with cost control in the 1990s', pp. 21–51 in David M. Thomas, ed., Canada and the United States: Differences that Count, 2nd edn. Peterborough, ON: Broadview Press.

Falardeau, Jean-Charles. 1960. Roots and Values in Canadian Lives. Toronto: University of Toronto Press.

Fedorowycz, Orest. 1995. 'Homicide in Canada—1994'. Juristat 15, 11. Catalogue 85-002. Ottawa: Statistics Canada.

Ferguson, Will. 1997. Why I Hate Canadians. Vancouver: Douglas and McIntyre.

Finke, Roger and Rodney Stark. 1992. The Churching of America, 1776–1990. New Brunswick, NJ: Rutgers University Press.

Fischer, David Hackett. 1989. Albion's Seed: Four British Folkways in America, vol. 1. New York: Oxford University Press.

Fitzpatrick, Rory. 1989. God's Frontiersmen: The Scots-Irish Epic. London: Weidenfeld and Nicolson.

Fleras, Augie and Jean Leonard Elliott. 1992. The Nations Within: Aboriginal–State Relations in Canada, the United States, and New Zealand. Toronto: Oxford University Press.

———. 2002. Engaging Diversity: Multiculturalism in Canada, 2nd edn. Toronto: Nelson Thomson Learning.

———. 2003. Unequal Relations: An Introduction to Race and Ethnic Dynamics in Canada, 4th edn. Scarborough, ON: Prentice Hall Allyn and Bacon.

Fleras, Augie and Roger Maaka. 2004 (in press). The Politics of Indigenity. Dunedin, NZ: University of Otago Press.

Foote, Shelby. 1989. Conversations with Shelby Foote. Edited by W.C. Carter. Jackson: University Press of Mississippi.

Forbes, H.D. 1987. 'Hartz-Horowitz at twenty: nationalism, Toryism, and socialism in Canada and the United States'. Canadian Journal of Political Science 20, 2 (June): 287–315.

Forse, Michel and Simon Langlois. 1994. 'Comparative structural analysis of social change in France and in Quebec', pp. 269–301 in Simon Langlois, Theodore Caplow, Henri Mendras, and Wolfgang Glatzer, Convergence or Divergence? Comparing Recent Social Trends in Industrial Societies. Montreal and Kingston: McGill-Queen's University Press.

Fournier, Marcel, Michael Rosenberg, and Deena White. 1997. Quebec Society: Critical Issues. Scarborough, ON: Prentice-Hall Canada.

Franklin, John Hope. 1956. The Militant South: 1800–1861. Cambridge, MA: Harvard University Press.

Freedman, Samuel. 2000. Jew vs. Jew: The Struggle for the Soul of American Jewry. New York: Simon and Schuster.

Frideres, James. 1988. Native Peoples in Canada, 3rd edn. Scarborough, ON: Prentice-Hall Canada.

———. 1998. 'Indigenous peoples of Canada and the United States of America: entering the 21st century', pp. 167–96 in Leen d'Haenens et al., eds, Images of Canadianness. Ottawa: University of Ottawa Press.

Fulford, Robert. 1993. 'A post-modern dominion: the changing nature of Canadian citizenship', pp. 104–19 in William Kaplan, ed., Belonging: The Meaning and Future of Canadian Citizenship. Montreal and Kingston: McGill-Queen's University Press.

Gagnon, Lysiane. 2003a. 'When ritual soothes'. The Globe and Mail, 9 June, p. A11.

———. 2003b. 'Chirac may send Muslim girls to purdah'. The Globe and Mail, 29 December, p. A19.

———. 2004. 'Canadians relate to Democrats'. The Globe and Mail, 8 March, p. A11.

Galbraith, John Kenneth. 1985. The Scotch. Toronto: Macmillan of Canada.

Gallup. 1996. The Gallup Poll, vol. 56, 33. 2 May. Toronto: Gallup Canada.

———. 2000a. The Gallup Poll, vol. 60, 28. 13 April. Toronto: Gallup Canada.

———. 2000b. The Gallup Poll, vol. 60, 58. 7 August. Toronto: Gallup Canada.

———. 2001a. The Gallup Poll, vol. 61, 17. 8 March. Toronto: Gallup Canada.

———. 2001b. The Gallup Poll, vol. 61, 22. 18 April. Toronto: Gallup Canada.

———. 2001c. The Gallup Poll, vol. 61, 41. 30 June. Toronto: Gallup Canada.

———. 2001d. The Gallup Poll, vol. 61, 48. 15 August. Toronto: Gallup Canada.

———. 2001e. The Gallup Poll, vol. 61, 56. 19 September. Toronto: Gallup Canada.

———. 2001f. The Gallup Poll, vol. 61, 56. 10 October. Toronto: Gallup Canada.

———. 2001g. The Gallup Poll, vol. 61, 71. 14 November. Toronto: Gallup Canada.

———. 2001h. The Gallup Poll, vol. 61, 85. 12 December. Toronto: Gallup Canada.

———. 2002a. The Gallup Poll, vol. 62, 1. 6 February. Toronto: Gallup Canada.

———. 2002b. The Gallup Poll, vol. 62, 6. 6 March. Toronto: Gallup Canada.

———. 2003. The Gallup Poll. 27–29 June. Princeton, NJ: The Gallup Organization. http://www.gallup.com/poll/releases/pr030703.asp?version=p, accessed June 2003.

Gannon, Maire. 2001. 'Crime comparisons between Canada and the United States'. Juristat 21, 11. Catalogue 85-002. Ottawa: Statistics Canada.

Garreau, Joel. 1981. The Nine Nations of North America. Boston: Houghton Mifflin Company.

Gartner, Rosemary. 1990. 'The victims of homicide'. American Sociological Review 55, 1 (February): 92–106.

Gastil, Raymond D. 1975. Cultural Regions of the United States. Seattle and London: University of Washington Press.

Gatehouse, Jonathan. 2003. 'Backlash: why does half of the country believe same-sex marriages shouldn't be legal?' Maclean's, 1 September, pp. 28–32.

Gee, Ellen M. and Steven G. Prus. 2000. 'Income inequality in Canada: A racial divide', pp. 238–56 in Madeline A. Kalbach and Warren E. Kalbach, eds, Perspectives on Ethnicity in Canada: A Reader. Toronto: Harcourt Canada.

Genovese, Eugene. 1974. Roll, Jordan, Roll: The World the Slaves Made. New York: Pantheon Books.

Gibbins, Roger. 1982. Regionalism: Territorial Politics in Canada and the United States. Toronto: Butterworths.

Giddens, Anthony. 1976. New Rules of Sociological Method. New York: Basic Books.

———. 1990. The Consequences of Modernity. Stanford: Stanford University Press.

———. 1994. Beyond Left and Right. Stanford: Stanford University Press.

Gillespie, Mark. 1999. 'Labor Day finds continued strong support for unions'. The Gallup Poll Monthly, September: 29–33.

Glatzer, Wolfgang and Richard Hauser. 2003. 'The distribution of income and wealth in European and North American societies', pp. 187–217 in Yannick Lemel and Heinz-Hebert Noll, eds, Changing Structures of Inequality: A Comparative Perspective. Montreal and Kingston: McGill-Queen's University Press.

Glenn, Norval. 1967. 'Massification versus differentiation: some trend data from national surveys'. Social Forces 46, 2 (December): 172–80.

Glenn, Norval and J.L. Simmons. 1967. 'Are regional cultural differences diminishing?' Public Opinion Quarterly 31, 2 (Summer): 176–93.

Globe and Mail. 2003. 'The New Canada: how the survey was carried out'. 6 July.

Goldstone, Jack A. 1987. 'Cultural orthodoxy, risk, and innovation: the divergence of East and West in the early modern world'. Sociological Theory 5: 119–35.

———. 1991. Revolution and Rebellion in the Early Modern World. Berkeley and Los Angeles: University of California Press.

————. 2000. 'The rise of the West—or not? A revision to socio-economic history'. *Sociological Theory* 18, 2 (July): 175–94.

Grabb, Edward. 1982. 'Sense of control over life circumstances: changing patterns for French and English Canadians'. *Canadian Review of Sociology and Anthropology* 19, 3 (August): 360–76.

————. 1994. 'Democratic values in Canada and the United States: some observations and evidence from past and present', pp. 113–39 in Jerry Dermer, ed., *The Canadian Profile: People, Institutions, Infrastructure*. North York, ON: Captus Press.

————. 1998. 'Democratic values in Canada and the United States: some observations and evidence from past and present', pp. 246–70 in Tom Wesson, ed., *Canada and the New World Economic Order*. North York, ON: Captus Press.

————. 2002. *Theories of Social Inequality: Classical and Contemporary Perspectives*, 4th edn. Toronto: Harcourt Canada.

————. 2004 (in press). 'Social inequality', in James J. Teevan and W.E. Hewitt, eds, *Introduction to Sociology: A Canadian Focus*, 7th edn. Toronto: Pearson Education Canada.

Grabb, Edward, Douglas Baer, and James Curtis. 1999. 'The origins of American individualism: reconsidering the historical evidence'. *Canadian Journal of Sociology* 24, 4 (Fall): 509–31.

Grabb, Edward and James Curtis. 1988. 'English Canadian–American differences in orientation toward social control and individual rights'. *Sociological Focus* 21, 2 (April): 127–40.

————. 1992. 'Voluntary association activity in English Canada, French Canada, and the United States: A multivariate analysis'. *Canadian Journal of Sociology* 17: 378–88.

————. 2002. 'Comparing central political values in the Canadian and American democracies', pp. 37–54 in Douglas Baer, ed., *Political Sociology: Canadian Perspectives*. Toronto: Oxford University Press.

Grabb, Edward, James Curtis, and Douglas Baer. 2000. 'Defining moments and recurring myths: comparing Canadians and Americans after the American Revolution'. *Canadian Review of Sociology and Anthropology* 37, 4 (November): 375–419.

————. 2001. 'On accuracy and big pictures: reply to Lipset'. *Canadian Review of Sociology and Anthropology* 38, 1 (February): 101–3.

Grabb, Edward and Margaret Poole. 1988. 'Sense of personal control among French and English Canadians: a reassessment and reformulation'. *Canadian Ethnic Studies* 20, 1: 95–111.

Gramsci, Antonio. 1928 [1971]. *Selections from the Prison Notebooks*. New York: International Publishers.

Granatstein, J.L. 1996. *Yankee Go Home? Canadians and Anti-Americanism*. Toronto: Harper Collins.

Granatstein, J.L. and Norman Hillmer. 1991. *For Better or for Worse: Canada and the United States to the 1990s*. Toronto: Copp Clark Pitman.

Granatstein, J.L. and Desmond Morton. 1989. *Marching to Armageddon: Canadians and the Great War, 1914–1919*. Toronto: Lester and Orpen Dennys.

Grantham, Dewey W., Jr. 1994. *The South in Modern America*. New York: Harper Collins.

Gregg, Allan. 2003. 'Bumpy ride'. *Maclean's*, 29 December, pp. 29–30.

Griffin, Patrick. 2001. *The People with No Name: Ireland's Ulster Scots, America's Scots Irish, and the Creation of a British Atlantic World, 1689–1764*. Princeton and Oxford: Princeton University Press.

Guindon, Hubert. 1978. 'The modernization of Quebec and the legitimacy of the Canadian state', pp. 212–46 in D. Glenday, H. Guindon, and A. Turowetz, eds, *Modernization and the Canadian State*. Toronto: Macmillan.

————. 1988. *Quebec Society: Tradition, Modernity, and Nationhood*. Toronto: University of Toronto Press.

Gwyn, Richard. 1985. *The 49th Paradox: Canada in North America*. Toronto: McClelland and Stewart.

————. 1995. *Nationalism Without Walls: The Unbearable Lightness of Being Canadian*. Toronto: McClelland and Stewart.

————. 2003. 'Farewell to old Conservative Party'. The Toronto Star, 7 December, p. A17.

————. 2004. 'An exchange of gestures at little cost'. The Toronto Star, 18 January, p. A15.

Habermas, Jürgen. 1984. The Theory of Communicative Action. Boston: Beacon Press.

Hackney, Sheldon. 1969. 'Southern violence'. American Historical Review 74 (February): 906–25.

Hagan, John. 1989a. 'Comparing crime and criminalization in Canada and the USA'. Canadian Journal of Sociology 14, 3: 361–71.

————. 1989b. 'Enduring differences: further notes on homicide in Canada and the USA'. Canadian Journal of Sociology 14, 4: 490–1.

————. 1991. The Disreputable Displeasures: Crime and Deviance in Canada, 3rd edn. Toronto: McGraw-Hill Ryerson.

————. 1994. Crime and Disrepute. Thousand Oaks, CA: Pine Forge Press.

Hagan, John and Jeffrey Leon. 1977. 'Philosophy and sociology of crime control: Canadian–American comparisons'. Sociological Inquiry 47: 181–208.

Hall, Anthony. 2003. The American Empire and the Fourth World. Montreal and Kingston: McGill-Queen's University Press.

Hallenstvedt, Abraham. 1974. 'Formal voluntary associations in Norway', pp. 219–30 in David Horton Smith, ed., Voluntary Action Research. Lexington, MA: Lexington Books.

Halliburton, R. 1977. Red over Black: Black Slavery among the Cherokee Indians. Westport, CT: Greenwood Press.

Halman, Loek, Thorleif Pettersson, and Johan Verweij. 1999. 'The religious factor in contemporary society'. International Journal of Comparative Sociology 40: 141–60.

Hamilton, Richard F. 1972. Class and Politics in the United States. New York: John Wiley and Sons.

Hampden-Turner, Charles and Alfons Trompenaars. 1993. The Seven Cultures of Capitalism. New York: Doubleday.

Hanna, Charles A. 1902 [1968]. The Scotch-Irish, 2 vols. Baltimore: Genealogical Publishing Company.

Harris, R. Cole and John Warkentin. 1974. Canada Before Confederation. New York: Oxford University Press.

Harrison, Trevor and John Friesen. 2004. Canadian Society in the Twenty-First Century: A Historical Sociological Approach. Toronto: Pearson Education Canada.

Hartz, Louis. 1955. The Liberal Tradition in America. New York: Harcourt, Brace, and World.

Hartz, Louis et al. 1964. The Founding of New Societies. New York: Harcourt, Brace, and World.

Harvey, Bob. 1996. 'Yes folks, we really are kinder and gentler'. Southam Newspapers report in the London Free Press, 30 October, p. A3.

Hatch, Nathan. 1989. The Democratization of American Christianity. New Haven: Yale University Press.

Hausknecht, Murray. 1962. The Joiners. New York: Bedminster Press.

Henry, Frances. 1989. 'Who Gets the Work in 1989?' Background Paper. Ottawa: Economic Council of Canada.

————. 2004. 'Two studies of racial discrimination in employment', pp. 285–94 in James Curtis, Edward Grabb, and Neil Guppy, eds, Social Inequality in Canada: Patterns, Problems, Policies, 4th edn. Toronto: Pearson Education Canada.

Henry, Frances and Effie Ginsberg. 1985. Who Gets the Work: A Test of Racial Discrimination in Employment. Toronto: The Urban Alliance on Race Relations and the Social Planning Council of Metropolitan Toronto.

Herman, Arthur. 2001. How the Scots Invented the Modern World. New York: Three Rivers Press.

Hill, David B. 2003. 'Homosexuality: ultimate wedge issue of 2004?' The Hill. http://www.hillnews.com/campaign/04003_pollsters.aspx, accessed May 7.

Hiller, Harry H. 2000. Canadian Society: A Sociological Analysis, 4th edn. Scarborough, ON: Prentice-Hall Canada.

Himes, Joseph, ed. 1991. The South Moves into the Future. Tuscaloosa and London: University of Alabama Press.

Himmelfarb, Gertrude. 1999. One Nation, Two Cultures. New York: Knopf.

Hobart, Charles and Frank Grigel. 1992. 'Cohabitation among Canadian students at the end of the eighties'. Journal of Comparative Family Studies 23, 3: 311–37.

Hofstede, Geert. 1980. Culture's Consequences. Beverley Hills, CA: Sage.

Hopcroft, Rosemary. 1994. 'The social origins of agrarian change in late medieval England'. American Journal of Sociology 99, 6 (May): 1559–95.

————. 1999. Regions, Institutions, and Agrarian Change in European History. Ann Arbor: University of Michigan Press.

Horowitz, Gad. 1966. 'Conservatism, liberalism, and socialism in Canada: an interpretation'. Canadian Journal of Economics and Political Science 32: 143–71.

Horowitz, Irving Louis. 1973. 'The hemispheric connection: a critique and corrective to the entrepreneurial thesis of development with special emphasis on the Canadian case'. Queen's Quarterly 80: 327–59.

Hou, Feng and T.R. Balakrishnan. 1996. 'The integration of visible minorities in contemporary society'. Canadian Journal of Sociology 21, 3: 307–26.

Houston, Cecil J. and William J. Smyth. 1990. Irish Emigration and Canadian Settlement: Patterns, Links, and Letters. Toronto: University of Toronto Press.

Hume, David. 1754 [1975]. The History of England from the Invasion of Julius Caesar to the Revolution of 1688. Chicago: University of Chicago Press.

Humes, Karen and Jesse McKinnon. 2000. 'The Asian and Pacific Islander population in the United States'. Current Population Reports. US Department of Commerce, Washington, DC, September.

Hung, Kwing and Sharon Bowles. 1995. 'Public perceptions of crime'. Juristat 15, 1. Catalogue 85-002. Ottawa: Statistics Canada.

Huntington, Samuel P. 1996. The Clash of Civilizations and the Remaking of World Order. New York: Simon and Schuster.

Hurst, Charles. 2001. Social Inequality: Forms, Causes, and Consequences, 4th edn. Boston: Allyn and Bacon.

Hutcheon, Linda. 1988. The Canadian Postmodern. Toronto: Oxford University Press.

Hyams, P.R. 1980. Kings, Lords, and Peasants in Medieval England. Oxford: Oxford University Press.

Ibbitson, John. 2004. 'Pluralism: the world wonders how we pulled it off'. The Globe and Mail, 6 February, p. A21.

Inglehart, Ronald. 1977. The Silent Revolution: Changing Values and Political Styles. Princeton: Princeton University Press.

————. 1990. Culture Shift in Advanced Industrial Society. Princeton: Princeton University Press.

————. 1997. Modernization and Postmodernization: Cultural, Economic, and Political Change in 43 Societies. Princeton: Princeton University Press.

Inglehart, Ronald and Wayne Baker. 2000. 'Modernization, cultural change, and the persistence of traditional values'. American Sociological Review 65, 1 (February): 19–51.

Inglehart, Ronald, Neil Nevitte, and Miguel Basanez. 1996. The North American Trajectory. New York: Aldine de Gruyter.

Inkeles, Alex.1997. National Character: A Psycho-Social Perspective. New Brunswick, NJ: Transaction Publishers.

————. 1998. One World Emerging? Convergence and Divergence in Industrial Societies. Boulder, CO: Westview Press.

Iton, Daniel. 2000. 'The backlash and the Quiet Revolution: the contemporary implications of race and language in the United States and Canada', pp. 141–64 in David M. Thomas, ed., Canada and the United States: Differences that Count, 2nd edn. Peterborough, ON: Broadview Press.

Jackson, Andrew. 2003. 'Why the 'big idea' is a bad idea: a critical perspective on deeper economic integration with the United States'. Canadian Centre for Policy Alternatives, June. http://www.policyalternatives.ca/publications/big-idea.pdf, accessed July 2003.

Jackson, Carlton. 1993. A Social History of the Scotch-Irish. Lanham, MD: Madison Books.

Jacob, Margaret. 1988. The Cultural Meaning of the Scientific Revolution. New York: Alfred Knopf.

Janigan, Mary. 2004. 'Cozying up to the Yanks'. Maclean's, 23 February, p. 13.

Johns, Elizabeth A. 1989. Review of Grady McWhiney, Cracker Culture. The Western Historical Review 25, 2 (May): 206–7.

Johnson, Harry M. 1960. Sociology: A Systematic Introduction. New York: Harcourt, Brace and World.

Johnson, Michael P. 1989. Review of Grady McWhiney, Cracker Culture. The Journal of Southern History 55, 3 (August): 488–90.

Johnstone, John C. 1969. Young People's Images of Canadian Society. Studies of the Royal Commission on Bilingualism and Biculturalism, No. 2. Ottawa: Queen's Printer.

Jones, Jeffrey M. 2003a. 'Support for the death penalty remains high at 74%'. The Gallup Poll Tuesday Briefing, 19 May, pp. 28–30.

———. 2003b. 'Understanding Americans' support for the death penalty'. The Gallup Poll Tuesday Briefing, 3 June, pp. 101–4.

———. 2003c. 'Nearly half of Americans say immigration levels should be decreased'. The Gallup Poll Tuesday Briefing, 10 July, pp. 18–22.

Kanji, Mebs and Neil Nevitte. 2000. 'Who are the most deferential—Canadians or Americans?', pp. 121–40 in David M. Thomas, ed., Canada and the United States: Differences that Count, 2nd edn. Peterborough, ON: Broadview Press.

Kearney, Hugh. 1989. The British Isles: A History of Four Nations. Cambridge: Cambridge University Press.

Kennedy, Suzanne and Steven Gonzalez. 2003. 'Government spending in Canada and the United States'. Department of Finance Working Paper 2003-05. Ottawa: Department of Finance, Economic and Fiscal Policy Branch.

Kennickell, Arthur. 2000. 'An examination of change in the distribution of wealth from 1989 to 1998: evidence from the Survey of Consumer Finances'. American Enterprise Institute Seminar Series on Understanding Economic Inequality. Washington, DC, 9 February.

Kerans, Roger. 2000. 'Two nations under law', pp. 359–76 in David M. Thomas, ed., Canada and the United States: Differences that Count, 2nd edn. Peterborough, ON: Broadview Press.

Kerridge, Eric. 1969. Agrarian Problems in the Sixteenth Century and After. New York: Barnes and Noble.

Khan, Sheema. 2003. 'Why does a head scarf have us tied up in knots?' The Globe and Mail, 28 September, p. A27.

Kilbourn, William, ed. 1970. Canada: A Guide to the Peaceable Kingdom. Toronto: Macmillan of Canada.

Kishlansky, Mark. 1996. A Monarchy Transformed: Britain 1603–1714. London: Penguin.

Klapp, Orrin. 1978. Opening and Closing. Cambridge: Cambridge University Press.

Knoke, David. 1986. 'Associations and interest groups'. Annual Review of Sociology 12: 1–21.

Knowles, Norman. 1997. Inventing the Loyalists: The Ontario Loyalist Tradition and the Creation of Usable Pasts. Toronto, Buffalo, and London: University of Toronto Press.

Kohn, Melvin, ed. 1989. Cross-National Research in Sociology. Newbury Park, CA: Sage.

Kolko, Gabriel. 1984. Main Currents in Modern American History. New York: Pantheon.

Koschmann, J. Victor. 1997. 'The nationalism of cultural uniqueness'. American Historical Review 102, 3 (June): 758–68.

Krauss, Clifford. 2003. 'In God we trust . . . Canadians aren't so sure'. The New York Times, 25 March.

Kritzer, H.M., N. Vidmar, and W.A. Bogart. 1991a. 'The aftermath of injury: cultural factors in compensation seeking in Canada and the United States'. Law and Society Review 25: 499–543.

———. 1991b. 'To confront or not to confront: measuring claiming rates in discrimination grievances'. Law and Society Review 25: 875–87.

Kunz, Jean Lock, Anne Milan, and Sylvain Schetagne. 2000. 'Unequal access: a Canadian profile of racial differences in education, employment, and income'. A Report Prepared for the Canadian Race Relations Foundation, by the Canadian Council on Social Development.

Kurzwell, Edith. 1980. The Age of Structuralism: Levi-Strauss to Foucault. New York: Columbia University Press.

Ladd, Everett. 1981. '205 and going strong'. Public Opinion 4 (June-July): 7–12.

Ladd, Everett and Charles Hadley. 1975. Transformations of the American Party System: Political Coalitions from the New Deal to the 1970s. New York: W.W. Norton.

LaFree, Gary. 1999. 'Declining violent crime rates in the 1990s: predicting crime booms and busts'. Annual Review of Sociology 25: 145–306.

Lambert, Ronald and James Curtis. 1983. 'Opposition to multiculturalism among Quebecois and English Canadians'. Canadian Review of Sociology and Anthropology 20, 2: 193–207.

———. 1988. 'The racial attitudes of Canadians', pp. 343–48 in Lorne Tepperman and James Curtis, eds, Readings in Sociology: An Introduction. Toronto: McGraw-Hill Ryerson.

Lamontagne, Leopold. 1960. 'Ontario: the two races', pp. 351–73 in M. Wade, ed., Canadian Dualism. Toronto and Quebec: University of Toronto Press and Les Presses Universitaires Laval.

Lane, Robert. 1959. Political Life: Why and How People Get Involved in Politics. New York: The Free Press.

Langguth, A.J. 1988. Patriots: The Men Who Started the American Revolution. New York: Touchstone.

Langlais, Jacques and David Rome. 1991. Jews and French Quebecers. Waterloo, ON: Wilfrid Laurier University Press.

Langlois, Simon. 2003. 'Research on class and stratification in Quebec and Canada', pp. 75–116 in Yannick Lemel and Heinz-Hebert Noll, eds, Changing Structures of Inequality—A Comparative Perspective. Montreal and Kingston: McGill-Queen's University Press.

Langlois, Simon, Jean-Paul Baillergeon, Gary Caldwell, Guy Frechet, Madeleine Gauthier, and Jean-Pierre Simard. 1992. Recent Social Trends in Quebec, 1960–1990. Montreal and Kingston: McGill-Queen's University Press.

Latouche, Daniel. 1995. 'Quebec in the emerging North American configuration', pp. 117–39 in Robert Earle and John Wirth, eds, Identities in North America: The Search for Community. Stanford: Stanford University Press.

Laxer, Gordon. 1985. 'The political economy of aborted development: the Canadian case', pp. 67–102 in Robert J. Brym, ed., The Structure of the Canadian Capitalist Class. Toronto: Garamond.

Laxer, James. 2003. The Border: Canada, the US, and Dispatches from the 49th Parallel. Toronto: Doubleday Canada.

Le Bourdais, C. and N. Marcil-Gratton. 1996. 'Family transformations across the Canadian/American border: when the laggard becomes the leader'. Journal of Comparative Family Studies 27, 3: 415–36.

Leger. 2003. 'How Canadians feel about military action against Iraq'. Report by Canadian Press/Leger Marketing. http://www.leermarketing.com/documents/spclm/030203eng.pdf, accessed July 2003.

Lemel, Yannick and John Modell. 1994. 'Is there a single pattern of social evolution?', pp. 23–42 in Simon Langlois, Theodore Caplow, Henri Mendras, and Wolfgang Glatzer, Convergence or Divergence? Comparing Recent Social Trends in Industrial Societies. Montreal and Kingston: McGill-Queen's University Press.

Lemieux, Denise and Marion Mohle. 2003. 'Gender inequality in five modern societies', pp. 333–68 in Yannick Lemel and Heinz-Hebert Noll, eds, Changing Structures of Inequality—A Comparative Perspective. Montreal and Kingston: McGill-Queen's University Press.

Lemieux, Thomas. 1993. 'Unions and wage inequality in Canada and the United States', pp. 69–107 in David Card and Richard Freeman, eds, Small Differences That Matter. Chicago and London: University of Chicago Press.

Lenton, Rhonda. 1989a. 'Homicide in Canada and the US: a critique of the Hagan thesis'. Canadian Journal of Sociology 14, 2: 163–78.

———. 1989b. 'The danger of disaggregation'. Canadian Journal of Sociology 14, 4: 487–9.

Leuchtenberg, William E. 1958. The Perils of Prosperity, 1914–1932. Chicago: University of Chicago Press.

Lévi-Strauss, Claude. 1968. Structural Anthropology. London: Allen Lane.

———. 1969. The Elementary Structures of Kinship. Boston: Beacon Press.

Leyburn, James G. 1962. The Scotch-Irish: A Social History. Chapel Hill: University of North Carolina Press.

Li, Peter. 1988. Ethnic Inequality in a Class Society. Toronto: Wall and Thompson.

———. 1996. The Making of Post-War Canada. Toronto: Oxford University Press.

———. 1998. The Chinese in Canada, 2nd edn. Toronto: Oxford University Press.

———. 2003. Destination Canada: Immigration Debates and Issues. Toronto: Oxford University Press.

Lian, Jason and Ralph Matthews. 1998. 'Does the vertical mosaic still exist? Ethnicity and income in Canada, 1991'. Canadian Review of Sociology and Anthropology 35, 4 (November): 461–82.

Lipset, Seymour Martin. 1963a. 'The value patterns of democracy'. American Sociological Review 28: 515–31.

———. 1963b. The First New Nation. New York: Basic Books.

———. 1964. 'Canada and the United States—a comparative view'. Canadian Review of Sociology and Anthropology 1: 173–85.

———. 1968. Revolution and Counterrevolution. New York: Basic Books.

———. 1979. 'Revolution and counterrevolution—some comments at a conference analyzing the bicentennial of a celebrated North American divorce', pp. 22–45 in Richard A. Preston, ed., Perspectives on Revolution and Evolution. Durham, NC: Duke University Press.

———. 1981. Political Man: The Social Bases of Politics. Baltimore: Johns Hopkins Press.

———. 1985. 'Canada and the United States: the cultural dimension', pp. 109–60 in Charles F. Doran and John H. Sigler, eds, Canada and the United States. Englewood Cliffs, NJ: Prentice-Hall.

———. 1986. 'Historical conditions and national characteristics'. Canadian Journal of Sociology 11, 2: 113–55.

———. 1989. 'Voluntary activities: more Canadian–American comparisons—a reply'. Canadian Journal of Sociology 14, 3: 377–82.

———. 1990. Continental Divide: The Values and Institutions of the United States and Canada. New York: Routledge.

———. 1994. 'The social requisites of democracy'. American Sociological Review 59, 1 (February): 1–22.

———. 1996. American Exceptionalism: A Double-Edged Sword. New York: W.W. Norton.

Lipset, Seymour Martin and Gary Marks. 2000. It Didn't Happen Here: Why Socialism Failed in the United States. New York: W.W. Norton.

Lipset, Seymour Martin, K.R. Seong, and John Charles Torres. 1993. 'A comparative analysis of the social requisites of democracy'. International Social Science Journal 36 (May): 155–75.

Literary Review of Canada. 1998. 'Comparing national identities'. Vol. 7, 4 (December), p. 7.

Locke, John. 1690 [1967]. Two Treatises of Government, 2nd edn. Cambridge: Cambridge University Press.

Loftus, Jeni. 2001. 'America's liberalization in attitudes toward homosexuality, 1973 to 1998'. American Sociological Review 66, 5 (October): 762–82.

Lower, A.R.M. 1946. From Colony to Nation. Toronto: Longmans, Green and Company.

Luebke, Paul. 1991. 'Southern conservatism and liberalism: past and future', pp. 236–53 in Joseph Himes, ed., The South Moves into the Future. Tuscaloosa and London: University of Alabama Press.

Lukes, Steven. 1973. Individualism. Oxford: Basil Blackwell.

Lunman, Kim. 2003. 'Canadians embracing patriotism, poll shows', from The Canada Page, http://www.thecanadapage.org/CanEmbPat.htm, accessed July 2003.

Lyons, Linda. 2003. 'US next down the aisle toward gay marriage?' The Gallup Poll Tuesday Briefing, 22 July, pp. 113–15.

McCarthy, Shawn. 2003. 'Social gap between Canada, US regional, pollster says'. The Globe and Mail, 11 December, p. A12.

McClelland, J.S. 1996. A History of Western Political Thought. London and New York: Routledge.

McCullough, David. 2001. John Adams. New York: Simon and Schuster.

McDonald, Forrest. 1988. 'Prologue', pp. xxi–xliii in Grady McWhiney, Cracker Culture: Celtic Ways in the Old South. Tuscaloosa and London: University of Alabama Press.

Macfarlane, Alan. 1978. The Origins of English Individualism: The Family, Property, and Social Transition. Oxford: Basil Blackwell.

McGregor, Gaile. 1985. The Wacousta Syndrome. Toronto: University of Toronto Press.

———. 1988. The Noble Savage in the New World Garden. Toronto: University of Toronto Press.

McIlwraith, Thomas. 2001. 'British North America, 1763–1867', pp. 207–34 in Thomas McIlwraith and Edward Muller, eds, North America: The Historical Geography of a Changing Continent, 2nd edn. Lanham, MD: Rowman and Littlefield Publishers.

MacIver, Robert. 1947. The Web of Government. New York: Macmillan.

McKinnon, Jesse. 2001. 'The black population: 2000'. Census 2000 Brief. US Department of Commerce, Washington, DC, August.

MacKinnon, Neil. 1986. This Unfriendly Soil: The Loyalist Experience in Nova Scotia. Montreal and Kingston: McGill-Queen's University Press.

MacLean, J.P. 1900 [1968]. Scottish Highlanders in America. Baltimore: Genealogical Publishing Company.

Maclean, R. 1976. 'The highland Catholic tradition in Canada', pp. 93–117 in W. Stanford Reid, ed., The Scottish Tradition in Canada. Toronto: McClelland and Stewart.

Maclean's. 1998. 'Taking the pulse of a nation'. 5 January, p. 45.

———. 2003a. 'A steady tide'. 3 February, p. 13.

———. 2003b. 'Just say yes'. 29 December, pp. 32–6.

MacMillan, David S. 1976. 'The Scot as businessman', pp. 179–202 in W. Stanford Reid, ed., The Scottish Tradition in Canada. Toronto: McClelland and Stewart.

McPherson, James. 1991. Abraham Lincoln and the Second American Revolution. New York: Oxford University Press.

———. 1998. 'Quebec whistles Dixie'. Saturday Night Magazine. Volume 113, 2 (March): 13–23, 72.

McRae, Kenneth. 1964. 'The structure of Canadian history', pp. 219–75 in Louis Hartz et al., The Founding of New Societies. New York: Harcourt, Brace, and World.

McRoberts, Kenneth. 1993. Quebec: Social Change and Political Crisis, 3rd edn. Toronto: McClelland and Stewart.

McWhiney, Grady. 1988. Cracker Culture: Celtic Ways in the Old South. Tuscaloosa and London: University of Alabama Press.

Manfredi, Christopher. 1997. 'The judicialization of politics: rights and public policy in Canada and the United States', pp. 310–40 in Keith Banting, George Hoberg, and Richard Simeon, eds, Degrees of Freedom: Canada and the United States in a Changing World. Montreal and Kingston: McGill-Queen's University Press.

———. 2000. 'Rights and the judicialization of politics in Canada and the United States', pp. 301–18 in David M. Thomas, ed., Canada and the United States: Differences that Count, 2nd edn. Peterborough, ON: Broadview Press.

Marchand, Philip. 2001. 'Why General Lee would fight for the fleur-de-lys'. The Toronto Star, 27 January, p. M2.

Marger, Martin. 1999. Social Inequality: Patterns and Processes. Mountain View, CA: Mayfield Publishing Company.

Marsden, Peter, John Shelton Reed, Michael Kennedy, and Kandi Stinson. 1982. 'American regional cultures and differences in leisure time activities'. Social Forces 60, 4 (June): 1023–49.

Martin, David. 2000. 'Canada in comparative perspective', pp. 23–33 in David Lyon and Marguerite Van Die, eds, Rethinking Church, State, and Modernity: Canada between Europe and America. Toronto: University of Toronto Press.

Martin, Patricia Yancey, Kenneth Wilson, and Caroline Matheny Dillman. 1991. 'Southern-style gender: trends and relations between men and women', pp. 103–48 in Joseph Himes, ed., The South Moves into the Future. Tuscaloosa and London: University of Alabama Press.

Martinez, Michael. 2000. 'Turning out or tuning out? Electoral participation in Canada and the United States', pp. 211–28 in David M. Thomas, ed., Canada and the United States: Differences that Count, 2nd edn. Peterborough, ON: Broadview Press.

Martire, Gregory and Ruth Clark. 1982. Anti-Semitism in the United States: A Study of Prejudice in the 1980s. New York: Praeger.

Martis, Kenneth. 2001. 'The geographical dimensions of a new nation, 1780s–1820s', pp.143–64 in Thomas McIlwraith and Edward Muller, eds, North America: The Historical Geography of a Changing Continent, 2nd edn. Lanham, MD: Rowman and Littlefield Publishers.

Marx, Karl, and Friedrich Engels. 1846 [1976]. The German Ideology, in Marx Engels Collected Works, vol. 5. New York: International Publishers.

Matthews, Ralph. 1983. The Creation of Regional Dependency. Toronto: University of Toronto Press.

Matyas, Joe. 2003. 'Numbers of non-believers on the rise'. The London Free Press. 14 May, p. A3.

Maxim, Paul, Jerry White, Dan Beavon, and Paul Whitehead. 2001. 'Dispersion and polarization of income among Aboriginal and non-Aboriginal Canadians'. Canadian Review of Sociology and Anthropology 38, 4: 465–76.

Maxim, Paul and Paul Whitehead. 1998. Explaining Crime, 4th edn. Boston: Butterworth-Heinemann.

Mayer, Egon, Barry A. Kosman, and Ariela Keysar. 2003. The American Religious Identification Study, 1990–2001. http://www.gc.cuny.edu/studies.key_findings.htm, June 2003.

Mayers, Adam. 2003. Dixie and the Dominion: Canada, the Confederacy, and the War for the Union. Toronto: The Dundurn Group.

Mazzuca, Josephine. 2002a. 'More accepting of homosexuals—Canada or US?' The Gallup Poll Tuesday Briefing, 6 August, pp. 1–2.

———. 2002b. 'American and Canadian views on abortion'. The Gallup Poll Tuesday Briefing, 24 September, pp. 95–6.

———. 2002c. 'The death penalty in North America'. The Gallup Poll Tuesday Briefing, 15 October, pp. 51–2.

———. 2002d. 'Worship call: do US, Canada, Britain answer?' The Gallup Poll Tuesday Briefing, 15 October, pp. 53–4.

Menzies, Charles. 2004. 'First Nations inequality and the legacy of colonialism', pp. 295–303 in James Curtis, Edward Grabb, and Neil Guppy, eds, Social Inequality in Canada: Patterns, Problems, Policies, 4th edn. Scarborough, ON: Pearson Education Canada.

Merelman, Richard. 1991. Partial Visions: Culture and Politics in Britain, Canada, and the United States. Madison: University of Wisconsin Press.

Milbrath, Lester. 1965. Political Participation: How and Why Do People Get Involved in Politics? Chicago: Rand McNally.

Miller, Kerby A. 1985. Emigrants and Exiles: Ireland and the Irish Exodus to North America. New York and Oxford: Oxford University Press.

Milner, Henry and Sheilagh Hodgins Milner. 1973. The Decolonization of Quebec. Toronto: McClelland and Stewart.

Mitchell, Susan. 1998. American Attitudes: Who Thinks What about the Issues that Shape our Lives, 2nd edn. Ithaca, NY: New Strategist Publications.

Monet, Jacques. 1971. 'The 1840s', pp. 200–25 in J.M.S. Careless, ed., Colonists and Canadiens. Toronto: Macmillan.

Montesquieu, Charles de Secondat. 1748 [1989]. The Spirit of the Laws. Translated by Anne M. Cohler, Basia Carolyn Miller, and Harold Samuel Stone. Cambridge: Cambridge University Press.

Moon, C. David, Nicholas Lovrich, Jr, and John Pierce. 2000. 'Political culture in Canada and the United States: comparing social trust, self-esteem, and political liberalism in major Canadian and American cities'. Social Science Quarterly 81, 3 (September): 826–36.

Moore, Christopher. 1994. The Loyalists: Revolution, Exile, Settlement. Toronto: McClelland and Stewart.

Moore, Wilbert E. 1971. American Negro Slavery and Abolition: A Sociological Study. New York: Third Press.

Morris, Raymond and C. Michael Lanphier. 1977. Three Scales of Inequality: Perspectives on French–English Relations. Don Mills, ON: Longman.

Morton, W.L. 1961. The Canadian Identity. Madison and Toronto: University of Wisconsin and University of Toronto Press.

———. 1963. The Kingdom of Canada. Toronto: McClelland and Stewart.

Myers, Gustavus. 1914 [1972]. A History of Canadian Wealth. Toronto: James Lewis and Samuel.

Myrdal, Gunnar. 1944. An American Dilemma. New York: Harper.

Naegele, Kaspar. 1961. 'Canadian society: some reflections', pp. 1–54 in Bernard Blishen, Frank Jones, Kaspar Naegele, and John Porter, eds, Canadian Society: Sociological Perspectives. Toronto: Macmillan.

Nelles, H.V. 1997. 'Review essay: American Exceptionalism—A Double-Edged Sword'. American Historical Review 102, 3 (June): 749–58.

Nelson, William. 1961. The American Tory. Boston: Beacon Press.

Nevitte, Neil. 1996. The Decline of Deference. Peterborough, ON: Broadview Press.

———. 2000. 'Value change and reorientations in citizen–state relations'. Canadian Public Policy 26 Supplement: S73–S94.

Nevitte, Neil, Miguel Basanez, and Ronald Inglehart. 1992. 'Directions of value change in North America', pp. 245–59 in Stephen Randall, Herman Konrad, and Sheldon Silverman, eds, North America Without Borders? Integrating Canada, the United States, and Mexico. Calgary: University of Calgary Press.

Nevitte, Neil and Roger Gibbins. 1990. New Elites in Old States. Toronto: Oxford University Press.

Newby, I.A. 1978. The South: A History. New York: Holt, Rinehart, and Winston.

Newman, F.W. 1889 [1969]. Anglo-Saxon Abolition of Negro Slavery. New York: Negro Universities Press.

Newman, Peter. 1995. The Canadian Revolution, 1985–1995: From Deference to Defiance. Toronto: Viking.

Newport, Frank. 1999. 'Some change in American attitudes towards homosexuality, but negativity remains'. The Gallup Poll Monthly 402 (March): 28–30.

———. 2003. 'Six in 10 Americans agree that gay sex should be legal'. The Gallup Poll Tuesday Briefing, 27 June, pp. 45–9.

Niemonen, Jack. 2002. Race, Class, and the State in Contemporary Sociology. Boulder, CO: Lynne Rienner Publishers.

Nisbett, Richard E. 1993. 'Violence and US regional culture'. American Psychologist 48, 4: 441–9.

Nisbett, Richard E. and Dov Cohen. 1996. Culture of Honor: The Psychology of Violence in the South. Boulder, CO: Westview Press.

Nish, Cameron. 1971. 'The 1760s', pp. 1–19 in J.M.S. Careless, ed., Colonists and Canadiens. Toronto: Macmillan.

Noel, S.J.R. 1990. Patrons, Clients, Brokers. Toronto: University of Toronto Press.

Nolan, Mary. 1997. 'Against exceptionalisms'. American Historical Review 102, 3 (June): 769–74.

Nunn, Clyde, Harry Crockett, and J. Allen Williams, Jr. 1978. Tolerance for Nonconformity. San Francisco: Jossey-Bass.

O'Connor, Julia. 1998. 'Social justice, social citizenship, and the welfare state, 1965–1995: Canada in comparative context', pp. 180–231 in Rick Helmes-Hayes and James Curtis, eds, The Vertical Mosaic Revisited. Toronto: University of Toronto Press.

O'Connor, Julia, Ann Shola Orloff, and Sheila Shaver. 1999. States, Markets, Families: Gender, Liberalism, and Social Policy in Australia, Canada, Great Britain, and the United States. Cambridge: Cambridge University Press.

Odum, Howard W. 1936. Southern Regions of the United States. Chapel Hill: University of North Carolina Press.

————. 1947. The Way of the South. New York: Hafner Publishing Company.

Odum, Howard W. and Harry Estill Moore. 1938. American Regionalism: A Cultural-Historical Approach to National Integration. New York: Henry Holt.

OECD. 2003. OECD Economic Outlook, no. 73, April.

Ogmundson, Richard. 2002. 'The Canadian case: cornucopia of neglected research opportunities'. The American Sociologist 33, 1 (Spring): 55–78.

Olsen, Gregg M. 2002. The Politics of the Welfare State: Canada, Sweden, and the United States. Toronto: Oxford University Press.

Ornstein, Michael. 1985. 'Canadian capital and the Canadian state: ideology in an era of crisis', pp. 129–66 in Robert J. Brym, ed., The Structure of the Canadian Capitalist Class. Toronto: Garamond.

————. 1986. 'The political ideology of the Canadian capitalist class'. Canadian Review of Sociology and Anthropology 23, 2: 182–209.

Ornstein, Michael and H. Michael Stevenson. 1999. Politics and Ideology in Canada. Montreal and Kingston: McGill-Queen's University Press.

Osborne, Brian S. and Donald Swainson. 1988. Kingston: Building on the Past. Westport, ON: Butternut Press.

O'Toole, Roger. 2000. 'Canadian religion: heritage and project', pp. 34–51 in David Lyon and Marguerite Van Die, eds, Rethinking Church, State, and Modernity: Canada between Europe and America. Toronto: University of Toronto Press.

Ouimet, Marc. 1999. 'Crime in Canada and the United States: a comparative analysis'. Canadian Review of Sociology and Anthropology 36, 3 (August): 389–408.

Palmer, Howard. 1976. 'Mosaic vs. melting pot? Immigration and ethnicity in Canada and the United States'. International Journal 31: 488–528.

Pammett, Jon. 1996. 'Getting ahead around the world', pp. 67–86 in Alan Frizzell and Jon Pammett, eds, Social Inequality in Canada. Ottawa: Carleton University Press.

Panetta, Alexander. 2003. 'Charest's first budget won't include tax cut'. The London Free Press, 17 April, p. A5.

Parker, John. 2003. 'A nation apart'. The Economist, 8 November, pp. 3–20.

Parsons, Talcott. 1951. The Social System. New York: The Free Press.

Paxton, Pamela. 1999. 'Is social capital declining in the United States: A multiple indicator assessment'. American Journal of Sociology 105: 88–127.

Pekelis, Alexander. 1950. Law and Social Action: Selected Essays. Ithaca, NY: Cornell University Press.

Pelletier, Rejean and Daniel Guerin. 1996. 'Postmaterialisme et clivages partisans au Quebec: les partis sont-ils differents?' Canadian Journal of Political Science 29, 1 (March): 71–109.

Pendakur, Krishna and Ravi Pendakur. 1998. 'The colour of money: earnings differentials among ethnic groups in Canada'. Canadian Journal of Economics 31, 3 (August): 518–48.

————. 2001. 'Colour my world: has the minority–majority earnings gap changed over time?' Strategic Research and Analysis, Department of Canadian Heritage, SRA-420.

Perkel, Colin. 2003. 'Canada sixth in economic freedom'. The London Free Press, 9 July, pp. C1 and C7.

Perlin, George. 1997. 'The constraints of public opinion: diverging or converging paths?', pp. 71–149 in Keith Banting, George Hoberg, and Richard Simeon, eds, Degrees of Freedom: Canada and the United States in a Changing World. Montreal and Kingston: McGill-Queen's University Press.

Perry, David. 2000. 'What price Canadian? Taxation and debt compared', pp. 52–67 in David M. Thomas, ed., Canada and the United States: Differences that Count, 2nd edn. Peterborough, ON: Broadview Press.

Pocklington, T.C. 1985. Liberal Democracy in Canada and the United States. Toronto: Holt, Rinehart and Winston.

————. 1994. Representative Democracy: An Introduction to Politics and Government. Toronto: Harcourt Brace.

Pocock, John. G.A. 1987. The Ancient Constitution and the Feudal Law. Cambridge: Cambridge University Press.

Ponting, J. Rick. 1986. Arduous Journey. Toronto: McClelland and Stewart.

Porter, John. 1965. The Vertical Mosaic: An Analysis of Social Class and Power in Canada. Toronto: University of Toronto Press.

———. 1967. 'Canadian character in the twentieth century'. Annals of the American Academy of Political and Social Science 370: 48–56.

———. 1975. 'Ethnic pluralism in Canadian perspective', pp. 267–304 in Nathan Glazer and Daniel P. Moynihan, eds, Ethnicity: Theory and Experience. Cambridge, MA: Harvard University Press.

———. 1979. The Measure of Canadian Society. Toronto: Gage.

Posgate, Dale and Kenneth McRoberts. 1976. Quebec: Social Change and Political Crisis. Toronto: McClelland and Stewart.

Presthus, Robert. 1973. Elite Accommodation in Canadian Politics. Cambridge: Cambridge University Press.

———. 1977a. 'Aspects of political culture and legislative behaviour: United States and Canada', pp. 7–22 in Robert Presthus, ed., Cross-National Perspectives: United States and Canada. Leiden: E.J. Brill.

———. 1977b. 'Political involvement and party allegiances in Canada and the United States', pp. 23–43 in Robert Presthus, ed., Cross-National Perspectives: United States and Canada. Leiden: E.J. Brill.

Pugliese, Donato. 1986. 'Introduction', pp. 3–14 in Volunteer Associations: An Annotated Bibliography. New York: Garland Publishers.

Putnam, Robert. 1995. 'Bowling alone: America's declining social capital'. Journal of Democracy 6: 65–78.

———. 2000. Bowling Alone: The Collapse and Revival of American Community. New York: Simon and Schuster.

Qian, Zhenchao. 1999. 'Who intermarries? Education, nativity, region, and interracial marriage, 1980 and 1990'. Journal of Comparative Family Studies, 30, 4: 579–97.

Quinley, Harold and Charles Glock. 1979. Anti-Semitism in America. New York: The Free Press.

Ramcharan, Subhas. 1982. Racism: Nonwhites in Canada. Toronto: Butterworths.

Rawlyk, George. 1971. 'The 1770s', pp. 20–40 in J.M.S. Careless, ed., Colonists and Canadiens. Toronto: Macmillan.

———. 1995. 'Religion in Canada: A historical overview'. The Annals of the American Academy of Political and Social Science 538 (March): 131–42.

Ray, Julie. 2003. 'Worlds apart: religion in Canada, Britain, US'. The Gallup Poll Tuesday Briefing, 12 August, pp. 108–9.

Reed, John Shelton. 1982. One South: An Ethnic Approach to Regional Culture. Baton Rouge: Louisiana State University Press.

———. 1983. Southerners: The Social Psychology of Sectionalism. Chapel Hill: University of North Carolina Press.

———. 1986. The Enduring South: Subcultural Persistence in Mass Society. Chapel Hill: University of North Carolina Press.

———. 1991. 'New South or no South? Regional culture in 2036', pp. 225–35 in Joseph Himes, ed., The South Moves into the Future. Tuscaloosa and London: University of Alabama Press.

———. 1992. 'The Mind of the South and Southern distinctiveness', pp. 137–56 in Charles W. Eagles, ed., The Mind of the South: Fifty Years Later. Jackson, MS and London: University Press of Mississippi.

Reed, Paul and L. Kevin Selbee. 2000. 'Distinguishing characteristics of active volunteers in Canada'. Nonprofit and Voluntary Sector Quarterly 29, 4: 571–92.

Reid, W. Stanford. 1976. 'The Scottish Protestant tradition', pp. 118–36 in W. Stanford Reid, ed., The Scottish Tradition in Canada. Toronto: McClelland and Stewart.

Reidy, Joseph. 1992. From Slavery to Agrarian Capitalism in the Cotton Plantation South. Chapel Hill and London: University of North Carolina Press.

Reimer, Samuel. 1995. 'A look at cultural effects on religiosity: a comparison between the United States and Canada'. Journal for the Scientific Study of Religion 34, 4: 445–57.

Reitz, Jeffrey. 1980. The Survival of Ethnic Groups. Toronto: McGraw-Hill Ryerson.

———. 1988. 'Less racial discrimination in Canada, or simply less racial conflict? Implications of comparisons with Britain'. Canadian Public Policy 14, 4: 424–41.

———. 1998. Warmth of the Welcome: The Social Causes of Economic Success for Immigrants in Different Nations and Cities. Boulder, CO: Westview Press.

Reitz, Jeffrey and Raymond Breton. 1994. The Illusion of Differences: Realities of Ethnicity in Canada and the United States. Toronto: C.D. Howe Institute.

Riddell, W. Craig. 1993. 'Unionization in Canada and the United States: a tale of two countries', pp. 109–47 in David Card and Richard Freeman, eds, Small Differences That Matter. Chicago and London: University of Chicago Press.

Riddell, William Renwick. 1920. 'The slave in Canada', reprinted from The Journal of Negro History 5, 3 (July), by the Association for the Study of Negro Life and History, Washington, DC.

Rioux, Marcel. 1971. Quebec in Question. Translated by James Boake. Toronto: James Lewis and Samuel.

Roberts, Julian and Loretta Stalans. 1997. Public Opinion, Crime, and Criminal Justice. Boulder, CO: Westview Press.

Roberts, Julian, Loretta Stalans, David Indermaur, and Mike Hough. 2003. Penal Populism and Public Opinion. Oxford and New York: Oxford University Press.

Rodgers, Bill. 2003. 'US ambassador cites tighter borders over pot'. The London Free Press, 2 May, p. A14.

Rodgers, Daniel T. 1987. Contested Truths: Key Words in American Politics since Independence. New York: Basic Books.

———. 1992. 'Republicanism: the career of a concept'. Journal of American History 79 (June): 12–38.

Roediger, David. 1991. The Wages of Whiteness: Race and the Making of the American Working Class. London: Verso.

———. 1994. Towards the Abolition of Whiteness: Essays on Race, Politics, and Working Class History. London: Verso.

Romano, Renee. 2003. Race Mixing: Black–White Marriage in Postwar America. Cambridge, MA: Harvard University Press.

Rosenfeld, Rachel and Arne Kalleberg. 1990. 'A cross-national comparison of the gender gap in income'. American Journal of Sociology 96, 1 (July): 69–106.

Rossides, Daniel. 1997. Social Stratification: The Interplay of Class, Race, and Gender, 2nd edn. Upper Saddle River, NJ: Prentice-Hall.

Rotolo, Thomas. 1999. 'Trends in voluntary association participation'. Nonprofit and Voluntary Sector Quarterly 28: 199–212.

Russo, Robert. 2004. 'Policies may be reviewed for a better "fit" with US'. London Free Press, 21 January, p. A5.

Ryan, Mary P. 1999. 'Civil society as democratic practice: North American cities during the nineteenth century'. Journal of Interdisciplinary History 29: 559–84.

Saez, Emmanuel and Michael Veall. 2003. 'The evolution of high incomes in Canada, 1920–2000'. Social and Economic Dimensions of an Aging Population (SEDAP) Research Paper No. 99. McMaster University, Hamilton, ON.

Saunders, Doug. 2004. 'Why Canadians are the new Americans'. The Globe and Mail, 3 January, p. F2.

Saussure, Ferdinand de. 1915a [1959]. Course in General Linguistics. Translated by Wade Baskin. New York: The Philosophical Library.

———. 1915b [1983]. Course in General Linguistics. Translated by Roy Harris. London: Gerald Duckworth and Co.

————. 1915c [1972]. Cours de Linguistique Generale. Paris: Payot.

Savoie, Josee. 2002. 'Crime Statistics in Canada 2001'. Juristat 22, 6. Catalogue 85-002. Ottawa: Statistics Canada.

Sayer, Derek. 1992. 'A notable administration: English state formation and the rise of capitalism'. American Journal of Sociology 97, 5 (March): 1382–415.

Schaff, Phillip. 1855 [1961]. America: A Sketch of Its Political, Social, and Religious Character. Edited by Perry Miller. Cambridge, MA: Belknap Press of Harvard University Press.

Schama, Simon. 2000. A History of Britain, vol. 1. New York: Hyperion.

————. 2001. A History of Britain, vol. 2. London: BBC Worldwide.

————. 2002. A History of Britain, vol. 3. Toronto: McClelland and Stewart.

Schlesinger, Arthur M., Sr. 1944. 'Biography of a nation of joiners'. American Historical Review 50: 1–25.

————. 1964. Paths to the Present. Boston: Houghton Mifflin Company.

Schlesinger, Arthur M., Jr. 1986. The Cycles of American History. Boston: Houghton Mifflin Company.

Schmidley, Dianne. 2003. 'The foreign-born population in the United States: March 2002'. Current Population Reports, P20-539, US Census Bureau, Washington, DC. http://www.census.gov/prod/2003pubs/p20-539.pdf, accessed July 2003.

Schwartz, S.H. and W. Bilsky. 1990. 'Toward a theory of the universal content and structure of values: Extensions and cross-cultural replications'. Journal of Personality and Social Psychology 58: 878–91.

Scott, John. 1995. Sociological Theory: Contemporary Debates. Aldershot, UK and Brookfield, VT: Edward Elgar Publishing Company.

Selbee, L. Kevin and Paul Reed. 2001. 'Patterns of volunteering over the life cycle'. Canadian Social Trends, 61 (Summer): 2–6.

Seljak, David. 2000. 'Resisting the "no man's land" of private religion: the Catholic Church and public politics in Quebec', pp. 131–48 in David Lyon and Marguerite Van Die, eds, Rethinking Church, State, and Modernity: Canada between Europe and America. Toronto: University of Toronto Press.

Senior, H. and W. Brown. 1987. Victorious in Defeat. Toronto: Methuen.

Shain, Barry. 1994. The Myth of American Individualism: The Protestant Origins of American Political Thought. Princeton: Princeton University Press.

Sharkansky, Ira. 1978. The Maligned States: Policy Accomplishments, Problems, and Opportunities, 2nd edn. New York: McGraw-Hill.

Shaw, Matthew. 2003. Great Scots! How the Scots Created Canada. Winnipeg: Heartland Associates.

Shenkman, Richard. 1988. Legends, Lies, and Cherished Myths of American History. New York: William Morrow.

Siddiqui, Haroon. 2001a. 'Census draws portrait of multi-hued Canada'. The Toronto Star, 25 April, p. A13.

————. 2001b. 'Media out of touch with pluralistic Canada'. The Toronto Star, 22 April, p. A13.

————. 2003. 'Arabs and West retreat into parallel worlds'. The Toronto Star, 26 October, pp. F1–F2.

Simeon, Richard and Elaine Willis. 1997. 'Democracy and performance: governance in Canada and the United States', pp. 150–86 in Keith Banting, George Hoberg, and Richard Simeon, eds, Degrees of Freedom: Canada and the United States in a Changing World. Montreal and Kingston: McGill-Queen's University Press.

Simon, Rita J. and James P. Lynch. 1999. 'A comparative assessment of public opinion toward immigrants and immigrant policies'. International Migration Review 33, 2 (Summer): 455–67.

Simpson, Jeffrey. 2000. Star-Spangled Canadians: Canadians Living the American Dream. Toronto: Harper Collins.

Skelton, W.G. 1965. 'The United Empire Loyalists: a reconsideration'. Dalhousie Review 45: 5–16.

Smidt, Corwin and James Penning. 1982. 'Religious commitment, political conservatism, and political and social tolerance in the United States: a longitudinal analysis'. *Sociological Analysis* 43: 231–46.

Smith, Allan. 1994. *Canada: An American Nation?* Montreal and Kingston: McGill-Queen's University Press.

Smith, David. 1973. *The Geography of Social Well-Being*. New York: McGraw-Hill.

Smith, David Horton. 1975. 'Voluntary action and voluntary groups'. *Annual Review of Sociology* 1: 247–70.

Smith, Jennifer. 2000. 'The grass is always greener: prime ministerial vs. presidential government', pp. 229–47 in David M. Thomas, ed., *Canada and the United States: Differences that Count*, 2nd edn. Peterborough, ON: Broadview Press.

Smith, Paul. 1968. 'The American loyalists: notes on their organizational and numerical strength'. *William and Mary Quarterly* 25: 259–77.

Smith, Timothy L. 1957. *Revivalism and Social Reform in Mid-nineteenth Century America*. New York: Abingdon Press.

Sniderman, Paul, Joseph Fletcher, Peter Russell, and Philip Tetlock. 1996. *The Clash of Rights: Liberty, Equality, and Legitimacy in Pluralist Democracy*. New Haven and London: Yale University Press.

Sniderman, Paul, David Northrup, Joseph Fletcher, Peter Russell, and Philip Tetlock. 1992. 'Working paper on anti-Semitism in Quebec'. Institute for Social Research, York University.

———. 1993. 'Psychological and cultural foundations of prejudice: the case of anti-Semitism in Quebec'. *Canadian Review of Sociology and Anthropology* 30, 2 (May): 242–70.

Srebrnik, Henry. 2000. 'Football, frats and fun vs. commuters, cold and carping: the social and psychological context of higher education in Canada and the United States', pp. 165–91 in David M. Thomas, ed., *Canada and the United States: Differences that Count*, 2nd edn. Peterborough, ON: Broadview Press.

Stanbridge, Karen A. 1997. 'England, France, and the North American colonies: an analysis of absolutist state power in Europe and in the New World'. *Journal of Historical Sociology* 1, 10 (March): 27–55.

Stanley, George F.G. 1976. 'The Scottish military tradition', pp. 137–60 in W. Stanford Reid, ed., *The Scottish Tradition in Canada*. Toronto: McClelland and Stewart.

Statistical Abstract of the United States: 1899–1900. Washington: US Census Bureau.

Statistical Abstract of the United States: 1910. Washington: US Census Bureau.

Statistical Abstract of the United States: 2001. Washington: US Census Bureau.

Statistics Canada. 2003a. CANSIM II, Tables 384-0002 and 385-0001. http:// www.statcan.ca/ english/ Pgdb/econ50.htm and http://www.statcan/english/Pgdb/ govt51b.htm.

———. 2003b. 'Proportion of foreign-born, Canada, provinces, and territories, 1991, 1996, and 2001'. http://www.statcan.ca/english/Pgdb/demo46a.htm.

———. 2003c. 'Visible minority population, provinces and territories'. http://www.statcan.ca/ english/Pgdb/demo40b.htm.

———. 2003d. 2001 Census of Population. 'Earnings groups, full-year, full-time workers, for males and females, for Canada, provinces, and territories—20% sample data'. http://www12.statcan.ca/english/census01/products/highlight/Earnings/Page.cfm?, accessed July 2003.

———. 2003e. 'Imports and exports of goods on a balance-of-payments basis'. http://estat.statcan.ca/content/english/articles/daily/020517a.shtml, accessed August 2003.

———. 2003f. 'Visible minority groups, 2001 counts, for Canada, provinces, territories, census metropolitan areas, and census agglomerations—20% sample data'. http://www12.statcan.ca/ english/census01/products/highlight/Ethnicity, accessed July 2003.

———. 2003g. 'Immigrant status by period of immigration, 2001 counts, for Canada, provinces, territories, census metropolitan areas, and census agglomerations—20% sample data'. http://www12.statcan.ca/english/census01/products/highlight/Immigration, accessed July 2003.

―――. 2003h. 'Ethnic Diversity Survey: portrait of a multicultural society'. Catalogue no. 89-593-XIE, September.

Steckel, Richard H. 2000. 'The African population in the United States, 1790–1920', pp. 433–81 in Michael R. Haines and Richard H. Steckel, eds, A Population History of North America. Cambridge: Cambridge University Press.

Stewart, Ian. 1990. 'New myths for old: the Loyalists and maritime political culture'. Journal of Canadian Studies 25, 2 : 20–43.

Stier, Haya and Noah Lewin-Epstein. 2003. 'Time to work: a comparative analysis of preferences for working hours'. Work and Occupations 30, 3 (August): 302–26.

Streib, Gordon F. 1991. 'The South and its older people: structural and change perspectives', pp. 69–99 in Joseph Himes, ed., The South Moves into the Future. Tuscaloosa and London: University of Alabama Press.

Strickland, Rennard. 1997. Tonto's Revenge: Reflections on American Indian Culture and Politics. Albuquerque: University of New Mexico Press.

Stuart, Reginald. 1988. United States Expansion and British North America, 1775–1871. Chapel Hill: University of North Carolina Press.

Studlar, Donley. 2001. 'Canadian exceptionalism: explaining differences over time in provincial and federal voter turnout'. Canadian Journal of Political Science 34, 2 (June): 288–319.

Stuhr, Macarie Leigh. 2003. 'Gender and visible minority status in the Canadian labour market: analysis over two decades'. Unpublished Master's thesis, Department of Sociology, University of Waterloo, Waterloo, ON.

Talman, James John, ed. 1946. Loyalist Narratives from Upper Canada. Toronto: The Champlain Society.

Talman, James John and Archibald Hope Young. 1934. Church Establishment and Endowment in Upper Canada. Toronto: Canadian Historical Review.

Tepperman, Lorne and James Curtis. 2004. Social Problems: A Canadian Perspective. Toronto: Oxford University Press.

Tervit, Trish. 1997. 'Quebecers fool around the most'. The London Free Press, 16 September, p. A1.

Thomas, David M., ed. 2000. Canada and the United States: Differences that Count, 2nd edn. Peterborough, ON: Broadview Press.

Thompson, Edgar T. 1975. Plantation Societies, Race Relations, and the South: The Regimentation of Populations. Selected Papers of Edgar T. Thompson. Durham, NC: Duke University Press.

Thompson, John Herd and Stephen J. Randall. 1994. Canada and the United States: Ambivalent Allies. Montreal and Kingston: McGill-Queen's University Press.

Thorner, Daniel. 1968. 'Peasantries', pp. 503–11 in David Sils, ed., International Journal of the Social Sciences, vol. 11. New York: Macmillan and the Free Press.

Tibbetts, Janice. 2002. 'US warns Canada not to relax drug laws'. The National Post. 18 July, p. A5.

Tocqueville, Alexis de. 1835 [1954]. Democracy in America, vol. 1. New York: Vintage Books.

―――. 1840 [1954]. Democracy in America, vol. 2. New York: Vintage Books.

―――. 1856a [1998]. The Old Regime and the Revolution, vol. 1: The Complete Text. Translated by Alan S. Kahan. Chicago: University of Chicago Press.

―――. 1856b [2001]. The Old Regime and the Revolution, vol. 2: Notes on the French Revolution and Napoleon. Translated by Alan S. Kahan. Chicago: University of Chicago Press.

Todorov, Tzevetan. 1984. The Conquest of America: The Question of the Other. New York: Harper Colophon.

Treble, Patricia and Barbara Wickens. 2003. 'Off the charts'. Maclean's, 18 August, pp. 30–1.

Tremblay, Manon. 2000. 'Gender and society: rights and realities—a reappraisal', pp. 319–37 in David M. Thomas, ed., Canada and the United States: Differences that Count, 2nd edn. Peterborough, ON: Broadview Press.

Tremblay, Marc. 1953. 'Orientations de la pensee sociale', pp. 193–208 in Jean-Charles Falardeau, ed., Essais sur le Quebec Contemporain. Quebec: Les Presses Universitaires Laval.

Tremblay, Sylvain. 1999. 'Crime statistics in Canada, 1998'. Juristat 19, 9. Catalogue 85-002. Ottawa: Statistics Canada.

Trent, John, Robert Young, and Guy Lachapelle, eds. 1995. Quebec–Canada: What Is the Path Ahead? Ottawa: University of Ottawa Press.

Triandis, H.C. 1973. 'Subjective culture and economic development'. International Journal of Psychology 8: 163–80.

Triandis, H.C., C. McCusker, and C.H. Chui. 1990. 'Multi-method probes of individualism and collectivism'. Journal of Personality and Social Psychology 59: 1006–20.

Truman, Tom. 1971. 'A critique of Seymour M. Lipset's article, "Value differences, absolute or relative: the English-speaking democracies"'. Canadian Journal of Political Science 4: 497–525.

Turner, Margey Austin, Michael Fix, and Raymond J. Struyk. 1991. Opportunities Denied, Opportunities Diminished: Discrimination in Hiring. Washington: Urban Institute Project.

Tylor, Edward. B. 1871. Primitive Culture. London: Murray.

Ujimoto, K. Victor and Gordon Hirabayashi, eds. 1980. Visible Minorities and Multiculturalism: Asians in Canada. Toronto: Butterworths.

Underhill, Frank. 1960. In Search of Canadian Liberalism. Toronto: Macmillan of Canada.

United States Mission to the European Union. 2002. 'Death penalty support dropping in US, growing in Europe'. 6 June. http://www.useu.be/Categories/Justice%20and%20Home% 20Affairs/June0602DeathPenaltyUSEurope.html, July 2003.

Upton, L.F.S. 1969. The Loyal Whig. Toronto: University of Toronto Press.

———. 1971. 'The 1780s', pp. 41–61 in J.M.S. Careless, ed., Colonists and Canadiens. Toronto: Macmillan.

Urmetzer, Peter and Neil Guppy. 1999. 'Changing income inequality in Canada', pp. 56–65 in James Curtis, Edward Grabb, and Neil Guppy, eds, Social Inequality in Canada: Patterns, Problems, Policies, 3rd edn. Scarborough, ON: Prentice Hall Allyn and Bacon Canada.

———. 2004. 'Changing income inequality in Canada', pp. 75–84 in James Curtis, Edward Grabb, and Neil Guppy, eds, Social Inequality in Canada: Patterns, Problems, Policies, 4th edn. Scarborough, ON: Pearson Education Canada.

US Census Bureau. 2000. 'Geographic comparison table'. Census 2000 Summary File 3, Matrices P53, P77, P82, P87, P90, PCT47, and PCT52.

US Department of Justice. 2002. 'Crime in the United States, 2001'. Bureau of Justice Statistics of the Federal Bureau of Investigation. http://www.fbi.gov/ucr/cius_01/01crime2.pdf, June 2003.

Vandello, Joseph and Dov Cohen. 1999. 'Patterns of individualism and collectivism across the United States'. Journal of Personality and Social Psychology 77, 2: 279–92.

Verba, Sidney, Kay Lehman Schlozman, and Henry E. Brady. 1995. Voice and Equality: Civic Voluntarism in American Politics. Cambridge, MA: Harvard University Press.

Waite, Peter. 1987. 'Between three oceans: challenging a continental destiny', pp. 279–374 in Craig Brown, ed., The Illustrated History of Canada. Toronto: Lester Orpen Dennys.

Wallot, Jean-Pierre. 1971. 'The 1800s', pp. 95–121 in J.M.S. Careless, ed., Colonists and Canadiens. Toronto: Macmillan.

Wanner, Richard. 2003a. 'Entry class and the earnings attainment of immigrants to Canada, 1980–1996'. Canadian Public Policy 29: 53–71.

———. 2003b. 'Shifting origins, shifting labour markets: trends in the occupational and earnings attainments of male immigrants to Canada, 1971–1996'. Annual meeting of the Canadian Population Society, Halifax.

Wanner, Richard and Michelle Ambrose. 2003. 'Trends in the occupational and earnings attainments of women immigrants to Canada, 1971–1996'. Canadian Studies in Population 30, 2: 355–88.

Watt, David Harrington. 1991. 'United States: cultural challenges to the voluntary sector', pp. 243–87 in Robert Wuthnow, ed., Between States and Markets: The Voluntary Sector in Comparative Perspective. Princeton: Princeton University Press.

Wayne, Michael. 1983. The Reshaping of Plantation Society. Baton Rouge: Louisiana State University Press.

Weakliem, David and Robert Biggert. 1999. 'Region and political opinion in the contemporary United States'. Social Forces 77, 3: 863–86.

Weber, Adna Ferris. 1967. The Growth of Cities in the Nineteenth Century. Ithaca, NY: Cornell University Press.

Weber, Max. 1911. 'Deutscher Sociologentag'. Verhandlungen 1: 39–62.

———. 1927 [1950]. General Economic History. Translated by Frank H. Knight. Glencoe, IL: The Free Press.

———. 1947. The Theory of Social and Economic Organization. Translated by A.M. Henderson and Talcott Parsons. New York: The Free Press.

Weiner, Myron. 1987. 'Empirical democratic theory', pp. 3–34 in Myron Weiner and Ergun Ozbudun, eds, Competitive Elections in Developing Countries. Durham, NC: Duke University Press.

Weinfeld, Morton. 1981. 'Myth and reality in the Canadian mosaic: "Affective ethnicity"'. Canadian Ethnic Studies 13: 80–100.

———. 1990. 'Canadian Jews and Canadian pluralism', pp. 87–106 in S.M. Lipset, ed., American pluralism and the Jewish Community. New Brunswick, NJ and London: Transaction Books.

———. 2001. Like Everyone Else . . . But Different: The Paradoxical Success of Canadian Jews. Toronto: McClelland and Stewart.

Wesley, Charles H. 1940. 'The Negro in the United States and Canada', pp. 72–86 in Charles H. Wesley, ed., The Negro in the Americas, vol. 1. Washington, DC: The Graduate School of Howard University.

Westhues, Anne. 2003. 'Social policy in Canada—return to an activist agenda?' The Reddin Symposium XVI: 1–16. The Canadian Studies Center, Bowling Green State University.

White, Jerry P., Dan Beamon, and Paul Maxim, eds. 2003. Aboriginal Conditions: The Research Foundations for Public Policy. Vancouver: University of British Columbia Press.

White, Morton. 1978. The Philosophy of the American Revolution. Oxford: Oxford University Press.

Wilensky, Harold. 2002. Rich Democracies: Political Economy, Public Policy, and Performance. Berkeley and Los Angeles: University of California Press.

Williams, Robin M., Jr. 1960. American Society: A Sociological Interpretation. New York: Knopf.

Wilson, Alan. 1971. 'The 1810s', pp. 122–48 in J.M.S. Careless, ed., Colonists and Canadiens. Toronto: Macmillan.

Wilson, Bryan. 1982. Religion in Sociological Perspective. London: Oxford University Press.

Wilson, Catherine Anne. 1997. 'The Scotch-Irish and immigrant culture on Amherst Island, Ontario', pp. 134–45 in H. Tyler Blethen and Curtis W. Wood, Jr, eds, Ulster and North America: Transatlantic Perspectives on the Scotch-Irish. Tuscaloosa and London: University of Alabama Press.

Wilson, P. Jackson, J. Gilbert, K. Kupperman, S. Nissenbaum, and D. Scott. 1996. The Pursuit of Liberty: A History of the American People, vol. 1, 3rd edn. New York: Harper Collins College Publishers.

Wilson, William Julius. 1999. The Bridge over the Racial Divide. Berkeley and Los Angeles: University of California Press.

Wise, S.F. 1971. 'The 1790s', pp. 62–94 in J.M.S. Careless, ed., Colonists and Canadiens. Toronto: Macmillan.

Wishart, David. 2001. 'Settling the Great Plains, 1850–1930: prospects and problems', pp. 237–60 in Thomas McIlwraith and Edward Muller, eds, North America: The Historical Geography of a Changing Continent, 2nd edn. Lanham, MD: Rowman and Littlefield Publishers.

Wolfe, Martin. 1972. The Fiscal System of Renaissance France. New Haven: Yale University Press.

Wolfson, Michael and Brian Murphy. 2000. 'Income inequality in North America: does the 49th parallel still matter?' Canadian Economic Observer, August. Catalogue No. 11-010-XPB. Ottawa: Statistics Canada.

Wood, Chris. 1999. 'The vanishing border'. Maclean's, 20 December, pp. 20–3.

Wood, Gordon S. 1992. The Radicalism of the American Revolution. New York: Knopf.

———. 2002. The American Revolution: A History. New York: Modern Library.

Wood, Michael. 1999. In Search of England: Journey into the English Past. Berkeley and Los Angeles. University of California Press.

Wood, Nancy. 1993. 'A reluctant welcome'. Maclean's, 4 January, p. 26.

Wright, Charles and Herbert H. Hyman. 1958. 'Association memberships of American adults: evidence from national survey samples'. American Sociological Review 23: 184–294.

Wright, Erik Olin. 1979. Class Structure and Income Determination. New York: Academic Press.

Wright, Erik Olin, Andrew Levine, and Elliott Sober. 1992. Reconstructing Marxism. London: Verso.

Wrong, Dennis. 1955. American and Canadian Viewpoints. Washington: American Council of Education.

Wu, Z. and Douglas Baer. 1996. 'Attitudes toward family life and gender roles: a comparison of English and French Canadian women'. Journal of Comparative Family Studies 27, 3: 437–52.

Wuthnow, Robert. 1991. 'Tocqueville's question reconsidered: volunteerism and public discourse in advanced industrial societies', pp. 288–308 in Robert Wuthnow, ed., Between States and Markets: The Voluntary Sector in Comparative Perspective. Princeton, NJ: Princeton University Press.

———. 1998. After Heaven: Spirituality in America since the 1950s. Berkeley: University of California Press.

Wynn, Graeme. 1987. 'On the margins of empire, 1760–1840', pp. 189–278 in Craig Brown, ed., The Illustrated History of Canada. Toronto: Lester and Orpen Dennys.

———. 2001. 'Realizing the idea of Canada', pp. 357–78 in Thomas McIlwraith and Edward Muller, eds, North America: The Historical Geography of a Changing Continent, 2nd edn. Lanham, MD: Rowman and Littlefield Publishers.

Young, Robert. 1995. The Secession of Quebec and the Future of Canada. Montreal and Kingston: McGill-Queen's University Press.

Zimring, Franklin. 2003. The Contradictions of American Capital Punishment. Oxford and New York: Oxford University Press.

Zimring, Franklin and Gordon Hawkins. 1997. Crime Is Not the Problem: Lethal Violence in America. New York and Oxford: Oxford University Press.

INDEX

aboriginal peoples, 78, 108, 203–5, 258, 259
Acadia, 90; see also French Canada
'achievement', 22
Adams, John, 63, 65, 67, 68, 76
Adams, Michael, 206, 232, 253, 269–71, 272
Adamson, Christopher, 115
affiliation, religious, 140–2
African Americans, 78, 79; see also blacks
agriculture, 104, 105–10
Ajzenstat, Janet, 126, 270
America: as term, 3; see also American North; American South; United States
American: as term, 3
American Civil War, 57, 69, 108, 109, 124–5, 263; Canadian participation in, 122n.
'American Creed', 22–3, 24, 48, 61, 64, 75, 97, 216–17
'American exceptionalism', 236
'Americanism', 22, 195
'Americanness', 81, 95
American North, 54, 255–9; crime in, 160–1; family and sexual values in, 146–53; as 'fragment', 13–15, 17–20; religion in, 141–5; 'Scotch-Irish' in, 102–3
American Revolution, 4, 5, 15, 54, 56–7; opposition to, 76–8; significance of, 20–2
American South, 54, 56–7, 131, 252; crime and law in, 159–61; family and sexual values in, 146–53; as 'fragment', 16; income distribution in, 178; influence of, 256–7; religion in, 141–5; 'Scotch-Irish' in, 101–5; slavery in, 105–10; the state and, 174–6; Tocqueville's view of, 42–4
Anglican Church, 96, 100, 112, 113–14
'Anglo-Irish', 100
anti-Americanism, 85

anti-Semitism, 209–11, 213
Appleby, Joyce, 62
'aristocracy', 42–3
Arnold, Benedict, 93
ascription, 22, 75
assertiveness, personal, 186–8
association(s): free, 38–9; voluntary, 234–45

Baer, Doug, 283
Baptists, 110
Berton, Pierre, 98
biculturalism, 196
bilingualism, 196
blacks, American, 106, 258; see also African Americans
Bonilla-Silva, Eduardo, 107
Breton, Raymond, 200, 202, 205, 207, 209, 214
Britain: assistance to Canada and, 119–21; settlers from, 93–105; see also England; Ireland; Scotland
British: as term, 50
Bryce, James, 73, 267
Buffalo, population of, 117
Bush, George W., 228, 261, 262

Caldwell, Gary, 237
Calvinists, 96–7
Canada: as term, 3; see also English Canada; French Canada; specific provinces
Canadian: as term, 3
Canadian Centre for Research and Information on Canada (CRIC), 208
Canadian Charter of Rights and Freedoms, 154–5
'Canadian Creed', 24–5
Canadian National Survey of Giving, Volunteering, and Participating, 237
capital punishment, 161, 163, 260
Carleton University Survey Centre, 232
Cartwright, Richard, 84–5

Catholics, 92, 112–13, 116, 140–2; Irish, 100
'Cavaliers', 104–5
'Celtic culture', 101–5
centralization, political, 123–7
change, attitudes about, 188–90
Chevalier, Michel, 72
Chicago, population of, 117
children, 183–6
Chrétien, Jean, 261
Christianity, 106–7; see also Catholics; Protestants; religion
'church and state', 115
Churchill, Winston, 31–4, 49, 53, 65
Church of England, 96; see also Anglicans
Church of Ireland, 100
citizenship, levels of, 198–9
Civil War, see American Civil War
Clark, S.D., 126
'clash of civilizations', 268
class: conflict, 13; loyalists and, 79–80; structure, 14, 87, 88–9, 108–9
climate: English, 35–6; statism and, 121–2
Clinton, Bill, 261
'collective consciousness', 28, 29
collectivism, 19, 25, 75, 166–7, 243; attitudes about, 180–92; 'egalitarian', 172; 'feudal', 175; 'hierarchical', 172; state and, 168–80
Common Law, 32, 35
Commons, John, 15
communalism, local, 68–73, 74, 176
conformity, community, 70, 71; see also communalism, local
'conservatism', 12
Constitution, American, 32–3
convergence: divergence and, 266–74
Co-operative Commonwealth Federation, 19
counter-revolution, 20–2
Craig, Gerald M., 78, 80
crime, 153–65, 244–5; attitudes about, 161–5; economic, 162, 164; non-violent, 157–8, 160; violent, 155–7, 158, 159, 160, 263
'cultural mosaic', 195–7
culture, concept of, 29
'culture of honour', 159
Curtis, James, 207, 208, 240

Dahrendorf, Ralf, 47
data sources, 136–8
death penalty, 161, 163, 260
deep structures, 26–58, 248–55
deference, 75, 219, 262
democracies, English, 46–58
Democracy in America, 37
discrimination, job, 202–3
dissent, civil, 220–5

distinctiveness: American South, 105–10; French Canada, 91–3
divergence: convergence and, 266–74
Dorchester, Lord, 84
Drucker, Peter, 235
Durham, Lord, 82
Durkheim, Emile, 29, 185

'economic freedom index', 171
economies, linked, 273
education, 115n.; immigrants', 200–1; spending on, 171
egalitarianism, 23, 24
elites, 98, 259–62; American, 67–8; English-Canadian, 83–6; political values and, 125–6; religion of, 113
elitism, 22, 24–5, 75
Engels, Friedrich, 267
England: influence of, 5, 31–53, 217; settlers from, 95–6; see also Britain
English: as term, 50
English Canada, 54, 255–9; crime in, 160–1; family and sexual values in, 146–53; as 'fragment', 13–15, 17–20; loyalist myth and, 74–86; religion in, 141–5; Tocqueville's view of, 44–5; values of, 83–6; see also specific provinces
equality, 22; freedom and, 186n.; gender, 149; legal, 32–3, 37, 48–9, 50, 70, 74, 248
equity, 32–3
Errington, Jane, 81, 114, 117–18
Espenshade, Thomas, 206
ethnic composition, 87, 89, 90, 110–11, 197–200; British origin of, 93–105; in French Canada, 90–3; see also immigrants; immigration
extremism, 262–6

Family Compact, 113
family values, 146–53
feudalism: American South and, 15–16, 42–3, 108–9, 110, 175; French Canada and, 15–16, 17, 45, 92
First Nations, 203–5; see also aboriginal peoples
fragments: founding, 11–20, 25; liberal, 13–15; feudal, 15–17
France: control by, 92; influence of, 55; religious symbols and, 255n.
freedom: equality and, 186n.; religion and, 112; political, 33–4
French Canada, 54, 55–6, 131; American invasion of, 92; American view of, 82; collectivism in, 171–4; crime and law in, 160; ethnic composition of, 90–3; family and sexual values in, 146–53; as 'fragment', 15–16, 17, 18; income distribution

in, 178; religion in, 112, 141–5, 152–3; Tocqueville's view of, 45; see also Quebec
fundamentalism, religious, 141

Gannon, Maire, 157
geography: English, 35–6; statism and, 121–2
Giddens, Anthony, 267
Gini coefficient, 178
globalization, 268
Globe and Mail, 208
'God and Society in North America Survey', 141n., 213
Goldstone, Jack A., 52
Gore, Al, 228, 262
government: role of in Canada, 119–27; spending by, 169–71, 173; see also state; statism
Gross Domestic Product, 171, 172
Gwyn, Richard, 81, 273

Hamilton, Alexander, 67
Hartz, Louis, 5, 9, 11–20, 23–4, 25, 45, 249; on American South, 56, 57, 108; on French Canada, 55; on Toryism, 75, 82, 83
health care, 171–2
Hempstead, Katherine, 206
Henry, Patrick, 65
Hispanics, 258
homicide, 155–6, 169
Hopcroft, Rosemary, 36, 46–7
Horowitz, Gad, 4, 9, 11, 17, 18–20, 25, 56, 249; on Toryism, 75, 82, 83
Hume, David, 33

immigrants: attitudes toward, 205–6; socioeconomic attainments of, 200–5
immigration, 89–90; British, 95–105; Canadian, 111; non-British, 110–11; patterns of, 197–200; tolerance and, 194, 196–7
incarceration, 155, 175
inclusion, social, 193–215, 243
income: distribution of, 177–8; immigrants' and minorities', 201–2
indicators, social, 284–5
individualism, 23, 25, 166–92, 243; attitudes about, 180–92; economic, 71; 'liberal', 66–7; 'moral', 24; myth of, 65–73; slavery and, 175; as term, 72
inequality, economic, 176–80
Inglehart, Ronald, 137
Inkeles, Alex, 270
International Crime Survey, 158
International Social Survey Program, 232
intolerance, religious, 52, 70
invasion, American, 92–3
Iraq, 272

Ireland, 100–1, 110–11
Iroquois, 78

Jefferson, Thomas, 63, 65, 67, 68
Jews, 152–3, 209–11, 213
justice, equal, see equality, legal
justice systems, comparison of, 154–5

Kingston, population of, 117
Knowles, Norman, 78–9, 82
Kohut, Andrew, 271–2

laissez-faire, 23, 24
Lambert, Ronald, 207, 208
'land hunger', 80
Langguth, A.J., 65
language: deep structures and, 28–30; shared, 30, 31, 38, 272–3
law, 153–65; English, 31–2; slavery and, 107–8
Laxer, James, 274
'left-liberalism', 12
Li, Peter, 198
liberalism, 11–15, 62, 64, 66; constraints on, 12–13, 24; American, 22–5
liberty, 23, 25, 40, 49–50, 70, 74, 248; civil, 154–5; economic, 48, 71; English, 34–7; 'natural', 12; political, 34–7, 48; pre-revolutionary concept of, 61–5; 'spiritual', 63
Lincoln, Abraham, 49
linkages, Canada–US, 81–3, 85, 122
Lipset, Seymour Martin, 5, 9–10, 20–5, 155, 196, 230; on divergence, 129–30, 147–8, 248–9, 267, 269, 272; on political interest, 216–17, 219, 225, 228; on voluntarism, 235, 236; see also 'American Creed'; statism; Toryism
'local communalism', 68–73, 74 , 176
Locke, John, 12–13, 23–4, 34, 62, 63–4
loyalism, 14–15, 75–6, 83–4
loyalists, 15, 17–18, 130, 249–50, 259; 'late', 77, 80; myth of, 56–7, 74–86; nature of, 77–80, 94–5; number of, 76–7; values of, 83–6
loyalty, oath of, 80
Luxembourg Income Study, 177

McClelland, J.S., 65
McDonald, Forrest, 103, 105
Macfarlane, Alan, 46
Maclean's/Decima poll, 208
McRae, Kenneth, 5, 9, 17–20, 25, 45, 55, 81, 82, 249
McWhiney, Grady, 103, 105
Magna Carta, 32–3, 35
marriage: interracial, 206–8; same-sex, 253, 259–60
Marsden, Peter, 238
Martin, Paul, 261

Martinez, Michael, 226
Marx, Karl, 1
masses, elites and, 83–6, 259–62
'melting pot', 195–7, 200
Methodists, 109–10, 114, 115
military, 172
minorities: loyalist, 78; as neighbours, 211–14; socioeconomic attainments of, 200–5; tolerance toward, 193–215; 'visible', 254
mobility, 70–1
Mohawks, 78
Montesquieu, Charles de Secondat, 34–7, 40, 63
Montgomery, Richard, 93
Montreal, 117, 254
moral issues, 140–65, 242–3, 244–5
mosaic: cultural, 195–7; vertical, 200
multiculturalism, 195–7, 199–200, 243, 260–1
Multiculturalism Act, 195–6
multivariate analyses, 283
Murphy, Brian, 178
Muslims, 213
myths, 132–3, 135–6, 247, 273; 'American individualism', 65–73; 'converging values', 269; historical, 59–60; 'loyalist', 74–86; national, 1–2, 4; 'Scotch-Irish', 99, 101

national pride, 230–2
nations, 'internal', 255–9
New Brunswick: loyalists and, 95; religion in, 114
New Democratic Party, 19
Newfoundland, religion in, 112–13
Niagara region, population of, 117
Noel, S.J.R., 81
non-Christians, 140–1; see also Jews; Muslims
North America: as term, 3
Nova Scotia, American immigrants and, 94–5

Old Regime and the Revolution, The, 41
Ontario: population of, 117–18; religion in, 113–14
Orange Order, 101
'origins thesis', 20–5

'parapolitics', 234
Parsons, Talcott, 22
Parti Quebecois (PQ), 172–4
patriotism, 230–2
Pew Research Center, 256, 271–2
plantation economy, 42–4, 105–10
pluralism, 35, 48, 49, 50, 51–2, 70, 74, 248, 250
Pocock, John G.A., 46

police, 158
'political culture', 216
politics, 244, 245; activity and, 219–25; attitudes toward, 216–33; confidence in, 227, 228–30; culture of, 118–22, 126–7, 216; organization of, 123–7; protest and, 220–5; rights and, 33–4; structures of, 216–17
population: foreign-born, 197–8, 199, 254, 258–9; non-white, 199; rural/urban, 69; size of, 116–7; see also specific groups
populism, 23, 24
Porter, John, 200
post-modernism, 253–4
poverty, 179–80, 265
Presbyterians, 96–7, 98, 114
prisons, 155, 175
protest, political, 220–5
Protestant ethic, 96–7, 99–101
Protestantism, 112–16; American South and, 109–10; British, 95–105; conservative, 148
Protestants, 39, 40, 140–2; see also specific groups
provinces, autonomy of, 123–4
punishment, capital, 161, 163
Puritans, 39, 40

Quebec, 55–6, 252–5; influence of, 256; 'old' and 'new', 150–3; state intervention in, 172–4; see also French Canada
Quebec Act, 92–3
Quiet Revolution, 150

race, concept of, 107–8
racism, 43–4, 107–8
Reed, John Shelton, 176
Reed, Paul, 237, 238
regions, 5–6; categorization of, 281–3; see also sub-societies
Reid, W. Stanford, 96–7
Reitz, Jeffrey, 200–1, 202, 205, 207, 209, 214
religion, 39–40, 111–16, 140–5, 152–3; American sectarianism and, 114–15; American South and, 109–10; as association, 235, 236, 237, 238–40; Catholic, 100, 112; local communalism and, 69–70; rights of, 92–3; Protestant, 95–105, 112, 113–16
religiosity, 142–5, 148
republicanism, 67–8
research questions, 138–9
revolution, see American Revolution
rights, political, 33–4
Roman Catholic Church, 92; see also Catholics
Romano, Renee, 208
Roosevelt, Franklin, 121

samples, research, 136–8
Saussure, Ferdinand de, 28–9
Schaff, Phillip, 72–3
Schlesinger, Arthur M., Sr, 270
'Scotch-Irish', 98–105
Scotland, 96–8
self-confidence, 186–8
servants, indentured, 107
Seven Years War, 90
Seward, William, 83
sexual values, 146–53
Shain, Barry, 62–3, 64, 65, 66, 69, 72, 78, 130, 132
Shenkman, Richard, 71, 132
Simcoe, John Graves, 84, 85
Simpson, Jeffrey, 269
slavery, 16, 42–4, 57, 105–10, 194, 250
slaves: population of, 90n., 106; runaway, 78
'social fact', 29, 30
socialism, 13, 19
'social protection', 171
sovereignty, popular, 38, 48, 49, 50, 70, 74, 248
state: autonomy of, 123–4; collectivism and, 168–80; role of, 167; see also government; statism
'states' rights', 69, 109
statism, 24, 171–80, 119–21, 123; attitudes about, 180–92; religion and, 112–13; see also government; state
Strachan, John, 113
structures, see deep structures
sub-societies, 53–8, 257–8; see also regions

taxation, 170, 171, 173
terminology, geographic, 3
theories: 'founding fragment', 11–20, 25; 'revolutionary origins', 2–25; 'deep structures', 26–58, 248–55
Thomas, W.I., 132–3
Thompson, Edgar T., 2, 105, 106
Thorner, Daniel, 52
Tocqueville, Alexis de, 9, 37–45, 49, 71, 82–3, 234, 266, 272–3; on American South, 57, 105, 106; on French Canada, 45, 55; on individualism, 72–3
tolerance, ethnic, 193–215, 243, 245
Toronto, population of, 117
Toryism, 18–20, 22–5, 74–6, 83–6, 101; French Canada and, 92; 'red', 19
'Tory touch', 14–15, 19, 56, 249
trust, interpersonal, 230–2
'tyranny of the majority', 71

unionization, 178–9
unions, 235, 236, 238–40
United Empire Loyalists, 15, 84; see also loyalists
United States: Declaration of Independence, 65; see also American North; American South
urbanization, 116–18

values, 20; 'American Creed', 22–4; 'Canadian Creed', 24–5; family and sexual, 146–53; systems of, 28, 29; see also collectivism; inclusion; individualism; religion; statism
'vertical mosaic', 200
veterans, benefits for, 120n.
victimization, rates of, 158
violence, political, 262–3; see also crime, violent
'visible minority', 198; see also minorities
'voluntarism', 235, 244
voluntary associations, 234–45
voting, 225–6, 228

War of 1812, 85–6, 132
Washington, George, 67
wealth, 179, 265
Weber, Max, 1, 36, 234
Weiner, Myron, 53
welfare state, 121
Wolfson, Michael, 178
Wood, Gordon S., 82
World Values Surveys (WVS), 6, 137, 238–42, 275–80, 281–3